Sir John Fortescue
and the
Governance of England

Sir John Fortescue and the Governance of England

MARGARET KEKEWICH

THE BOYDELL PRESS

First published 2018
The Boydell Press, Woodbridge

ISBN 978 1 78327 350 8

The Boydell Press is an imprint of Boydell & Brewer Ltd
PO Box 9, Woodbridge, Suffolk IP12 3DF, UK
and of Boydell & Brewer Inc.
668 Mt Hope Avenue, Rochester, NY 14620–2731, USA
website: www.boydellandbrewer.com

A CIP catalogue record for this book is available
from the British Library

This publication is printed on acid-free paper

FOR PETER

Contents

Illustrations

The author and publishers are grateful to all the institutions and individuals listed for permission to reproduce the materials in which they hold copyright. Every effort has been made to trace the copyright holders; apologies are offered for any omission, and the publishers will be pleased to add any necessary acknowledgement in subsequent editions.

Acknowledgements

I am most grateful to the staff of The National Archives, Rare Books and Manuscripts in the British Library, the Warburg Institute, Lambeth Palace Library and the Institute of Historical Research in London, the Bodleian Library in Oxford and Cambridge University Library for their assistance. Some debts to individuals are recorded in footnotes, but, over a considerable period, I have received advice and support from Gladys Bland, Nigel Ramsay, Colin Richmond, Susan Rose, Malcolm and Margaret Summers and members of the Late Medieval Seminar at the Institute of Historical Research, University of London. Mary Ruskin translated the Latin passages in *The Declaration upon certain writings* and Cath D'Alton has made the genealogies. Alan Cromartie and Hannes Kleineke read the mansucript before it was sent to the publisher and made many constructive suggestions. The staff at Boydell & Brewer have always been kind and considerate and devoted great care to the project, in particular, Rob Kinsey, Caroline Palmer, Christopher Feeney and Rebecca Cribb. My husband, Peter Fawcett, has supported me in many ways and I am deeply grateful to him.

Abbreviations

BIHR	*Bulletin of the Institute of Historical Research*
BJRL	*Bulletin of the John Rylands Library*
BL	British Library
BnF	Bibliothèque nationale de France, Paris
Bodl.	Bodleian Library, Oxford
CCR	*Calendar of Close Rolls*
CFR	*Calendar of Fine Rolls*
CIPM	*Calendar of Inquisitions Post Mortem*
CPR	*Calendar of Patent Rolls*
CSPM	*Calendar of State Papers, Milan*, I
Devon RO	Devon County Record Office
EETS	Early English Text Society
EHR	*English Historical Review*
Foedera	*Foedera*, ed. T. Rymer, 10 vols (The Hague: 1739–45)
HMC	Historical Manuscripts Commission
KB	The National Archives, King's Bench
NMS	*Nottingham Medieval Studies*
ODNB	*Oxford Dictionary of National Biography*, ed. H.C.G. Mathew and B. Harrison, 60 vols (Oxford: 2004)
PL (Davis)	*Paston Letters*, ed. N. Davis, R. Beadle and C. Richmond, 3 vols (Oxford: 2004–5)
PL (Gairdner)	*Paston Letters*, ed. J. Gairdner, 6 vols (London: 1904)
PPC	*Proceedings and Ordinances of the Privy Council*, ed. N.H. Nicolas, 6 vols (1835)
PROME	*Parliament Rolls of Medieval England, 1275–1504*, ed. C. Given-Wilson, 16 vols (Woodbridge and Leicester: 2005)
RC	Record Commission

RP	*Rotuli Parliamentorum*, ed. J. Strachey, J. Pridden and E. Upham, 7 vols (London: 1832)
RS	Rolls Series
Seipp	*An Index and Paraphrase of Printed Year Book Reports, 1268–1535*, compiled by D.J. Seipp (Boston University: 2007), online resource
TNA	The National Archives, London
TRHS	*Transactions of the Royal Historical Society*
VCH	*Victoria History of the Counties of England*

Editorial note

Titles are modernised. Quotations from texts retain the original spelling. Translations, unless described otherwise, are by the author.

Chronology

Date	Political Events	Sir John Fortescue Life and Works
c. 1395–1400		Born in Devon
1399	Accession of Henry IV	
1413	Accession of Henry V, who revived the Hundred Years War	
Before 1420		Admitted to Lincoln's Inn
1420	Treaty of Troyes	
1421		MP for Tavistock
1422	Death of Henry V Accession of Infant Henry VI Death of Charles VI Dukes of Gloucester and Bedford made Protectors of England and France	
Before 1423		Married Elizabeth Brytte
1424–26		Governor of Lincoln's Inn. Elizabeth Brytte died in 1427
1428–29		Governor of Lincoln's Inn
1429	Coronation of Henry VI at Westminster Protectorates of Bedford and Gloucester ended	
1429–30		Pensioner and Governor of Lincoln's Inn

Date	Political Events	Sir John Fortescue Life and Works
1431	Coronation of Henry VI at Paris	
1432		Apprentice for Duchy of Lancaster MP for Totnes
1435	Congress of Arras. Death of John, duke of Bedford	
Before 1436		Married Isabella Jamyss
1436		MP for Wiltshire
1437–8		Serjeant-at-Law
1441		King's Serjeant
1442		Chief Justice of the King's Bench; knighted
1444	Truce of Tours	
1445	Henry VI married Margaret of Anjou	
1447	Death of Humphrey, duke of Gloucester	
1448	Surrender of Anjou and Maine	
1450	Trial of William de la Pole, duke of Suffolk Loss of Normandy Suffolk beheaded by rebels Jack Cade's rebellion	Fortescue and other justices consulted on Suffolk's case Fortescue named and condemned in rebel poem
1450–53		Fortescue probably composed *The Commodities of England*
1453	Final loss of Gascony and Guyenne Henry VI temporarily insane Birth of Prince Edward	
1454		Consulted by Lords in Thorpe's case

Date	Political Events	Sir John Fortescue Life and Works
1454–55	First Protectorate of Richard, duke of York	
1455	First battle of St Albans	Richard Fortescue killed in battle of St Albans
1456	Second Protectorate of Richard, duke of York	
1457		Appointed to commission to investigate means by which the King might pay his debts in gold and silver
1458	'Loveday', temporary reconciliation between Lancastrians and Yorkists	
1459	Battle of Blore Heath Coventry parliament. Attainder of Yorkists	Helped draft attainder of Yorkists, and probably the *Somnium Vigilantis*
1460	Battle of Northampton Richard duke of York claims the throne Battle of Wakefield, duke of York killed	Consulted with other justices concerning duke of York's claim. They declined to give an opinion
1461	Second Battle of St Albans Edward IV proclaimed King Battles of Towton, Ryton and Brancepeth	Fortescue appointed Chancellor by Lancastrians Fortescue present at all three battles Attainted Exiled to Scotland with Henry VI and Margaret of Anjou
1461–63		In exile in Scotland Wrote *De Titulo Edwardi Comitis Marchie*, *Defensio Juris Domus Lancastrie*, *Of the Title of the House of York*, *Replication to the Claim of the duke of York*
1462–63		Estates forfeited by attainder

Date	Political Events	Sir John Fortescue Life and Works
1463	Fortescue sailed with Queen Margaret and Prince Edward from Bamburgh to Sluys, and they settled at Koeur in Bar	
1463–68		Probable date of composition of *De Natura Legis* *Naturae*
1464	Edward IV married Elizabeth Woodville	
1468–70		Wrote *De Laudibus Legum Anglie* and a series of memoranda to Louis XI
1470	Agreement between Louis XI, earl of Warwick and Margaret of Anjou at Angers Warwick invaded England, and Edward IV flees to Burgundy. Henry VI freed from Tower of London	Summoned with Queen Margaret and Prince Edward to Paris by Louis XI Wrote *Articles sent by Edward, Prince of Wales to the earl of Warwick*
1471	Edward IV returned to England Queen Margaret, Prince Edward and Fortescue landed at Weymouth Battle of Barnet, Warwick killed, Henry VI captured Battle of Tewksbury. Prince Edward killed, Queen Margaret and Fortescue captured. Henry VI died (probably murdered) in the Tower	Given general pardon Appointed to Edward IV's council
1471–73		Wrote *Declaration upon Certain Writings* and final version of *The Governance of England*
1473		Attainder reversed

Date	Political Events	Sir John Fortescue Life and Works
1474		Gained possession of manor of Ebrington, Gloucestershire
1475	England briefly at war with France	
1476		Delivered assize roll to Exchequer
*c.*1479		Died and buried in the church at Ebrington

Genealogy 1 The Fortescues

Taken from T. Clermont, *A History of the Family of Fortescue in all its Branches* *(London: 1869) with additions and corrections.*

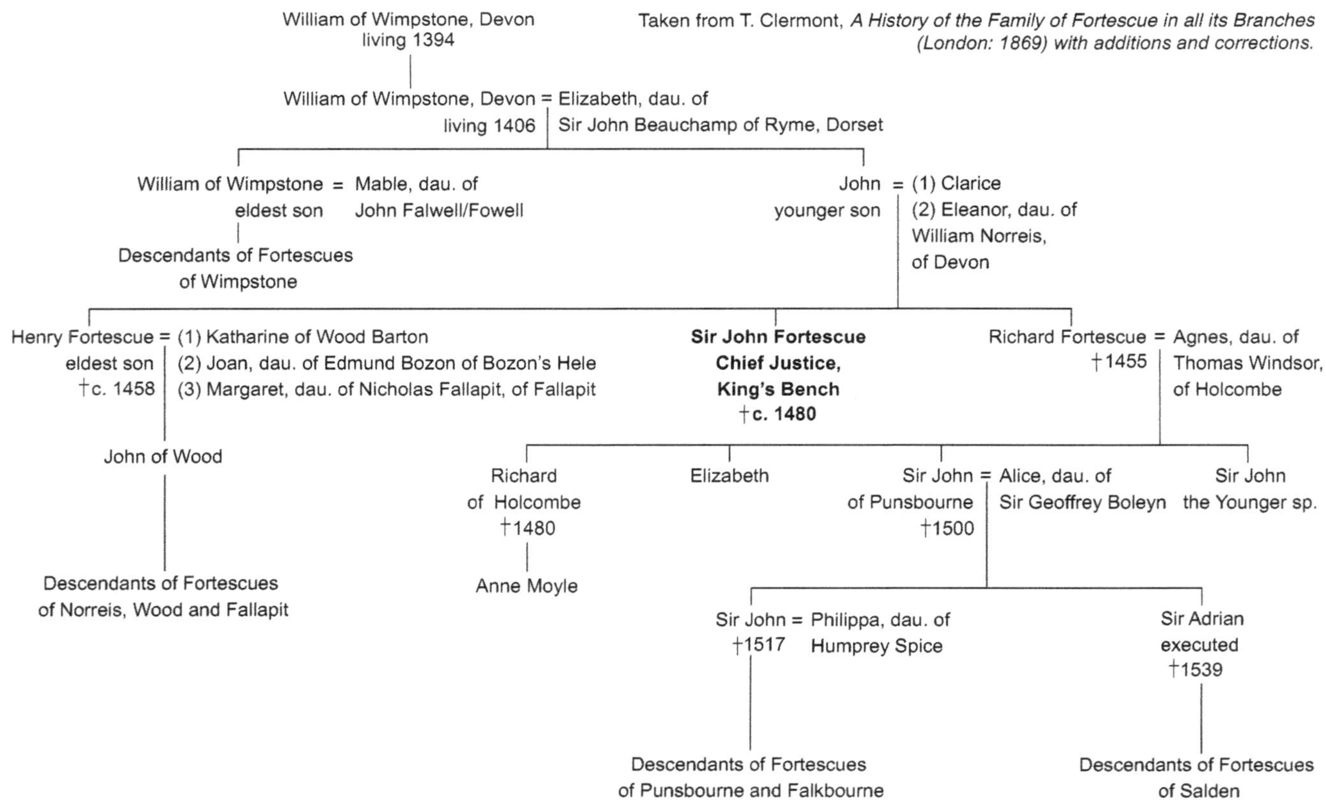

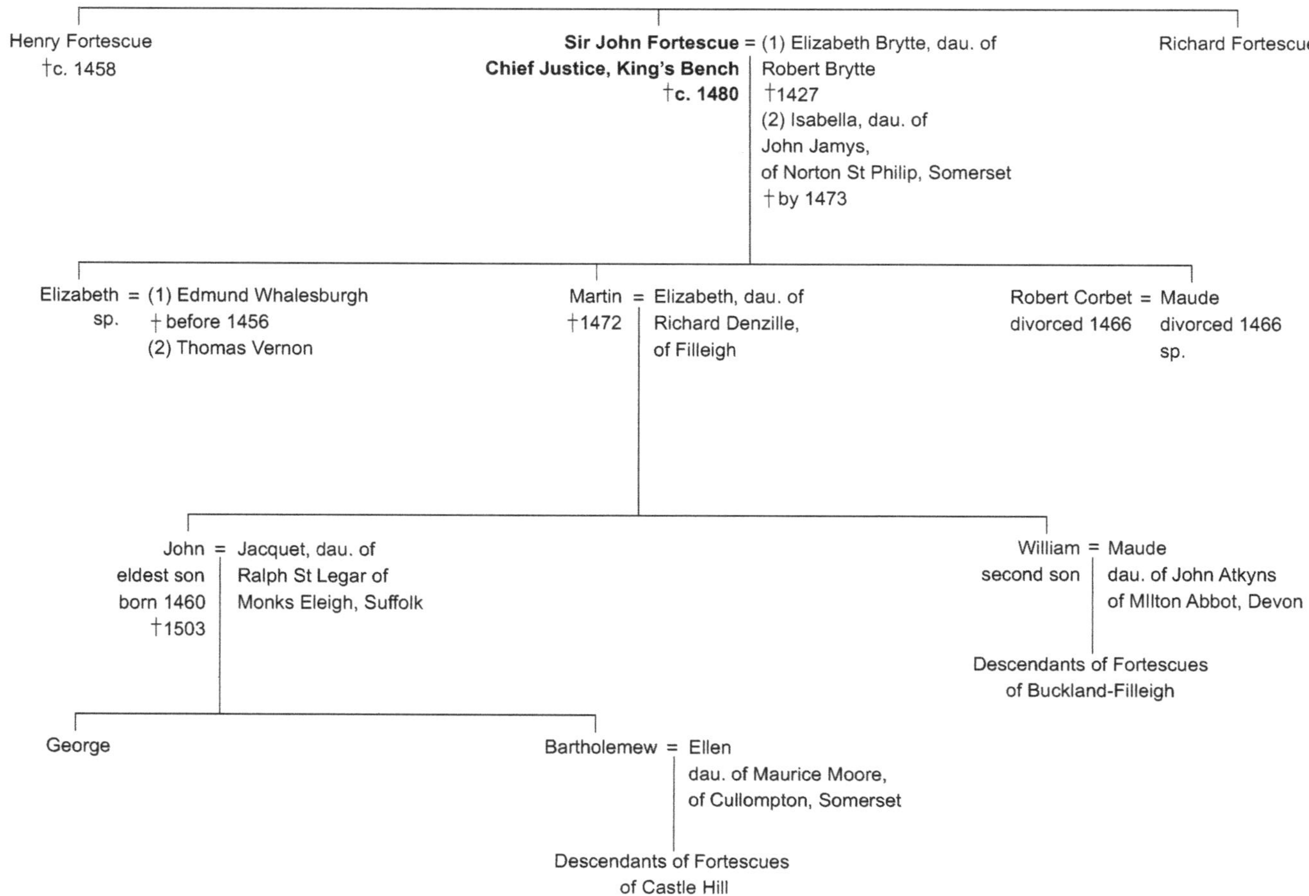
Henry Fortescue
†c. 1458
Sir John Fortescue = (1) Elizabeth Brytte, dau. of Robert Brytte †1427
Chief Justice, King's Bench
†c. 1480
(2) Isabella, dau. of John Jamys, of Norton St Philip, Somerset †by 1473
Richard Fortescue
Elizabeth = (1) Edmund Whalesburgh †before 1456
sp.
(2) Thomas Vernon
Martin = Elizabeth, dau. of Richard Denzille, of Filleigh
†1472
Robert Corbet = Maude
divorced 1466
divorced 1466
sp.
John = Jacquet, dau. of Ralph St Legar of Monks Eleigh, Suffolk
eldest son
born 1460
†1503
William = Maude
second son
dau. of John Atkyns of MIlton Abbot, Devon
Descendants of Fortescues of Buckland-Filleigh
George
Bartholemew = Ellen
dau. of Maurice Moore, of Cullompton, Somerset
Descendants of Fortescues of Castle Hill

Genealogy 2 The Rival Claims of Lancaster and York to the Throne of England

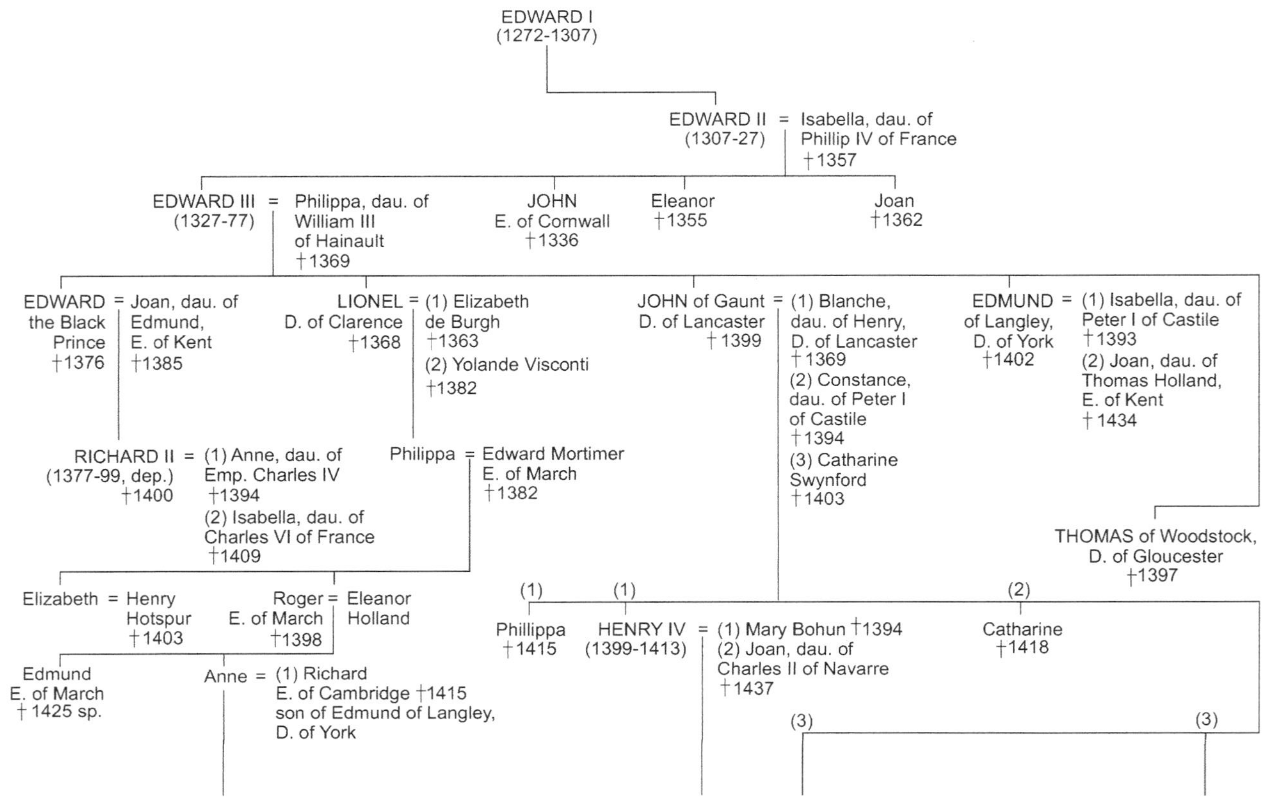

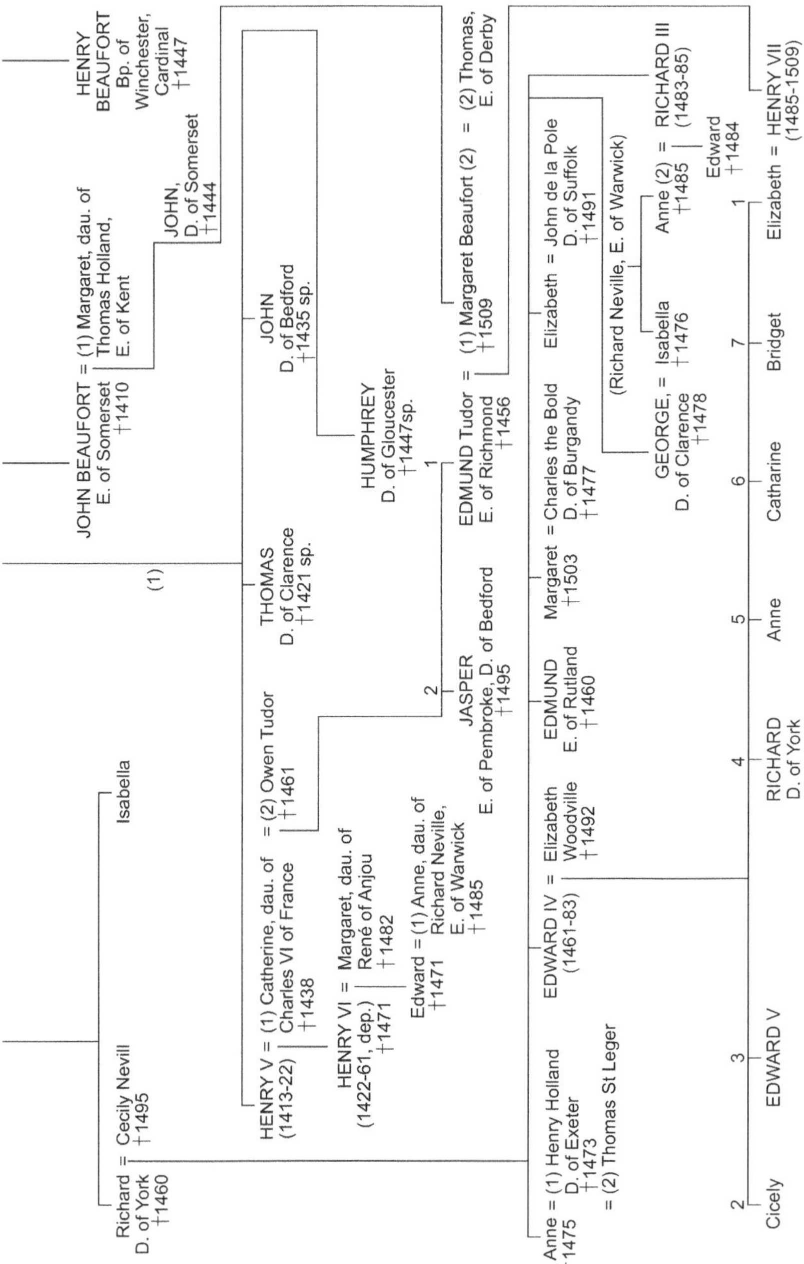
HENRY BEAUFORT
Bp. of Winchester, Cardinal
†1447
JOHN BEAUFORT = (1) Margaret, dau. of Thomas Holland, E. of Kent
E. of Somerset
†1410
JOHN,
D. of Somerset
†1444
Richard = Cecily Nevill
D. of York
†1460
†1495
Isabella
(1)
HENRY V = (1) Catherine, dau. of Charles VI of France = (2) Owen Tudor
(1413-22)
†1438
†1461
THOMAS
D. of Clarence
†1421 sp.
JOHN
D. of Bedford
†1435 sp.
HUMPHREY
D. of Gloucester
†1447sp.
HENRY VI = Margaret, dau. of René of Anjou
(1422-61, dep.)
†1471
†1482
Edward = (1) Anne, dau. of Richard Neville, E. of Warwick
†1471
†1485
2
JASPER
E. of Pembroke, D. of Bedford
†1495
1
EDMUND Tudor = (1) Margaret Beaufort (2) = (2) Thomas, E. of Derby
E. of Richmond
†1456
†1509
Anne = (1) Henry Holland
†1475
D. of Exeter
†1473
= (2) Thomas St Leger
EDWARD IV = Elizabeth Woodville
(1461-83)
†1492
EDMUND
E. of Rutland
†1460
Margaret = Charles the Bold
†1503
D. of Burgandy
†1477
Elizabeth = John de la Pole
D. of Suffolk
†1491
(Richard Neville, E. of Warwick)
GEORGE, = Isabella
D. of Clarence
†1478
†1476
Anne (2) = RICHARD III
†1485
(1483-85)
Edward
†1484
2 Cicely
3 EDWARD V
4 RICHARD
D. of York
5 Anne
6 Catharine
7 Bridget
1 Elizabeth = HENRY VII
(1485-1509)

Introduction

This book is about the life and works of Sir John Fortescue, the most important political thinker of fifteenth-century England. His major treatises remain the starting point for an understanding of ideas about kingship, law and government during the Caroline civil wars and their aftermath. Yet in his lifetime Sir John Fortescue was a prominent man but not remarkable. The dates of his birth (*c.*1395) and death (*c.*1479) have to be prefaced by *circa* because none of his contemporaries thought to record them for posterity. He was sometimes referred to in the *Paston Letters* informally, almost in a jocular tone, despite the fact that he was, at the time, Chief Justice of King's Bench.[1] In exile (1461–70) he was Chancellor to the Lancastrians but was swept aside in favour of the more powerful claim of Bishop George Neville when Henry VI was briefly restored to the throne. His contemporaries might well have been surprised at the weight that later generations gave to his opinions. Recent scholarship can account for this and bring new evidence to bear on Fortescue's career and thought.

The Fortescue family promoted the rapid posthumous growth of his reputation, assisted by local historians and the heralds from the College of Arms who visited his descendants and obligingly awarded their remote ancestors a distinction that they had never possessed.[2] His great-nephew Sir Adrian Fortescue was an admirer and assiduously copied at least one of the works, *The Governance of England*, before his disgrace and death during the reign of Henry VIII.[3] The new art of printing fed a growing demand by lawyers and political commentators for Fortescue's *De Laudibus Legum Anglie*.[4] A century later the book could provide support

1 *Paston Letters and Papers of the Fifteenth Century*, ed. N. Davis, and vol. 3, ed. R. Beadle and C. Richmond, 3 vols (Oxford: 2004, 2005), 'The Chief Justice is right herty and seith ful weel and kyndely of my maister', vol. 2, 187, also 210 and 221.

2 See below, Chapter 1; N. Ramsay, ed., *Heralds and Heraldry in Shakespeare's England* (Donington: 2014) *passim*.

3 Oxford, Bodleian Library MS Digby 145, ff. 131b–159a.

4 Sir John Fortescue, *De politica administratione; et legibus civilibus florentissimi regni Anglie commentarius*, pub. Edward Whitechurch (London: 1545/6).

to both sides in the confrontation between kings and parliament over where sovereignty should lie.

Fortescue's reputation as a political guru continued to flourish into the eighteenth century, assisted by the three editions of *The Difference between an Absolute and Limited Monarchy* by John Fortescue Aland.[5] It was further enhanced by the work of Charles Plummer in the late nineteenth century when he demonstrated that *The Governance of England*, the title he gave to *The Difference between Absolute and Limited Monarchy*, was even more central to constitutional debate than the *De Laudibus*.[6] The interest in Fortescue as a political theorist was underpinned by the publication in 1869 of a family history and all his then known works by Thomas Fortescue, Lord Clermont.[7] Articles and the works by historians such as Stanley Chrimes kept interest going throughout the twentieth century until the writings of, amongst others, J.G.A. Pocock, Quentin Skinner, Maurizio Viroli, Jean-Philippe Genet, Christine Carpenter and John Watts put Fortescue at the centre of studies of the language of politics, the pressure of events on theorists and normative expectations of political conduct.

Lord Clermont's edition of Fortescue's works included a brief but well-documented biography: it recounted the main facts about his life that were then known, but eschewed any kind of interpretation of his ancestor's contribution to late medieval political ideas.[8] Charles Plummer also wrote thirty-two biographical pages in his 1885 edition of the *Governance* and appended a list of Fortescue's works, an assessment of his sources, character, legal and political significance.[9] This last included praise for Fortescue's 'confidence in the capacities of parliamentary government',[10] opening up a rich vein that was to be enthusiastically mined by generations of historians. S.B. Chrimes drew heavily on both Clermont and Plummer for his brief outline of Fortescue's life, adding

[5] *The Difference between an Absolute and Limited Monarchy as it more particularly regards the English Constitution by Sir John Fortescue Knight*, ed. J. Fortescue Aland of the Inner Temple (London: 1714, 1719, 1724).

[6] *The Governance of England by Sir John Fortescue*, ed. C. Plummer (Oxford: 1885). It will be referred to as *The Governance of England* in this book as that is the title used by modern writers.

[7] Thomas Fortescue, Lord Clermont, *The Works of Sir John Fortescue, Knight, A History of the Family of Fortescue in all its Branches*, 2 vols (London: 1869), referred to here as *Works* (vol. 1) and *Family* (vol. 2). It is also available from University Microfilms International (Ann Arbor, MI: 1981).

[8] Clermont, *Works*, 3–55.

[9] Plummer, *Governance of England*, 40–73, 96–105.

[10] *Ibid.*, 103.

any newly discovered facts: beyond these works no comprehensive account has been attempted.[11] The increased attention that scholars in recent decades have paid to the social, ideological and political context in which writers functioned makes the production of a new biography timely.

Part I of this book examines Fortescue's origins and career and how they may have contributed to the development of his political ideas. Two chapters trace his life from his membership of the junior branch of an unremarkable Devonian gentry family via a meteoric rise in the law to become the Chief Justice of King's Bench. His common-law learning is illustrated by the *Year Books*, which provide insights into Fortescue's activities during the last eighteen years of his legal career and throw light on his capacities and on how innovative he might have been as a justice. His powerful friends and patrons, his network of regional and business contacts, his expanding property holdings and his servants all served to enhance his status. The increasingly unstable political situation in the 1440s and 1450s and his duty to preserve royal authority might have undermined him but the high mortality rate amongst the Lancastrian nobility and royal household and his shrewd response to the situation had made him a principal counsellor to Henry VI and Margaret of Anjou by 1460.

The third chapter discusses the long years of exile, first in Scotland and then in the duchy of Bar (which lay between Eastern France and the Empire), which saw the emergence of Fortescue as a formidable polemicist for Lancaster. The limited personnel in the small court of Queen Margaret and Prince Edward, 1463 to 1470, entailed Fortescue exercising other talents: as a diplomat seeking to raise support for the Lancastrian cause in Europe and as a tutor to the Prince. By the close of the decade the prince was regarded as a young adult and at that stage became an asset that his house had previously lacked: a potential military leader and an attractive suitor on the marriage market. His union with the daughter of the earl of Warwick, seemingly engineered by Fortescue, proved a decisive factor in the political revolution that once more set Henry VI on the English throne from late 1470 to early 1471. The disastrous end to the Lancastrian restoration, when both Henry and his son Prince Edward were destroyed, could also have ruined Fortescue but he proved remarkably resilient. After disowning his previous opinions on

[11] *Sir John Fortescue 'De Laudibus Legum Anglie'*, ed. S.B. Chrimes (Cambridge: 1942) lix–lxxv, a chronology and a brief life. See Chapter 6 for further discussion of Fortescue's early editors.

the rights of succession in England and France in the *Declaration upon certain writings late sent out of Scotland*, he ended his life as a respected adviser to Edward IV and the Yorkists: a man of affairs who lived in a fine property that that had been restored to him.

Although Fortescue's principal works are examined in Part II a polemical tract against the Yorkists, the *Somnium Vigilantis*, which is associated with him but was probably written by others, is discussed in Part I. It is closely related to the political environment and specific period in which it was produced and stands apart from the more coherent corpus of his polemical tracts, legal and political treatises.

Part II of the book examines Fortescue's writings in roughly chronological order, first dealing with his little paper, *The Commodities of England*, which was probably destined for Henry VI's council in the early 1450s. Four tracts justifying the Lancastrian right to the English crown which were produced in Scotland (1461–63) survive, although two of them are fragmentary. The longer *De Natura Legis Naturae* is a hybrid: a philosophical justification for the use of the law of nature to determine the succession in sovereign kingdoms and then its application to an imaginary situation where the brother of a dead king rather than the king's daughter or her son had the right to the throne.

Throughout the later years of exile, Fortescue explained in his *De Laudibus Legum Anglie*, he had been attempting to instruct Edward of Lancaster in the joys of the common law. His experience of conducting learning exercises for generations of students in Lincoln's Inn must have helped him in the daunting task of engaging a martially minded teenager of probably limited intelligence.[12] Yet it was a necessity if, as Fortescue showed in the work, the Prince was to be convinced that it was preferable to rule politically with a regard for the laws and customs of England, the former promulgated in parliament, rather than regally led by his own will. The work also had the more general aims of stressing the values that Fortescue wished the Lancastrians to cherish and providing a handbook for future rulers to consult about the relationship between the laws and the governance of England.

The *Governance of England* seems to have been completed in its final form in the early 1470s and was offered to Edward IV as a summation of Fortescue's long experience of the largely dysfunctional royal regime of Henry VI and as a model of how governance should be reformed. It is suggested in this study that, rather than being the constitutional programme that was described by nineteenth- and some

[12] See below, Chapter 3, p. 124, n. 65.

twentieth-century historians, it recommended a strong council of professionals who could interpret and implement the royal will. Any suspicion that this might pose a threat to the royal prerogative was dissipated by the closing reassurance 'he may leve this order whan hym liste'.[13] In Fortescue's time the prerogative, the right of kings to exercise unlimited power, had never been seriously questioned. This did not mean that subjects expected them to ride roughshod over laws, customs and religion: only tyrants would do so and, ultimately, they could expect divine retribution in this world or the next. What was distinctive about Fortescue's advice was that he went into great detail about the bureaucratic arrangements needed to help monarchs to rule wisely, and in particular rejected the leading role of great lords in the royal council.

The seeming inconsistency of remarks such as the above about leaving 'this order', which followed pages of advocacy of conciliar government, has been one of the reasons why political commentators with widely differing views have been able to claim support from Fortescue's ideas. The final chapter traces this process from the esteem Fortescue enjoyed among earnest sixteenth-century legal students via the opposing camps in the vigorous controversies that ended in the Civil War of the mid-seventeenth century to the servile seekers of preferment of the eighteenth century. Only with Charles Plummer in the late nineteenth century were Fortescue's ideas related to the political environment in a fashion that modern historians would recognise. Armed with his edition of the *Governance*, the *De Laudibus* published by Chrimes in 1942, their modernised versions brought out by Shelley Lockwood and the collection of political manifestos and tracts, including the *Governance* and three shorter works by Fortescue called *John Vale's Book* which appeared in the mid-1990s, the debate amongst historians continues.[14]

Writing in 1942, when England was at war with Germany, Stanley Chrimes described Fortescue's works as 'the authentic voice of English character'.[15]After due allowance has been made for the patriotic fervour that was informing his opinion, the grounds for his assertion will be examined through his subject's works, at a time when the question of English national identity is a major concern. His early life in the West of England, where regular expeditions departed to fight for Henry V's rights in France, and the subsequent humiliation of defeat both fed into

[13] *The Politics of Fifteenth-Century England: John Vale's Book*, ed. M.L. Kekewich, C. Richmond, A.F. Sutton, L. Visser-Fuchs and J.L. Watts (Stroud: 1995) 250.

[14] *Ibid.*; S. Lockwood, *Sir John Fortescue 'On the Laws and Governance of England'* (Cambridge: 1997).

[15] Chrimes, *De Laudibus*, cviii.

the xenophobia that informed his later works. Nine years of exile when the Lancastrians were largely dependent on the good will of ambivalent French princes, especially the intransigent Louis XI, and experience of life in Bar and in France seem to have confirmed Fortescue's opinion about the superior merits of the English polity.

Fortescue's preoccupations diverged to some extent from contemporary writers both in England and on the Continent who still largely adhered to the ethical 'mirror for princes' formula.[16] In both the *De Laudibus* and the *Governance of* England he adopted a comparative method when examining legal and political institutions contrasting, in the first case, the civil law that was widely used on the Continent with the English common law. The strength of the latter resided in its organic relationship with the society with which it had been associated from time immemorial: predictably Fortescue felt that its interpretation was safe in the hands of virtuous and well-educated judges. The English political system was closely related to the common law since it too had remained unchanged since the time of the legendary King Brutus and was defined by custom and statutes: kings swore at their coronation to uphold the system and only bad ones would damage themselves and their subjects by abrogating it. The baleful effects of the unlimited exercise of the royal will could be observed in the abject state of much of French society.

Appendix 1 contains the English translation of Fortescue's Latin tract *Of the Title of Edward earl of March* and Appendix 2 is devoted to the *Declaration upon certain writings late sent out of Scotland.* Both tracts are printed for the first time since Clermont's edition of 1869 and both are essential to an understanding of Fortescue's thought and career. The first is the only complete version of his arguments about the succession before he composed the much longer *De Natura Legis Naturae* and gives some intimations of how his political ideas might develop. The *Declaration* contains evidence about Fortescue's personality and circumstances towards the end of his life, his methods of working and the earlier tracts that he was disowning.

The origins of Fortescue's political ideas, it is suggested, are to be found in his own long experience of the law and government and in some measure from the education that he received as a child and young adult.

[16] John Watts has made the point that 'mirrors for princes' by the late middle ages could 'depict a polity in which the king was the vehicle of a communal enterprise for the realisation of communal interests', but he goes on to say that for Fortescue only the king's independent will could guarantee a single common interest and the unity of the realm. J. Watts, *Henry VI and the Politics of Kingship* (Cambridge: 1996) 21–31.

Two contemporary influences led him to build on those and to adopt an innovative approach to political ideas: works by Italian humanists that were already current in England and popular agitation against perceptions of misrule voiced in petitions and pamphlets and which sometimes filtered far enough up the social scale to be expressed in parliament. The extent to which Fortescue's work showed the impact of humanism is controversial but it is claimed here that it was more than modish window-dressing. As Chief Justice Fortescue was in the eye of the storm that was Jack Cade's revolt in 1450; he also regularly attended parliament for nearly forty years: some of the demands of dissident subjects and members of parliament found their way, almost verbatim, into his treatises. Following generations of readers and commentators have thus been challenged to make sense of a thinker who was simultaneously highly respectful of tradition but also prepared to question many of the basic tenets of the English polity, in particular the unlimited supremacy of the royal prerogative and of the nobility who were still seen by many as the natural rulers of the land under the king.

Part I
LIFE

CHAPTER I

c. 1395–1442

The Fortescue Family in Devon

A biographical study of Sir John Fortescue, Chief Justice of King's Bench, must start in the early modern period rather than the fifteenth century. This is because the high-achieving and numerous descendants and collaterals of the great man felt that they had to endow his ancestors with an eminence and a lustre that they had not in fact possessed. The family contained several notable lawyers, politicians and capable historians and they, assisted by the heralds on visitations in the sixteenth and seventeenth centuries and sycophantic antiquarians, produced an impressive account of the Fortescues from the time of the Norman Conquest. To his credit Thomas Fortescue, Lord Clermont, in his account of the family expressed scepticism about some of the most erroneous claims.[1] As Christine Carpenter has remarked, 'genealogies can be very revealing about the sense of lineage when they are in error or fail to tell the truth'.[2] More recently Sir John Baker has made a similar point, 'the pedigree rolls of ascendant families may be more interesting now for what they tell us about a family's claims and pretensions than for factual information about a family's remoter origins'.[3]

The original accounts of the Fortescue family produced in the sixteenth and seventeenth centuries put their ancestors in a prominent place in the history of England. They had Richard Strongshield (Fortéscu) fighting for William the Conqueror at the battle of Hastings and being richly rewarded.[4] Some of his family returned to Normandy, where they still flourished in the fifteenth century, but the rest settled in Devon and Cornwall, where they served the monarchy loyally and often

[1] Clermont, *Works*, 3–6; T. Fortescue, Lord Clermont, *A History of the Fortescue Family in all its Branches*, second edition (London: 1880) ix–x.

[2] C. Carpenter, *Locality and Polity: A Study of Warwickshire Landed Society, 1401–1499* (Cambridge: 1992) 247.

[3] J. Baker, 'Tudor Pedigree Rolls and Their Uses', *Heralds and Heraldry*, 105–24.

[4] Clermont, *Works*, 3.

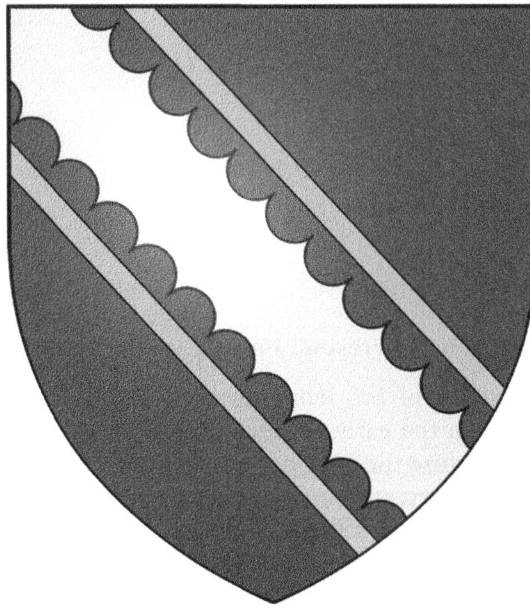

1 The Fortescue arms. Azure (blue), a bend engrailed argent (silver) cottised or (gold).

achieved knightly status. Sir John's 'grandfather', also called John, was knighted and made Governor of Meaux after it was conquered by the English. An extra generation was inserted into the family in the shape of Henry Fortescue, called the father of John junior, the subject of this book (Henry was actually his older brother).[5] Not only John junior[6] but Henry and their younger brother Richard were knighted.[7]

The real history of the Fortescue family insofar as it can be recovered is rather more prosaic. In the late fourteenth century the principal manor held by William Fortescue, the head of the English branch of the family, was at Wimpstone in the parish of Modbury in Devon. He was probably an esquire (a member of the gentry who could bear arms,

[5] Typical of the roseate version are J. Prince, *Danmonii Orientales Illustres* or *The Worthies of Devon* (Exeter: 1701) 304–7; T. Westcote, *A View of Devonshire in MDCXXX with a Pedigree of Most of its Gentry*, ed. G. Oliver and P. Jones (Exeter: 1845) 626.

[6] Sir John Fortescue CJKB was often referred to in the rolls in his early years as 'John junior' and his father, who was never knighted, as 'John senior'.

[7] A more detailed discussion of Sir John's origins and early life may be found in M.L. Kekewich, 'John Fortescue Junior: An Upwardly Mobile Gentleman, *c.*1400–1442', *Southern History*, 17 (1995) 1–23.

ranking immediately below a knight), as that was the rank of his son, John senior.[8] His family had owned this manor from at least 1209 and deeds link the family to Modbury from the late twelfth century, so the tradition that they had first come over from Normandy at the time of the Conquest is credible, especially as they had a French name. William also held Combe in the nearby parish of Holbeton and some other lands, but these were not extensive properties and would not have by themselves given their owner high standing in the county. William left Wimpstone to his oldest son, William, and Combe to his second son, John senior, who married twice, his first wife Clarice was probably the mother of his sons Henry, John junior and Richard. John senior's second wife was Eleanor Norreis, daughter of William Norreis of North Huish Devon, and she is not recorded until 1421, by which time her stepsons were adults.[9] Since they were all married and active in local society by the early 1420s it is reasonable to assume that they were born during the last years of the previous century and that their early years were probably spent at the manor of Combe.

The process by which the Fortescues provided themselves with a distinguished ancestry may be traced to the Herald's Visitation to Devon in 1564/5, a time when several members of the family held offices or were about to gain them in government, the royal household or the law. John Fortescue of Spridleston, Devon, for example, had two sons, Nicholas and Lewis, who were respectively a groom porter and a baron of the Exchequer under Henry VIII. Later in the century Sir John Fortescue of Salden, Oxfordshire, achieved even greater distinction as a privy councillor to Elizabeth I and Chancellor of the Exchequer under both the Queen and James I.[10] Nigel Ramsay's edited collection *Heralds and Heraldry in Shakespeare's England* has recently confirmed the suspicion that many medieval pedigrees were 'improved' with the collusion of

[8] *CPR*, Henry VI, 1422–29, 108. Four references to William Fortescue during the later reign of Richard II show him busy with local affairs and legal disputes and raising taxes for the Crown but none declare his social status, TNA, C 54/232, mem.20d; C 60/189, mem.20; C 66/322, mem.11d; C66/324.

[9] *Register of Edmund Stafford, Bishop of Exeter, 1395–1419*, ed. F.C. Hingeston-Randolph (London: 1886) 8 May 1412, 275. No surname or parent is assigned to Clarice in this one known reference to her; *Register of Edmund Lacy, Bishop of Exeter, 1420–1455, Registrum Commune*, ed. G.R. Dunstan, 5 vols (Torquay: 1963–72) 1, 35; Clermont, *Family*, 7–8, 42; see below (p. 24 n. 49) for somewhat impressionistic accounts of Richard's age in 1433 and 1442.

[10] J. Broadway, *'No historie so meete': Gentry Culture and the Development of Local History in Elizabethan and Early Stuart England* (Manchester: 2006) 150–78; Clermont, *Family*, 11, 312–416.

2 Combe farm, ancient walls, Holbeton, Devonshire.

visiting heralds.[11] London, BL Harley MSS 889 and 1091 tell the same inaccurate tale: 'Sir' John Fortescue was the second son of William of Wimpstone and served Henry V in France as captain of Meaux in Brie.[12] His son was Henry Fortescue, Chief Justice in Ireland, who had three sons, Henry the eldest, Sir John Fortescue Chief Justice of England, the second and Richard the third son.[13] The herald, William Harvey, Clarenceux King of Arms, thus inserted a non-existent generation into the pedigree and awarded Meaux to John Fortescue senior.

Political society in Devon in the early fifteenth century presented considerable challenges to the gentry, knights and nobles who participated in local governance. The success with which they navigated its opportunities and pitfalls would determine whether they could ascend to fortune and favour in the county and at a national level. The Fortescues and their like were fortunate that the leader of their society was Edward

[11] Ramsay, *Heralds and Heraldry*, *passim*.

[12] London, BL MS Harley 889, f. 49a, dated 1565; MS Harley 1091, ff. 58a–59b, copied by Jacob Chaloner, a Jacobean arms painter with additions by John Saunders. Richard Fortescue was credited with a knighthood

[13] London, BL MS Harley 1538, f. 94a, dating from the early seventeenth century.

Courtenay, earl of Devon. He had backed Henry Bolingbroke when he seized the throne in 1399 and his house remained loyal to the dynasty (with one brief aberration in the mid-1450s) until it was destroyed in 1471. The honour and power that the earl enjoyed also enhanced the fortunes of his affinity and their friends and families in Devon. The problem by the second decade of the century, however, was that the earl was blind and aged and could no longer exercise the authority that had originally put him in such a commanding position. Martin Cherry has traced the sorry story of how fissures appeared in the community of Devon and how these were compounded when Earl Edward died in 1419, only to be followed by a short-lived heir who was then succeeded by a young child, Earl Thomas, in 1422.[14]

These developments did not necessarily have to be disastrous; Simon Payling, Nigel Saul, Susan Wright and Simon Walker amongst others have discussed magnate lordship as conceived as a vertical system but also suggested that counties could be effectively governed by independent gentry establishments in which dominant bonds were horizontal.[15] Proliferating county studies in recent decades have shown that some could function reasonably well without a great magnate. Yet several factors made the case of Devon and Cornwall as a dysfunctional area during the reign of Henry VI intractable. Hannes Kleineke has argued that the absence of a strong royal presence in the duchy of Cornwall for most of the century as well as its remoteness from London was compounded by problems such as the innate lawlessness and predisposition to violence of the shipmen, tinners and others who were greedy for the wealth of the mines.[16] Piracy was thriving in the West. There

[14] M. Cherry, 'The Courtenay Earls of Devon. The Formation and Disintegration of a Late Medieval Aristocratic Affinity', *Southern History*, 1 (1979) 71–97; H. Kleineke, '"Þe Kynges Cite": Exeter in the Wars of the Roses', *The Fifteenth Century VII: Conflicts, Consequences and the Crown in the Late Middle Ages*, ed. L. Clark (Woodbridge: 2007) 137–56. When Earl Thomas came of age in 1435 he was backed by the Beauforts in his conflict with Sir William (later Lord) Bonville, eventually subsumed into the rivalries of the Wars of the Roses.

[15] N. Saul, *Knights and Esquires: The Gloucestershire Gentry in the Fourteenth Century* (Oxford: 1981) 260–2; S.M. Wright, *The Derbyshire Gentry in the Fifteenth Century* (Chesterfield: 1984) 235–61; S.K. Walker, *The Lancastrian Affinity* (Oxford: 1990); S. Payling, *Political Society in Lancastrian England: The Greater Gentry of Nottinghamshire* (Oxford: 1991) 105–8. See also the overview by Watts, *Henry VI*, 91–101.

[16] H. Kleineke, 'Why the West Was Wild: Law and Disorder in Fifteenth Century Cornwall and Devon', *The Fifteenth Century, III: Authority and Subversion*, ed. L. Clark (Woodbridge: 2003) 75–93. The custom that gave the duchy of Cornwall

was, for example, the case of the notorious *Mackerel* of Fowey, a pirate barge that belonged to the duke of Exeter, the Admiral of the West.[17] Another factor that made for turbulence was that the far West was a fertile ground for recruitment during the Hundred Years War with France. If the war kept some potentially violent men out of the counties for several decades, their return full of discontent in its last stages was to compound a dangerous situation.

Another consequence of the West's engagement with the war in France was an increased consciousness of the distinctive character of England and the English. Andrea Ruddick has traced the growth of this tendency from the late thirteenth century and throughout the fourteenth century: a climate of opinion that was well established when the young Fortescues were growing up.[18] John junior's two brothers were actively involved in the reconquest of Normandy and John probably lived in a climate of patriotic, if not xenophobic, opinion as a child and a young adult.[19] This seems to have influenced his attitudes in later life, especially those expressed in his best known works the *De Laudibus Legum Angliae* and the *Governance of England.*

The Fortescue family was confronted by the same opportunities and temptations as other lawyers and minor gentry in Devon and Cornwall in the early decades of the fifteenth century and on the whole did rather well out of the situation. John Fortescue senior, the father of the subject of this study, was probably in his forties when he was appointed as one of the stewards of Edward, earl of Devon, in about 1413.[20] In that year John senior made his one recorded journey abroad when he obtained a safe-conduct to sail on a ship commissioned at Plymouth by the Courtenays to convey pilgrims to the shrine of St James of Compostela in Galicia.[21] In 1416 he was given the office of escheator for the counties

---

to the heir to the throne ensured that it was ruled by a minor and his household or council for most of the fifteenth century. One exception was when Henry of Monmouth (later Henry V) was prince of Wales.

17 N.A.M. Rodger, *The Safeguard of the Sea: A Naval history of Britain, 660–1649* (London: 1997) vol. 1, 147–9.

18 A. Ruddick, *English Identity and Political Culture in the Fourteenth Century* (Cambridge: 2013).

19 See below, Chapter 4, p. 185, nn. 91, 92, for English anti-French propaganda during the fifteenth century.

20 L.S. Woolger, 'John Fortescue', *The History of Parliament: The House of Commons, 1386–1421*, 4 vols, ed. L. Clark, C. Rawcliffe and J.S. Roskell (Stroud: 1992) vol. 3, 109.

21 Calendar of the French Rolls, *The Forty-Fourth Annual Report of the Deputy Keeper of the Public Records* (London: 1883) 545.

of Cornwall and Devon.[22] There is no evidence that he had any military ambitions;[23] his activities seem to have been confined to property transactions, legal work and estate management. When in 1419 Hugh Courtenay succeeded as earl of Devon, he appointed John Fortescue senior as one of his stewards or possibly allowed him to retain the post he had held under the previous earl.[24]

Henry Fortescue, John senior's oldest son, made a promising start to his career when he served Sir Hugh in 1419 (before he became earl) as his squire (*scutifer*) on an expedition to Normandy in the spring.[25] In the following year he served Hugh, who had by then succeeded his father as earl of Devon, as a man-at-arms on the *Grace Dieu*, the flagship of the fleet that was defending the English Channel.[26] He sat in the parliament of 1421 as a knight of the shire for Devon.[27] He was, however, soon to show the forceful, impetuous tendencies that characterised his conduct from time to time and seem to have affected his promising legal career that is discussed below. The Patent Rolls record that on 3 July 1422 William Cheyne and others were sent into Devon on a commission of oyer and terminer to investigate a charge by Thomas Gylle of Dodbrook that he had been assaulted by Henry Fortescue and 'other evildoers'. They had besieged and broken his houses and pursued him to Dodbrook town market with drawn swords and later lain in ambush to kill him so that he dared not approach his houses. This was how a violent and arrogant man, back from the war in France and belonging to the affinity of the earls of Devon, thought that he would settle a property dispute.[28]

Whilst the English Fortescues were doing well in Devon, the French branch of the family was still flourishing in Normandy. It is worth

22 *CCR*, Henry V, 1413–19, 454.

23 I am grateful to Anne Curry, Professor of Medieval History at the University of Southampton, who some years ago consulted her database which records the names of those who are known to have been involved in the wars of the English in France. She wrote: 'I doubt whether … John Fortescue was ever captain of Meaux. So far there seems to be no proof that he ever served in France.'

24 *CCR*, Henry VI, 1422–29, 39, an order to the escheator of Devon to take the fealty of various feoffees holding property for Hugh, late earl of Devon. They include John Fortescue, esquire, 'then his steward', and Henry Fortescue. See below, p. 28, n. 69.

25 TNA, Issue Roll, Henry V, Pasch., E403/640, 20 May 1419.

26 R.W. Dunning and L.S. Woodger, 'Henry Fortescue', *House of Commons, 1386–1421*, 3, 108.

27 *Ibid.*

28 *CPR*, Henry V, 1416–22, July 3 1422, 447.

remarking on this as their careers may provide an explanation for the myth surrounding 'Sir' John Fortescue, governor of Meaux. One of them died fighting for Charles VI at Agincourt, but his brother Jean made a smooth transfer of allegiance to Henry V. He was appointed as captain and administrator general of maritime affairs in the Cotentin, subsequently held several offices, was knighted and given a command in the English army in 1429.[29] It is easy to see how his career could have been confused with that of his contemporary, John Fortescue senior. Although John Fortescue junior was later to write about social and economic conditions in Normandy, he did not refer to his French relatives. He must have been aware of their existence and the reasons for his silence can only be a matter for speculation.

The Fortescue family, like many of their gentry contemporaries, improved their status and prospects through their legal expertise in the early fifteenth century. John senior and his sons Henry and John used their professional knowledge of the law very effectively to enhance their family's interests. Many young men, often the sons of gentry, spent time at the Inns of Chancery and Inns of Court to complete their education and acquire sufficient knowledge of the law to pursue the business of their estates.[30] The large number of statute books owned by private individuals, men and women, in the late middle ages indicates a widespread interest and engagement in the law, principally motivated by the need to protect families' property interests.[31]

The fragmentary records of Lincoln's Inn before 1422 cannot provide a full account of the Fortescues' membership, but the manuscript as well as the printed version of the first *Black Book* indicates that there was a John senior and that John junior (later Sir John Fortescue, the subject of this book) was also there and very active by the 1420s.[32] Henry

[29] Clermont, *Family*, 322–56; *The Forty-First Annual Report of the Deputy Keeper of the Public Records* (London: 1880) 756.

[30] J.H. Baker, *The Legal Profession and the Common Law: Historical Essays* (London: 1986) 95–6.

[31] D.C. Skemer, 'Reading the Law: Statute Books and the Private Transmission of Legal Knowledge in Late Medieval England', *Learning the Law: Teaching and Transmission of Law in England, 1150–1900*, ed. J.A. Bush and A. Wijffels (London and Rio Grande: 1999) 113–31.

[32] *Records of the Honourable Society of Lincoln's Inn: The Black Books*, vol. 1, *Admissions from 1422 to 1586* (London: 1897) 1–4; see also the manuscript of the first volume held in Lincoln's Inn, London. On f. 7v there is a reference to 'Johannes ffortescu junior'. This implies that the senior Fortescue shared the same name of 'John' and was Sir John's father rather than his older brother Henry. The two Johns were sometimes distinguished in other documents in the same way.

Fortescue made no identifiable appearance but he must have received a legal training, probably at Lincoln's Inn, as he was sufficiently versed in the intricacies of land tenure to figure with his father in legal documents from the early 1420s and to receive a high legal office.[33]

In 1426 Henry Fortescue was appointed Chief Justice of Kings Bench in Ireland. The move may well have been dictated by the demise of the last adult earl of Devon, which stopped for the immediate future a local source of employment and patronage: Henry held office for three years before returning to England.[34] He acquired some modest property through his three marriages: first to Katherine, of Wood Barton before 1421, second to Joan, daughter of Edmund Bosom of Bosomzeal before 1424 and third, by 1437, to Margaret daughter of Nicholas Fallapit of Fallapit.[35] Henry had several children including an heir, John, but none of his marriages were to bring him wealth or important contacts, either in the West or nationally, and that obscurity makes it hard to trace all the details of his career.

Lincoln's Inn was not mentioned in 1388 when there was a call of sergeants from the Inner and Middle Temples and Gray's Inn, which indicates that it could have been established after that date, M. McGlynn, *The Royal Prerogative and the Learning of the Inns of Court* (Cambridge: 2003) 15–16.

[33] *CPR*, Henry VI, 1422–29, 108; *CFR*, Henry VI, 1422–30, 79–80, Henry Fortescue was described as 'gentleman'; *CCR*, Henry VI, 1422–29, 39. J. Baker, *The Men of Court, 1440–1550*, 2 vols (London: 2012) vol. 1, 699 suggests that 'Fortescue senior' was Henry rather than his father John. No reference to 'Fortescue senior' is to be found in the *Black Books*, but his existence is implied by the references to 'Fortescue junior', who certainly was our John Fortescue. Baker may have based his assumption on the entries in the *Records of the Honourable Society of Lincoln's Inn*, 2 vols (London: 1896) vol. 1, 2, which lists a Fortescue senior (Henry) and a Fortescue junior (John). Given the vestigial records before 1422 it is possible that both John senior and his son Henry attended the Inn for a time. Several later Fortescues, including the scholarly Sir Adrian, were members.

[34] *Rotulorum Patentium et Clausorum Cancellariae Hiberniae Calendarium* (Dublin: 1828) vol. 1, 241, 243, 246, 248–9; F. Elrington Ball, *The Judges in Ireland*, 2 vols (London: 1926) vol. 1, 100, 157, 175. Clermont stated that he was Chief Justice of Common Pleas, *Family*, 42, but Elrington Ball cites him in the list of Chief Justices of Kings Bench. This is confirmed in the *Rotul: Patentium … Hiberniae*, 249, where he is described as 'C.J. Hib', and another, James Alleyn knight, is given as 'C.J. de C.B.', Communi Banco/Common Bench or Pleas.

[35] Clermont, *Family*, 45; 'Lacy Register', vol. 1, p. 20, where Henry and his wife Katherine were granted permission to hold divine service in their house called 'Le Wode in the parish of Wodelegh' in 1420–21, Katherine's surname is not known; *ibid.*, vol. 2, 70, the same permission was given to Henry and Margaret his wife in 1437. See also *House of Commons, 1386–1421*, vol. 3, 108–9.

A statement by Sir John Fortescue in the *De Laudibus Legum Anglie* has led some writers to calculate that he must have been born between 1385 and 1395.[36] This conviction arose from the passage he wrote about the office of Serjeant-at-Law:

> Nor has anyone been admitted to this estate and degree who has not first completed sixteen years at least in the general study of the law; and as a sign that all justices have so graduated, each of them, when seated in the court of the king, will wear a coif of white silk, which is the primary and principle of the sartorial insignia with which serjeants-at-law are decorated at their creation.[37]

The evidence was eventually reassessed and it indicates that the date at which Fortescue became a Serjeant-at-Law should be changed from 1430, the year previously favoured, to 1437/8. Originally a case in the *Year Book* for the eighth year of Henry VI involving Fortescue and others, all referred to as 'apprenticii' (barristers), was taken by William Dugdale and succeeding writers to mean that he must already have become a serjeant.[38] They thought that only those who had become serjeants could plead at adjourned assizes, but S.E. Thorne and Sir Ronald Roxburgh have argued that apprentices were allowed to plead. Roxburgh went on to cite entries from the *Black Books* of Lincoln's Inn showing that Fortescue was resident there when he surrendered his keys to the Inn in July 1437, and then presumably followed the traditional practice on promotion of transferring to one of the serjeants' inns.[39] This allows him to have been in his sixties and seventies rather than ten years older during the violent upheavals of the civil wars, when he went into exile and produced many of his works.

Fortescue's birth is likely to have occurred in the last years of the fourteenth century rather than after 1400. The *Black Books* record him as one of the Governors of Lincoln's Inn in 1424–25, 1425–26, 1428–29

[36] Plummer aired the possibilities in 1885, *Governance of England*, 40, n. 4.

[37] Chrimes, *De Laudibus*, 125.

[38] *Medieval English History: An Index and Paraphrase of Printed Year Book Reports, 1268–1535*, compiled by D.S. Seipp (Boston: 2007) (http://www.bu.edu/law/faculty-scholarship/legal-history-the-year-books/) 1430.076.

[39] S.E. Thorne, *Readings and Moots at the Inns of Court in the Fifteenth Century* (London: 1954) vol. 1, lix–lx, lxxi, n. 12; R. Roxburgh, *The Records of the Honourable Society of Lincoln's Inn: The Black Books*, vol. 5, *Two Postscripts* (London: 1977) 19–22; J.H. Baker, *The Order of Serjeants* (London: 1984). There were two serjeants' inns, one in Fleet Street and the other in Chancery Lane.

3 Sir John Fortescue, the Salden portrait. An engraving from an anonymous portrait on canvas probably dating from the mid-sixteenth century

and 1429–30.[40] The Governors had considerable responsibilities and only a lawyer of some seniority could expect to be so honoured. On the other hand, boys as young as fifteen were admitted to the Inns and John Fortescue's considerable abilities, ambition and, perhaps, influential friends could have led to his preferment rather more rapidly than was usual.[41] The surviving portraits of Fortescue date from the sixteenth or the seventeenth centuries, and the Salden portrait was owned by the Fortescue family.[42] They are sufficiently similar to have been based on an original which from the clothing, long hair and shaven face probably dates from the early Tudor period, they show a vigorous and reasonably youthful man, an image that is repeated on his tomb in Ebrington Church, Gloucestershire.

John senior's third son, Richard, did not apparently receive a legal training, since he worked as a mercer and then took advantage of the opportunities presented by the French campaigns. He was an apprentice to Everard Flete, a London mercer, 1409/10 to 1418/19 but seems to have abandoned his long training in favour of the excitement of the wars in France.[43] He appeared in the French rolls in 1421 as 'Richard Fortescu, of Ermyngton, Devon', in the retinue of Richard Hankeford, a fellow Devonian who had made a successful career as one of Henry V's captains.[44] Richard Fortescue had married: he and his wife, Agnes, daughter of Thomas Windsor and granddaughter of Richard Holcombe, were mentioned in an indenture and a letter relating to a dispute with

[40] *Black Books*, vol. 1, 1, 2, 3, 4. He was referred to as 'Pensioner' for 1429–30. Pensioners collected the dues from Fellows to pay for their expenses at the Inn.

[41] E.W. Ives, *The Common Lawyers of Pre-Reformation England, Thomas Kebell: A Case Study* (Cambridge: 1983) 36.

[42] In 1869 the Salden portrait was owned by Francis Fortescue Turville, Esq. It survives in a private collection and could have been commissioned during the sixteenth century, when a later Sir John Fortescue lived at Salden and was Chancellor of the Exchequer to Elizabeth I and James I. Clermont printed an anonymous engraving of the picture in his *Works* and an engraving by William Faithorne, *c.*1663, of another portrait of Fortescue. This was destroyed by a fire at the Fortescue residence of Castle Hill, Devon in 1936. Nineteenth-century copies of it are held at Castle Hill and Lincoln's Inn. I am grateful to Lady Arran and Megan Dunmall, Archivist at Lincoln's Inn, for this information. The painters of both portraits are unknown. L. Fagan, *A Descriptive Catalogue of the Engraved Works of William Faithorne* (London: 1888) 36.

[43] *The Medieval Account Books of the Mercers of London*, ed. L. Jefferson, 2 vols (Aldershot: 2008) vol. 1, 228–9, 308–9. The books contain no other references to Richard Fortescue.

[44] *Forty-Fourth Annual Report of the Deputy Keeper of the Public Records*, 632.

Thomas Chaucer and other feoffees of Thomas Stonor I in 1424 over the manor of Ermington, Devon.

John Fortescue junior had assisted in drafting the indenture dealing with Ermington, showing that he was putting his legal skills to work for his family.[45] The dispute concerned a petition filed in Chancery by Thomas Chaucer and his fellow feoffees. They protested that they were seised of the manor and hundred of Ermington until Richard Fortescue of great malice and forethought made a forcible entry and broke down hedges and ditches. The indenture seems to have been a compromise agreement made by the cool judgement of John junior, his father and Thomas Stonor. Richard and his wife waived their rights of pasture within the manor in exchange for twelve acres of land adjacent to their own property. A draft of a reasonably affable letter from Thomas Stonor to John Fortescue senior confirms this interpretation; his lawyer son figures again: 'And seeth that youre forseyde son Rychard duly ensile the same endenture, for youre son Jonys honestie hanketh theron.' This settlement did not last and in 1438 Henry and then his brother John Fortescue were called in to arbitrate but the dispute continued.[46]

Richard may have built on his first sortie into France and earlier work for the mercers to establish business connections as, in February 1425/6, he was described as 'Richard Fortescu of Halcombe, Devon, alias citizen and mercer of London', travelling in the retinue of the duke of Bedford.[47] Like his brother Henry, Richard seems to have had a disputacious, even violent side to his nature. Apart from the legal wrangle with the Stonors, he was associated with Henry in an affray that probably took place in 1431.[48] Despite the dubious side to his character, Richard was regularly called upon to act as a juror, eight times for inquisitions post mortem

[45] *Kingsford's Stonor Letters and Papers, 1290–1483*, ed. C. Carpenter, 2 vols (Cambridge: 1996) vol. 1, 36–9.

[46] H. Kleineke, 'Richard Fortescue' (d.1480, the son of Richard Fortescue and the nephew of John junior), *The History of Parliament: The House of Commons, 1422–1461*, ed. L. Clark, forthcoming. I am grateful to the Trustees of the History of Parliament for allowing me to use this material.

[47] *The Forty-Eighth Annual Report of the Deputy Keeper of the Public Records* (London: 1887) vol. 2, 240.

[48] See below, p. 29 n. 72. The dispute at Ermington revived in the 1460s between Richard Fortescue, the oldest son of Richard, John junior's brother, and Thomas Stonor II and his friends and servants. His bailiff, John Frende, was physically menaced and imprisoned by Richard, who seems to have inherited his father's disputacious temperament. The Fortescues would have been weakened at that time by the disgrace and exile of Sir John. In the reign of Henry VIII an act of parliament confirmed the Stonors' right to various manors

between 1432 and 1447. On two occasions his age was recorded; in 1433 he was described as '43 years and more', but in 1442 his age was given as '40 and more'. He was reputedly the youngest of the three brothers, so, despite the rather vague accounts of his age, this tends to push John's birth, as the middle brother, back into the 1390s.[49]

John Fortescue's early career

Unlike his father and older brother John Fortescue junior seems to have focussed his ambitions on the capital city from an early stage in his career. Thomas Tanner stated that he attended Exeter College, Oxford, but no evidence for this has been found.[50] Dr John Maddicott, the college historian, writes: 'Sir John Fortescue's membership of the college is an often-repeated myth. There is absolutely no evidence for it. If he was a fellow this would almost certainly show up in the records; and his birth *c.*1385 would make him of undergraduate age before the college began to take undergraduates (who in any case were very few and far between in the early years).'[51] The skill of his later writings together with the good grounding in scholastic works that they display indicate that Fortescue had been well taught, although nothing is known of his early years. John Prince wrote of 'the learned works he published, which we can hardly suppose should be written with so much art, without the assistance of an academical education'.[52] Although he does not seem to have attended a university hall it is quite possible that Fortescue's knowledge of scholastic works could be explained by his family's employment of a tutor who had studied in Oxford or Cambridge. His manifest intelligence and application (in contrast to his rather thuggish brothers) would have made it worth their while to do so. If this was the case his tutor might have given him some grounding in civil law since this was taught at both universities, whereas common law was taught in London in the courts

including Ermington, *Kingsford's Stonor Letters*, *passim*; A. Hanham, 'Pleas, Pigs and Peascods: Three Unpublished Stonor Accounts', *The Ricardian*, 24 (2014) 113–19.

[49] *CIPM*, 11–15 Henry VI, 1432–37, no.124, 110; *CIPM*, 21–5 Henry VI, 1442–47, no.146, 85.

[50] T. Tanner, *Bibliotheca Britannico-Hibernica sive de scriptoribus* (London: 1748) 293; but see Chrimes, *De Laudibus*, lxx, who dismissed the idea.

[51] I am very grateful to Dr Maddicott for this information given in an e-mail of 31 July 2012.

[52] Prince, *Worthies*, 305.

and their inns.[53] Fortescue's first major treatise, the *De Natura Legis Naturae*, shows a decent knowledge of civil law.

Once Fortescue reached Lincoln's Inn he would have benefited from a fine higher education: regular readings and moots were held supervised by senior members. Together with private study of legal treatises and manuals and regular experience of the practicalities of pleading in the Westminster courts, they provided a level and quality of instruction not to be found elsewhere and which compared favourably with what was offered by the universities.[54] Fortescue paid tribute to it in the *De Laudibus Legum Anglie*:

> In these greater inns, indeed, and also in the lesser, there is, besides a school of law, a kind of academy of all the manners that the nobles learn. There they learn to sing and to exercise themselves in every kind of harmonics. They are also taught there to practise dancing and all games proper for nobles, as those brought up in the king's household are accustomed to practise. In the vacations most of them apply themselves to the study of legal science, and at festivals to the reading, after the divine services, of Holy Scripture and of chronicles. This is indeed a cultivation of virtues and a banishment of all vice. So for the sake of the acquisition of virtue and the discouragement of vice, knights, barons, and also other magnates, and the nobles of the realm place their sons in these inns, although they do not desire them to be trained in the science of the laws, nor to live by its practice, but only by their patrimonies.[55]

It is, however, suggested below, in Chapter 5, that many of Fortescue's reminiscences in the *De Laudibus* sound like the rose-tinted memories of an exile and that they were also intended to press a positive view of the common law of England on Prince Edward of Lancaster.

One way in which an ambitious young lawyer could enhance his career prospects was to accept posts from powerful ecclesiastical or lay bodies. John junior did precisely this when when he was recorded acting as an undersheriff for the City of London's Sheriff's Court in 1423/4. He was paid 16s 8d in total for participating in an action between the

[53] P. Brand, 'Learning English Customary Law: Education in the London Law School, 1250–1500', *Vocabulary of Teaching and Research between Middle Ages and Renaissance*, ed. O. Weijers (Turnhout: 1995) 199–213.

[54] Baker, *Legal Profession*, 22–3; J.H. Baker, *Readers and Readings in the Inns of Court and Chancery*, Selden Society (London: 2000) 4–11.

[55] Chrimes, *De Laudibus*, 119. Fortescue, perhaps in order to recommend the study of the law to Edward of Lancaster, exaggerated the status of many of its students in this passage.

Tailors' Company and a parson: the reason for this remuneration was not given, and could have related to one sum or a series of smaller payments, perhaps for giving counsel and/or acting on the Company's behalf in the Westminster courts.[56] Later in the decade he was to achieve a more lucrative post in the duchy of Lancaster [57] and he was a counsel for the city of Canterbury from 1429 and for the city of Exeter in the 1430s.[58]

It was probably in the early 1420s that John Fortescue junior married Elizabeth Brytte, a local heiress to a modest estate in Leigh Peverell and Compton, Devon. This linked the Fortescues to the powerful family of the Champernouns, who owned a mansion in the centre of Modbury, as well as other estates in Devon and Cornwall.[59] Elizabeth died on 2 May 1427 while still a minor; she was without issue so her interest in that Champernoun inheritance reverted to her sister Margaret, who was of age, the wife of Thomas Wyse, who was later to appear in several transactions with John junior.[60] It is possible that the severing of such a personal link with his neighbourhood confirmed John junior's interest in London and the powerbrokers who were to be found there rather than in the narrower attractions of Devon, although it was not unusual for lawyers to practise in London and retain their regional links.

The whole Fortescue family had suffered a setback in 1422 with the premature death of earl Hugh Courtenay. His young son and heir, Thomas, would be in no position to exercise patronage for over a decade and, in the meantime, John senior had lost his post as steward. In the

[56] P. Tucker, *Law Courts and Lawyers in the City of London, 1300–1550* (Cambridge: 2007) 279–80.

[57] See below, pp. 36–7, n. 102.

[58] Baker, *Readers and Readings*, 106; see below, pp. 30–1, n. 79.

[59] G.A. Cawse, *Modbury* (London: 1860) 14–16, 22–3; Elizabeth and her sister Margaret were the great granddaughters of Agnes Dodescombe who had married Adam Bramscombe as her first husband. She had a daughter by him whose son, Robert Brytte, was the father of the Brytte sisters. Agnes had married Richard Champernoun as her second husband but their son, Otis, was without issue, so when he died Margaret and Elizabeth inherited his lands in Leigh Peverell and Compton. *CFR*, Henry VI, 1422–30, 42–3, an order to the escheator in the county of Devon on 30 May 1423 for the disposition of the Champernoun property; *CIPM*, 1–5 Henry VI, 1422–27, no.141, 163–5, no. 332, 176–7.

[60] *CFR*, Henry VI, 1422–30, 111. Writ of 'diem clausit extremum' after the death of Elizabeth, late wife of John Fortescue the younger. TNA, Inquisitions Post Mortem, C 139/43/6, 8 Henry VI (1429). Thomas Wyse was a member of Lincoln's Inn, *Records*, 1, 2; Baker, *Men of Court*, vol. 2, 1724; H. Kleineke, 'Thomas Wyse', *House of Commons 1422–1461*.

terms discussed above this changed the power structure in Devon from a vertical system based on the lordship of a great magnate to a horizontal one of gentry establishments. However, John Watts has asked whether, even when a magnate (or the monarch) dominated a county, such hegemony was invariably as significant as some historians have imagined.[61] The earl's cousins, the Courtenays of Powderham, and the Bonvilles gravitated to the circle of Walter, Lord Hungerford, which was establishing itself as a power centre in the West.[62] Under the deteriorating conditions for the enforcement of royal authority nationally, the area was to become increasingly wild during the following decades.[63] The gentry in such situations were by no means invariably on the side of what modern observers would call 'law and order', and this was to be true of the Fortescues as they tried to hold on to their property and look after their family.[64]

The John Fortescue of London 'gentilman', who figured in 1426 as a mainpernor (surety) for John Wyse (probably the father of Thomas Wyse) and Richard Trevaignon, was almost certainly John junior, although the mid and late 1420s and early 1430s are the most difficult period in which to distinguish father and son from each other.[65] Use of the descriptions 'senior' and 'junior' lapsed, and some of the 'John Fortescues' could, in any case, refer to John of Wimpstone, the son of William junior, or to Henry Fortescue's son John of Wood Barton. The remainder of the career of John senior can, therefore, only be tentatively suggested. In May 1430 he was probably controller of the coinage of tin in Devon and Cornwall: this could have been a post obtained for him by his increasingly influential son John.[66] In July 1432 when John Merston, Keeper of the King's Jewels, was given the post he was to receive the same fees and wages as his predecessor, who was probably dead by then.[67]

John Fortescue senior was unquestionably dead by 1436 since in that year his sons, Henry and John, and John junior's second wife Isabella (also called 'Elizabeth'), agreed to a transfer of various properties in

[61] Watts, *Henry VI*, 91–2.

[62] See below, pp. 34–7, for Lord Hungerford.

[63] R.L. Storey, *The End of the House of Lancaster* (Stroud: 1986) 84–92, 98–99, 165–75.

[64] P.C. Maddern, *Violence and Social Order: East Anglia 1422–1442* (Oxford: 1992).

[65] *CFR*, Henry VI, 1422–30, 154–5; L.S. Clark, 'John Wyse', *House of Commons, 1386–1421*, vol. 4, 933–4.

[66] *CPR*, Henry VI, 1429–36, 54.

[67] *Ibid.*, 203.

Devon from the former to the latter: they were described by Henry as 'formerly belonging to my father John Fortescue'.[68] In 1441 the escheator of Somerset was ordered to give Henry Fortescue, the only surviving feoffee, livery of the manor of Crewkerne so that it might be passed to Thomas Courtenay, earl of Devon (by then an adult). The abstract of this document, which attests to the decease of John Fortescue senior, is worth quoting as it is the strongest piece of evidence for his career as it has been outlined above, as opposed to the 'glorious captain of Meaux' version of earlier histories:

> on Wednesday 4 June 9 Henry V [1422] Hugh Courtenay, late earl of Devon gave the said manor (among other things) to Hugh Courtenay of Haccombe, knight, his uncle, Hugh Lutrell, knight, his cousin, John Fortescue esquire then his steward, Thomas Hendeman, Richard Aldrynton clerks, John Selman, William Dawny, Richard Bamfyle and the said Henry [Fortescue] for forty years from Midsummer day then next, and that on 30 June following he made a quitclaim therof to them, their heirs and assigns, in their possession being, that after he died, and those feoffees assigned the said manor to the countess in dower, that the other feoffees are dead, and the reversion of the manor belongs to the said Henry only and to his heirs and assigns.[69]

Henry Fortescue's career as Chief Justice of King's Bench for Ireland had been looking promising: in 1426 he received a salary of forty pounds per annum, later altered to forty pence a day, and a grant of the custody of some manors but, never one to avoid trouble, he was proactive on behalf of the English settlers. By the end of 1429 he had been relieved of the post of Chief Justice, and Stephen Bray, who he had superseded three years earlier, had been reappointed. The reason for this is not known, although it could be significant that Henry Fortescue had been a member of two delegations to the English government to state the grievances of the settlers in Ireland and during their first mission they appear to have been involved in an affray.[70] This scandal can hardly have

[68] Devon County Record Office, Exeter, 1262, M/T, 570. Quitclaim of messuages (sites for dwellings) and lands in Overcombe, Efford and Alston by Henry Fortescue to John, his brother and John's wife Isabella. Clermont stated that Richard Fortescue inherited Punsborne in Hertfordshire from his father in about 1435 but the *VCH* records that in 1441 John Kirkeby died seized of it and that it was purchased by Sir John Fortescue in 1447/8. It passed to John, son of Sir John's brother Richard, later in the century, Clermont, *Family*, 151; *VCH*, Hertfordshire, vol. 3, 105, 422; see below, Chapter 2.

[69] *CCR*, Henry VI, 1435–41, 418.

[70] Clermont, *Family*, 42–3.

been welcome to the royal council, preoccupied with the French war and the damaging animosity between the Protector Gloucester and Cardinal Beaufort. The fuss must also have embarrassed Henry's brother John, who was by the late 1420s associated with the interests of Walter, Lord Hungerford, an influential member of the council.

In 1430 Henry was a feoffee for James Butler, earl of Ormonde, one of the foremost nobles in Ireland and potentially an influential patron.[71] Henry did not abandon all his Irish associates, for it was probably in 1431 that another embarrassing affray took place. Together with his brother Richard Fortescue and 'grete peuple of Irysshemen and othere in the maner of were arraide', he was accused of breaking into the house of Richard and Margery Sackville in pursuit of a claim to their property in Nethercombe, Devon. They protested that their furniture had been damaged, Richard Sackville had been arrested without a warrant, their children had been cast out 'al naked' and Margery had been beaten so severely that she had miscarried. The unfortunate Sackville had been kept in prison in London for more than three years at the time of the petition (probably 1434) and it is possible that the good offices of John Fortescue junior could have been invoked to support his brother's claims:[72] as is so often the case, the final result of this sorry affair is not recorded.

There seems to have been a streak of instability in Henry's character: his alienation of property to John was perhaps an indication of failing fortune and there are unanswered questions about his career in Ireland. In 1434 he appeared with his brother Richard amongst the gentry of Devonshire to whom the bishop of Exeter, Roger Champernoun and Philip Carey administered oaths not to maintain peace-breakers. They were in the company of other notorious denizens of the wild West including members of the Courtenay and Bonville families. This was part of a huge exercise set up by act of parliament to administer oaths to potential trouble-makers throughout the country.[73] In the case of the Fortescues it just might have worked, since in the same year Henry was considered to be sufficiently respectable to participate in a commission of oyer and terminer in defence of the interests of the dean and chapter of Exeter Cathedral.[74] Whilst it was possible for a gentleman to act lawlessly and continue to prosper (see below, Chapter 2, for the career of William

[71] *CPR*, Henry VI, 1429–36, 27. Henry Fortescue is described as 'esquire'.

[72] *Calendars of the Proceedings in Chancery in the Reign of Queen Elizabeth with Earlier Proceedings from Richard II*, 4 vols (London: 1830) vol. 2, xviii–xix.

[73] *RP*, Henry VI, iv, 455–7; *PROME*, 11, 149–50; Lacy, 1, 273–8.

[74] *CPR*, Henry VI, 1429–36, 358, 399.

Tailboys), he would usually enjoy the protection of a powerful patron. The authors of Henry Fortescue's biography have pointed out that his career, after years in the doldrums, only picked up with his appointment as sheriff of Devon in 1446 and 1452 and of Cornwall in 1447, after his brother John had become Chief Justice of King's Bench.[75] So after his early promise his career lapsed into decent provincial respectability; Richard Fortescue prospered sufficiently to leave his heirs a good estate, whilst John Fortescue's progress in the law was an uninterrupted success story.

Alan Cromartie has observed that anything that the court of Common Pleas 'ever did had a potentially didactic function' and the same could be said of the other courts that sat in Westminster Hall: King's Bench and Chancery.[76] It has been suggested above that the young men who lived in the Inns and listened to the cases that were heard in the courts profited from a demanding and rigorous education that was unparalleled in any other institution, including the universities. Senior barristers regularly held readings, lectures on legal points arising from the statutes of the realm, for their benefit.[77] The moots, mock court sessions in which cases were discussed, were more lively and relatively junior lawyers could participate – they facilitated advocacy and thinking on one's feet. From the late thirteenth century some of the most useful discussions in Common Pleas and, less frequently, King's Bench were recorded in the *Year Books*. Direct experience of the law, teaching by seniors, debate and private reading of treatises such as the *Modus Componendi Brevia*, *Natura Breviarum*, *Hengham Parva* and *Curia Placita* provided young men with excellent opportunities.[78] Some, such as Fortescue senior and John Paston II, would apply their knowledge in administering their own and others' estates, lawyers like Henry and John Fortescue junior could use their knowledge to rise to high office.

John Fortescue was growing in importance. By 1437/8, for example, he felt that it was beneath his dignity to accept a mere 13s 4d from the city of Exeter as a retained counsel. He did, however, remain on the city's payroll, although the increase of the fee to £2 in 1440/1 indicates

[75] R.W. Dunning and L.S. Woodger, 'Henry Fortescue', *House of Commons, 1386–1421*, vol. 3, 108.

[76] A. Cromartie, *The Constitutionalist Revolution: An Essay on the History of England, 1450–1642* (Cambridge: 2006) 11.

[77] Baker, *Readers and Readings*, 4–11; P. Brand, *The Origins of the English Legal Profession* (Oxford: 1992) 114–19.

[78] Brand, *Origins*, 118.

that his status as a serjeant was being recognised.[79] The situation changed dramatically from 1439 as far as references in the *Year Books* are concerned; previously he had featured rarely, but the reports for that year covered eleven cases in which he participated and no less than seventy in 1440, cases invariably held in the Court of Common Pleas. Simultaneously records of his other public activities increase with membership of several commissions for the peace, one for oyer and terminer and one gaol delivery.[80] In 1441, the year in which he was made King's Serjeant, he was enormously busy, mentioned in no fewer than fifty-five cases as well as sitting on commissions for the peace in four counties and carrying out a gaol delivery.[81] It was customary for prominent figures to be named to sit on commissions that they did not invariably attend, but Fortescue's frequent appearance on the lists shows how highly he was regarded by the early 1440s.

The evidence of the *Year Books* does not indicate a low level of legal activity by Fortescue before 1439, since their compilers habitually only recorded the names of senior lawyers and justices. They do not and never were intended to give official or comprehensive accounts of cases in the Westminster courts and the majority of their reports relate to Common Pleas.[82] The main concern of the legal students and clerks who seem to have compiled them was to note the technical arguments about points of law and often the conclusion to a case was not recorded. A substantial number were also postponed to a later date. Both the arguments and the judges' decisions, when they were recorded, could form precedents for later cases, which promoted a strong sense of collective memory and, by the fifteenth century, had the force of law.[83]

John Fortescue belonged to a family in which his father and older brother had also undertaken a legal training and he came from the South West of England, which was peculiarly litigious, perhaps as a result of its lawlessness. Later in life the crises that afflicted the Lancastrian

[79] N. Ramsay, 'Retained Legal Counsel, *c.*1275–1475', *TRHS*, 35 (1985) 95–112; *CCR*, Henry VI, 1435–41, 250, John Fortescue 'serjeant at law' witness to a recognisance of 2,000 marks with Lord Hungerford, Sir Edmund Hungerford, etc., March 1439.

[80] *CPR*, Henry VI, 1436–41, 378, 413, 579.

[81] *CPR*, Henry VI, 1436–41, 579, 583–4, 589–90. There were three or four King's Serjeants who were paid a small retainer by the Crown to do its business. The rest of the time they continued their private practices; most eventually became judges.

[82] Ives, *Common Lawyers*, 148.

[83] A. Musson and W.M. Ormrod, *The Evolution of English Justice: Law, Politics and Society in the Fourteenth Century* (Basingstoke: 1999) 145.

government were to propel Fortescue into an increasingly prominent political role as his high legal status involved him in decisions where impartiality was simply not an option. He had spent decades in training and pleading as a junior barrister and this experience of the practicalities of the common law seems to have affected his later theories of how England should be governed. Most of the discussion recorded in the *Year Books* is highly technical, which is hardly surprising as this was what interested those who compiled them, but occasionally Fortescue expressed an opinion that could be seen in a wider context.

At the Court of Common Pleas in Michaelmas term 1440, for example, whilst Fortescue was arguing for the plaintiff in a fairly standard case of debt on arrears of rent, the question of jurisdiction in Wales came up. Here he treated the court to a fine historical distinction 'between Wales, which was a separate kingdom at one time, and Lancaster, Chester and Durham, which were derived out of the Crown, and were at one time at common law all one kingdom'.[84] The following year he was to make a long speech justifying the separate rights of the Irish government – did this reflect views he had formed whilst his brother Henry was Lord Chief Justice there?[85] These cases anticipate by twenty years arguments based on historical precedent that were to run through all his major works, a natural enough device for a common lawyer.

Once Fortescue had been appointed a King's Serjeant it was to be expected that he would try to protect the royal prerogative in cases where it was called in question, and he was to do exactly that in the Exchequer Chamber in Easter 1441. A defendant rector prayed to be discharged from paying any tithes because Henry IV had exempted his predecessor from any taxes. Fortescue argued for the King's power to rescind any grant made by his predecessor and his fellow serjeants and justices agreed that a judgment in favour of the rector could lead to many more such claims.[86] Such close involvement with the interests of the monarchy, soon to be followed by his appointment as Chief Justice of King's Bench, may well have widened Fortescue's political horizons beyond the concerns of the Inns of Court.

If John Fortescue junior initially undertook a legal career as a partisan for his family's interests in Devon, his ambitions progressively rose to include a national dimension. He lived in a period when the House of Commons was increasingly seen as an avenue for advancement by upwardly mobile lawyers and he successfully embraced that means of

[84] Seipp, 1440.049.
[85] *Ibid.*, 1441.073.
[86] *Ibid.*, 1441.028.

making contacts.[87] From 1421 to 1432 he was regularly returned for Devon boroughs as a member of parliament: he sat for Tavistock in 1421 (twice), 1423 and 1425, for Totnes in 1426, for Plympton in 1429 and for Totnes in 1432.[88] The frequency with which John junior sat for parliament suggests that he was laying the foundations for a career in government as well as the law and gaining the experience that was to be used with such formidable effect in his writings in later decades.

During John Fortescue's first parliament in May 1421 he had an opportunity to see his king, Henry V, in person. In later decades of the century the political nation looked back nostalgically on his short reign as a time of power abroad and prosperity and good governance in England. It took them a long time to realise that his successor was to be an unfit receptacle for the great authority invested in him and for Fortescue to come up with an alternative model of a king advised by a strong council. Conciliar government, however, was the solution which Henry V's brothers, the dukes of Bedford and Gloucester, and the great lords and administrators of the realm adopted after the king's untimely death on 31 August 1422 and the succession of his infant son, Henry VI. Apart from the bruising confrontations between Gloucester and his supporters on the one hand, and Bedford, Bishop Beaufort and their sympathisers on the other, England and English France were remarkably well ruled during the next fourteen years. Gloucester, Bedford and Beaufort generally compromised with each other's aspirations and limitations and, supported by the rest of the lords, parliament, the gentry and the great merchants worked to safeguard the achievements of their dead king. Yet the initial success of the uncles of Henry VI in defending and extending English conquests in northern France made it difficult for the government to persuade the Commons that more taxation was needed.

[87] J.R. Roskell, 'The Social Composition of the Commons in a Fifteenth-Century Parliament', *Parliament and Politics in Late Medieval England*, 3 vols (London: 1981–3) vol. 1, 152–172; H. Kleineke, 'The Widening Gap: The Practice of Parliamentary Borough Elections in Devon and Cornwall in the Fifteenth Century', *Parchment and People: Parliament in the Middle Ages*, ed. L. Clark (Edinburgh: 2004) 121–35. He makes the point that this process was facilitated in the West by the patronage of the duchy of Cornwall: S. Payling, 'The Rise of Lawyers in the Lower House, 1395–1536', *ibid.*, 103–20.

[88] *Accounts and Papers Printed by Order of the House of Commons* (1878) vol. 62, 297, 299, 305, 308, 310, 315, 321; J.J. Alexander, 'Devon County Members of Parliament: The Later Plantagenet Period (1399–1485)', *Report and Transactions of the Devonshire Association*, 46 (1914) 478–96. Henry Fortescue was a knight of the shire for Devon in 1421.

It is rare for individual members of the Commons to be identified in the parliamentary rolls.[89] Fortescue was not named until, two decades later, he became Chief Justice and a trier of petitions. During the years when he was a burgess, representing boroughs in Devon, Fortescue witnessed the strengths and weaknesses of conciliar rule during a long minority. If his later writings were influenced by what he experienced, they left him with a high regard for the public spirit and good sense of members of the House of Commons and a faith in the benefits of a strong royal council provided that it was not dominated by the self-interests of a great lord or faction. He also possessed a realistic appreciation of the need for a strong financial position to prosecute a successful foreign policy and safeguard trading interests. It would be a long time before John Fortescue would be in a position to offer such advice to the royal government and, after the death of the last adult Courtenay earl in 1422, he urgently needed a powerful patron to support his ambitions.

A powerful patron

For a period of ten years starting in 1428 the rolls record the involvement of John Fortescue in a substantial number of transactions which concerned the property interests of Lord Hungerford. These mostly related to the extensive estates he owned in Wiltshire and Somerset: Fortescue acted on various occasions as a surety, witness and feoffee.[90] In 1437 he was a member of parliament again but this time he was a knight of the shire for Wiltshire: a sign of his progressive disengagement from Devon and that his status was rising, probably as a result of the patronage of Hungerford.[91] Any further progress through parliament was thwarted by his elevation to the rank of Serjeant in 1437. Simon Payling has remarked on how this advancement in the law truncated the parliamentary activities of Fortescue and two other lawyers.[92]

Walter Hungerford, lord of Heytisbury and Hommet, had been a loyal supporter of the Lancastrian dynasty from its earliest days. He

[89] S. Payling, 'Identifiable Motives for Election to Parliament in the Reign of Henry VI: The Operation of Public and Private Factors', *The Fifteenth Century VI: Identity and Insurgency in the Late Middle Ages*, ed. L. Clark (Woodbridge: 2006) 90, 89–105.

[90] *CPR*, Henry VI, 1422–29, 526; *CPR*, Henry VI, 1436–41, 152, 300; *CCR*, Henry VI, 1422–29, 395, 397, 445–6, 459, 467–8; *CCR*, Henry VI, 1429–35, 43, 50, 53–6, 66–7, 163, 248, 252, 309; *CCR*, Henry VI, 1435–41, 35, 50, 61, 250.

[91] *Accounts and Papers*, 331.

[92] S. Payling, 'The Rise of the Lawyers', *Parchment and People*, 112, n. 39.

was a companion-in-arms to Henry V and fought for him at Agincourt: the King gave him the barony of Hommet in Normandy in 1418. He enjoyed a prominent position at court as a soldier and statesman entering the English peerage in 1426 as a baron.[93] Described as a 'self-propelling counsellor', he regularly sat on the royal council throughout the minority of Henry VI and was one of the young king's guardians.[94] A small group of prelates and laymen, including Cardinal Beaufort and Lord Hungerford, dominated the three great offices of state and principal household posts for twenty years from 1422 to 1442, ensuring a remarkable degree of political stability.[95] In the course of his long career Hungerford acquired large amounts of land in England, especially in Wiltshire and Somerset, and in France. His first wife Katherine Peverell (who died in 1422) was the daughter of a niece of Hugh Courtenay, earl of Devon and a Cornish squire and held considerable property in the county, so there was a link with the Fortescue family's patron. Sir Walter was one of the royal retainers who filled the vacuum that Earl Edward Courtenay's incapacity created in Devon in the early fifteenth century.[96] Hungerford was cultured, possessing a knowledge of poetry and theology, he was a benefactor of Merton College, Oxford and a generous donor to a number of religious foundations.[97] By his political eminence, his connection with the West and the Courtenays and his excellence as a role model, Lord Hungerford was just the sort of patron that John junior needed.

The patronage of Hungerford confirmed John Fortescue's attachment to the house of Lancaster and also to members of the council who opposed attempts by Henry VI's uncle, the duke of Gloucester, to exercise the powers of a regent. These included not only Hungerford but also Cardinal Beaufort, the great-uncle of the young Henry VI, and

93 K.B. McFarlane, 'The Hungerford Family and the Hundred Years War', *The Nobility of Later Medieval England: The Ford Lectures for 1953 and Related Studies* (Oxford: 1973) appendix B, 126–8; J.S. Roskell, *Parliament and Politics in Late Medieval England*, 3 vols (London: 1981–3) vol. 2, 'Sir Walter Hungerford', 95–135.

94 E.F. Jacob, *The Fifteenth Century, 1399–1485* (Oxford: 1961) 331–2; R.A. Griffiths, *The Reign of King Henry VI: The Exercise of Royal Authority* (London: 1981) 33–41.

95 G.L. Harriss, *Cardinal Beaufort: A Study of Lancastrian Ascendancy and Decline* (Oxford: 1988) 389.

96 Cherry, 'Courtenay Earls', 93, 96.

97 M. Hicks, 'St Katherine's Hospital, Heytesbury: Prehistory, Foundation and Re-foundation, 1409–1478', *Richard III and His Rivals: Magnates and Their Motives in the Wars of the Roses* (London: 1991) 119–32.

Lord Cromwell, a wealthy and hard-headed councillor. In 1432 the duke had Hungerford dismissed from his post of Treasurer as he perceived him to be hostile to his interests: the issues in dispute were growing suspicion of Gloucester's ambition and, increasingly, his unwillingness to contemplate any concessions to France that might lead to an end to the expensive and inconclusive war. Gloucester's enmity could have extended to Hungerford clients such as Fortescue and no evidence has been found that he enjoyed any signs of the duke's favour during the next fifteen years. Fortescue had been a member of a number of parliaments that had colluded in the limitation of Gloucester's powers and probably shared misgivings about him.

Lord Cromwell was associated with Fortescue in business transactions and the lawyer was subsequently to act as one of his executors.[98] Cromwell was dismissed as Lord Chamberlain in 1432, although he was made Treasurer in the following year, a post he held for the next ten years.[99] His prudent policies, undermined by household opposition and the drain of the war in France, could have influenced Fortescue's later recommendations for sound fiscal measures.[100] Fortescue's experience of the stable and generally successful governance by the council in the early decades of the reign of Henry VI must have informed other aspects of his political ideas as they developed. Despite the hostility of Gloucester, Hungerford and Cromwell continued to be powerful and influential until old age overtook them.

The coherence of the Duchy of Lancaster declined after the removal of the strong hand of Henry V; it was increasingly viewed simply as a convenient source of revenue but remained attractive to ambitious lawyers such as John Fortescue.[101] In 1432 Fortescue was retained as an apprentice for the Duchy of Lancaster by the feoffees of Henry V; Lord Hungerford had been Chief Steward of the Duchy estates south of the Trent and in Wales since 1413 and was appointed Duchy Chamberlain in 1425. As an executor of Henry V he was in a good position to extend its patronage to John Fortescue, who from 1439 to 1442 was employed

[98] *CCR*, Henry VI, 1454–61, 197.

[99] K.H. Vickers, *Humphrey Duke of Gloucester: A Biography* (London: 1907) 230; Rymer, *Foedera*, IV, iv.177.

[100] R.L. Friedrichs, 'Ralph, Lord Cromwell and the Politics of Fifteenth Century England', *NMS*, 32 (1988) 207–27.

[101] H. Castor, *The King, the Crown and the Duchy of Lancaster: Public Authority and Private Power, 1399–1461* (Oxford: 2000) 40–1.

as one of its serjeants-at-Law.[102] Lord Hungerford also used Fortescue as a personal legal adviser.[103] On four occasions between 1434 and 1441 he sat on Commissions for the Peace in Somerset, probably reinforcing the dominance of his patron in that county.[104] Fortescue's ascent up the professional ladder was assisted by Hungerford, but his posts were all legal ones where there was some expectation that he would be even-handed. Yet the cases discussed below in Chapter 2, when he had become Chief Justice, did not always show him to have been impartial.

Fortescue undertook a steady flow of work on behalf of Hungerford up to 1438 and his association with the family continued after he became a serjeant-at-law in 1437. On 11 May 1442, just after he had been made Chief Justice of the King's Bench, Fortescue, Sir Robert Hungerford (Walter's son), Sir Richard Newton, Chief Justice of Common Pleas, and others demised to Sir William Estefield and others: 'All their meadow adjoining their messuage called "Bosammes Ynne" on the west, and their land called "Clementes ynne mede" on the north, reserving a foot path for their servants to go by the said meadow from the gate of the said messuage towards London.'[105] The reference to the movement of servants indicates that Fortescue (who would have left a serjeants' inn on his promotion) and Hungerford were residents of the inn, which in turn implies a degree of intimacy between them.[106]

His interest in 'Bosammes Ynne' raises questions about John Fortescue's personal circumstances and places of residence during this stage in his career. By the early 1440s 'Bosammes Ynne' (the name derived from

[102] R. Somerville, *The History of the Duchy of Lancaster*, vol. 1, *1265–1603* (London: 1953) 451, 453.

[103] *ODNB*, 20, 461.

[104] TNA, Exchequer payments to sheriffs for the services of JPs, E101/586/10, m.1, 1434, m.2, 1436, m.3, 1437, m.4, 1441. I am grateful to Hannes Kleineke for giving me this reference.

[105] C.L. Kingsford, 'Historical Notes on Medieval London Houses', *London Topographical Record*, 10 (1916) 44–144; E. Williams, *Early Holborn and the Legal Quarter of London*, 2 vols (London: 1927) vol. 1, 819–20, records that the justices of King's Bench and Common Pleas, including Fortescue, contributed to improvements in their parish church of St Andrew in 1457. See also *CCR*, Henry VI, 1447–54, 364, which confirms Fortescue's tenure of 'Bosomysynne' and the 'Elmefeld' in the parish of St Giles of the Lepers in 1452. It was subsequently rebuilt and then demolished to make way for the Aldwych.

[106] Sir Robert Hungerford, Lord Hungerford after his father Walter's death in 1449, died in 1459. His oldest son, Sir Robert Hungerford (Lord Moleyns from 1445 and Lord Hungerford from 1459) was also a close associate of Fortescue and shared his exile until his death after the battle of Hexham in 1464.

4 Tomb of Robert, second baron Hungerford (*c.*1460), in Salisbury Cathedral.

John Bosham, a previous owner) could have been his principal London home, conveniently situated between the City and Westminster. It seems to have been rebuilt at about that time and was later known as 'New Inn' or 'St Mary Inn' and was one of three Inns of Chancery held in trusteeship by Fortescue and his fellow justices, the others were 'Angel Inn' and 'Clement's Inn'.[107] The Fortescue family seem to have kept an interest in the first inn for the rest of the century as it was presumably the same property which in 1487 was occupied by John Fortescue's nephew, Sir John Fortescue of Punsborne.[108] Earlier in his career Fortescue would have lived in Lincoln's Inn and then moved to a serjeants' inn when

[107] In his *De Laudibus Legum Anglie* Fortescue mentioned ten inns of chancery. Students attended them to learn the basics of law before they were admitted to one of the four Inns of Court (Grey's and Lincoln's Inns, the Inner and Middle Temples), Chrimes, *De Laudibus*, 116.

[108] Kingsford, 'Historical Notes', 122–3; Williams, *Early Holborn*, vol. 2, 1470, 1474.

he achieved that rank.[109] His residence in London would have been punctuated by visits to the growing number of properties which he was acquiring and by his frequent service on assizes. He expected to be in London during the high summer months of 1436 to 1439 because he promised to be available during harvest time, probably to teach junior lawyers. His oath and the penalty of 20 shillings to be paid whenever he defaulted are duly recorded in the *Black Books* of Lincoln's Inn.[110] Fortescue had other property interests in London, for example, in 1429 and again in 1440 a plaint of intrusion was made against him, Adam Summayster, Hugh Cavendish and others in respect of a free tenement in the parish of St Dunstan in the East.[111]

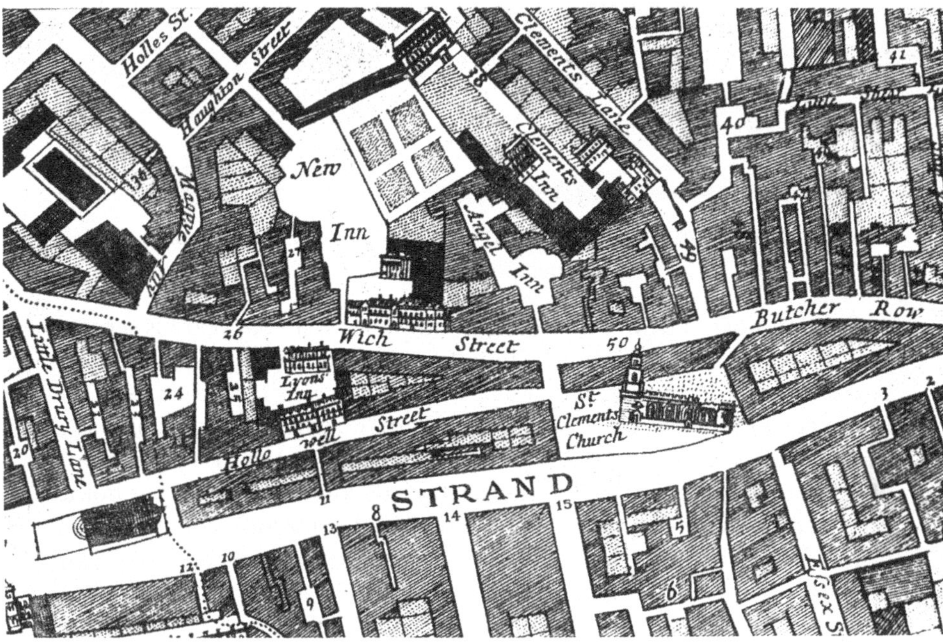

3 Devereux Court
5 Crown Court
10 Strand Bridge
12 Three Halbert Court
13 Savoy Alley
14 Surrey Street
20 Denham Yard
23 Bell Inn
24 Ogdens Court
26 Wich Alley
27 Wickhams Court
36 Sherbourne Court
38 Horse Shoe Court
40 Boswell Court
49 Lamb Inn

5 Map showing New Inn and Clement's Inn in 1755.

[109] Plummer, *Governance of England* 44–5, n. 4.

[110] *Black Books*, vol. 1, 6.

[111] *Calendar of the Plea and Memoranda Rolls Preserved among the Archives of the Corporation of the City of London at the Guildhall*, vol. 4, *A.D. 1413–1437*, ed. A.H. Thomas (Cambridge: 1943) 224; vol. 5, *A.D. 1437–1457*, ed. P.E. Jones (Cambridge: 1954) 24.

6 New Inn (Bosamme's Inn) in 1850. The style suggests the Queen Anne period.

By 1436 Fortescue was no longer a widower, for in that year his second wife, Isabella Jamys, daughter of John Jamys esquire, of Norton St Philip, Somerset, figured with him in a deed. In 1437 he was described as 'John Fortescue of Norton, co. Somerset, gentleman', when he was acting as a surety.[112] This shows that his wife had brought to the marriage property of sufficient substance for her husband to take on the name of her home (and she also owned property in Wiltshire). Fortescue's concentration of his provincial interests in Somerset and Wiltshire in the 1430s was presumably connected with his patron Lord Hungerford's importance in those counties.[113] The deed of 1436 which first mentioned Isabella Jamys as his wife also showed him in the process of acquiring property in Devon, the quitclaim which was made by Henry Fortescue in favour of his brother John and his wife for messuages, lands and tenements at Overcombe, Efford and Alston.[114]

At this stage it seems that Henry's career was trailing that of his younger brother: his initial advantage as the oldest son who would have inherited most of his father's lands seems to have been dissipated. In

[112] *CCR*, Henry VI, 1435–41, 112.

[113] Clermont, *Family*, 46.

[114] See above, pp. 27–8, n. 68.

7 Fortescue arms still displayed on the Fleur-de-Lys public house in Norton St Philip.

1441, letters of attorney from Henry again delivered seisin of lands (they originally belonged to William de Combe in Holbeton) to John Fortescue and his wife Isabella for her jointure.[115] This records the alienation of the family home of Combe manor from Henry to his successful younger brother: on the back of the document it is noted that the transactions took place in the church in Ermington in the presence, amongst others, of the vicar, Henry and Richard Fortescue and John Gogh, the latter presumably representing the interests of their absent brother John.[116] Other properties which John Fortescue acquired during his long career were widespread throughout the western and eastern counties. Most of them would have provided him with income and status rather than places of residence.[117] The evidence cited above indicates that he lived at Norton St Philip after his second marriage. It could have remained his principal country seat until the time when, after his return from exile in 1471, he finally gained the reversion of the manor of Ebrington in Gloucestershire in 1474.[118]

[115] Devon County Record Office, 1262 M/T 571.

[116] See below, p. 60, n. 59, for Fortescue's associate John Gogh.

[117] See below, Chapter 2, for details of his other property holdings.

[118] Devon County Record Office, 1262 TG 10.

John Fortescue's three surviving children, Martin, Elizabeth and Maud, were probably born in the late 1430s or the early 1440s, since in 1450 Maud (still a minor) was married to Robert Corbet.[119] From the deeds in which the names of John and Isabella Fortescue are associated, their marriage appears to have been a conventional and harmonious gentry alliance in which property and the interests of the family were paramount. The provision John made for his wife before he joined the Lancastrian army in 1461 might indicate a tender concern or could simply have been a prudent legal device to safeguard some of his assets.[120] The low opinion of women, especially of their fitness to exercise sovereign power, which emerged from his writings on the succession might suggest some negative personal experiences. On the other hand, it could be that he was simply rationalising a political stance by tapping into a well-known misogynist literary theme which had no relation to his personal feelings or circumstances.

Fortescue seems progressively to have disengaged himself from Devonian affairs and to have cultivated a wide circle of business, legal and political acquaintances in London and Westminster. From time to time he was still associated with the Courtenays[121] and other Devon families and his property interests there continued although he made his purchases elsewhere. His instincts were to prove sound, since he was soon to make the most spectacular advance in his career.

Sir John Hody, who was described by Lord Campbell as a 'very obscure' man, had only been appointed Chief Justice of the King's Bench in 1440, he was promoted directly from the position of Serjeant, which was unusual as the post was normally awarded to men who were already justices.[122] Hody did Fortescue two favours, for he seems to have created a precedent and then conveniently died late in 1441 before Lord Hungerford's influence waned (he ceased attending the royal council regularly from 1444).[123] Fortescue was not the kind of man to allow such an opportunity to pass him by, especially with such a convenient

[119] Devon County Record Office, 1262 M/FS 1. Her husband was also a minor at the time of their marriage.

[120] C.L. Scofield, 'Sir John Fortescue in February 1461', *EHR*, 27 (1912) 321–3. See below, Chapter 2.

[121] For example, he acted as a feoffee with Sir Philip Courtenay for Sir Walter Hungerford in 1439, *CPR*, Henry VI, 1436–41, 300; later in the same year he sat on commissions of oyer and terminer with him in Devon, *ibid.*, 370, 448.

[122] J. Campbell, *Lives of the Chief Justices of England*, 2 vols (London: 1849) vol. 1, 141; L. Clark, 'John Hody', *House of Commons, 1386–1421*, vol. 3, 384–6.

[123] R. Virgoe, 'The Composition of the King's Council, 1437–1461', *BIHR*, 43 (1970) 134–60.

precedent. The Close Rolls record his appointment to the highest legal office in the land: 'By writ of 20 January last the king willed that the said John be chief justice to hold pleas before the king, commanding him to busy himself about that office.'[124]

John Fortescue's father had improved the fortunes and status of his branch of the family by receiving stewardships from two earls of Devon and holding several public offices. He probably attended Lincoln's Inn and two of his sons trained in the law. Henry seems to have been too fond of the company of wild and lawless men to prosper at a crucial stage in his career in the late 1420s and early 1430s. John junior, on the other hand, while not ignoring the interests of his turbulent siblings, found himself powerful friends in Lord Hungerford and Lord Cromwell, two major forces on the minority council of Henry VI.[125] He also appears to have had outstanding gifts as a lawyer which led to his unusually fast promotion. Yet no gentleman who wished for a role in national life could be immune from the political rivalries that existed in the vacuum that was the personal rule of Henry VI. Economic decline, failure in France and, most toxic of all, the resurgence of a dynastic dispute were to make the work of the Chief Justice of King's Bench increasingly difficult and dangerous. The troubled times were also to lead him to apply his considerable intellectual gifts to the dilemma of how good governance could be secured for England.

[124] *CCR*, Henry VI, 1441–47, 16.

[125] G.L. Harriss, *Shaping the Nation: England 1360–1461* (Oxford: 2005) 596.

CHAPTER 2

1442–1461

Part 1: The Chief Justice

Sir John Fortescue, as he must be called from 1442 since he was knighted in the course of the year, had become a person of consequence in both the political and legal world.[1] He had accumulated a decent amount of property during the two previous decades, he knew a number of the most powerful men at the King's court and he was a loyal supporter of the house of Lancaster. During the next two decades, before that loyalty caused his dismissal in early 1461, did he become influential as well as prominent? The first part of this chapter seeks to answer that question through an examination of his record as Chief Justice of the King's Bench and participant in the business of government.

By the 1440s the political importance of Lord Hungerford, Fortescue's patron, had diminished. He was ageing and had ceased attending the council regularly; moreover he was closely associated with the martial feats of the early century which did not appeal to Henry VI.[2] Lord Cromwell was still a councillor although he remained his own man, not closely linked with any group at court. Henry had assumed direct control after his long minority and the political momentum had to a large extent passed to members of his household and others close to the young, impressionable King and they exercised considerable influence over him.[3] The conflict between Cardinal Beaufort and the duke of Gloucester had been effectively resolved in favour of the former and his policy of making a settlement with France which Henry wanted. The formation of rival factions concentrated on Henry, his household and the Beauforts on the one hand and on the duke of York and the Nevilles on the other, was to be a phenomenon of the 1450s rather than the 1440s. For the time being there was no serious conflict between

[1] *CPR*, Henry VI, 1441–46, 137, 7 December 1442, when he was first referred to as 'knight'.

[2] Virgoe, 'The Composition of the King's Council', 157.

[3] Griffiths, *Henry VI*, 278–88 and *passim.*

Fortescue's role as the servant of the Crown and his loyalty to past and present patrons such as Thomas, earl of Devon, the Hungerfords and Lord Cromwell.

Henry VI married Margaret of Anjou in 1445 as part of the predominant party's policy of making peace with France. This was largely instigated by Henry's favourite councillor, the earl of Suffolk, and Adam Moleyns, bishop of Chichester, Keeper of the Privy Seal, who had taken over Cardinal Beaufort's role as leaders of the peace faction. They received poor terms from the wily Charles VII of France that were to stack up grave problems for the royal government in coming years. Recent scholarship has shown how marriage normally enhanced the status of a monarch: but long years without an heir did nothing to calm fears about Henry VI's virility.[4] The suspicious death of the duke of Gloucester in February 1447 led to further criticism of Henry VI and his French queen. The continuing climate of discontent with the King and his advisers made the work of the judges charged with the maintenance of royal authority ever more challenging.

The earl of Suffolk was pre-eminent in the favours of Henry VI and Sir Walter Hungerford was related to him by marriage, whilst his younger son, Sir Edmund, was his close associate.[5] No records have been found that link Fortescue with Suffolk, but he might have benefited from the Hungerford relationship with the earl, although he would have been embarrassed by the antics of some of his followers. Fortescue continued to associate with Sir Walter's sons as the old lord gradually withdrew from public affairs, but his connection with Lord Cromwell could have been less advantageous as the decade wore on. Cromwell was present at the council forty-four times between 1443 and 1446, eighteen between 1447 and 1449 and nine between 1450 and 1453.[6] He had usually supported Cardinal Beaufort but, as the prelate aged (he died in 1447), Cromwell was progressively alienated from Suffolk, upon whom, in some respects, Beaufort's mantle had fallen. Cromwell also had a connection with the duke of York, who was paying him an annuity in 1441.[7]

[4] J.L. Laynesmith, *The Last Medieval Queens: English Queenship 1445–1503* (Oxford: 2004) 30–6; H.E. Maurer, *Margaret of Anjou: Queenship and Power in Late Medieval England* (Woodbridge: 2003).

[5] J.S. Roskell and C. Kightly, 'Sir Walter Hungerford', *House of Commons, 1386–1421*, vol. 3, 446–53.

[6] Virgoe, 'The Composition of the King's Council', 157–8.

[7] Friedrichs, 'Ralph, Lord Cromwell', 219.

At the end of the decade, when law and order were particularly precarious, Suffolk supported his client William Tailboys, a thuggish Lincolnshire gentleman and esquire of the royal household, against Cromwell, his hapless neighbour at Tattershall. Fortescue was involved in the dispute and the violent, lawless actions that had preceded it for much of his time as Chief Justice and it illustrates the dangerous political climate in which he had to operate. What follows is mainly based on the masterly study in which Roger Virgoe dissected the career of Tailboys.[8] During the 1440s Tailboys, together with his followers, seems to have murdered at least three men and committed other assaults, robberies and trespasses and this put them on a collision course with the court of King's Bench. In 1448 he made the mistake of assaulting John Dymoke, a servant of Lord Robert Willoughby, the nephew by marriage of Lord Cromwell. Fortescue had been appointed to a commission of oyer and terminer in that year to investigate Tailboys and his servants but it achieved nothing, probably due to pressure from Suffolk:

> Touching all evildoers adhering to William Tailboys late of Kyme, co. Lincoln, esquire, and the tenants and servants of William, who have committed murders, felonies, trespasses, robberies, plundering, extortions, misprisions,[9] homicides, maimings, rapes of women, maintenances, rebellions, insurrections, confederacies, conspiracies, champerties,[10] oppressions, unlawful entries, congregations, gatherings, prostrations of houses, riots and routs.[11]

On 14 July, however, a new commission was issued to Fortescue and other justices to investigate Dymoke's complaint but this also seems to have achieved little. On 16 October indictments were sent to the King's Bench but through the intercession of Suffolk Tailboys was pardoned for not appearing to answer Dymoke's charges, although the other charges against him remained.[12]

In Trinity Term 1449 writs of *exigent* were issued against Tailboys and about 150 of his men but Suffolk put pressure on the sheriff of

[8] R. Virgoe, 'William Tailboys and Lord Cromwell: Crime and Politics in Lancastrian England', *BJRL*, 55 (1972–73) 459–82.

[9] Failure to report a crime.

[10] Illegal proceeding whereby a party not truly engaged in a suit intervenes to help the plaintiff or defendant.

[11] *CPR*, 1446–52, 187–8.

[12] TNA, King's Bench, Ancient Indictments, KB 9/260/92, 95.

Lincolnshire not to pursue them.[13] On 28 November it was alleged that Tailboys and some of his 'slaughterladdes' tried to murder Cromwell at a council meeting in the Star Chamber at Westminster.[14] This inept episode may have had Suffolk's approval, and Ralph Griffiths, like Virgoe, believes that it could have encouraged Cromwell to take a hand in the Duke's subsequent impeachment by parliament: two charges involved the wrongdoing of Tailboys.[15] The fact that a member of the household could behave so riotously in the King's palace testifies to the dysfunctional nature of his government and the difficulties experienced by the justices in upholding the law.

In early 1450 Suffolk was impeached, exiled and murdered and this enabled Fortescue and his fellow justices finally to punish Tailboys, who was imprisoned for several years. Lords Cromwell and Willoughby were respectively awarded £2,000 and £650 in damages against him and Dymoke was awarded £1,000.[16] It seems, however, that he never paid any of these sums to the plaintiffs and prison did not curb his ability to make mischief. Before his death in July 1452 Lord Willoughby witnessed the confession of John Stanes, the chaplain of Tailboys, who had been asked by his master to write libellous bills about Cromwell which were posted up throughout the land.[17] When these failed to ruin Cromwell, Tailboys gave Stanes a bag of gunpowder to blow up the house next to Cromwell's London residence. The plan was that the 'slaughterladdes' of Tailboys would murder him whilst his servants were preoccupied with the results of the explosion. The confession indicates that the chaplain belatedly repented of work so far removed from the normal duties of a priest and no harm came to Cromwell.

Cromwell died in 1455, as the various cases against Tailboys made their way slowly through King's Bench, but not a penny did any of the injured parties (including the widows of two of the murdered men) receive from him. Yet lacking a powerful protector he was no longer as threatening as he had been a decade earlier: Fortescue and his fellow

[13] TNA, KB 27/754, plea, rot. 111; 753, rex, rot. 18; E.28/78/103; E.159/226, Mich. Brevia Directa, rot.18.

[14] *RP*, vol. 5, 200–1; *PROME*, vol. 12, 147–9.

[15] Griffiths, *Henry VI*, 580–1.

[16] TNA, KB 27/755, plea rot.d; KB 27/755, plea rot. 26, 30.

[17] He quoted a stanza from the bill:

York and Norfolk come rescewe Caleys
And we will go with you bothe more and lesse.
That as Somersett hath eten Fraunce and Normandie
So Cromwell lereth to ete Gasconye and Guyan.

TNA, Chancery Miscellanea, C 47/7/8, rot.2.

executors of Cromwell's estate seem to have recognised that there was no point in wasting further time and money on someone who was probably incapable of paying the huge damages required. In 1457 they made a settlement in which they recorded, probably to Fortescue's satisfaction, that Tailboys had been condemned for the harm done to Lord Cromwell and had been in prison for many years. He was released from the sum he still owed, and promised to behave well in the future for a bond of 1,000 marks and not to harm Cromwell's former servants or any of the jurors involved in the cases against him: 'To be from hensforth of good, peasible and restfull rule in his contre of Lincolnshire and elleswhere as is fitting and according for a man of his degree.'[18]

Cases involving Tailboys troubled Fortescue and King's Bench for most of the time when he was Chief Justice; those concerning his patron Lord Cromwell were particularly burdensome. Other occasions when politics became involved with the administration of the law will be discussed below, but the rampages of Tailboys both in Lincolnshire and London challenged Fortescue's exalted opinion of the system as expressed in his later writings and the dignity of his own position. He could have had rogues like Tailboys in mind when he later condemned the undue influence of the king's household in *The Articles sent by Edward, Prince of Wales, to the earl of Warwick concerning the government of England.*[19]

The practice of the common law

The environment in which Fortescue worked is well known both from an illumination that was possibly made during his time as Chief Justice and because it changed little over several centuries, during which period it was vividly described on a number of occasions.[20] The Court of King's Bench shared Westminster Hall with Common Pleas and Chancery as well as various shops, booths and a general bustle of officials, courtiers and commoners. The Court sat for three hours a day, from 8 to 11 in the morning: litigants could later attend in chambers to confer with serjeants-at-law and their other counsel. Fortescue claimed that

[18] *CCR*, 1454–61, 197–8.

[19] *Vale's Book*, 223.

[20] Ives, *Common Lawyers*, 167–9; J.H. Baker, 'Westminster Hall, 1097–1997', *The Common Law Tradition: Lawyers, Books and the Law* (London and Rio Grande: 2000) 247–62.

8 The Court of King's Bench, *c.*1460.

the judges used their ample free time to study the law and read the Holy Scriptures.[21]

The Court measured no more than thirty feet by fifty-six feet and had to accommodate up to five judges and about twenty other people – officials, counsel, litigants and defendants as well as spectators, legal students and sometimes a jury. One advantage of this proximity was that it encouraged learned discussion between judges and counsel: part of the process by which cases were made and judgment delivered, promoting developments and improvements in legal practice. These are well recorded in the *Year Books* and it was this aspect of the work of the courts that most interested the students of law and clerks who are thought to have compiled them. The judges in all three courts had participated in the education of young lawyers in their inns but they continued and extended their teaching role by these discussions of the law and its application before making judgments. The seriousness with which they regarded establishing the law precisely is illustrated by the practice of retiring to the Court of the Exchequer Chamber, which met in any chamber of council near to the Exchequer at Westminster. The *Year Books* regularly record that justices from all three courts and other senior lawyers would go there to consult each other over matters of difficulty.

It was suggested in Chapter 1 that some of Fortescue's opinions that were recorded in the *Year Books* when he was a serjeant and King's Serjeant might have anticipated ideas that later emerged in his political writings. Once he became Chief Justice of the King's Bench his role changed since, as the title implies, he was working directly for the monarchy in its own Court. The long, academic discussions on technical points of law which had characterised the work of Fortescue and his fellows in Common Pleas continued but the end result had to be the maintenance of royal power. By no means all the work of King's Bench concerned the King and in those cases it was business as usual. On the other hand, an early example of the new Chief Justice's wish to define the nature and extent of royal powers occurred in Michaelmas 1442 and concerned a case of Trespass:

> One cannot prescribe to have jurisdiction, nor fines nor issues that are forfeited to the king, because when such things have accrued to the king by matter of record [contained in the rolls of courts of record such as King's Bench] one cannot have them by prescription [a right which existed by reason of lapse of time] etc. but other things that belong to the

[21] Chrimes, *De Laudibus*, 129.

> king and the title of the king do not accrue to him by matter of record, the law is otherwise, as of waif, stray, wreck of the sea, treasure trove and so of like things.[22]

The great majority of the cases dealt with by Fortescue as Chief Justice and recorded in the *Year Books* (although there were doubtless many more) do not touch on wider political issues. There were 132 from 1442 to 1460 (as well as a number of cases in 1442 which were heard in Common Pleas, where Fortescue was still described as 'Serjeant'); only those referring to him as 'Chief Justice' have been counted.[23] Two cases in Michaelmas 1456 touched on the rights of the King. In the first, when a hapless defendant pleaded that someone had borrowed £60 from him and given him jewels for security, he claimed that he did not know that they belonged to the King. In the second case the same defendant argued that it was the custom of London that pledged goods should not be restored until the debt (in this case a massive £300 presumably incurred on behalf of the King) had been paid. Unfortunately for him all the justices, including Fortescue, meeting in the Exchequer Chamber agreed that the King should have his jewels back. This was a clear case of the royal prerogative being allowed to override custom and the common law.[24]

An example of a type of argument which anticipated those later used in Fortescue's writings occurs in 1456, although it was not concerned with the worsening political situation which was soon to turn his world upside down. In a case in Trinity term heard in the Exchequer Chamber, adjourned from Common Pleas, a writ of *Quare Impedit* (issued in cases of a disputed presentation to a benefice) involved a conflict between canon law and common law. The plaintiff had presented his clerk to a benefice after a vacancy and the defendant bishop had refused him. In an attempt to resolve the issue Fortescue resorted to the kind of philosophical distinctions that were later to help him through intractable arguments in the *De Natura Legis Naturae*:

> It would be hard if the law of Holy Church made within time of memory should bar our law which is and has been in force since time immemorial.

[22] Seipp, 1442.149 abr.

[23] Presumably the 1442 cases where he was still described as 'serjeant' were those he had undertaken before his promotion since he cannot have continued to plead afterwards, when they were passed to others. Alternatively, those appearing in 1442 could simply have been misdated in the *Year Books*. I am grateful to Sir John Baker for his advice on this matter.

[24] Seipp, 1456.087, 1456.105ss.

> *Quare impedit* is partly purely temporal and partly purely spiritual, all the process and everything done since, that is, the institution, induction and admission, is purely spiritual; and as to what is said that the law of Holy Church is such, we have no regard for that, because we are still in temporal proceedings.[25]

The most constant guidance to Sir John Fortescue's public duties as Chief Justice is given by the Patent, Close and Fine Rolls which record many of his activities and the official rewards that he received for carrying them out. These are supplemented by the parliament rolls, *Black Books*, references in the *Paston Letters*, bishop's registers, the *Year Books*, the *Proceedings and Ordinances of the Privy Council* and the records of the law courts held in The National Archives.[26] The problem of distinguishing between the various Johns in the Fortescue family arises again: three nephews and at least one cousin bore the same name. Fortunately the title 'Sir' and description 'Chief Justice' put many references beyond doubt, otherwise context and links with known associates must serve to identify him. Evidence for some of his activities as well as for his views and personality can also be derived from Fortescue's own writings.

As Chief Justice of the King's Bench, Sir John Fortescue could expect a regular income, which probably totalled about £250 per annum.[27] Five days after his appointment in January 1442, he was awarded 180 marks annually from the customs receipts at London, Bristol and Kingston upon Hull and 106s 11¼d and a sixth of a halfpenny yearly at Christmas for a robe and fur and 66s 6d for a robe and linen at Whitsuntide. In February he received an annuity of 40 marks from the petty customs at Bristol and a tun of wine. In the following year he was given an additional tun of wine from the same port.[28] Other rewards were available to him as a high legal officer, some coming from work he was given because of his status, and he might also be persuaded to act favourably in some cases, as is suggested below, in return for direct or indirect benefits.

One of Fortescue's duties as Chief Justice was to attend the royal council from time to time, often in company with the Chief Justice of the Common Pleas: much routine business was carried out by the council

25 *Ibid.*, 1456.103ss.

26 R.C. Palmer, 'The Construction of an Online Digital Archive: The Anglo-American Legal Tradition Website Project', *Law, Lawyers and Texts: Studies in Medieval Legal History in Honour of Paul Brand*, ed. S. Jenks, J. Rose and C. Whittick (Leiden: 2012) 361–78.

27 See below, p. 69, n. 90.

28 *CPR*, Henry VI, 1441–46, 37, 38, 194. See below for a discussion of Fortescue's total income.

advised by experts such as the most senior lawyers. The council records for 1442 to 1443 are fuller than those for subsequent years and give some indication of the role performed, as occasional members, by the Chief Justices who seem to have attended when legal affairs were in question.[29] On 23 March 1443, for example, Fortescue and Judge Westbury, were required to 'declaren all their demenyng at Norwich and in Norfolk' where they had recently held a commission of oyer and terminer. On 10 May in the same year they were summoned to deal with complaints from Cardinal Kemp, one of the King's most influential advisers, that his property in Yorkshire was being damaged by lawless persons. They were required by the King to report back on the following day and duly did so with the recommendation that the justices of the peace in the East and West Ridings should arrest the rioters and that a commission of oyer and terminer should be sent to the area.

Only one mention is made of Sir John Fortescue's presence at the council between 1443 and 1461, but it is inconceivable that he did not attend from time to time. The scanty records sometimes list the most important councillors on a particular date and then add 'and others' or 'etc.'.[30] Many meetings were unrecorded but their transactions are implied, without naming particular persons, from entries in the Patent Rolls or warrants issued under the Privy Seal. Fortescue's contribution to the work of government is likely to have been primarily reactive. He was carrying out commands rather than personally dispensing patronage or developing policies, the prerogative of the King and his advisers. Only where the technicalities of the law were concerned might he have been able to suggest initiatives. He enjoyed some respect amongst his legal peers and junior members of the profession, but in the court and council he would, at this early stage, have been regarded as a superior servant rather than an equal.

Fortescue was an industrious Chief Justice: laziness was never a charge levelled against him when he subsequently became embroiled in political conflict. An outline of his recorded activities, 1442–43, shows the workload typical of a conscientious senior legal officer, even if he did not invariably sit on all the commissions to which he was nominated. In 1442 he certified four pardons and was a trier of petitions in parliament:

[29] *Proceedings and Ordinances of the Privy Council of England*, ed. H. Nicholas, 6 vols (London: 1835) vol. 5, 247, 249, 256–8, 266–7, 268–70, 304. Griffiths, *Henry VI*, 284, suggests that the scanty records kept after 1443 reflect the decline in the council's importance.

[30] *PPC*, vol. 6, 31, 37, 39, 74, 85, 90, 98, 101, 131, 143, 144, 152, 161, 166, 177, 258, 260, 274, 316, 322, 330–1.

a role he performed in most parliaments until 1461.[31] In January he was appointed a justice of assize, in company with William Paston, in Hertfordshire, Essex, Kent, Surrey, Sussex and Middlesex.[32] He frequently worked on this South-Eastern circuit but Somerset and other counties were often added to it and he presumably took advantage of appointments to the West to visit his home and family in Norton St Philip. In March he was charged with others with raising a loan for the King in Bristol and in May with raising another in Somerset.[33] In October the royal council ordered him to investigate some indictments which had been issued against Robert Wellys, 'abbot of Tourhill beside London'.[34] He was also a member of commissions of the peace in 1442 in Kent (April), Essex (May and November), Somerset (May and June), Suffolk (August) and Sussex (October).[35] In the *Year Book* for 1442 he appeared as Chief Justice in ten cases.[36]

For the remainder of the decade Fortescue carried out similar duties to those recorded for 1442. Their description mostly makes for tedious reading, but some incidents throw a more intimate light on the Chief Justice or show how his standing as a servant of the Crown was slowly enhanced. On 28 January 1444 a passage in *The Paston Letters* provides an instance of the former when James Gresham, a lawyer, wrote to Justice William Paston:

> The Chief Justice of the Kyngges Benche recomaundeth hym to yow and is right sory of the matier that is cause of your noun comyng hedir, but [he] wole do al that he can or may for yow. He hath had a cyetica that hath letted hym [a gret while] to ride, and dar not yet come on non horses bak. And therfor he hath spoke to the lordes of the conseill and enformed hem of your sekenesse and his also, that he may not ride at these next assises to Estgrynsted; and though thoe assises discontynue *per [noun] venu dez*

[31] *CPR*, Henry VI, 1441–46, 76, 81, 127, 130; J.C. Wedgwood and A.D. Holt, *History of Parliament, 1439–1509*, 2 vols (London: 1936–38) vol. 2, 31, 57, 74, 101, 131, 159, 195, 230; G. Dodd, *Justice and Grace: Private Petitioning and the English Parliament in the Late Middle Ages* (Oxford: 2007), 193–4, shows that the work was not confined to the life of a parliament but could preoccupy triers afterwards.

[32] *CPR*, Henry VI, 1441–46, 38.

[33] *Ibid.*, 62, 68.

[34] *PPC*, vol. 5, 215.

[35] *CPR*, Henry VI, 1441–46, 470, 472, 477, 478–9.

[36] Seipp, *passim*.

Justicez he hopeth to be excused, [and ye also]. And as for the remenaunt of the assises he shall purvey to be ther by water.[37]

If Fortescue's heavy workload took its toll, even temporarily, it did not prevent the King and council from continuing to burden him with commissions. The weakening hold of the English on their French possessions and the growing unpopularity of Henry VI's household and favourites such as Suffolk made the government ever more reliant on their senior law officers to maintain order. R.L. Storey has recorded evidence that popular dissatisfaction even extended, in some cases, to the King himself, expressed in the opinion that he was too childish to rule effectively.[38] In the short term, Fortescue and his fellows were capable of upholding royal authority, but only until the crisis of 1449–50.

Fortescue was deeply involved in 1444 in the case of Thomas Kerver. This has been described by C.A.F. Meekings and is worth considering as it is the most accessible and detailed account of Fortescue's early activities as Chief Justice and the way in which he could be affected by political pressures.[39] The outcome of the case was clearly considered to be of great importance in protecting the reputation of King Henry and demonstrating his power and prestige. In April 1444 Thomas Kerver of Reading (probably the abbot of Reading's bailiff) cited with approval the Palm Sunday text, 'Ve regno cui puer Rex est'.[40] He later said to Thomas Codryngton, a servant of the abbot, and others that it would have been worth more than £100,000 to England if the King had never been born. On that day and on other occasions he compared Henry VI unfavourably with the martial dauphin of France. These unwise remarks formed the basis for an indictment for treason, drafted by Thomas Tresham, a royal servant who was Speaker of the Commons on several occasions. On 3 July Fortescue presided over the trial, held in King's Bench. It took place before a grand jury that found Kerver guilty of treasonable intention and of specific utterances but not of attempting to enlist others. However, this verdict was apparently insufficiently damning and Fortescue delayed his judgement.

Meekings believed that the royal council, advised by Fortescue, decided to conduct a new trial under a writ of oyer and terminer so that the articles of the indictment could be reformulated to increase the

37 *PL* (Davis) vol. 2, no. 432, 13–14.

38 Storey, *End of the House of Lancaster*, 33–35.

39 C.A.F. Meekings, 'Thomas Kerver's Case, 1444', *EHR*, 90 (1975) 331–46. See also Storey, *End of the House of Lancaster*, 34, 36 and B.P. Wolffe, *Henry VI* (London: 1981) 17, 128, 132, 138.

40 'Woe to thee, O land, when thy king is a child' (Ecclesiastes 10:16).

likelihood of a conviction. This procedure was 'a very rare expedient' which seems 'to betray the mind of Fortescue who, on such technical legal matters, must have been the council's main adviser on the range of instruments required'.[41] The charge of attempting to enlist others was 'sexed-up' and the unfortunate Thomas Codryngton was indicted for failing to report Kerver immediately. The new trial was held at Reading in early August, and the commission included Fortescue, Sir Richard Newton, Chief Justice Common Pleas and several royal servants. This time Kerver was found guilty of all charges and Codryngton's misprision was condemned. Kerver was sentenced to be paraded publicly in various towns in Berkshire and then hung, drawn and quartered.

At that stage the government's purposes in taking such trouble and incurring such expense to punish an obscure, if loose-tongued, person became apparent. On 4 August King Henry pardoned Kerver his life but he was still to be paraded and hung up and then imprisoned during the King's pleasure. The King warned that 'in any like case the offenders, even if of the blood royal, could expect neither favour nor grace but due punishment'.[42] This letter signalled that the King and council's true target was their most prominent critic, the duke of Gloucester, who would ascend the throne should Henry VI die. Like Kerver, he deplored the lacklustre response of Henry VI's government to the danger of losing English possessions in France. The propaganda value of the public humiliation of a traitor in the vicinity of London and the royal residence of Windsor was considerable, as was the display of princely magnanimity. In September Henry pardoned Thomas Codryngton.[43]

The whole Kerver episode sheds little lustre on Fortescue, who seems to have acted as a royal agent rather than as an impartial judge prepared to accept the verdict of a properly constituted grand jury. Rather than see the original indictment fail on one count, he allowed the jurisdiction of his own court to be devolved to a commission of oyer and terminer. On the other hand, he could be defended on the grounds that he upheld royal prestige without anyone dying. He was a new Chief Justice from an unimportant family and it would perhaps be unrealistic to expect him to act otherwise. Campbell recounts the fates of three Chief Justices who were either killed or disgraced during the reigns of Richard II and Edward IV for perceived political independence.[44] Technically the law

[41] Meekings, 'Kerver's Case', 337.

[42] *Ibid.*, 339; S. Bentley, ed., *Excerpta Historica or Illustrations of English History* (London: 1831) 280–1.

[43] *CPR*, Henry VI, 1441–46, 295.

[44] Campbell, *Lord Chief Justices*, vol. 1, 105–6, 111–12, 144.

had not been violated even if its spirit had been ignored, but Fortescue had not heard the last of Thomas Kerver as he languished in Wallingford castle in Oxfordshire.

Kerver's fate may have scared some local people but it could not quieten widespread anxieties about the King's character and appearance. Several men were reported for saying that he still looked like a child and one for saying that he foolishly played with a stick with a bird on it. In 1448 Fortescue investigated an alleged conspiracy involving a servant of the royal household and one John Hartlepool but it did not result in any charges.[45]

Fortescue's affiliation to his two powerful friends continued. In 1444 he was involved in transactions as a feoffee for the estates of Lord Cromwell and Sir Walter Hungerford. In Michaelmas Term in the previous year a case came before Fortescue in King's Bench in which Thomas Hungerford (Sir Walter's grandson) and his wife Elizabeth, as plaintiffs, brought a writ of trespass against one Robert for taking away a villein belonging to Elizabeth. The Chief Justice intervened several times with opinions favourable to the plaintiffs, who won the case.[46] It cannot be proved whether Fortescue acted impartially in this case, but Michael Hicks has observed that lawyers were: 'retained ...even the royal justices, whose services can readily be imagined; legislation forbidding judges to be retained was only partially effective and did not prevent Chief Justice Fortescue from serving the Hungerfords'.[47]

By 1445 Fortescue was capable of 'pulling rank' in Lincoln's Inn: the *Black Books* for that year record his request that John Pointz should be admitted to repasts whenever Fortescue was present. He also asked that Robert Aspare should be excused from keeping vacations when he was riding out of town with the Chief Justice.[48] These are the requests of a busy and important man who wanted his servants and associates to be readily available. Robert Aspare, alias Asper, seems to have been of fairly humble condition as he rode out of town at Fortescue's behest. He had been admitted to Lincoln's Inn in 1442 and was a King's Bench reporter who recorded some of Fortescue's decisions in the *Year Books*.[49] He must have been the 'Robert Asspur, gentleman', of the county of Yorkshire,

[45] Storey, *End of the House of Lancaster*, 33–5.

[46] Seipp, 1443.108.

[47] M. Hicks, *Bastard Feudalism* (London: 1995) 56.

[48] *Black Books*, vol. 1, f. 61r.

[49] Baker, *Common Law Tradition*, 148, n. 77.

who acted as mainpernor together with Fortescue when the manor of Farington Gurney, Somerset was committed to them in 1443.[50]

John Pointz (Poyntz, Poynes) may have enjoyed a rather higher status than Aspare since Fortescue evidently valued his company at dinner. At least two men of that name were active during the middle years of the century, one in Gloucestershire and the other in Essex. Given that the former was a member of Lincoln's Inn and that Fortescue was developing property interests in Gloucestershire through his dealings with the Corbets, it is likely that he was the man who became the Chief Justice's client. He figures several times in the rolls concerning his inheritance and the holding of an inquisition *post mortem* in Gloucestershire in 1460.[51] Invariably described as 'esquire', he was to become a man of property.[52] Fortescue would have found the clientage of a relatively young local squire who was knowledgeable in the law very useful. Fortescue also employed a number of servants, including quasi-professionals such as scribes and stewards, and some of those are referred to below.

In 1447 the government recognised Fortescue's continued good service by granting an additional annuity of £40 per annum to 'maintain his estate'. Like earlier grants it was to be financed from the issues of the customs of the ports of London, Bristol and Kingston upon Hull.[53] But under the dysfunctional rule of Henry VI such benefits came at a heavy price. In the summer the Kerver case re-emerged. On 25 August the King wrote to archbishop Stafford, the Lord Chancellor:

> Right Reverend fader in god Right trusty and welbeloved. We grete you wele. And how be hit that we now late sent unto oure trusty and welbeloved Knight Sir John ffortescu our chief Justice charging hym to deliver oute of oure Castel of Walyngford in our behalve Thomas Kerver, which by oure commaundement hath long tyme been in ward in the prison of oure said Castel, yet natheles the said John ffortescu hath do us to understande that

[50] *CFR*, Henry VI, 1437–45, 263, 292; Baker, *Men of Court*, vol. 1, 237.

[51] *CPR*, Henry VI, 1452–1461, 562; Baker, *Men of Court*, vol. 2, 1261–2.

[52] In 1457 Thomas Pointz enfeoffed Nicholas and John Pointz and Alice, the latter's wife, with a moiety (half) of the manor of Nimsfield, co. Gloucester. Three years later both Thomas and Nicolas were dead and Robert and John respectively were named as their sons and heirs. An order to the escheator in the county of Gloucestershire in October 1460 gave John, heir of Nicolas, full seisin of his lands, *CPR*, Henry VI, 1452–61, 357; *CFR*, Henry VI, 1452–61, 212, 242, 282, 293; John Pointz died in 1466 and was succeeded by his son Robert who was a minor, *CPR*, Henry VI, 1467–77, 23.

[53] *CPR*, Henry VI, 1446–52, 26.

> he hath no pouair so to do in any wise. Wherfore we wolling for certain causes and consideracions especially moeving us, the forsaid Thomas to be in brief tyme delivered out of the said prison without any firther delay charge you that ye do make oure writting in due fourme directed to the Counestable of our said castel.[54]

Fortescue was to write some twenty-three years later: 'The justice shall swear among other things that he will do justice without favour, to all men pleading before him, friends or foes alike, that he will not delay to do so even though the king command him by his letters or by word of mouth to the contrary.'[55]

Meekings explains Fortescue's refusal to act in terms of the improper request made to him by the King.[56] Kerver was no longer in the custody of the King's Bench and only a writ from Chancery could release him, as Henry's letter to Stafford belatedly recognised. The main theme of the *De Laudibus* was to be the importance of the King knowing the laws of England. Yet in this case there could have been more to Fortescue's rejection of the King's request than a legal technicality: on other occasions the Chief Justice did not appear to be so particular. The trouble and expense incurred by the government had been for the purpose of delivering an exemplary punishment in a strategically vital area of the realm.[57] Simply to release a man convicted of treason a mere three years after the offence negated to a large extent the benefit from the manipulation of the law in which Fortescue had colluded. Royal government was weaker and Henry's prestige was lower in 1447 than it had been in 1444 and his excessive generosity was one of the problems which were posing ever greater dangers to royal servants. Fortescue seems to have been gaining in confidence in his office and, in Kerver's case, could risk putting the law before the royal will. Earlier in the year the duke of Gloucester had died under suspicious circumstances whilst in royal custody. Fortescue never commented on the matter to defend or condemn it, but the legality of what was done was questionable and it was on his watch as Chief Justice. Was this a belated attempt to assert himself?

It was evidence of Fortescue's increasing prestige that in February 1448 he was given the keeping of two-thirds of the manors of Flete Damerlle and Holbeton in Devon for Henry Holland, duke of Exeter,

[54] Bentley, *Excerpta Historica*, 390.
[55] Chrimes, *De Laudibus*, 127.
[56] Meekings, 'Kerver's Case', 344.
[57] *Issues of the Exchequer, Henry III to Henry VI*, ed. F. Devon (London: 1837) 454.

who was a minor. Profits could be made from the manors and Fortescue's standing in his native parish would be enhanced. It was a mark of high favour that he should be entrusted with some of the affairs of a magnate who was so closely related to the Plantagenets that he could dispute with the duke of York any claim to be the heir to the childless King. The two gentlemen who were the mainpernors for the commitment of the Holland property in Devon to Fortescue were often associated with him in business deals and they can be added to the group of clients and servants who were attached to him. John Gough (Gogh) came from Kilkhampton, Cornwall and held various clerical posts in King's Bench, and John Nicholl (Nicoll) came from Malmesbury, Wiltshire: they could have been respectively involved in the Courtenay and Hungerford followings.[58] Fortescue and Gogh surrendered the Flete Damerlle and Holbeton property in May 1448 to Nicholl and Thomas Povy (described as Fortescue's clerk in 1461).[59] This is a further sign that as he increased in affluence and importance Fortescue relied on a network of agents and servants to safeguard his wide-ranging and politically sensitive connections as well as his property interests.

The death of Lord Hungerford in 1449 was less harmful to Fortescue than if it had occurred at an earlier stage in his career. Hungerford's demise only involved Fortescue in routine property transactions in Wiltshire and Dorset.[60] At the same time he also purchased land from the duke of York, who, despite his wealth, needed to raise money before his departure for Ireland, where he had been appointed Lord Lieutenant. Fortescue paid 100 marks for Easton in Gordano, Gloucestershire, which he turned into a life interest for another of his associates, Thomas Younge.[61] York also granted his manor of Hambledon, Rutland to Fortescue and others but this looks like an enfeoffment rather than a sale.[62] The duke sold a considerable amount of property at this time: the fact that Fortescue was one of the purchasers need have no particular political significance beyond the fact that it indicates that normal relations existed between York and the Chief Justice.

The rapid promotion of John Fortescue to the position of Chief Justice in 1442 probably took him by surprise and he seems to have been subservient to the King and his advisers during his early years. Before his fall, Suffolk successfully frustrated the efforts of the plaintiffs and

[58] *CFR*, Henry VI, 1445–52, 86; Baker, *Men of Court*, vol. 1, 762, 2, 1162.

[59] *CFR*, Henry VI, 1445–52, 88–9.

[60] *CCR*, Henry VI, 1447–54, 147–8.

[61] P.A. Johnson, *Duke Richard of York, 1411–1460* (Oxford: 1988) 62–3.

[62] *CPR*, Henry VI, 1446–52, 218.

the court of King's Bench to bring Tailboys to justice, but Fortescue and his fellows did exact eventually some kind of retribution when Tailboys was weaker and they were stronger. The case of Thomas Kerver also demonstrates that Fortescue's early willingness to bend to the will of his masters was overtaken by 1447 by his insistence on the letter of the law when the King made an improper request for Kerver to be released without a writ from Chancery. Fortescue's wishes that he should have the company of his favoured companions and servants and his purchases of property in Wiltshire and near London show a man finally at ease in the high office he occupied. Yet the King and Queen were surrounded by the group of household men and self-seeking magnates that Fortescue was to condemn in his later writings. It would involve the cataclysm of 1450 and the outbreak of civil war with the toll it took on those close to the royal family to give the Chief Justice real political influence.

A proto-Renaissance lawyer?

The period when Fortescue presided over the court of King's Bench saw a number of practical modifications to the English common law but did these emanate from enthusiasm for continental, humanist ideas about legal reform or a desire to make an unwieldy system more workable? Meekings asked

> if it was the development of the equity side of the Chancery that stimulated the King's Bench to develop the classic bill [bill of Middlesex] under Chief Justices Fortescue, Markham, Billyng and Huse; or rather, whether the development of the equity (and later prerogative-court) bill and the classic King's Bench bill are not part of an early-Renaissance development of new ways of litigation.[63]

With hindsight we know that the law was one of the means used by the early Tudor monarchs, Henry VII and his son, to enhance their authority, especially to curb the powers of the 'overmighty subjects' whose wealth and ambitions had been one of the reasons for the civil wars at the end of the fifteenth century. The *Prince* of Niccolò Machiavelli in the early sixteenth century, which encouraged rulers to evade the restraints of custom and ethics to enjoy supreme power, was the Renaissance text that summarised the new, ruthless approach to tradition. Italian humanists had already subjected many authorities on history and the law to searching analysis and often found them wanting and in need of reform.

[63] C.A.F. Meekings, 'King's Bench Files', *Legal Records and the Historian*, ed. J.H. Baker (London: 1978) 106, 97–139.

The commons of Kent were to include the reform of legal procedure in their demands in 1450, for complaints about the operation of the law were as common then as they are now. Recourse to the common law was fraught with difficulties for ordinary men and women by the mid-fifteenth century.[64] The courts were mired in endless procedural complexities which could delay cases for years; it was extremely hard to get defendants into court to answer charges laid against them in writs and the penalties for non-appearance (seizure of goods or outlawry) were difficult to enforce. If a case did actually come to court and a jury was required, there were limited ways of ensuring their attendance. In these circumstances it was costly for litigants to initiate cases and few ever came to a satisfactory conclusion. This was the creaking system over which Sir John Fortescue was to preside for nearly twenty years: despite the very favourable account he was to give of it in his treatise *De Laudibus Legum Anglie*, in practice, like many of his contemporaries, he devised ways of coping with its anomalies.[65]

From the early years of the fifteenth century litigants and their attorneys had increasingly pursued justice by outflanking the constraints of the common law. One way in which they did this was by taking their cases to the court of Chancery, where verdicts could be based on equity (or 'reason' as it was often called in the fifteenth century). There common sense rather than precedent was the norm, and the conduct of cases could cut through the worst procedural delays and considerably reduce the expense of an action.[66] Meekings saw the increasing resort to Chancery as a possible part of the process of introducing early Renaissance learning into the English legal system. Perhaps it was rather, along with developments in practice in King's Bench, a realistic response led by Fortescue and his fellow justices to a system that was no longer fit for purpose.

The business of King's Bench involving private individuals (there were also cases brought by the Crown) was mainly concerned with breaches of the peace, while Common Pleas (or the Common Bench) dealt with most property cases. The latter court was obliged to remain fixed in one place by the provisions of Magna Carta; King's Bench was still technically peripatetic although by the fifteenth century it was based in Westminster. The Crown's cases were usually dispatched reasonably

[64] M. Blatcher, *The Court of King's Bench, 1450–1550: A Study in Self-Help* (London: 1978) 26.

[65] See below, Chapter 5, 'Edward of Lancaster', pp. 198–216.

[66] D.R. Klinck, *Conscience, Equity and the Court of Chancery in Early Modern England* (Farnham: 2010).

promptly, so what was needed was a means of satisfying private plaintiffs in complaints of assault and trespass and a device for diverting some of the business away from Common Pleas for the profit of King's Bench. The solution lay in the 'bill of Middlesex', by means of which a plaintiff could initiate a case through a bill rather than be forced to acquire a writ from the sheriff in the actual county where it was claimed the offence took place.[67] The county of Middlesex included Westminster and its courts, and bills alleging that offences of trespass had occurred there were often sued irrespective of the real facts. Defendants were then taken into the marshal's custody or bailed under the court's jurisdiction and the real grounds for the action could then be declared.[68]

The use of 'bills of Middlesex' in preference to writs pre-dated Fortescue's time as Chief Justice but became more frequent during his tenure of office. This proved an effective alternative to appeals to Chancery: Common Pleas and King's Bench courts had been in danger of forgoing their lucrative fees by losing too many cases. Blatcher gave the credit for stemming the tide and extending their court's jurisdiction to the King's Bench prothonotories (chief clerks), since she believed that the judges were too 'Olympian' to concern themselves in such matters.[69] Fortescue took two important decisions to facilitate the system: Kempe's case in 1448 (a bill may lie against a prisoner who has been unlawfully arrested) and Selby's case in 1452/3 (when the court allowed bail to be treated as custody).[70] 'Custody' was a legal fiction but it did permit actions to proceed when the defendant was not physically present and it was combined with the fiction that a trespass had been committed in Middlesex. Taken together, they enabled the court of King's Bench to hear the real cause of the action, often for debt, rather than for it to go through the lengthy and expensive procedure by a writ, acquired from a county sheriff, in Common Pleas. Fortescue's time in the Sheriff's Court of London might have given him the experience of working with greater flexibility than was the case with the royal courts at Westminster.[71] This led him to encourage the kind of legal sleight of hand that

[67] 'Bills' in this sense were petitions addressed directly to a court in order to start an action.

[68] Meekings, 'King's Bench Files', 105–6.

[69] Blatcher, *Court of King's Bench*, 109 but see S. Jenks, 'Bills of Custody in the Reign of Henry VI', *Journal of Legal History*, 23 (2002) 197–222, who believes that Blatcher placed too much emphasis on the importance of the 1450s in the development of the 'bill of Middlesex'.

[70] J.H. Baker, *An Introduction to English Legal History* (London: 1990) 49–51; Seipp, 1448.035, 1452.024.

[71] Tucker, *Law Courts and Lawyers*, 369–70.

made it less risky for plaintiffs to bring fictitious allegations of trespass to get defendants into the custody of King's Bench.

Had it not been for these legal developments Magna Carta would have prevented such cases from being tried in King's Bench. Here is an extract from Fortescue's judgement in 1452/3 in Selby's case, rescued by Clermont from the complexities of old French and Latin. It shows the Chief Justice embracing the legal fiction. A bill of trespass had been presented in King's Bench by David Selby against a person who was in custody there:

> As it seems to me, it is enough: for although the cause of his being in prison does not appear, it shall be supposed for a legal reason; for it may be for some offence done to the Court, or some other suggestion made to us; of which things we never should make record. And many people are often in this place committed to prison; which proceeding shall be supposed legal rather than otherwise. And therefore recover your damages etc.[72]

'The legal fiction has always been an important method by which common-law machinery has been adjusted!' Blatcher in her dissection of the growth of the 'bill of Middlesex' showed how Chief Justices colluded in such legal fictions but was comforted by the thought that they were only the latest of a string of devices used to expedite legal processes.[73]

The whole question of the legal uses of bail had been addressed in a statute in 1445; in a preamble the many extortions and oppressions practised by sheriffs were condemned.[74] One remedy provided was to enact that they might only charge 20d for bailing a prisoner and their junior officers could expect no more than 4d. With a few exceptions, sheriffs were required to release their prisoners on bail promptly pending court action. It may have been just a coincidence that this measure was passed three years after Fortescue became Chief Justice but it does show a detailed knowledge of the workings of the law at county level such as he possessed. It also ties in with the apparent aims of King's Bench to clarify the law, hasten its operation and attract business away from Common Pleas and Chancery. A dismissive tone was adopted by Fortescue in 1458 when he was passing judgment based on an absurd precedent: 'Sir, the law is as I say it is, and so it has been laid down ever since the law began; and we have several set forms which are held as law, and so held and used for good reason, though we cannot at present

[72] Clermont, *Works*, *Year Book*, 30 Henry VI, Michaelmas Term, 22–3.
[73] Ives, *Common Lawyers*, 196; Blatcher, *Court of King's Bench*, 111–24.
[74] *Statutes of the Realm*, 11 vols (London: 1810–23) vol. 2, 23 Hen. VI, c.9, 334–6.

remember that reason.'[75] Faced with such anomalies Fortescue dealt with them with characteristically wry humour.

Scholarship on the processes of arbitration has shown that this was another means by which disputants could avoid the delays and expense of the common law. Profits could still, however, be made by lawyers through these procedures and from the Chancellor downwards they participated in arbitration. The case of John Shillingford, mayor of Exeter, is well documented and throws a useful light on a high-profile case of arbitration involving the Chancellor and the Chief Justices (Fortescue and Newton).[76] Between 1447 and 1448 Shillingford tried to bring a long-running dispute over jurisdiction between Edmund Lacy, bishop of Exeter, and the city to a conclusion. There seems to have been no political issue at stake and the case shows the great officers operating principally as lawyers. It had been taken to Common Pleas with a writ of trespass on Church lands sued by the bishop, so Shillingford, at considerable expense, went to London accompanied by the city recorder, Nicholas Radford, and other attorneys. The Chancellor, John Stafford, archbishop of Canterbury, captivated perhaps by a magnificent present of fish (tench and pickerel), was well disposed and, warning them against continuing the case in Common Pleas, suggested that the matter should be settled through arbitration by himself and the Chief Justices.

The arbitration took over a year to complete and involved the city of Exeter in a number of payments for food, wine, bribes and the regular expenses of travel and sending messages. Fortescue discussed the case over a meal with the Chancellor on 6 November 1447.[77] Later, after 19 April 1448, Nicholas Radford went to pay his respects to Fortescue and reported, 'my lord Fortescue said many things as me thoghte, and onys I herde hym seye, with right a gladde spyrute, "And my lord Chaunceller woll be endyfferent, we shall have a gode ende I truste to Almyghty God and owre lady", and sone after departed'.[78] Fortescue had been retained for some years as an attorney by Exeter and was a local man, so it was to be expected that he would be favourable to their cause. The City Receiver's Account, 1447–48, also shows that they took care of his

[75] W.S. Holdsworth, *The History of English Law*, 17 vols (London: 1922) vol. 3, 626; *Year Book* 36 Henry VI pl. 21.

[76] *Letters and Papers of John Shillingford, Mayor of Exeter, 1447–1450*, ed. S.A. Moore (London: 1871) *passim*.

[77] *Ibid.*, 18.

[78] *Ibid.*, 62.

servants, 'Item dato Johannoi Goff servienti Johannis Fortescu Chivaler eodem tempore xl d. Item dato clerico suo iiiid.'[79]

When a settlement was finally reached in December 1448, it represented a compromise between the city and the bishop. The cathedral and churchyard were recognised to be under the jurisdiction of the latter but reasonable incursions by city officials in pursuit of malefactors were to be allowed. The earl of Devon and Lord Bonville had also become involved, and it is impossible to know the precise nature of the negotiations as only the account of some of the city's dealings (involving at a late stage a large box of anchovies) survive. Shillingford seldom makes it clear which Chief Justice he is referring to, but the Chancellor and Newton rather than Fortescue seem to have taken the most active part. Did Fortescue confine himself to uttering comforting generalities, collecting whatever payments were forthcoming and eating the fish or was he of practical assistance to his fellow Devonians? He was unlikely to have wished to offend the bishop and, like the Chancellor, probably welcomed an outcome in which both sides gained something: an aim that Edward Powell has attributed to the royal government and magnates concerned with cases of arbitration.[80]

Simon Payling described another arbitration in Nottinghamshire in 1449 in which Fortescue was involved and which had a good end. Lord Cromwell invited Fortescue as Chief Justice of the King's Bench and John Portington, a justice in Common Pleas, to arbitrate in a dispute between Robert, the heir of the Willoughby estate, and his stepmother. It was a familiar tale of a landowner trying to provide for his children by a second wife and in the process threatening the rights of the issue of his first marriage. In 'a masterly document', probably drafted by Fortescue, the return awarded the heir most of the lands but with sufficient given to the stepmother to placate her. The arbitrators wished to avoid future conflict and provided in the document against every possible reason for dispute that might arise between the parties.[81] These transactions throw a positive light on Fortescue, who seems to have adopted a practical and humane approach to conflicts between apparently irreconcilable parties.

[79] *Ibid.*, 148.

[80] E. Powell, 'Settlement of Disputes by Arbitration in Fifteenth Century England', *Law and History Review*, 2 (1984) 21–43; C. Rawcliffe, 'The Great Lord as Peacekeeper: Arbitration by English Noblemen and Their Councils in the Later Middle Ages', *Law and Social Change in British History*, ed. J.A. Guy and H.G. Beale (London: 1984) 34–54.

[81] Payling, *Political Society in Lancastrian England*, 208–11.

While Fortescue was open to procedures that made justice more accessible, such as 'the bill of Middlesex' and arbitration, there was a darker side to his record as Chief Justice. The Fastolf papers contain evidence of what can only have been a bribe given to Fortescue at some time before Fastolf's death in 1459, when Thomas Howes was released from King's Bench gaol: 'Item datum in regardo cuidam Capitali Justiciarii domini regis...unam robam panni auri de crymson velwet ut dictus Judex esset plus favorabilis in judicio suo prefato Thome Howys quando imprisonatus fuit in le kyngysbynche – vi li xiii s iiii d.'[82] The case arose from a writ of *capias* (arrest) obtained against Howes by John Andrew of Baylham, Suffolk in 1455. Howes, together with John Paston I, had been granted the wardship of Thomas Fastolf of Cowhaugh, Suffolk in the previous year and this was to involve the 'preest innocent in such a cause' in all sorts of trouble.[83] The rival contender for the wardship was the influential Sir Philip Wentworth, the king's carver, and he was backed up by notorious local strong-arm men such as John Heydon and Thomas Daniel.[84]

The way in which such problems were dealt with is demonstrated in a letter from Sir John Fastolf to his stepson, Stephen Scrope, of 30 October, 1457:

> The parson Ser Thomas Howes cometh up at this tyme by the grevous pursewte of John Andreus and Heydon, to apere be fore the right worschepeful ser, my right wel be-loved brother your fadir [Sir Richard Bingham, the father of Scrope's wife] and other the Kynges juges of the Kynges Bench; I prey you hertily that ye wille have in remembraunce for to recomaund me to hym whan ye speke with hym, and for to thank hym for his rightful favour shewed in Sir Thomas matier, and in alle other matiers that toucheth me wheche ben attained in that hey courte.[85]

In this case the family connection may have negated the need for a bribe but it was a different matter with Fortescue. One of his tasks was gaol delivery: if some prisoners paid him so lavishly it constituted a good

[82] Oxford, Magdalen Coll. Fastolf Paper 42 m.4; Ives, *Common* Lawyers, 309; K.B. Macfarlane, 'William Worcester', *Studies Presented to Sir Hilary Jenkinson*, ed. J. Conway Davies (Oxford: 1957) 196–221, 214, 'Item, given in reward to the Chief Justice of the Lord King ... a robe of cloth of gold and crimson velvet that the said judge should be more favourable in his judgement to the aforesaid Thomas Howys when he was imprisoned in the King's Bench – £6 13s 4d.'

[83] *PL*, ed. Davis, vol. 2, nos. 525, 576, 118, 177.

[84] See below, pp. 93–4, nn. 196–200.

[85] *PL*, ed. Davis, vol. 3, no. 1035, 168.

source of income. Thomas Howes was a priest and a useful servant to Sir John Fastolf, but one wonders if such a generous payment was intended to elicit other favours as well: the kind of 'matiers' referred to in Fastolf's letter to Scrope. It was probably in 1456, for example, that Fastolf wrote to John Paston I about a property dispute in which he had been assisted by Fortescue: 'the Chif Justice of England, as I am enformed, recitid the matier in Parlement by-fore the Lordes'.[86] Fortescue was insistent in his *De Laudibus* that English judges were incorruptible, but as in other claims he made in that treatise there seems to have been a considerable gap between ideal and reality.[87]

There was, of course, a grey area between bribes when the conduct of the recipient was definitely affected by the gift and favours, goods or money that might be offered in the hope that benefits would follow and those occasions when they did not. With draconian sanctions applied in modern Western societies against any whiff of corruption it is hard to penetrate the thinking of late medieval commentators on the subject. Fortescue, however, made his disdain for the practice of bribery very clear in his *De Laudibus*, but he was the man who had used the civil law at length in the *De Natura* only to condemn it in the *De Laudibus.*[88]

Fortescue wrote the *De Laudibus* when he had long been in exile, not burdened with the need to make the creaking system of the common law work or, indeed, tempted by the opportunities for lining his pockets with bribes and gifts. His main objective in the treatise was to convince the Lancastrian heir to the throne to whom it was addressed of the need to understand the principles of the common law and to recognise its superiority over continental civil law. Fortescue wished to wean the Prince away from what he perceived to be the autocratic practices of his Valois mother's family and instil in him a respect for political and regal government, where the sovereign had an obligation to observe the laws and customs of his English realm: he also hoped that his treatise would be used by subsequent rulers. Even if as Chief Justice he had been, in practice, all too aware of the shortcomings of the common law he also knew that it was flexible enough to be amended. Whilst he can scarcely be hailed as a precursor of a legal renaissance, as a supreme pragmatist he had presided over a period when the Westminster courts had adapted to face external challenges and their own shortcomings.

86 *PL*, ed. Davis, vol. 2, no.569, 166–8.

87 Chrimes, *De Laudibus*, 129. A cynic might find his words ambiguous: 'Nor was it ever found that any of them was corrupted with gifts and bribes.'

88 See below, Chapter 4 and Chapter 5.

A man of property

Sir John Fortescue was a prosperous man by the late 1440s, owning several properties and enjoying a substantial disposable income:

> [J]udges were in a uniquely advantageous position to exploit the local land market. First, the excess capital provided by judicial salaries and other legal fees ... provided the necessary cash for outright purchases ... Second, the legal training and position of a judge gave him the skill and connections to defend his purchases against rival claimants who so often made life difficult for the purchasers of land in late medieval England.[89]

Fortescue's property provided him with rents and goods, and as Chief Justice it was possible to earn about £250 a year from his salary, robes, court fees and continuing private practice.[90] Eric Ives, when he calculated a judge's income, took no account of the yield from bribes: the evidence from the Fastolf gift suggests that this could have been very lucrative. An examination of Fortescue's property transactions from the mid-1440s to 1461 shows him concerned further to increase the value of his holdings. He was also influenced by other considerations: conventional piety, his family interests and the shift of focus in his personal life from the West to the vicinity of London.

E.T. Callahan has drawn attention to the innovative nature of Fortescue's theory of the origin of property.[91] It was formulated most explicitly in the *De Natura Legis Naturae*, taking the Genesis text 'In the sweat of thy brow thou shalt eat bread' as his starting point.[92] Making a departure from canon, civil and common law, he took this to mean that personal property, whether created by the owner or his forebears, was sanctioned by divine as well as natural law.[93] Fortescue's actions and theories, both in his capacity as a judge, in private as a wealthy landowner and in his

89 Payling, *Political Society in Lancastrian England*, 31.

90 Ives, *Common Lawyers*, 321–9, based on calculations made for the 1480s.

91 E.T. Callahan, 'Blood, Sweat and Wealth: Fortescue's Theory of the Origin of Property', *History of Political Thought*, 17 (1996) 21–35; D. Wood, *Medieval Economic Thought* (Cambridge: 2002) 118, draws similar conclusions to Callahan, characterising Fortescue's approach as 'economic nationalism' – no realm could prosper under a poor king.

92 Clermont, *Works*, vol. 1, 291.

93 Janet Coleman traced the proliferation of justifications of property rights in the works of the late scholastics from the thirteenth century. These responded not only to theory but to current legal and economic practices, '*Dominium* in Thirteenth and Fourteenth-Century Political Thought and its Seventeenth-Century Heirs: John of Paris and Locke', *Political Studies*, 33 (1985) 73–100.

Governance of England, bore out his commitment to this belief. He appears to have devoted considerable thought, energy and resources to retaining what he had and improving the landholdings and wealth of his family by buying new properties.

Fortescue acquired property in Hertfordshire: he bought Gacelyns in 1447/8 and probably purchased Punsbourne at the same time,[94] and seems to have owned the manor of Bayford. In 1441 John Kirkeby had died seised of lands formerly belonging to Robert Punsbourne, so Clermont was incorrect in stating that the manor was ever owned by John Fortescue senior, who left it to his son Richard. It did eventually pass to his son John, esquire to the body of King Edward IV, later in the century, probably whilst Sir John Fortescue was still in exile. At some point the manors of Gacelyns and Punsbourne seem to have been merged.[95] By 1454/5 Sir John also owned a tenement, Potterells Grove in the manor of North Mimms.[96] In Middlesex by 1455 he owned the tofts (homesteads) of Geffrons and Bovyngdons (also known as Pounses) which were to form part of the manor of South Mimms by the sixteenth century. In 1457 Fortescue and others granted a house and forty-three acres in Hendon to the prior of the Hospital of St Mary within Cripplegate, London.[97] It must have been Fortescue's property holdings in Middlesex that led him in the mid-1440s to entrust some valuable service books to John Holwill. They were deposited in the church at Enfield, from where they were subsequently stolen:

> William Frekys late of Enfield, holywater clerk, and Thomas Grene late of London, chaplain and Austin friar, in the feast of the Circumcision of Our Lord [1 January 1447] 25 Henry VI broke into the parish church of Enfield at Enfield and stole there two books called antiphoners worth £20, a book called 'A temporell legent' worth £10, a psalter, a primer covered in velvet worth 100s and another primer worth 40s from the goods and chattels of John Fortescu kt.[98]

[94] *VCH*, Hertfordshire, vol. 3, 102.

[95] Clermont, *Family*, 151; *VCH*, Hertfordshire, vol. 3, 105, 422. In 1538 the Fortescues sold the reversion to the Lord Admiral, Thomas Seymour.

[96] *VCH*, Hertfordshire, vol. 2, 255.

[97] *VCH*, Middlesex, vol. 5, 21–2, 275; *CPR*, Henry VI, 1452–61, 473.

[98] TNA, KB9/255/1 m.8. I am grateful to Isobel Harvey, who sent me this reference.

Fortescue also owned property in Wiltshire, which was mentioned in the inquisition of 1468, seven years after he had been attainted.[99] This comprised lands and messuages (suitable lands for a dwelling or containing a house) in Kingston Deverell, Trowbridge, Hilperton, Bradford-on-Avon, Chippenham and Sutton Benger: it had been all transferred to Sir John Wenlock. These holdings probably dated from transactions in the 1430s when he had been very active in that area on behalf of Sir Walter Hungerford.

On 12 February 1443 Fortescue made provision for his widowed mother-in-law in Somerset. An Inspeximus (a charter confirming an earlier charter) confirmed that Sir John Fortescue, his wife Isabella and her mother Margery Jamys had been given a charter by the late prior of the Carthusian house at Hinton granting them lands, a house 'wherein Margery now dwells' and other property at Norton St Philip in return for an annual rent of 13s 4d: should John and Isabella die without heirs male it would all revert to the prior.[100] It is impossible to know where Sir John and Lady Fortescue lived at this time, although it was suggested above that during the early years of their marriage they were based at Norton St Philip. They now had three children, all of them fairly young, and the estate of a Chief Justice to maintain. It is probable that the family was based nearer to London, perhaps in one of the properties in Hertfordshire or Middlesex that Sir John was so anxious to safeguard for his wife in early 1461.[101]

In 1456 Lady Fortescue made over her jointure in Devon to her son Martin and his wife. This could simply have been a sign that his parents no longer wished to concern themselves with so remote a property. It could, however, have been part of the process noticed above, by which they attempted to avoid the consequences of Sir John's possible disgrace. Since those lands were in Martin and Elizabeth's possession and passed to their oldest son John as the inquisition dated 1502 recorded at the time of his death, they succeeded.[102] The property was specified as having formed part of Lady Fortescue's jointure in a deposition made by three witnesses in 1480, which probably formed part of the settlement of Sir John's estates after his death.[103]

99 *CIPM*, viii, 1422–85, no. 285, 214; TNA, C 145/323/50. 7 Ed.IV, 1468; *CPR*, Edward IV, 1467–88, 99.

100 *CPR*, Henry VI, 1441–46, 170.

101 See above, Chapter 1, and the second part of the present chapter.

102 *CIPM*, Henry VII, 2, 388–90. The manor of Combe was worth 10 marks per annum in 1502.

103 *CCR*, Edward IV, Richard III, 1476–85, 199.

On the feast of the Purification of the Virgin Mary (2 February) 1450, a marriage settlement of two manors was agreed between Sir John Fortescue on behalf of his daughter Maud, the bride, and Sir Robert Corbet, who held the manors, on behalf of his son Robert, the groom. Since the couple were still children, the settlement included elaborate provisions for their keeping until, in the first instance, Robert attained eleven years of age but the arrangements extended until he was twenty-one. Sir Robert was to take most of the profits of the manors, but when the children were in Fortescue's custody, he was to draw an income sufficient for their maintenance. When he was twenty-one Robert would be granted the manor of Little Downham (co. Norfolk) but he would have to wait until his father died for King's Bromley (co. Stafford). Fortescue, with Sir Edmund Hungerford, Thomas Younge and John Gogh, was among the feoffees charged with carrying out the complex provisions of the settlement.

The agreement envisaged the possibility of an annulment, but only up to the time when Robert was fourteen. In that case, Fortescue could draw profits to the value of 300 marks before they were returned to Sir Robert Corbet.[104] The feoffment was witnessed, amongst others, by Robert Hungerford, Lord Moleyns, Thomas Povy, Fortescue's clerk, and Richard Fortescue, who in 1450 could either have been Sir John's brother or one of his nephews, the sons of Henry and Richard.[105] It is hard to estimate from the evidence available the annual yield of Fortescue's property, but the mention of 300 marks, the assumed profits of Corbet's two manors over an indeterminate period, gives some idea of what the value of such holdings might have been.

Robert Corbet served on commissions of the peace in Suffolk in 1445: in March he was plain 'Robert Corbet', by November he bore the title of 'knight'. He seems to have been principally based in East Anglia, where, apart from the manor of Little Downham, he owned several other properties (see below) and sat on a number of commissions between 1445 and 1452.[106] The rolls also give a good indication of how he came to enjoy a prominent position in Suffolk and why he attracted Fortescue as a potential father-in-law for his daughter. In 1438 the escheator for that

[104] Devon Record Office, Indenture: 1262 M/FS 1.

[105] *Ibid.*, Feoffment: 1262 M/TZ 16.

[106] *CPR*, Henry VI, 1441–46, 431, 479. A Corbet (no first name) is mentioned in the *Black Books* of Lincoln's Inn as one of those keeping the first vacation in 1438, f. 35r.; *CPR*, 1446–52, 440, 595; *CFR*, 1445–52, 171. Another Corbet (again no first name) was admitted to Lincoln's Inn in 1463, this could have been Maud's husband Robert, Baker *Men of Court*, vol. 1, 523.

county, investigating the estates of Robert Corbet's parents, Guy and his widow Joan, found that on payment of a fine he could inherit the manor of Assington as well as lands, meadows, woods and rent.[107] Corbet also owned the manors of Gedinghall in Suffolk as well as Stoke Nayland, Bures St Mary, Mount Bures, Wiston, Polstead and Boxford.[108] In 1444 he was allowed to take possession of the manor of Standlake in Oxfordshire, the manor of Farncote in Gloucestershire (where he also owned the reversion of the manor of Ebrington) the manors of Hadley and Hatton in Shropshire and the manor of King's Bromley in Stafford.[109] Sir Robert Corbet was a wealthy man and, like Fortescue, had property interests in a number of counties.

The most significant piece of business that Fortescue transacted with Corbet, apart from the marriage of his daughter, was his purchase of the reversion of the manor of Ebrington, Gloucestershire. This agreement was specifically linked to another, the enfeoffment of Corbet with Gedinghall in 1455, when Fortescue, John Gough, John Nicoll and Thomas Povy made a final concord before John Prysot, Chief Justice of Common Pleas, and other justices. Fortescue paid Sir Robert Corbet

9 Fortescue's signature on Paris, BnF Ms. fonds fr., f. 175.

200 marks, and the endorsement, dated 1457, on the other side of the deed laid out the terms:

> J. Fortescu and his co feffees with ynne w[ritten] in Michell' terme anno xxxv^{to} *Henrici* vi^{ti} yn t[he] kynges Benche *rotulo* cviii^{o} enrolled their deed [by] which they enfeffid Sir Robert Corbet, Knyg[ht] and other which

[107] *CFR*, Henry VI, 1437–45, 62.
[108] *CCR*, Henry VI, 1447–54, 398–9.
[109] *CCR*, Henry VI, 1441–47, 242, 245–6; *CFR*, Henry VI, 1437–45, 315.

10 The manor of Ebrington, Gloucestershire. Mostly rebuilt in the early seventeenth century. The arms over the doorway were erected by Mrs Lucy Fortescue in the eighteenth century. The family still lives there.

he desired to be enfeffid wi[th] hym of the manor[Gedinghall] withynne written yn f[orm] acordyng to certeyne covnantes made by writing upon the sale of the revercion of the maner of Ebrighton. J. Fortescu with myne owne hande.[110]

The 'certeyne covnantes' no doubt explained the exact nature of the deal and the link between the enfeoffment of Sir Robert Corbet with Gedinghall and his receipt of 200 marks for Ebrington. This document, as well as supplying a well-authenticated autograph belonging to Fortescue, is quite specific that there was a connection between the two transactions.

The grant to Fortescue of the reversionary right to Ebrington also survives in the Devon Record Office at Exeter: Corbet waived all interest he or his heirs might have in favour of Fortescue and his heirs.[111] A life tenant, Dame Joyce (Jocosa) Beauchamp, widow of John Greville, was actually in possession of the manor. At about the same time she wrote to Fortescue in deferential terms: 'ingoodfeith Sir I am right well plesyd and gladde to be youre tenant for I trust verily that hit shall hereafter

[110] Devon Record Office, 1262 M/TSU 2 and transcription.
[111] *Ibid.*, 1262 M/TG 6.

be to me grete comfort, herts ease and suerte'.[112] Fortescue and his family had no opportunity to enjoy Ebrington before his exile, since Joyce Beauchamp was probably younger than her deceased husband and survived to the 1470s. The Patent Rolls for 1462 record the transfer of the attainted Fortescue's property in Middlesex and Hertfordshire and elsewhere within the realm, together with the reversion of Ebrington, to John Lord Wenlock.[113]

The Corbets seem to have regretted their close association with the Fortescue family, which is the construction that must be put upon the divorce of Robert Corbet from Maud Fortescue in 1466. Blomefield in his *History of the County of Norfolk* asserted that they were never divorced[114] but that directly contradicts the trust deed that settled an income on her after the annulment of her marriage, 'withynne a monyth after that a lawfull devorce of marriage is made and had by the lawe of holy chirche by twene the said Robert Corbet and Mawde now his wyf the doughter John Ffortescue knight'. The deed also makes it clear that there were no surviving children from the marriage and that Robert expected to have issue by a subsequent union.[115] Sixteen years had elapsed since the original marriage settlement in 1450, so Robert must have been considerably older than fourteen years, the age before which he could seek an annulment by the terms of the agreement. Perhaps incompatibility or Maud's failure to produce a surviving heir were factors that exacerbated the political embarrassment of this union for the Corbets. The period of the divorce, however, was a time when political affiliations were particularly problematical for the nobility and gentry, who were unsure whether to back the increasingly unpopular Edward IV, the disaffected Warwick or even the Lancastrians.[116]

Fortescue and his wife had made good material provision for the future of their only son Martin and his wife by the grant in 1456 of the manor of Combe and lands, rents and other properties in Holbeton, Overcombe, Nethercombe, Battokysburg, Efford and Alston in Devon,

[112] *Ibid.*, 1262 M/TG 7. John Greville was a merchant of Gloucestershire who had married Sybil Corbet. Her uncle Guy Corbet, who owned the reversion of Ebrington, was the father of the Sir Robert Corbet who was the father-in-law of Maud Fortescue. Joyce Beauchamp was presumably the second wife of John Greville and thus in possession of the manor.

[113] *CPR*, 1461–67, 192.

[114] F. Blomefield, continued by C. Parkin, *An Essay Towards a Topographical History of the County of Norfolk*, 11 vols (London: 1805–10) vol. 9, 479.

[115] Devon Record Office 1262 M/TN1; Corbet subsequently married Lettice, daughter of John Shirewood of Coventry, and had two children.

[116] See below, Chapter 3.

which had been Isabella's jointure.[117] The original Fortescue family estate, which John had acquired from his brother Henry after the death of their father, was to be held by his son: a sign perhaps that he wished to disengage himself from the cares of property in remote Devon. Martin's wife Elizabeth was the daughter and heiress of Richard Denzille of Filleigh, Wear-Giffard and Buckland Filleigh, north Devon. It was an extensive estate, some of which (now called Castle Hill) the Fortescue family still owns. Apart from these properties, the inquisition *post mortem* held in 1473 after the death of Martin makes it clear that Elizabeth also brought other property with her into the marriage.[118] Martin and Elizabeth had two surviving sons, John, who inherited Ebrington (where the senior branch of the Fortescue family still lives), and William.[119]

Martin Fortescue never held any kind of office, even a minor one, and did not figure independently of his wife and parents in any legal document.[120] His low profile could be explained by the fact that, like his sister Maud, he was very young when he married and only reached maturity under Edward IV, when, as a traitor's son, he would have been wise to court obscurity. He died too soon to profit from his father's rehabilitation, 1471–73, possibly always having experienced delicate health. He might even have suffered from some form of mental or physical incapacity, in which case Fortescue seems to have used his wealth and prominent position to tempt a squire and his apparently capable daughter into the marriage. Fortescue's daughters both made good marriages, respectively to sons of a man of affairs and a courtier, and it seems odd, when he was at the height of his powers, that he could not ally his only son to a more prominent family. At least Martin's obscurity safeguarded his father's original family lands, which duly descended to his heirs.

Little can be learnt about the life of Fortescue's other daughter, Elizabeth. Clermont stated that in about 1456 she married Edmund, son of

[117] See above, p. 71. n. 104; *CIPM*, Henry VII, Inquisition on John Fortescue of Were esq., 388–9; Clermont, *Works*, 7, stated that the marriage took place on 10 September 1454. This information was derived from a manuscript he had seen, the *Stemmata Fortescuana*, which had been compiled in 1795 by Mr Incledon.

[118] TNA, C 140/41 39: 'Okehampton …, Plympton …, Lamerton, manerium, Brodesbray, manerium, Brokeland, manerium, Hertelegh, messuagia et terrae, Lordesyend iuxta Criditon [Crediton], messuagia et terrae, Bredewike, yerd et fen, Mukford, messuagia et terrae.'

[119] Clermont, *Family*, 47.

[120] *CCR*, Henry VI, 1454–61, 212–13. He was associated with his wife Elizabeth and John (probably their son) in 1457 in receiving a quitclaim for a messuage and land in Efford in the parish of Holbeton, Devon.

Thomas Whalesburgh, an esquire of the king's body and master of the game of the king's deer in Cornwall.[121] But a quitclaim dated 1456 in The National Archives indicates that Edmund was dead by that date and that his widow had married Thomas Vernon, a member of the Derbyshire gentry family resident at Haddon.[122] Thomas Whalesburgh was a member of a commission to investigate complaints of piracy involving the port of Fowey in 1448 and was sheriff of Cornwall in 1453.[123] Griffiths describes this appointment as part of a deliberate policy to install gentlemen in the King's employment in the regions to counterbalance the influence of the duke of York.[124]

In 1448 Fortescue had been one of the witnesses to a quitclaim issued by Thomas Whalesburgh, who was heir to some property in Somerset: he was a man of some substance in the West and part of the Lancastrian establishment and it is easy to see why Fortescue made an alliance with his family.[125] In 1452 an indenture between John Trevelyan and Thomas Whalesburgh for Trevelyan's marriage to Thomas's daughter, who was one of his heirs, referred to: 'Lands and tenements to the yerly value of xx li of the which the said Thomas hath made a lesse to Elizabeth, doughter of John Fortescu, knyght, for the tyme of her lyf, in the shires of Cornwayle and Devon.'[126] Her first husband seems to have been dead by that time as he was not mentioned and Thomas was making provision for his widowed daughter-in-law: there is no sign of any issue. In 1456 Thomas Whalesburgh was on a commission of array in Cornwall and in 1473 Thomas 'Whalisburgh' accompanied John Fortescue, sheriff of Cornwall (the son of Richard Fortescue), and others in their assault, on behalf of Edward IV, on St Michael's Mount where the earl of Oxford was ensconced.[127] So this family appears to have made a smooth transition from service to Lancaster to vigorous support of York.

121 Clermont, *Family*, 46; *CPR*, 1441–44, 170.

122 I am grateful to Hannes Kleineke for bringing this second marriage to my notice, TNA, CP 25/1/293/73/411. Thomas Vernon was probably a brother or a son of Sir William Vernon, a staunch Lancastrian and Treasurer of Calais, 1451–60. He made his peace with the Yorkists in 1461 but was later accused of participating with his son in violent affrays. He died in 1467, Wedgwood, *Biographies*, 908.

123 *CPR*, Henry VI, 1446–45, 187; *CFR*, 1452–61, 74.

124 Griffiths, *Henry VI*, 720–1, n. 34.

125 *CCR*, Henry VI, 1447–54, 442.

126 *Trevelyan Papers Prior to 1588*, ed. J. Payne Collier (London: 1857) part 1, 38.

127 *CPR*, Henry VI, 1452–61, 309; *CPR*, Edward IV, 1467–77, 399–400. Despite his reconciliation with the house of York, Thomas Whalesburgh failed to acquire the manor of Alford in Somerset. He claimed to have inherited it from his uncle

During his early years as a Chief Justice, Fortescue seems to have obeyed the King's advisers complacently. He also avoided potential pitfalls such as the need to discipline Suffolk's turbulent follower Tailboys and helped to preserve the influence of his friend, Lord Cromwell, without alienating the duke. His grasp of the complexities of the common law and his application of it vindicated the decision that had been made to appoint him before he had completed the customary duties that preceded elevation to Chief Justice. By the end of the decade Fortescue was more confident in his actions: he was well known in government circles and had amassed sufficient wealth to be a useful patron in counties such as Devon and Somerset, as well as in London. His expectation must have been that he would continue to prosper and retain respect as a learned judge. However, the 1450s proved to be a time when very few could count on prospering or acquitting themselves honourably. Like most Chief Justices, Fortescue had not enjoyed an important political role but the crises of the 1450s were to propel him into greater prominence.

Part 2: The Crisis in Governance

Between the summer of 1449 and the summer of 1450 the stability of life in England came under serious threat from the deteriorating situation in France. The whole of Normandy was lost, leaving only Gascony, Guyenne and Calais of all the territory that Henry VI had inherited in 1422 in English hands, and this was to have a devastating impact on the rule of law. A series of military expeditions to France were mounted in futile attempts to retrieve the situation, all of them inadequately financed by successive parliaments. The constant presence of disaffected soldiers, seamen and uprooted settlers in and around the southern ports encouraged the already rebellious disposition of many of the commons of Kent, Sussex, Hampshire and the other southern counties.[128] The King and his council, supported by their law officers and representatives in the counties, developed no coherent policies to deal with the crisis. In his later writings Fortescue never engaged closely with the mechanics of popular unrest, preferring to deal in general terms with the factors that might lead subjects to rise against their princes.[129] In the case of the *Governance* Fortescue had good reason to avoid embarrassing refer-

Simon de Ralegh but John Fitzjames seems to have held it over the long period of the dispute, 1455 to 1480, *VCH*, Somerset, vol. 10, 77.

[128] I.M.W. Harvey, *Jack Cade's Rebellion of 1450* (Oxford: 1991) *passim*.

[129] *Vale's Book*, 'Governance', ch. 12, 240–2.

ences to his Lancastrian past, but no such constraint applied when he wrote the *De Laudibus*. The dismal first response to the crisis by the Lancastrian regime and the further erosion of its authority during the next decade surely contributed to his two later studies of governance with their prescriptions for avoiding financial meltdown and consequent political strife.

The year 1450 started badly for Henry VI and his household. On 9 January one of its most influential members, Adam Moleyns, bishop of Chichester and Keeper of the Privy Seal, was hacked to death at Portsmouth by mutinous soldiers. Parliament, which had been sitting since the previous November, was seething with indignation as English France bled away. The King and council were desperate for the grant of a subsidy to pay for the next campaign, so on 7 February they had to endure a thoroughgoing indictment of the duke of Suffolk, who was impeached for his treasonable alienation of royal lands in France.[130] On 17 March Suffolk was condemned to five years of exile before a Great Council at Westminster Palace: on 2 May, whilst sailing from Dover, he was intercepted and murdered by shipmen.

Fortescue's presence was not recorded amongst the members of the Great Council on 17 March although he was probably there. He had certainly been consulted about Suffolk's case on 27 January, together with the other justices, and the careful opinion he had offered on the preliminary charges levelled against the duke reflected the fact that the King and council had not yet realised how serious the situation had become. Fortescue advised against imprisoning Suffolk for:

> In thiese generall termes, Rumoir, and noyse of sclaundre and Infamie, may many things be understand; that is for to sey, mesprisions or trespasses; for which causes it nedeth not by the lawe to committe hym to warde; or elles Felonyes or Tresons. And for asmoche as the wordes been generall and noothing in speciall declared, he [Fortescue] wold common with his Felawes, and bryng an answere what the lawe therin will after her conceytes. And afterward all the lordes from the lowest to the highest, held in maner oon opinion; that for cause there was noo speciall mater of sclaundre and Infamie putte upon hym, that he shuld not be committed to warde till the specialte were declared and shewed.[131]

The other recorded intervention by Fortescue in the Suffolk case occurred on 13 March. It fell between a first inconclusive meeting

[130] *RP*, vol. 5, 177; *PROME*, vol. 12, 94–8.
[131] *RP*, vol. 5, 176–7; *PROME*, vol. 12, 93.

between the King, the Great Council and the duke on the previous day and the session of 17 March which condemned him to exile:

> The xiii day of Marche then next folowyng, the Chief Justice rehersed to all the Lordes by the Kynges commaundement, saiying, that it is well in youre remembraunce in what wyse the Duke of Suffolk demeaned hym here yesterday; and upon that he axed a question, what advise the Lordes wold geve to the Kyng, what is nowe to doo furthermore in this mater, which advis was differred unto Monday then next commyng, on the which Monday [16 March] was noo thing doon in that matier.[132]

Fortescue's unwillingness to proceed against the duke in January was probably a reaction against the popular outcry; to succumb to pressure from such a source would set an extremely bad precedent. By mid-March the situation had become so dangerous that the Council was prepared to sacrifice Suffolk; the time had come to disregard the common law and opt for an 'equitable' solution to the crisis. The language in which Fortescue conveyed the King's ambivalent wishes implied that the Chief Justice was as alarmed as the rest of the government, 'what is nowe to doo furthermore in this mater'. His care in avoiding sentiments which could later be held against him anticipated an equally reserved answer that he and his fellow justices were to make to the duke of York's claim to the throne a decade later.[133]

Fortescue had good reason to be afraid – he was on the 'hit list' in a subversive poem called *The Dirge Made by the Commons of Kent in the Time of their Rising.* All those who were associated with Suffolk ('Jack Napes', a reference to his badge of an ape chained to a log) were portrayed singing a dirge for his soul using phrases from the office for the dead and the psalms. There was an implicit threat that the mourners would soon meet the same fate as their friend. Fortescue was mentioned in a verse that included Sir Thomas Hoo, John Hampton, Ralph Butler, Lord Sudeley, and John, Lord Stourton, all household men who were believed to have feathered their own nests at the expense of the Crown. Richard Woodville, Lord Rivers, had fought for Lancaster in France and been richly rewarded. He was soon to be prominent in brutally suppressing the aftermath of Jack Cade's rebellion:

> *Expectans expectavi*, seyth Sir Thomas Hoo,
> *Complaceat tibi*, begynneth John Hampton.
> *Beatus que intelligit* and dredit also,

[132] *RP*, vol. 5, 182; *PROME*, vol. 12, 105; Wolffe, *Henry VI*, 223–8.

[133] See below, p. 103–5.

Seyth John Fortescw, all this fals treson.
Sana Domine oure wittes with reson,
The Lorde Sudeley devoutly prayeth.
Quem admodum desiderat, ye Lord Stowrton,
Sitivit anima mea, for hym lyeth,
The lord Ryvers all onely seythe
Requiem eternam, God grawnt us to se,
A pater nostar ther must be in feyth,
For Jack Napis sowle *placebo* and *dirige*.[134]

The Articles of the Captain of Kent, issued in the summer during Jack Cade's revolt, were to demand that the extortions of King's Bench should be suppressed 'whiche ys so grevefull to the shire of Kente'.[135] This conveyed the unambiguous message that the court of King's Bench, over which Fortescue presided, was discredited. Several prominent and hated royal servants were to be murdered during this troublous time, including Bishop Aiscough, Lord Saye and William Crowmer. Fortescue doubtless remembered the fate of a previous Chief Justice in 1388, when Sir Robert Tressilian was executed in shameful circumstances after he had upheld the royal prerogative against the demands of the Lords Appellant. The judges, 'were liable to be entangled when the political questions which divided the state assumed a legal aspect ... [they] either chose or were compelled to take the side of the crown'.[136] The pressures on judges remained as severe in the unquiet reign of Henry VI as they had been during the troubled regime of Richard II.

In late March 1450 Fortescue was appointed to sit on a commission of oyer and terminer to deal with treasons and felonies in London. The lawlessness of the capital both before and during Jack Cade's revolt involved him in two more commissions, on 6 May and 1 July, as well as commissions in April for Surrey and in May for Oxford.[137] On 28 July, only two weeks after the capture and death of Cade, Fortescue was named to head a commission of oyer and terminer in Devon:

> touching the names of the malefactors who with Robert Wenynton of Clyfton Dertemouth Hardenesse, co. Devon, 'marchaunt', assaulted and imprisoned Walter Reynell at Clyfton Dertemouth Hardenesse, so that his life was despaired of, and kept him in prison until he delivered to

[134] *Three Fifteenth Century Chronicles*, ed. J. Gairdner (London: 1880) 102.
[135] *Vale's Book*, 206.
[136] Holdsworth, *History of English Law*, vol. 2, 560.
[137] *CPR*, Henry VI, 1446–52, 320, 381, 385–6.

Robert a writing whereby he released to Robert all personal actions and John Purchas, prisoner of John Lake.[138]

The Fine Rolls record that both protagonists in this affair were office holders in Devon. Robert Wenynton was collector of customs and subsidies in Exeter, Dartmouth and district, 1446–47, and searcher of ships in the same areas in 1447.[139] Walter Reynell, who was described as 'esquire' in 1449,[140] clearly enjoyed royal favour in 1450 and kept it as he was escheator for Devon and Cornwall in 1452 and represented the county of Devon in parliament in the following year.[141] In 1454 he was on a commission of array with Henry Fortescue and on another 'to arrest and commit to prison all persons in Devon who oppress, rob and kill therin and all their favourers', with a galaxy of local worthies including Courtenays, Bonvilles and Champernouns.[142] On the same day as Fortescue's commission of 28 July 1450, Thomas Wyse (his brother-in-law) and others, including Walter Reynell, were ordered to arrest Wenynton and bring him before the King and council.[143]

This all looks rather odd. On 30 July a commission of oyer and terminer was issued to the archbishops of York and Canterbury, the duke of Buckingham, John Prysot, Chief Justice Common Pleas and a cadre of lawyers to go into Kent to investigate alleged malpractices by members of the royal household and government servants in the aftermath of Cade's revolt.[144] Yet the greatest legal officer in the realm was concerned in a dispute between minor officials in the distant and permanently wild West immediately after the worst rebellion England had known for seventy years. The *Paston Letters* confirm that Fortescue did, in fact, leave London: 'The Chief Justice is not here, ne noon other iustice, except Danvers is now mad iuge of the Commune Place and is forth in to Kent with the Lords etc.'[145] Fortescue's next recorded presence in London was not until 6 November, when he was a trier of

[138] *Ibid.*, 387.

[139] *CFR*, Henry VI, 1445–52, 52, 54, 56, 61.

[140] *Ibid.*, 148.

[141] *Ibid.*, 252.

[142] *CPR*, Henry VI, 1452–61, 171, 652.

[143] *CPR*, Henry VI, 1446–52, 388.

[144] *Ibid.*, 388; R. Virgoe, 'Some Ancient Indictments in the King's Bench Referring to Kent, 1450–52', *Documents Illustrative of Medieval Kentish Society*, ed. F.R.H. Du Boulay (Ashford: 1964) 215–16, 214–65.

[145] *PL*, ed. Davis, 2, no. 455, 40–2.

petitions for the new parliament.[146] He was probably in the West for most of August and September and perhaps part of October as well.

Two explanations for the government's decision to send Fortescue to the West can be offered. The Reynell/Wenynton affair was significant since Wenynton, a member of parliament for Dartmouth and ship-owner, had been appointed in 1449 to safeguard English shipping after the recommencement of the war with France. Instead, true to the privateering ways of the wild West, he violently seized the neutral Bay fleet of Dutch and Hanseatic vessels and took them back to Southampton. This sparked off a huge diplomatic crisis and led to the imprisonment of English merchants and the loss of their ships and goods throughout the Hanseatic world. The English government, which desperately needed political friends and decent revenues from trade, attempted to placate the duke of Burgundy, the Hansards and the High Master of the Order of Teutonic knights. Wenynton had influential friends, courtiers like Thomas Daniel and John Trevelyan, and he evaded any consequences for his actions until their position was threatened by Cade's rebellion. But his original offence was presumably too far-ranging not to be addressed even in such troubled times so, besides his dismissal from his post as a customs collector, the Chief Justice was sent to head a commission to attempt to punish him for the assault on Reynall. Cherry assigns Reynell to Lord Bonville's faction that was ranged against the earl of Devon and at this time the royal household would have been likely to back Bonville and his clients in any dispute.[147] Wenynton managed to evade this and two later attempts by Reynell to bring him to justice by simply sailing away to Portugal. In the 1450s he resumed office as a collector of customs, became mayor of Dartmouth (for the second time) and eventually transferred his loyalty to the Yorkists, under whom he prospered.[148]

Another explanation for why Fortescue was sent to the West could be, as Griffiths suggested, that he had been allowed by the council to distance himself from gestures of reconciliation in the aftermath of the revolt when the commission to Kent in the summer of 1450 contained less controversial figures. He had been named as a possible target so

[146] *RP*, vol. 5, 210; *PROME*, vol. 12, 173.

[147] M. Cherry, 'The Struggle for Power in Mid-Fifteenth-Century Devonshire', *Patronage, the Crown and the Provinces*, ed. R.A. Griffiths (Gloucester: 1981) 123–44, 133.

[148] H. Kleineke, 'Robert Wenynton alias Cane of Dartmouth, Devon', *House of Commons, 1422–1461*. I am grateful to the trustees of the History of Parliament Trust for allowing me to refer to this material.

any commission at that time which included him would have run the risk of being seen as biased by the men of Kent. [149] There were plenty of rebels who had not been pardoned and it was wise to keep the unpopular Fortescue in reserve to deal with them when the time came.

Fortescue was next appointed to a commission of oyer and terminer in Sussex on 14 October and on 24 December he was finally assigned to Kent.[150] Whatever the explanation for his absence from London in the aftermath of Cade's revolt may have been, it was not caused by lack of commitment to the regime. In the autumn and winter he participated fully in the continued pursuit and punishment of the rebels and the suppression of any signs of disorder. In this he joined the earls of Devon, Salisbury and Warwick as well as the dukes of York and Exeter (the latter having achieved his majority). The government did not fully succeed in re-establishing law and order in southern England until 1452, and the long-term implications of the preceding years were grave. Up to that period lawyers such as Fortescue had recognised a formula for government which assumed that a large measure of authority was exercised by the Crown, underpinned by its respect for the laws and customs of the realm. When the King was absent on campaign or a minor, his authority could be successfully devolved to a royal council. The personal weaknesses of Henry VI after he assumed direct control of his kingdoms, combined with the losses in France, displayed the fallacy in this formula.[151] It was to take another twenty years and the fall of Lancaster for Fortescue to come up with a theory which could meet the case of either a weak king or one with tyrannical inclinations.

In the meantime, only two elements in the nation emerged with any credit from 1450: the merchants and gentry who had ultimately held the line against Cade and his supporters in London and the southern counties. The turning point in the rebellion had come when some of the merchants, tired of the depredations of the rebels, refused them entry into the city on 5 and 6 July.[152] The gentry, through their representatives in the House of Commons, had proposed two remedies for the grievances which had plunged the country into chaos: the removal of Suffolk and the resumption of the gifts with which the King had alienated too much of the royal estate. Fortescue with his gentry origins was to give due weight to their political significance in his later writings and to the

[149] Griffiths, *Henry VI*, 641, n. 218.

[150] *CPR*, Henry VI, 1446–52, 590, 596; he was appointed to Kent again on 5 April 1451, 590.

[151] See Watts, *Henry VI, passim*.

[152] Harvey, *Jack Cade's Rebellion*, 95–7.

institutions that allowed them a role in government. The inadequacy of Henry VI and his household, who had retreated to the safety of Leicester, in the summer of 1450 did not reach the standard Fortescue was to set for monarchy in his *De Natura Legis Naturae*: 'the king, as St. Thomas says, is given for the kingdom, and not the kingdom for him, inasmuch as he is related to the kingdom, as the thing caused to the cause, he ought to surrender himself to all sorts of dangers, rather than that the kingdom perish'.[153]

The King had proved to be less than kingly by the late 1440s. Ironically the situation was to push Fortescue into justifying the exercise of greater rather than less *ius regale*, royal rule uncontrolled by the law. The same chapter in the *De Natura* which has been quoted above conceded that, 'Nevertheless, there are other cases, and very many of them, in which it is sometimes right and expedient for a king governing politically to act *regaliter* against some of his people; as if his people has risen in arms against him.'[154] This presumably covered episodes such as the arbitrary decision taken by Henry VI to banish the duke of Suffolk in 1450: an action which, however timely, was not the result of any recognisable legal process.[155] A year later Henry reversed an undertaking, made in a memorandum to the duke of York only a few months earlier, that he would rely upon the advice of his council.[156] The exigencies of the time forced Fortescue and his fellow justices into colluding with royal actions which were calculated to reactivate the grievances that had caused the crisis in the first place. Political imperatives identified them ever more closely with the fortunes of Henry, his ministers and the royal household.

The situation of Sir John Fortescue in London on 2 January 1451, before his departure into Kent to root out the dissidents who had survived the rising of the previous year, was graphically described by Sir John Fastolf's servant John Bocking: 'The Chief Justice hath waited to ben assauted all this sevenyght nyghtly in hes hous, but nothing come as yett, the more pite etc.'[157] A Paston letter of 1444, mentioned above, when Fortescue voiced his concern for Justice William Paston's health, indicated that good relations existed between the Chief Justice and the Paston family at that time. Seven years later the dysfunction at the heart

[153] Clermont, *Works*, vol. 1, 216.
[154] *Ibid.*, 215
[155] Wolffe, *Henry VI*, 227–8.
[156] *Ibid.*, 244–5; *Vale's Book*, 190.
[157] *PL*, (Davis) iii, no. 1001, 118.

of government was reflected in the animosity voiced by Bocking against a member of a previously cohesive group of lawyers and gentlemen.[158]

Apart from the Kent commission of oyer and terminer that engaged him in early 1451, Fortescue sat on another in May in Southampton and Wiltshire. He was involved in two others, led by the duke of Exeter, in London in April and October which fulfilled the government's commitment to the Cade rebels to investigate malpractices amongst royal servants.[159] As the King and his advisers grew more confident that the worst was over, they seemingly risked using the unpopular Chief Justice in these sensitive enquiries. Both commissions dealt with men who had shared the odium heaped on him in *The Dirge Made by the Commons of Kent*: John Trevelyan ('*Qui Lazarum resussitasti*, Trevilyan shall singe') and Thomas Daniel ('*Manus tue*, Danyell thow shalt synge. For Jake Napis sowle *placebo* and *dirige*') were both hated servants of the royal household.[160] Despite the commissions, Trevelyan and Daniel continued to flourish in the 1450s: the former had a family link with Fortescue through the Whalesburghs and the latter was one of those who joined with him to draft the bill of attainder against the Yorkist lords at the Coventry parliament in 1459.[161]

Henry VI was probably present in person for some of the legal proceedings conducted by the commissions in Kent in January and in Wiltshire in July 1451.[162] According to Wolffe he was more active than usual in dealing with the two major petitions presented by the parliament which met from January to March and in May.[163] He made some half-hearted attempts to meet the first petition that thirty members of his court should be exiled. These included the duke of Somerset, who was rapidly replacing Suffolk in popular demonology, but the King specifically refused to touch any peers. He did, however, consent to the other petition which demanded a more effective act of resumption than that in the previous year, which had been largely negated by the high number of exemptions.[164] The parliamentary debates and the backstage

[158] See above, p. 54–5, n. 37; the animosity towards Fortescue could be linked to his friend Robert Hungerford, Lord Moleyns's seizure of the Pastons' manor of Gresham, H. Castor, *Blood and Roses: The Paston Family in the Fifteenth Century* (London: 2004) 44–59.

[159] *CPR*, Henry VI, 1446–52, 444–5, 477, 532.

[160] *Three Fifteenth Century Chronicles*, 101.

[161] *PL* (Davis) vol. 2, no. 609, 210.

[162] Virgoe, 'Ancient Indictments'.

[163] Wolffe, *Henry VI*, 244–8.

[164] See M. Hicks, *Warwick the Kingmaker* (Oxford: 1998), 76, for a discussion of the impact of resumption on one noble family.

discussions which culminated in these measures (allied with the popular agitation which had initially promoted them) surely informed Fortescue's later advice on the governance of England.

The government finally felt strong enough to deal with those it perceived as presenting a threat to its authority, even when they had not actually rebelled. Just before the dissolution of the 1450–51 parliament a motion by Thomas Younge, a business associate of Fortescue, proposed that the duke of York should be formally recognised as the still-childless King's heir.[165] The Lords rejected the proposal and Younge was sent to the Tower. It is impossible to know what Fortescue thought of the disgrace of his erstwhile associate but the subsequent fracas in the wild West between some of his friends and patrons could only have embarrassed him. The duke of York intervened in September 1451, without royal consent, to try and end the latest round in the violent dispute between the earl of Devon (at that time his supporter) and Lord Bonville. The King summoned the leaders of the confrontation, including Lord Bonville and Robert Hungerford, Lord Moleyns, to London and imprisoned them for a month, but the earl of Devon refused to come and York also stayed away. Henry VI was acting with rather more sense of direction than before or after this period but his underlying weakness was subjecting the loyalty of his principal servants such as Fortescue to intolerable strains.[166]

In 1452 in March, July, twice in September and in December Fortescue was appointed to commissions of oyer and terminer in Wiltshire, Bristol, Wiltshire again, the eastern and midland counties and Cornwall.[167] He was also appointed to commissions of the peace in Sussex in March and Surrey in June and held an inquisition in December into the slaying of a yeoman of the chamber at Kingston Lacy, Dorset.[168] Much of this was likely to have been a damage-limitation exercise after the duke of York's abortive attempt to overthrow the duke of Somerset at Dartford in early March. Yet Fortescue did not accompany the King on his great judicial progress, which lasted from June, when he left his palace at Eltham, to September, when he returned there. He traversed much of the West and the Midlands, making a particular point of doing justice in Devon and at York's town of Ludlow. Followers of the duke of

[165] Johnson, *Duke Richard*, 98–100; Younge and Fortescue in association occur as follows: *CPR*, Henry VI, 1441–46, 62; 1446–52, 221; *CCR*, Henry VI, 1435–41, 245; Henry VI, 1441–47, 50, 218–19, 229; *CFR*, Henry VI, 1437–45, 242.

[166] Griffiths, *Henry VI*, 688–92.

[167] *CPR*, Henry VI, 1446–52, 539, 581, 584; Henry VI, 1452–61, 54, 59.

[168] *CPR*, Henry VI, 1446–52, 596; Henry VI, 1452–61, 58.

York and the earl of Devon were punished, an effective demonstration of the King's authority on the home ground of those who had sought to subvert it.

Fortescue's absence could be explained by the generally lawless state of the country and a policy that he would give weight to judicial commissions where the King could not be present. Yet it could also reflect the fact that the earl of Devon, even when disgraced, was not a man Fortescue or his family, who mostly lived in the county, would wish to affront. Another lord with whom Fortescue had a long-standing connection was also beleaguered in the course of 1452. John Wilkins, who had led a rising in Kent in favour of the duke of York, was reputed to have incriminated Lord Cromwell, the Lord Chamberlain, as he was being led to execution. Cromwell was obliged to withdraw from council meetings and obtain sworn testimonies to his loyalty before Henry VI accepted that he was innocent.[169] At this time Fortescue received a life grant of two tuns of wine yearly from the port of London in lieu of a previous grant from Bristol. This was a confirmation that, despite the dubious activities of some of his friends and associates, he still enjoyed the confidence of the King and his servants.[170]

An undermighty king

The 1450s demonstrate the volatility of English politics and the difficulty for government servants in assessing how far they might safely combine loyalty to the crown with personal advantage. Initially the triumph enjoyed by Henry VI and his advisers over the duke of York in 1452, when he failed in a bid to become the King's principal counsellor, ensured that the parliament that met in the following year would be docile. Fortescue was a trier of petitions and witnessed the series of punitive measures that were passed against York's supporters.[171] The Speaker, Thomas Thorpe, was one of the duke of Somerset's affinity and did all he could to promote his patron's interests.[172] All seemed to be well: Queen Margaret was proving to be a powerful supporter for Somerset and she was pregnant, the unrest of 1450–51 had been quelled and York had been put in his place by the decisive exercise of royal authority.

[169] Wolffe, *Henry VI*, 258–9; Harvey, 167–8; *CPR*, Henry VI, 1452–61, 93–102. Virgoe, 'William Tailboys and Lord Cromwell', suggested that Tailboys could have had a hand in this libel.

[170] *CPR*, Henry VI, 1452–61, 86.

[171] *RP*, vol. 5, 227; *PROME*, vol. 12, 229.

[172] Johnson, *Duke Richard*, 130–1.

In August 1453 the precarious nature of the fragile peace under the aegis of an undermighty king was demonstrated by the total mental and physical collapse of Henry VI. For the following seventeen months he remained in seclusion, mostly in Windsor Castle, and the political nation had to devise a means by which his authority could be exercised.[173] The heavily pregnant Queen was incapacitated for political intervention and Somerset repeated York's mistake of the previous year: he failed to ensure the support of a sufficient number of magnates during the crisis.[174] In the autumn, with York once more politically ascendant, Somerset was deprived of his position on the council and imprisoned on a charge of treason harking back to the loss of the French lands.

The situation of Chief Justice Fortescue in the middle of these rapid reversals of fortune was unenviable. His personal opinion of Henry VI can only be inferred from his later writings, for there are plenty of passages in the *De Laudibus*, the *Articles sent to Warwick* and the *Governance* which can be read as critical of the King's capacities. Yet in October 1453 the Queen produced a male heir, Prince Edward, and in the following January she again established herself as a force to be reckoned with by (unsuccessfully) demanding powers that would have made her Regent. By the 1450s much of the political nation was probably ready to accept the relegation of their incompetent King to some form of tutelage. The problem for Fortescue, as for the rest of the nobility and gentry, was that there were now two feasible contenders for the custody of Henry VI. A queen consort and her son could not simply be destroyed like the duke of Suffolk. On the other hand, the military and political prestige of the duke of York and the support that he enjoyed from the earl of Salisbury and his son, the earl of Warwick and large areas of the country, were unavoidable facts of life and in March 1454 he was appointed Protector by the council.[175] It is a moot question as to whether the magnates divided according to where they believed their personal interests lay as K.B. McFarlane and his followers would suggest, or whether some at least were motivated by a wish to uphold good governance despite the weakness of the monarch.[176]

Fortescue was personally embroiled in one of the earliest consequences of the latest change in the balance of power. During the parliament's recess (probably in the Michaelmas Term, 1453) York had Thomas Thorpe, the Speaker, arrested and imprisoned on a charge of trespass.

[173] Griffiths, *Henry VI*, 715.
[174] Johnson, *Duke Richard*, 122–4.
[175] Watts, *Henry VI*, 301–12.
[176] McFarlane, *Nobility*, *passim*; Watts, *Henry VI*, *passim*.

When they reconvened the Commons asked the Lords to uphold their privileges so that their Speaker might be restored to them:

> To the which question, the chefe Justicez, after sadde communication and mature deliberation hadde amonge theim, aunswered and said; that they ought not to aunswere of that question, for it hath not be used afore tyme, that the Justicez shuld in eny wyse determine the Privelegge of this high Court of Parlement; for it is so high and so mighty in his nature, that it may make law, and that that is lawe it may make noo lawe; and the determination and knowlegge of that Privelegge belongeth to the Lordes of Parlement, and not to the Justices ... After which aunswere and declaration, it was thorowly agreed, assentid and concluded by the Lordes Spirituelx and Temporelx, that the seid Thomas, accordyng to the lawe, shuld remayne stille in prison for the causes abovesaid.[177]

The first references in the passage are to the 'chefe justicez', later to the 'chief Justice' (not quoted), so it is reasonably certain that the words were Fortescue's. He strongly endorsed the powers of parliament to the extent that they were being deprived of their own Speaker in the name of those powers! The inescapable conclusion must be that Fortescue and his fellow justices were placating the prevailing power, in this case York, and producing an answer which interpreted precedent to legalise a situation which was essentially the product of political pressure. In this they were re-enacting Suffolk's condemnation in 1450 and anticipating their response to York in the autumn of 1460. The interesting evidence for the development of Fortescue's thought is that he was already emphasising the powers of parliament, a theme that was to recur in his major political treatises:[178] 'Nor can the king ... impose tallages, subsidies, or any other burdens whatever on his subjects, nor change their laws, nor make new ones, without the concession or assent of his whole realm expressed in his parliament.'[179]

York's predominant position within the royal government was not necessarily against Fortescue's personal interests in 1454. With hindsight we know that he was to be one of the most vociferous supporters of the exiled Henry VI a few years later, but in 1454 no one was questioning the King's right to rule. The Protectorate of a great lord of the royal blood, of proven military ability and great personal wealth, could have presented a solution to the problems of the previous decade, when

[177] *RP*, vol. 5, 239–40; *PROME*, vol. 12, 254–5.

[178] *De Laudibus*, chapters 18, 36, Chrimes, 41, 87; *Governance*, chs 3, 14, 15, 19, *Vale's Book*, 228, 243, 246, 249.

[179] Chrimes, *De Laudibus*, 87.

decisive leadership had been lacking, replaced by an unedifying struggle to gain honours and wealth from the suggestable King. York had recently worked with two of Fortescue's associates in the West and London, the earl of Devon and Robert Hungerford, Lord Moleyns, and the duke had several times been involved in business with the Chief Justice who was an associate of his man, Thomas Younge.[180]

York also regarded another of Fortescue's associates, Lord Cromwell, as a potential supporter: his pleas for exemption on the grounds of age and sickness were swept aside and he was appointed to the council during the first Protectorate.[181] He needed York's good lordship in pursuit of his case against Henry Holland, duke of Exeter, who was celebrating his majority by staging a rebellion and making depredations on Cromwell's estates. The 'Amptill Dispute' is another example of how an undermighty king failed to protect his loyal followers from lawless assaults on their property and persons.[182]

The duke of Exeter was not the only disaffected subject to seize the opportunity of the King's illness to seek personal aggrandizement.[183] In 1454 Fortescue was busy on commissions of the peace in Essex, Hertford, Kent, Somerset, Middlesex, Surrey and Sussex and also held a commission of oyer and terminer in Newcastle upon Tyne.[184] Even if, as was probable, he was unable to service all these commissions, the fact that he was so frequently named shows him to have been actively supporting the regime by enforcing the rule of law. He could have resorted to Cromwell's plea of age or sickness had he been disinclined to work with the duke of York in attempting to govern the realm effectively. York's Protectorate was brought to an abrupt close in early 1455 by the recovery of Henry VI, described by Storey as 'a national disaster'.[185] Fortescue's position does

[180] See above, p. 60, nn. 62, 63; Robert Hungerford, knight, was keeper of Cranborne Chase for York, 1452–53, for a fee of £5 per annum, Johnson, *Duke Richard*, 233.

[181] S. Payling, 'The "Grete Laboure and Long and Troublous Tyme": The Execution of the Will of Ralph, Lord Cromwell, and the Foundation of Tattershall College', *The Fifteenth Century XIII: Exploring the Evidence: Commemoration, Administration and the Economy*, ed. L. Clark (Woodbridge: 2014) 1–30.

[182] R.A. Griffiths, 'Local Rivalries and National Politics: The Percies, the Nevilles and the Duke of Exeter, 1452–1454', *King and Country: England and Wales in the Fifteenth Century* (London: 1991) 321–64; Friedrichs, 'Ralph, Lord Cromwell', 207–27; S. Payling, 'The Amptill Dispute: A Study in Aristocratic Lawlessness and the Breakdown of Lancastrian Government', *EHR*, 104 (1989) 881–907.

[183] Storey, *End of the House of Lancaster*, especially chs 10 and 11.

[184] *CPR*, Henry VI, 1452–61, 177, 665, 667–8, 671, 676, 678–9.

[185] Storey, *End of the House of Lancaster*, 159.

not seem to have been affected adversely by his former co-operation with York's regime: most of his fellows had done the same thing. The rapidity with which Edmund, duke of Somerset was restored to power by the influence of the Queen and York and his friends were stripped of their offices destroyed any hope of a peaceful accommodation.

The first battle of St Albans in May 1455 reversed political fortunes again and the death of Somerset seems to have changed the agenda for many, including Fortescue. Up to that time they had been faced with a decision concerning which of two rival magnates, who were attempting to dominate the King, they should support, while each side incessantly proclaimed their loyalty to the monarchy. The vacuum left in the household by the removal of Somerset was effectively filled by Margaret of Anjou. As mother to the heir to the throne and wife to the enfeebled King, who doted on her, she enjoyed a unique status, and York was to discover during the next five years how difficult it would be to impose his will and remain a loyal subject at the same time. Lord Cromwell was a spent force and died two years later, in early 1456. The other great associates of Fortescue, the Hungerfords, were to support the King in ensuing confrontations.

From 1455 the Chief Justice had a personal reason for giving his allegiance to the Lancastrian king and queen. John Stow reported during the first battle of St Albans that there: 'were slaine on the Kinge's party, Lordes of name: Edmonde duke of Somerset, Henry Earle of Northumberland, the Earle of Stafford, the olde Lorde Clifforde, Sir Robert Vere,[186], Bartin Entewsell, William Chamberlaine, Richard Fortescue, and Ralph Ferrers knightes etc.'.[187] Sir John Fortescue remained involved with the fortunes of the other members of his family: the later transfer of the Punsborne estate and a share of Bosamme's Inn to Richard's descendants testifies to this, as does the survival of his papers in the hands of Sir Adrian Fortescue, his great nephew, Richard's grandson, early in the following century. As Plummer wryly remarked, his brother's death was 'not likely to have made him more favourably inclined towards the Yorkists'.[188]

In the meantime, whatever his private views might have been, the Chief Justice doggedly carried out the administration of the law.

[186] He actually survived until 1461 and is mentioned six times in the *CPR*, Henry VI, 1452–61, in the intervening years.

[187] J. Stow, *The Annales of England* (London: 1605) 661. No contemporary evidence has been found to support the attribution of a knighthood to Richard Fortescue, but he could have possessed one by 1455.

[188] Plummer, *Governance of England*, 51.

Throughout 1455 he was frequently appointed to commissions: of oyer and terminer: in Middlesex (twice), London, Devon and Cornwall; and of the peace in Essex, Hertford, Kent, Middlesex, Surrey and Sussex, as well as carrying out the other duties that were part of his job.[189] He also had to provide for the rehabilitation of York's loyal follower, Sir William Oldhall, who had been attainted just before the second appointment of the duke as Protector and was in sanctuary awaiting the reversal of his outlawry.[190] Fortescue was a trier of petitions in the new parliament, which passed a more draconian measure of resumption than had been possible on earlier occasions when the King and his household advisers had been in a position to modify the legislation. The Lords, however, diluted it when it passed to them and Fortescue managed to safeguard the grant of his two tuns of wine that had been made soon after he became Chief Justice.[191]

In February 1456 the duke of York resigned his office of Protector: gradually the Queen and her supporters (such as Henry the new young duke of Somerset and the household men who depended on her good will) were regaining the ground that they had lost since the first battle of St Albans. The immediate cause of York's eclipse seems to have been his failure to secure the effective measure of resumption that he and the Commons urgently desired and this strengthened the hand of the Queen in gaining control of the government.[192] Throughout the year Fortescue's vigorous activity as Chief Justice emphasised both the lawless state of a society, undermined by divisions within the ruling order, and his own commitment to the Lancastrian dynasty. He sat on commissions of oyer and terminer in Devon, Somerset (twice), Dorset (twice), London and its suburbs, Middlesex, Kent, Sussex and Bodmin.[193] He was on commissions of the peace in London, Kent, Middlesex and Sussex and one for *de wallis et fossatis* on Thameside, Middlesex and certified ten pardons.[194] He was also involved in the longstanding dispute between Sir Philip Wentworth, the King's carver, and John Paston I, over the wardship of the latter's kinsman, Thomas Fastolf of Cowhaugh in Nacton, Suffolk.[195]

[189] *CPR*, Henry VI, 1452–61, 223, 255–6, 258, 300, 665, 667–8, 671, 678–9.

[190] *PL* (Gairdner) vol. 3, no. 287, 33.

[191] *RP*, vol. 5, 317; *PROME*, vol. 12, 420.

[192] Watts, *Henry VI*, 317–31.

[193] *CPR*, Henry VI, 1452–61, 300, 304, 306–9.

[194] *Ibid.*, 277, 281, 290, 299, 324, 327, 668, 671, 679.

[195] *PL* (Davis), vol. 1, no. 51, 83–4; see also Davis's index for numerous references to this case. See also above, p. 67.

The Wentworth affair provides evidence of the way in which the lawsuits over which Fortescue presided were conducted during a time of weak and partial government. Sir Philip Wentworth, a Yorkshireman, had been granted the lucrative wardship by the King, when good sense would have indicated that it would have been more harmoniously administered by the minor's family based in Norfolk. Endless litigation and expense ensued over a period of thirteen years: the matter seems finally to have been concluded politically rather than legally in favour of the Pastons when the Lancastrians were defeated in 1460–61. In 1456, when power was fairly evenly balanced between York and the court, there seems to have been some hope of a settlement as John Bocking wrote to his master, Sir John Fastolf, on 9 February:

> As to youre matier of Wentworthe, the trety contynueth, and is putte by the arbitrours in Fortescu and Yelverton, and we have day of newe til Friday come sevenyght. God graunte it take a good ende. The lawe is with us clerly, as weel in th'atteynte as therinne as yette, blessid be Our Lord, hoo have you in hise most noble gouernaunce.[196]

Part of this arbitration process was probably recorded in the roll of expenses of John Paston I, 1458–59, in which he paid 23d for wine and spices for Wentworth and Fortescue.[197] The expenditure seems to have been wasted: as soon as Yorkist power was eclipsed by the summoning of the Coventry parliament of 1459, Wentworth presented a successful petition to the Commons that the rights claimed by his opponents should be annulled.[198] The difficulty lawyers and their clients experienced at this time in concluding such cases, when the balance of political power shifted so frequently, was one of the reasons for a progressive loss of confidence in the possibility of achieving a safe verdict through legal process.[199]

An additional problem for Fortescue and his fellow justices was the tendency, which emerged in the course of 1456, for the royal family to stay for most of the year on their estates in the Midlands, rather than in London or the Thames Valley, since they were able to enjoy a reasonable measure of security there.[200] Yet the state of law and order in the rest of the country was dependent on whoever had the local power to

196 *Ibid.*, vol. 3, no. 1029, 162.

197 *PL* (Gairdner), vol. 1, no. 321, 434; Castor, *Blood and Roses*, 105–8.

198 *PL* (Davis), vol. 2, no. 886, 535–7.

199 C. Richmond, *The Paston Family in the Fifteenth Century: The First Phase* (Cambridge: 1990) 241–3.

200 Griffiths, *Henry VI*, 777–85.

maintain or flout it. Fortescue was involved in a commission of oyer and terminer in Devon to deal with the aftermath of the feuding of William, Lord Bonville, and Thomas Courtenay, earl of Devon. In August 1456, he entered the city of Exeter in company with the head of the commission, the earl of Wiltshire 'with a right great fellowship'.[201] Fortescue's family had profited from their dependent relationship with the earls of Devon for decades, they also had business dealings with Lord Bonville. Yet again the weak regime, which had virtually abdicated responsibility for large tracts of the country, was placing its servants in an impossible situation. A petition in parliament questioned the impartiality of Fortescue and his fellow commissioners and requested that both the earl and lord Bonville should be kept in prison: 'tyll your Commission of Oier and Determyner be direct to endifferent Commissioners, to enquere, here and determine all the premises'.[202]

The Commons were correct in their assumption that justice would not be done in Devon. The earl, who by that time had deserted York for the royal family, paid no penalty for his lawless acts. In the following year Fortescue certified a royal pardon for his son, Sir Thomas Courtenay, who had murdered Nicholas Radford, the prominent lawyer and adviser to Lord Bonville who had figured in the Shillingford case described above. The fact that Sir Thomas was to wed Marie de Maine, the Queen's kinswoman, later in 1457 must have been a factor in securing his escape from any penalties for a particularly brutal killing.[203] In the following year Fortescue was one of the executors when the earl of Devon died: the Chief Justice seems to have had no wish to distance himself from the violent Sir Thomas who succeeded to the earldom.[204]

During 1457 and 1458 the opposing parties had reached a kind of stalemate. In March 1458 a Love-day was held in which the leaders of the two factions, including Margaret of Anjou, went hand in hand to St Paul's for a ceremony of reconciliation. This might have been engineered by Henry VI himself and recognised a situation in which neither side was sufficiently powerful or sufficiently resolute to destroy the other. The noble combatants at the first battle of St Albans promised compensation for those who had been killed (mainly Lancastrians).[205] The relatively

201 Storey, *End of the House of Lancaster*, 165–75.

202 *RP*, vol. 5, 332; *PROME*, vol. 12, 444.

203 Griffiths, *Henry VI*, 802; M.L. Kekewich, *The Good King: René of Anjou and Fifteenth-Century Europe* (Basingstoke: 2008) 124–5.

204 Watts, *Henry VI*, 338, n. 329, Fortescue was one of the earl's executors.

205 A.H. Thomas and I.D. Thornley, eds, *The Great Chronicle of London*, microprint (Gloucester: 1983) 190; M.L. Kekewich, 'The Attainder of the Yorkists in

low level of judicial activity on Fortescue's part in contrast to the previous years may have reflected this fragile peace. His membership of a commission in December 1457 to decide how many archers the county of Middlesex should provide for the defence of the realm indicates, however, the government's anxiety that it should be ready for trouble in the future.[206] It seems to have been part of a policy which also included the stockpiling of arms: a sign that the Queen and her advisers were planning to move against York when the time was right.[207]

The time seemed to be right in the summer and autumn of 1459. York and his allies wrong-footed themselves by failing to answer a summons to a meeting of the great council at Coventry in late June: 'And after the feast of St John the king held a great council at Coventry, the queen and the prince were present, the archbishop of Canterbury, the duke of York, the earls of Salisbury and Warwick etc. did not attend the council.'[208] This led to an indictment for their non-appearance and later to the charge that they had intended to waylay the King at Kenilworth.[209] Writs were issued for a parliament which was to be held at Coventry in November. Meanwhile the Yorkists were bested but not destroyed by the armed encounter at Ludford Bridge.

The loyal Lancastrians, including Fortescue, who met at Coventry in November had to embark on the risky business of attainting a number of great lords who were still at liberty. York fled to Ireland, where he was Lord Lieutenant and enjoyed considerable influence. Even more dangerous for the government was the fact that the earls of Salisbury, Warwick and March, York's oldest son, were ensconced in Calais, the ideal springboard for an invasion of England.[210] A year later on 24 October 1460 the knowing Friar Brackley reported to John Paston I the risks and opportunities that had faced Fortescue and his fellow lawyers at this crucial point in his career:

> Doctour Aleyn seyn after the parlement of Covintré that yf the lordys that tyme reynyng and now discessid myte haf standyn in gouernauns,

---

1459: Two Contemporary Accounts', *BIHR*, 55 (1982) 25–34, 25; H.E. Maurer, 'Margaret of Anjou and the Loveday of 1458: A Reconsideration', *Traditions and Transformations in Late Medieval England*, ed. D. Biggs, S.D. Michalove and A. Compton Reeves (Leiden: 2002) 109–24.

206 *CPR*, Henry VI, 1452–61, 406.

207 Wolffe, *Henry VI*, 317; Storey, *End of the House of Lancaster*, 186–7.

208 *John Benet's Chronicle for the Years 1400–1462*, ed. G.L. and M.A. Harriss, Camden Miscellany 24 (London: 1972) 223.

209 Wolffe, *Henry VI*, 317.

210 Hicks, *Warwick*, 154–77.

> that Fortescu the Justise, Doctowr Moreton, Jon Heydon, Thorp, and he schuld be made for evir: and yf it turnyd to contrary wyse it schuld growe to here fynal confusyon and uttyr destruccyon, for why, the parlyows writing and the myschevous inditing was ymaginid, contrivid and utterly concludid by here most vengeable labowr.[211]

Up to this time Fortescue had managed adroitly to serve the predominant power at each turn in the fortunes of York and Lancaster, without compromising his career, his family's interests or his personal safety. His close association with figures such as Thorpe and Heydon who were detested by the Yorkists, together with his work on drafting the bill of attainder which condemned the leading Yorkists and 'corrupted their blood', was an irrevocable commitment to the house of Lancaster.

There are signs that Fortescue's decision to engage himself so closely with Lancaster at this time arose from conviction as well as from the force of circumstances. He was old by the standards of the time, about sixty years of age and given that Coventry was remote from London and his properties in the West he could have absented himself from the parliament, had he wished to do so. Yet he was already making policy for the royal family rather than simply following the directions of their powerful advisers. Since the carnage of St Albans the latter had been distinctly thin on the ground and Fortescue seems to have been ready to fill the vacuum. It is well attested that he exercised considerable influence in the Lancastrian government in exile and the *Paston Letters* suggest that this could have started as early as 1459. Griffiths observed that the property confiscated from the Yorkists was managed far more prudently than had been the case with earlier windfalls. Instead of large-scale gifts and leases, most was 'assigned to royally-appointed stewards, receivers, and bailiffs who could exploit them for the crown's benefit'. The York, Neville and Clinton estates were absorbed into the royal demesne and only a modest quantity of annuities and leases were granted.[212] This change in practice seemingly originated from some new influence brought to bear on royal counsels and as Fortescue was the most eminent of the men named by Brackley as busying themselves with the attainder, it is a tenable hypothesis that he was the moving spirit behind the new approach. He was to advocate precisely that kind of

[211] *PL* (Davis), vol. 2, no. 617, 221–2; no. 609, 209–10.

[212] Griffiths, *Henry VI*, 825–7; Hicks, *Warwick*, 172, specifically associates Fortescue with such a policy.

procedure some twelve years later when the final version of the *Governance* was probably composed.[213]

The Somnium Vigilantis

It is hard to demonstrate whether or not Fortescue had a hand in the composition of the *Somnium Vigilantis*. This is an anonymous tract, mostly in English, from which the preamble is missing, which was issued to justify the attainder of the Yorkists at the Coventry parliament.[214] Over three decades ago this writer gave some thought to the authorship of the *Somnium* and suggested, mainly on stylistic grounds, that Fortescue was unlikely to have composed it. Two decades later J.P. Genet subjected the *Somnium* (and other works) to a factorial analysis which indicated that it was probably not written by Fortescue.[215] It has not been possible subsequently to arrive at a definitive conclusion on the matter, but what is certain is that Fortescue was closely associated with the whole process of attainder and was one of those who formulated the bill. The way in which it was justified does, therefore, have an interest for the study of the development of his political thought.

The structure adopted by the author or authors of the *Somnium* used the time-honoured 'Aunt Sally' ploy of allowing the opposition to make a brief, weak statement of the Yorkist case in a debate conducted before the King which was then demolished by a strong argument presented by the pro-Lancastrian orator. He refuted the Yorkist claim for clemency on the grounds that they had defied the royal will on several previous occasions: to show mercy would be a denial of all the principles of justice. To the plea that although they had done wrong it would be more harmful to the realm to destroy them than to pardon them, the Lancastrian orator answered that 'it is more nedefull to the reyaume that they be eternally depulsed and utterly destroyed than to reconsile hem in eny wyse'.[216]

[213] *Vale's Book*, chs 15 and 19, 244–6, 248–9.

[214] London, BL MS Royal 17 D xv, ff. 302–11 is the only surviving copy of the tract; J.P. Gilson, 'A Defence of the Proscription of the Yorkists in 1459', *EHR*, 26 (1911) 512–25; P. Strohm, *Politique: Languages of Statecraft between Chaucer and Shakespeare* (Notre Dame, IN: 2005) 12–17.

[215] Kekewich, 'Two Accounts'; A. Gross, *The Dissolution of the Lancastrian Kingship: Sir John Fortescue and the Crisis of Monarchy in Fifteenth-Century England* (Stamford: 1996) 58–60, 73, 97–100; J.P. Genet, 'New Politics or New Language? The Words of Politics in Yorkist and Early Tudor England', *The End of the Middle Ages? England in the Fifteenth and Sixteenth Centuries*, ed. J.L. Watts (Aberystwyth: 1996) 23–64.

[216] Gilson, 'A Defence', 518.

The response to the third Yorkist excuse that they had acted for the common wealth of all the realm at a time of great uncertainty contained an unambiguous account of how authoritative decisions should be taken:

> alle controversies and debates civile or criminalle, realle or personale, ben decided by the kynges laws without maintenance or wylfull interrupcion of the cours of justice, and in cas that ony thinge falle of the whiche the determinacion is not expressed in the common lawe, than the prince most be asked and inquired and by his excedyng auctorite and prudens of his conseyle an expikan[217] shalbe made tharopon, and so that no thinge be done by singular wylle and sencell affeccion.[218]

This passage with its reference to prudent counsel is compatible with the views that were later to be aired by Fortescue in the *De Laudibus* and *Governance*: it reflects his deep respect for the law together with a recognition that royal authority must always prevail. It also echoes a reply given to the duke of York's remonstrances with the royal government in 1450, 'we have determyned in our owne sowle to stablisshe a sadde and a substanciall counseile', and may represent continuity of policy from the time of cardinal Kemp, then a chief minister of the King.[219] In both cases the 'excedyng auctorite' of the King was to be balanced by the 'prudens of his conseyle', but it was clear that his regal power (or prerogative) was predominant: this was to be the advice Fortescue gave in all three of his great political treatises.

The fourth Yorkist apology was grounded on the claim that they had only harmed those who were public enemies, any others who had suffered were unintended victims. The Lancastrian response was to produce a catalogue of the Yorkists' crimes and renew the demand for their punishment. The fifth claim for mercy was based on England's need for defenders against external adversaries, the high birth of the lords and their popularity with the common people. All these points were peremptorily rejected with scathing references to 'the grete varyablenes of the peple and of thyncertitude of thaire oppynions'.[220] The final Yorkist point was a threat rather than a plea: the lords should be pardoned whilst they were prepared to submit, otherwise they would take by force what was not yielded willingly. This elicited from the royal orator a final and more vehement call for their condemnation. The last part of the pamphlet, which was written in French, was close in form

[217] *Ibid.*, n. 19, perhaps 'explicacion'.
[218] *Ibid.*, 518.
[219] *Vale's Book*, 190.
[220] Gilson, 521.

to a judicial review and verdict which was unsurprisingly awarded in favour of the King and his followers.

Doubts must remain that Fortescue could have been the principal author of the *Somnium* since the style of the English prose is at variance with the two surviving English tracts on the succession which he composed only about two years later in the early 1460s. In all his works Fortescue wrote in a clear, straightforward and unornamented fashion, his choice of vocabulary was conventional and he avoided imprecise phrases and colloquialisms. The *Somnium* abounded in florid prose sequences and inelegant phrases such as 'who ever says nay', it also contained words such as 'appreciable' and 'recay' which were either unknown or, at least, unusual at the time.[221] Yet the testimony of the *Paston Letters* is persuasive. Fortescue was closely concerned with the attainder, so might he not at least have taken an interest in the apologia for that piece of legislation? This raises the possibility that the *Somnium* was designed by a committee.[222] Fortescue was unlikely to have agreed that that the King's followers should be richly rewarded, the reverse of the views he expressed in the *Advice to the earl of Warwick* in 1470/1.[223] He was also disposed to hold a more favourable view of the common people than that expressed in the *Somnium*. Another less eminent colleague or group probably wrote the pamphlet, perhaps using some Latin phrases and sentiments supplied by the learned Chief Justice.

Paul Strohm in 2006 made a close reading of the *Somnium* to demonstrate how it contributed, amongst other writings, to a new language of practical politics in which both sides deployed the notion of 'public good'.[224] Strohm did not come to any firm conclusions about the authorship of the tract and neither did Daniel Wakelin in the following year but, in the course of his study of the penetration of humanism into English literature in the late middle ages, he discovered that the *Somnium* was based on a passage in Sallust's history of Catiline.[225] After the plot against Rome came to light a debate was held in the Senate about the fate of the conspirators who had been captured. Julius Caesar spoke in favour of mercy but M. Porcius Cato demanded severity and, menaced by Catiline, who was still at liberty, the Senate had them executed.[226]

221 *Ibid.*, 513.
222 Kekewich, 'Two Accounts', 30.
223 *Vale's Book*, 222–25.
224 Strohm, *Politique*, 12–17.
225 D. Wakelin, *Humanism, Reading and English Literature, 1430–1530* (Oxford: 2007) 165–8.
226 *The Catiline of Sallust*, ed. G.H. Nall (London: 1948) 40–54.

Wakelin commented on the self-conscious humanism of the *Somnium*: not only did it have a classical model but the loyalist orator was given more eloquent phrases than the Yorkist, who was instructed to observe due decorum in his speech.

Fortescue apparently had few reservations about the part he chose to play in the attainder of the Yorkists. His family had served Lancaster since the dynasty assumed power at the beginning of the century, and their patrons the Courtenays and the Hungerfords were identified with the line. Most of the advances the Fortescue family had made were derived from the royal government and its servants and Sir John was later to admit that he was a 'partial man' in pursuing his loyalty to Lancaster, even to exile.[227] Intellectual conviction seems to have coincided with self-interest: despite later claims that he advocated some sort of constitutional limitation on the prerogative, it will be argued in Chapter 5 that he believed that the best safeguard for stability was a strong, well-advised, authoritative monarchy. This sentiment is to be found in the *Somnium* with its recipe for solving civil unrest by, 'the prince ... by his excedyng auctorite and prudens of his conseyle'. Even if the prince was an unfit receptacle of such power, it was the duty of the political nation to ensure that he was advised by counsellors who could exercise it on his behalf.

The collapse of Lancaster

Despite the dangerous business that he had undertaken at Coventry, Sir John Fortescue seems to have been in a positive frame of mind in early December 1459, as John Bocking reported in the *Paston Letters*, 'The Chief Justice is right herty and seethe ful weel and kyndeley of my maister.'[228] His activities during the first half of the following year look like a response to the dismayed popular reaction to the attainder of the Yorkists.[229] He sat on commissions of oyer and terminer in London and the suburbs and in Kent, both areas known to be sympathetic to the exiled duke and to be at risk from an invasion by his supporters in Calais. He was also appointed to commissions of oyer and terminer in Wales and the Marches, Stafford, Salop, Worcester, Gloucester,

[227] *Declaration*, appendix 2, 298.

[228] *PL* (Davis), vol. 2, no. 584, 187.

[229] 'William Gregory's Chronicle of London', *The Historical Collections of a Citizen of London*, ed. J. Gairdner, 3 parts (London: 1876) part 3, 57–239, 206, 'the more parte of thys londe hadde pytte that they were attaynte and proclaymyd trayters'.

Hereford, York, Kingston upon Hull, Kent, Oxford, Wiltshire, Berkshire, Southampton, Somerset, Devon and Cornwall and was appointed to commissions of the peace in Kent and Sussex. The fact that these took him out of his customary circuits as well as sending him to the West and South-East and their sheer number indicate that the royal government was relying on a diminishing number of servants.[230] It is unlikely that Fortescue would have had time to participate in all these commissions before the Yorkist victory at the battle of Northampton on 10 July 1460. The commissions to Wales, the Marches and the West Midlands were concerned with treasonable activities in the forfeited lands of the duke of York and the earls of Warwick and Salisbury and, if efficiently executed, could further have damaged Fortescue's future standing with them.

The evidence shows that Fortescue did not, in fact, suffer unduly for his support of the Lancastrians after the battle of Northampton as the new regime, led by the duke of York, consolidated its power during the second half of the year. He remained Chief Justice and continued to enjoy his property, privileges and emoluments. The Yorkists were all too vulnerable, with the Queen and her supporters planning a counterattack, and they needed to preserve as much continuity as possible within the royal government. Henry VI was still technically king, even if he was virtually a prisoner of the Yorkists. The preservation of the precarious situation depended on the support of the lords and their followers, public servants and Londoners, who were not, at that stage, prepared to see him dethroned. The full extent of Fortescue's role in drafting the attainder, and possibly orchestrating propaganda to support it, may not have been known to the Yorkists or, if it was, they chose to ignore it, since *Gregory's Chronicle* records that they replaced several other great officers of state such as the Chancellor and Treasurer.[231] His obscure birth and status as a legal expert may have hidden from them the fact that he was becoming one of the Lancastrians' main political activists. Although Margaret Hastings made the point that it was most unusual for justices to be sacked when regimes changed in the fifteenth century, he was skating on thin ice.[232]

After Northampton, Fortescue was not appointed to any more commissions, a sign that he was not entirely trusted by the new regime. He could, for example, have been embarrassed by the fact that his close

[230] *CPR*, Henry VI, 1452–61, 562, 564–5, 609, 611, 613, 668, 679.

[231] 'Gregory's Chronicle', 207.

[232] M. Hastings, *The Court of Common Pleas in Fifteenth-Century England: A Study of Legal Administration and Procedure* (Ithaca, NY: 1971) 91–5.

associate, Robert, Lord Hungerford, was holding the Tower of London for Lancaster. The damage done by the bombardment to which he and lord Scales subjected the Londoners made a devastating impression.[233] Fortescue could, nonetheless, capitalise on his venerable status as a long-serving Chief Justice and his past contacts with Yorkists, including the duke himself, and he was still associated with Thomas Younge in dealing with the affairs of a chantry in Bristol.[234]

On 18 October 1460 Fortescue and his fellow judges had an opportunity either to ingratiate themselves with the new regime or to make a stand on behalf of the Lancastrian dynasty. In either case, despite the risks, they could have enhanced the force of the common law and their own powers as its ministers. Two days earlier the duke of York's supporters had presented a full statement of his claim to the throne to the Lords in parliament. The Lords in reply raised five objections to York's claim: they had all (including York) sworn oaths of loyalty to Henry VI, acts of parliament had confirmed the Lancastrian title to the throne and entails had vested the succession in royal heirs male. York bore the arms of Edmund of Langley, Edward III's fifth son, rather than those of Lionel of Clarence, his second son, through whom he made his claim. When Henry IV took the throne in 1399 he declared that he did so as the heir to Henry III, not as a conqueror: these arguments were to be taken up by Fortescue soon afterwards when he wrote his polemical tracts. The majority of the Lords were thus unwilling to dismiss Henry VI as a usurper, so they temporised by submitting the claim first to the King, who prevaricated, and then to the judges. The judges replied that:

> they were the Kyngs Justices, and have to determyne such maters as com before theym in the lawe, betwene partie and partie, and in such maters as been betwene partie and partie they may not be of Counseill; and sith this mater was betwene the Kyng and the seid Duc of York as two parties, and also it hath not be accustumed to calle the Justices to Counseill in such maters, and in especiall the mater was so high, and touched the Kyngs high estate and regalie, which is above the lawe and passed ther lernyng, wherfore they durst not enter into eny communication therof, for it perteyned to the Lordes of the Kyngs blode, and th'apparage of this his lond, to have communication and medle in such maters; and therefore they humble bysought all the Lordes, to have theym utterly excused of eny avyce or Counseill, by theym to be geven in that matier.

[233] *Benet's Chronicle*, 226.

[234] *CPR*, Henry VI, 1452–61, 601.

The King's Serjeants and Attorney gave a similar answer citing the opinion of the Justices as their precedent.[235]

For the third time since he had become Chief Justice, Fortescue had avoided the chance of extending the authority of the law and, in so doing, placing it above temporary political pressures. The full formulation of a theory in which the judicature could act as a constitutional counterbalance to the legislature had to await Montesquieu and the eighteenth century. Yet the place of the law in the definition of precedent as a means of determining political rights was inherent in the writings of some contemporary Italian humanists and Fortescue was to show an awareness of their work in all his major treatises.[236] Ironically he shunned repeated opportunities to enhance the constitutional role of the law in the state: it could be objected that this was a necessary means of preserving the impartiality of the judges, but in October 1460 impartiality looked more like impotence. On the other hand, Fortescue's stance was quite compatible with his later writings where he never suggested that the law should have a more central role in governance, only that it should be administered justly. He was also serving the Lancastrian interest by preventing the judges from endorsing the Yorkist succession. The situation in October 1460 will resonate with those who experienced the debates in the autumn of 2016 concerning the authority of the English High Court to determine whether parliament should be able to vote on the referendum decision to leave the European Union.

Chrimes pointed out that there is no evidence that Fortescue actually delivered the judges' opinion, yet he also referred to a very similar statement that he later made in his *Declaration upon Certain Writings*:

> They concernen the right of succession in kyngedoms, whiche is the grettest matier temporall in all the worlde, they oughten to be treted and declared by the mosste profounde and grettest lerned men that can be gotten tharto, and not by men of my simpleness that have not moche labored or studied in any faculte except the lawes of this londe, in whiche the studientes lerne full lytell of the right of succession of kingdoms.[237]

[235] *RP*, vol. 5, 376; *PROME*, vol. 12, 518.

[236] Chrimes, *De Laudibus*, xc–xciii including notes. Contemporaries of Poggio Bracciolini and Leonardo Bruni (authors used by Fortescue), particularly Maffeo Vegio, Ambrogio Camaldolese and Niccolo Niccoli, were working on the *Digest* and establishing legal studies as a proper concern for humanists.

[237] See below, Appendix 2, p. 298; S.B. Chrimes, *English Constitutional Ideas in the Fifteenth Century* (Cambridge: 1936) 22–3.

Fortescue's presence in London on 16 October and 4 November can be assumed since he certified the issue of pardons on those days.[238] He was likely, as the most senior and influential judge, to have guided the other justices to come to their inconclusive conclusion. The inability of the King or the judges to put up a convincing defence against York's claim eventually led the Lords to adopt a compromise. On the model of the 1420 treaty of Troyes between Henry V and Charles VI of France, the reigning king was to continue to rule but his son, Edward Prince of Wales, was disinherited in favour of the house of York. Could the spate of works in defence of the Lancastrian succession that Fortescue produced during the next few years have been an attempt to expiate for his failure to make a stand on the issue in October 1460?

The death of the duke of York at the battle of Wakefield in late December and the retrieval of Henry VI by his followers at the second battle of St Albans on 17 February 1461, appeared to change the balance of power between the factions yet again. London inclined towards the Yorkists and entry was refused to Margaret of Anjou and her reputedly lawless northern army.[239] Ten days after her victory at St Albans, on 26 February Edward, earl of March, York's oldest son, and his followers were admitted to London. They immediately announced that Henry VI was responsible for the renewal of the conflict by reneging on his agreement that the house of York should succeed him on the throne and the earl of March was proclaimed king as Edward IV.

Fortescue was in London as late as 29 January 1461, for that was the date of his last recorded act as Chief Justice of the King's Bench, when he certified the issue of a pardon to one Simon Lodbroke, 'wever' late of Reading.[240] Cora Scofield established that he was still in or near London about two weeks before the second battle of St Albans on 17 February since it was then that he tried to safeguard some of his property by declaring that it was his wife's jointure.[241] The witnesses to the deposition of 1480 remembered that she had surrendered her original jointure in Devon to their son Martin and his wife, so Fortescue ordered his

[238] *CPR*, Henry VI, 1452–61, 624, 627. Fortescue featured in the *Year Books* during Trinity 1460, Siepp, 1460.025. There were three final references to him for Trinity and Michaelmas but it is not clear that he was in court in person.

[239] C. Barron, 'London and the Crown, 1451–61', *The Crown and Local Communities in England and France in the Fifteenth Century*, ed. J.R.L. Highfield and R. Jeffs (Gloucester: 1981) 88–109; B.M. Cron, 'Margaret of Anjou and the Lancastrian March on London, 1461', *The Ricardian*, 11 (1999) 590–615.

[240] *CPR*, Henry VI, 1452–61, 641–2.

[241] Scofield, 'Fortescue in February 1461'.

steward, John Knyghton, to read a deed in North Mimms and deliver for her benefit seisin of his properties in Hertfordshire and Middlesex to Thomas Younge (the choice of that pro-Yorkist was surely not accidental) and Thomas Povy (one of Fortescue's clerks).[242] Fortescue would not have dallied in pro-Yorkist London to witness the proclamation of Edward's right to the throne from his own King's Bench in Westminster Hall on 4 March 1461.[243]

By 29 March Fortescue was in an unfamiliar and dangerous place. The parliament rolls recording his subsequent attainder, along with a number of other prominent Lancastrians, stated that they:

> in a feld bitwene the Townes of Shirbourne in Elmett and Tadcaster in the seid Shire of York, called Saxtonfeld and Tawtonfeeld [Towton], in the Shire of York, accompanyed with the Frenshmen and Scotts, the Kynges Ennemyes, falsely and traiterously agenst their feith and Liegeaunce, there rered werre agenst the same Kyng Edward, their rightwise, true and naturall Liege lord, purposyng there and then to have distroyed hym, and deposed hym of his Roiall Estate, Coroune and Dignite.[244]

The preamble to the act of attainder went on to name Fortescue as one of those who were involved in a later skirmish with Yorkist troops at Ryton and Brauncepeth in Durham on 26 June 1461. In both the attainder references Fortescue was simply given the title of 'knight': before 13 May he had been dismissed as Chief Justice of the King's Bench and his colleague, Sir John Markham, had been promoted in his place.[245] Activities of at least forty years duration in the law, in the business community of London and the West, in parliament and in the service of the Crown and of noblemen had come abruptly to a halt. Fortescue, already an old man, was soon to be exiled and condemned as a traitor: all the assumptions about law and governance upon which his long service to the Lancastrians had been based were now called into question. Yet he was to prove one of the greatest assets that the dynasty possessed. His second career as a polemicist, diplomat, tutor and adviser to prince Edward of Lancaster and author of treatises on law and government was about to begin.

[242] *CCR*, Edward IV, Edward V, Richard III, 1476–85.

[243] C.A.J. Armstrong, 'The Inauguration Ceremonies of the Yorkist Kings and Their Title to the Throne', *TRHS*, 30 (1948) 51–73.

[244] *RP*, vol. 5, 477–8; *PROME*, vol. 13, 42–5; 'Gregory's Chronicle', 217.

[245] *CPR*, Edward IV, 1461–67, 14.

CHAPTER 3

1461–*c.*1479

Exile in Scotland

The defeat of the Lancastrians at Towton on 29 March 1461 is now seen as a turning point in their fortunes, but this was not necessarily apparent to them at the time. Subsequently the career of Sir John Fortescue and his decrepit master, Henry VI, was to be fraught with dangers, yet they and the other members of their band may only gradually have come to accept that England was lost to them. They fled to Scotland after their military defeat and negotiated the provision of shelter and military aid from the Regent for young James III, his mother, Mary of Guelders. The other great power in the land, James Kennedy, archbishop of St Andrews, was also well disposed towards them.[1] In return it was rumoured that they had agreed to surrender the border fortress of Berwick to the Scots and promised to cede Carlisle: this was unlikely to commend them to unaligned opinion in England but they really had no alternative.[2]

In late June 1461 a group of Lancastrian lords recrossed the border, taking Henry VI with them. Fortescue was also in the party. The act of attainder passed in the parliament later in the year stated he was present at the skirmishes of Ryton and Brauncepeth: both were fiascos for the invaders, who beat a hasty retreat to Scotland. This seems to have ended Fortescue's involvement with martial activities for the next decade and encouraged him to turn to the *metiers* at which he excelled – political writing and diplomacy. It is unlikely that he had played an active part

[1] R. Nicholson, *Scotland: The Later Middle Ages* (Edinburgh: 1974) 399–400. Margaret of Anjou had already visited Scotland, probably from December 1460 to early January 1461, and had discussed at Lincluden the possibility of a marriage between her son and Mary, a sister of James III.

[2] M. Hicks, 'A Minute of the Lancastrian Council at York, 20 January, 1461', *Northern History*, 35 (1999) 214–21, establishes that an agreement (details unspecified) had been made at Lincluden on 5 January 1461. The Scots never took Carlisle.

either at Towton or in these later skirmishes, although the possibility cannot be entirely discounted. One of the rewards of attempting to trace Fortescue's career and works is his constant capacity to surprise.

Fortescue might already have been given the office of Chancellor before the Lancastrians retreated to Scotland after Towton. They claimed that they retained the Great Seal after King Henry's escape from Yorkist tutelage on 17 February 1461 and they would not have recognised Edward IV's Chancellor, George Neville, bishop of Exeter.[3] Hannes Kleineke, however, has pointed out that George Neville was unlikely to have surrendered the Seal to the Lancastrians. Fortescue might have had a separate royal seal for the King's Bench and have used this as a substitute for 'the real thing'.[4] The Lancastrian presence in the North and subsequently their status in diplomatic negotiations would be enhanced by the presence of the greatest officer of state: Fortescue may well have held the title for a few weeks whilst he was still on English soil. Despite the fact that it was unusual for a layman to hold the office the decision to appoint him was a wise one. The documents bearing his name in the French royal archives recognized him as, 'Le Chancellier d'Angleterre'.[5] During the complex and demanding diplomatic exchanges of the next decade he was to justify his promotion to the apparently empty title.

The long-term prospects which faced the Lancastrians in Scotland were extremely unpromising. The Regent had to steer a course between violently hostile factions, a situation that Edward IV had been swift to exploit by exerting maximum pressure on her to agree to a truce and then a peace. Part of such a settlement would certainly be the withdrawal of all support from the Lancastrians and ultimately their expulsion. An embassy from Philip the Good of Burgundy, a friend of the Yorkists, had already succeeded in destroying the project for a marriage between Edward of Lancaster and Mary of Scotland.[6] Henry, duke of

[3] Letter from Margaret of Anjou to Ormonde in Portugal, 13 December 1464, which mentioned that the Chancellor had sufficient authority under the King's Great Seal to bind the realm of England to repay Alfonso V of Portugal for costs he might incur in aiding the Lancastrians, Clermont, *Works*, 27.

[4] Hannes Kleineke, comments in a personal communication of 29 February 2016. See also 'The London Journal', which refers to a Lancastrian Great Seal on 22 February 1461, London, Corporation of London Record Office, 'London Journal', 6, f. 458.

[5] J. Calmette and G. Périnelle, *Louis XI et l'Angleterre, 1461–1483* (Paris: 1930) e.g. 69, n. 5.

[6] M.R. Thielemans, *Bourgogne et Angleterre: Relations politiques et économiques entre les Pays-Bas bourguignons et l'Angleterre, 1435–1467* (Brussels: 1966) 386.

Somerset, Robert Hungerford, Lord Moleyns, still a close associate of Fortescue, and Sir Robert Whittingham had been sent by Margaret of Anjou to negotiate for support from the new king of France, Louis XI. Despite the fact that he was first cousin to both Henry and Margaret he proved a very different proposition from his father, Charles VII, and kept the envoys as virtual prisoners until the following year.[7] Their grim report was copied in the *Paston Letters* and contained at the end a list of the meagre following that remained with the royal family.[8] Henry VI was at Kirkcudbright with four men and a child and Margaret was at Edinburgh accompanied by twenty-four men. Apart from Fortescue several of the others were obscure people, but they did include some household men such as Sir Edmund Hampden and William Tailboys and one nobleman, Lord Roos.

Henry VI, Margaret of Anjou and their followers were left in a state of suspended animation during the autumn and winter of 1461/2 by the detention of their delegation in France. Plummer identified their residence during this period as the guest house of the Blackfriars in Edinburgh.[9] This was regularly used by the Scots royal family and the Lord Chamberlain usually reimbursed the friars for their expenses. If this was done for the Lancastrians it must have given some relief to the impoverished group: apart from any valuables that they had taken into exile all sources of income had dried up. In 1462 in a letter of introduction to Louis XI for, 'nostre amie et loial chancellier Jehan Fortescu, chivalier', Henry mentioned his gratitude for the financial support that he was receiving from his Chancellor.[10] It is intriguing that this was possible. The man who set such store by solvency had managed to retain some resources, but by the end of 1464 these were exhausted, if his letter to John Ormonde is to be believed.[11] During his time in Scotland Fortescue worked on the polemical pamphlets which refuted the Yorkist claim to the English throne. They are discussed in Part II but it is relevant to note here an indication that they were produced with the co-operation of the Scots court. The contribution of William Fratour, the prebendary

[7] Marie of Anjou was his mother, the sister of Margaret of Anjou's father, King René. Henry VI's mother, Catherine of France, was the sister of Charles VII.

[8] *PL* (Davis) vol. 2, no. 646, 252–3.

[9] Plummer, *Governance of England*, 58; W. Moir Bryce, 'The Black Friars of Edinburgh', *The Book of the Old Edinburgh Club* (Edinburgh: 1910) vol. 3, 46; Wolffe, *Henry VI*, 333.

[10] Paris, BnF fonds fr. 4054, f. 176b.

[11] See below, pp. 122–3.

of Aberdeen, implies that the Lancastrians were receiving help with their propaganda campaign as well as material support.

Just as the Lancastrians were prey to the turbulent, faction-ridden politics of Scotland, so they were enmeshed by the conflict of interests between those whom they saw as their natural allies on the Continent: France, Burgundy and Brittany. The death of Charles VII in 1461 posed the question of the alignment of his heir, Louis XI. As dauphin he had frequently been at odds with his father and could not be counted on to follow Charles's generally pro-Lancastrian policy, as his detention of their delegation had swiftly demonstrated. He was more interested in seeking means of limiting the capacity of neighbours such as Burgundy and Brittany to harm France than to enquire into the rights and wrongs of the English succession.[12] He was progressively inclined to share Philip the Good's wish for peace with the Yorkist regime for if he dissented he could become dangerously isolated. Philip's son Charles, count of Charolais, followed the traditional Valois pattern by defying his father and pursuing, as far as he could, an independent policy of supporting Lancaster. This was the minefield into which Fortescue and the other Lancastrian envoys were precipitated.[13]

The diplomatic offensive was initiated by Margaret of Anjou in April 1462 as she made her way to France via Brittany: Somerset, Hampden and Hungerford were still detained in France but were allowed to participate in the negotiations. Jasper Tudor, titular earl of Pembroke, was also involved, as was Fortescue: rumour in England made him one of the leaders of a three-pronged attack on Wales, East Anglia and Kent.[14] A letter to Louis XI from the authorities in Rouen, dated 13 June, stated that Pembroke and Fortescue had obtained a recommendation from the count of Charolais, but they needed safe-conducts to go as ambassadors to Paris and instructions were required as to whether they should be allowed to proceed.[15] No information has been found about what decision was taken, but Fortescue's name was not on the treaty of Tours agreed by Margaret of Anjou and King Louis at the end of the month.[16] On the security of the town of Calais (which neither participant held), Louis produced sufficient money for a small invasion force but all this

[12] Technically he was suzerain of these duchies but, in practice, they could both take independent political lines.

[13] Kekewich, *The Good King*, 201–9.

[14] Griffiths, *Henry VI*, 885–8; *PL* (Davis) vol. 2, no. 662, 272–3.

[15] BnF fonds fr. 4054, f. 177a, 'sont entrez par (?) en ceste ville de Rouen le comte Pennebroc et mess. Jehan Forescu "chlr" chancelier du Roy Henry dangleterre'.

[16] Chrimes, *De Laudibus*, lxxiv.

enabled the Lancastrians to do was to take a few castles in Northumberland and, by early 1463, they had all been recaptured for Edward IV. Later in the spring they were taken again for Lancaster, providing some kind of a base from which an invasion of England could be launched.

In June 1463 the English and Scots royal families led an invasion south over the border, but this force was easily routed by Warwick and his brother, John Neville, Lord Montague, who pursued it for sixty miles back into Scotland. The Lancastrians desperately needed an effective military commander who could match such exploits but it was to be another seven long years before they found one. After this fiasco little more help could be expected from the Regent, and Margaret of Anjou found it timely to depart for the Continent, taking her son and most of the small court, including Fortescue, with her.[17] King Henry had returned to Scotland, where he proved an embarrassment to the government, which was inclined to make a settlement with the Yorkist regime. The problem was solved in 1464 when Somerset, after a brief accommodation with Edward IV, returned to his true allegiance and occupied parts of Northumberland. Bishop Kennedy, who had exercised the greatest authority in the country since the recent death of the Regent, was able to send Henry VI over the border to join his kinsman and a few months later a fifteen-year truce was concluded between Scotland and England.[18] By that time Somerset had been defeated at Hexham, although Henry was to be sheltered by well-wishers in the north for another fourteen months before he was captured and taken to London. Robert Hungerford, Lord Moleyns, was executed after the battle, so Fortescue's long-standing attachment to his family was broken.

Fortescue would never see Henry VI again. Since he had been appointed King's Sergeant and then Chief Justice he had been in regular contact with the King and this contact must have been fairly intimate after the second battle of St Albans. Yet although Fortescue was to remain loyal to Lancaster for as long as loyalty could reasonably be expected of him, none of his many statements on the governance of the realm of England betrayed any personal affection or admiration for Henry VI, to whom he referred in conventionally deferential terms. Indeed much that he wrote in the *De Natura*, *De Laudibus*, *Articles to Warwick* and *Governance of England* was censorious of his rule.[19] Margaret of Anjou was far from the ideal leader (Fortescue cannot have approved of her

[17] Ross, *Edward IV*, 50–4.

[18] Nicholson, *Scotland*, 404–6.

[19] B.P. Wolffe identified his inanity and perverse wilfulness as a major cause of the outbreak of the civil war, 'The Personal Rule of Henry VI', *Fifteenth Century*

11 Henry VI.

readiness to dispose of prize towns such as Berwick and Calais) but at least she was vigorous, determined and blessed with useful contacts on the Continent. It was in the Queen and her son, Prince Edward of Lancaster, that he invested his hopes for a Lancastrian restoration.

The chances of a restoration were minimal when Margaret of Anjou and the other exiles landed at Sluys in the Low Countries in July 1463.

England, 1399–1509: Studies in Politics and Society, ed. S.B. Chrimes, C.D. Ross, R.A. Griffiths (Manchester: 1972) 29–48.

12 Margaret of Anjou.

Matters further deteriorated during the coming months, for Louis XI was unimpressed by the dismal failure of the expedition to the North of England from Scotland in the previous year and in June 1463 he engaged in negotiations for a settlement with Edward IV. The French king was coming to realise that the pitiful amounts of aid he had given to his 'dear cousin' were not reciprocated by enthusiasm for her cause in England. On the other hand, Edward IV had the power to cause him great inconvenience and would become more dangerous as he took full control of his kingdom. If Louis wished to maintain friendly relations with the obstinately pro-Yorkist Philip of Burgundy a change of direction was indicated.

Chastellain's *Chronique* gives a vivid and extensive account of the desperate attempts made by Margaret of Anjou at St Pol, on 30 August 1463, to prevent the duke of Burgundy from joining a truce with Edward

IV and Louis XI and to divert him to supporting the Lancastrians.[20] The Queen had to be satisfied with polite but noncommittal words, a banquet, the gift of a fine diamond and money on her departure. She retreated to Bruges, where she received more hospitality from the count of Charolais, who genuinely wished her well. But neither of them could block the process, which was concluded at St Omer on 8 October when a year's Anglo-French truce was agreed that included Burgundy and Brittany.[21] Fortescue did not accompany the Queen to St Pol, indeed accounts make much of the fact that she went poorly dressed, with only a few women as companions. Yet it is unlikely that even his subtle arguments could have persuaded Philip that there was any advantage to be had in supporting Lancaster: the duke had seen the futility of the French and Scottish attempts over the past two years.

Exile in the Duchy of Bar

In September 1463 Margaret of Anjou retreated to the castle of Koeur near St Mihiel. The castle belonged to her father King René, duke of Anjou, and the duchy of Bar was one of the many places he claimed to rule that he actually governed. The duchy was situated between France and the Holy Roman Empire: the eastern half owed allegiance to the Emperor, the western to the king of France but in practice they were both happy to leave René to deal with its turbulent nobility. He and his first wife, Isabelle of Lorraine, had also ruled the adjacent duchy of Lorraine but on her death it had been inherited by his eldest son, John, duke of Calabria.[22] Margaret's retreat to Bar was an admission that little more could be done for the time being on the diplomatic front, 'ut ibi expectaret eventus mundi'.[23]

Financial problems must have been one reason for the choice of such an unpromising, remote location for there, with help from her father, she could sustain her son and a little court of between fifty and 200 people.[24] No surplus was available to mount lavish embassies or indulge

[20] G. Chastellain, *Oeuvres*, ed. K. de Lettenhove, 8 vols (Brussels: 1863–6) vol. 4, 278–99.

[21] Calmette and Périnelle, *Louis XI et l'Angleterre*, 42–5; Thielemans, *Bourgogne et Angleterre*, 382–402.

[22] Kekewich, *The Good King*, *passim*.

[23] 'There she waited upon the affairs of the world', *Letters and Papers Illustrative of the Wars of the English in France*, ed. J. Stevenson, 2 vols (London: 1861, 1864) vol. 2, 781.

[24] *Ibid.* Worcester estimated the number at 200; Griffiths, *Henry VI*, 888, says about fifty. People and their servants came and went and some locals were employed,

in finery, the kind of shows that might impress European princes that the Lancastrians were a viable government in exile.[25] The abortive campaigns in the North had been costly in terms of their prominent English supporters – the duke of Somerset, Robert Hungerford, Lord Moleyns, Lord Roos and Tailboys were all killed after Hexham and the de Veres, father and son, had already been executed. The Yorkists also possessed two human assets which were not available to the Lancastrians: an attractive young king and the magnetic personality and formidable military skills of Warwick. Yet the Lancastrian case was not entirely hopeless, Edward IV was attractive but he was also inexperienced and would make mistakes. The Queen and her son also had the intangible but appreciable asset of three very clever and persistent lawyers: Dr John Morton, Dr Ralph Makerell and Sir John Fortescue.

Life at Koeur must have been dreary even after the dangers, constant journeys and discomforts that the exiles had endured for the past three years. It is hard to recover the ambience of the fifteenth-century castle, which was accidentally destroyed by fire in 1783, since little survives above ground. Much of it was presumably recycled in the houses that cover part of the site, although a small field that could have formed part of the precinct might contain some foundations. The castle was large and well appointed: Dumont recorded twenty-four principal rooms, besides a great chamber with eighteen windows and a kitchen with the usual subsidiary offices. King René had arranged for suitable furniture to be brought from his other properties in anticipation of his daughter's arrival and pleasant gardens stretched on one side down to the canal.[26] Yet the village of Koeur and the neighbouring town of St Mihiel must have seemed very provincial to the Queen and her following, accustomed as they were to the palaces and great estates of England, Scotland, France and Burgundy. Fortescue had mainly spent his adult life in London, latterly as the greatest lawyer in the land surrounded by his family, friends, associates, clients and servants. In the mid-1460s he was either in his sixties or early seventies, a considerable age by the standards of the time. To be deprived of the comforts he enjoyed in his

so numbers varied, probably to somewhere between these two figures.

[25] C.M.J. McGovern, 'Lancastrian Diplomacy and Queen Margaret's Court in Exile, 1461–1471', unpublished BA dissertation (University of Keele: 1973); M.L. Kekewich, 'The Lancastrian Court in Exile', *The Lancastrian Court*, ed. J. Stratford (Donington: 2003) 95–110.

[26] C.E. Dumont, *Les ruines de la Meuse*, 5 vols (Paris and Nancy: 1869) vol. 2, 313–87. There are two villages of Koeur, 'la petite' and 'la grande'; the castle was situated in the former.

own homes and the stimulation of the news and business that his life in London had provided must have been a sore trial. Yet he was to prove as resilient and persistent in urging the claims of Lancaster as was Queen Margaret herself and used Koeur as a base for deploying two very effective weapons: his pen and his diplomatic skills.

The bishop of St Asaph, Thomas Bird, his chaplain and the Queen's chaplains were in St Mihiel by July 1463, presumably helping to prepare for the arrival of Margaret and her following. These priests enjoyed very cordial relations with the monks of the abbey in St Mihiel. One of the sources of information about the life of the exiles is the record of dinners to which they were regularly entertained there.[27] René of Anjou visited his daughter in October and the following January she spent some time with him at Louppy-sur-Marne. They may well have been discussing the financial support which she could expect from him: he was a prince whose titles far exceeded his actual revenues. He did, however, manage to provide her with a pension of 6,000 crowns per annum and from 1465 this was supplemented by a pension of 4,000 or 5,000 francs from Louis XI.[28] René was one of the most important princes in France, a great-grandson of King Charles V, and he had for many years aspired to make good the claim that the house of Anjou held to the throne of Naples. This claim was still being pressed by his son, John, duke of Calabria, but the family did not receive sufficient revenues either adequately to support his campaigns or to finance the Lancastrians' attempts to reconquer England. They also suffered from the replacement of Charles VII by Louis XI. The old king and René had been life-long friends and allies but Louis did not consider that their family ties automatically entitled them to assistance.[29]

In 1464 the Queen and her son fell ill and René sent them his physician. Margaret seems to have recovered quickly but a second visit of nineteen days was necessary for the physician to cure her eleven-year-old son. The Queen visited Anjou in 1466, probably to seek more diplomatic or financial assistance from her father. The following year

[27] C.E. Dumont, *Histoire de la ville de Saint Mihiel*, 4 vols (Paris and Nancy: 1860–4) vol. 1, 175–8.

[28] C.L. Scofield, *The Life and Reign of Edward IV*, 2 vols (London: 1923) vol. 1, 367–8; Paris, BnF Collection de Lorraine Ms 26, f. 45, 1464, Quittance from Margaret of Anjou to Olivier Haloret, maitre de la Chambre aux deniers to King René, for the sum of 687 livres tournois and 10 sous for her expenses in June and July. Signed by the Queen at Bar, 'Delabarre'.

[29] The classic French account of King René is A. Lecoy de la Marche, *Le Roi René: Sa vie, son administration, ses travaux artistiques et littéraires*, 2 vols (Paris: 1875); see also J. Favier, *Le Roi René* (Paris: 2008), which has a good bibliography.

some internal repairs were carried out in the castle and its external defences were strengthened. No one could have foreseen how long it would be the principal residence of the exiles. The other reason for the works could have been the reviving prospects for their cause. Once they became more dangerous to Edward IV he could have attempted their capture or harm through his friends and agents on the Continent. A far more immediate threat to their prospects was presented in the same year by the serious illness of Prince Edward. He probably had smallpox, as a carpenter was paid to surround his bed with planks of wood to prevent draughts or bright light affecting him. Had he not recovered it is doubtful that the Queen and the Chancellor would have been able to persuade any English nobles or European princes to take risks for the ageing and unprepossessing captive, Henry VI.

The intellectual influences that contributed to Fortescue's writings in the 1460s and 1470s are discussed in Part II. One possible source, however, has not previously been seriously considered, which is the flourishing culture of the court of King René, itself linked to the Valois court in the Loire valley. By the mid-1460s René was almost permanently resident in Provence, the only remaining part of the once great Angevin kingdom of Naples and Sicily.[30] There he promoted an eclectic mixture of art and literature derived from native traditions, the Italian Renaissance and the Low Countries. René himself was an author and patronised the work of those who frequented his court. Anthoine de la Sale composed the *Salade* for his son, John of Calabria, the uncle of Edward of Lancaster, in which he offered good advice about how a young prince should govern himself and his subjects. De la Sale had accompanied Margaret of Anjou to England for her wedding in 1445 and was probably known to Fortescue.[31] In London, Anjou and Koeur Fortescue had been exposed to the ethos of the court of the Angevins, and while he showed no sign of imbibing King René's love of chivalry and grand ceremonies the more serious work of authors such as de la Sale could have influenced the advice he offered. He referred to recent treatises by early Florentine Renaissance authors, Poggio Bracciolini and Leonardo Bruni, in his major works and the Angevins could have been one conduit by which these became known to him.[32]

Craig Taylor has subjected Fortescue's polemical works to close scrutiny with a view to discovering how far he could have been influenced by or could himself have affected the formidable body of work that

[30] Kekewich, *The Good King*, *passim*.

[31] *Ibid.*, 101.

[32] See below, Chapter 5.

had been generated in the debate over the rival dynastic claims in the Hundred Years War.[33] More will be said about this in Part II but here it should be noted that Fortescue visited France several times during his exile and was in touch with the Chancery of Louis XI, the place where some of the tracts on the French succession had originated. Margaret Blaney devoted much thought to whether Fortescue was the translator of Alain Chartier's *Treatise of Hope* (*Traité de l'Espérance*), called by Clermont *The Dialogue between Understanding and Faith*, although no conclusion has been reached.[34] He certainly had plenty of opportunities to encounter the work of the polemicists as well as eminent writers such as Chartier, Christine de Pisan and Philippe de Mézières.[35]

The Financial Consequences of Disgrace

The provision that Fortescue tried to make for his wife, Isabella Jamys, from his Hertfordshire and Middlesex properties in February 1461, has been mentioned above.[36] Some of the lands which they owned had already been given to his son Martin in 1456 as part of his marriage settlement. An inquisition *post mortem* taken on Martin's possessions in 1473 showed him to have been peacefully holding the manor of Combe and lands in Overcombe, Efford and elsewhere which had formed the nucleus of his father's early property acquisitions.[37] Humphrey, Lord Stafford, and Sir Philip Beaumont, acting as arbitrators, found in favour of Martin and Elizabeth Fortescue in 1466 in a dispute with Thomas Wyse, presumably Sir John's brother-in-law, and John Wyse over lands in Lamerton, Devonshire.[38] Transactions such as this ensured that the wealth Fortescue had so diligently accumulated over the space of forty years would not all be forfeited. The reversion of the manor of Ebrington and the remainder of Fortescue's lands had been alienated by the act of attainder of 4 December 1461 and granted to Yorkist supporters, but

[33] Craig Taylor, 'Sir John Fortescue and the French Polemical Treatises of the Hundred Years War', *EHR*, 114 (1999) 112–29; 'War, Propaganda and Diplomacy in Fifteenth Century France and England', *War, Government and Power in Late Medieval France*, ed. C. Allmand (Liverpool: 2000) 70–91; *Debating the Hundred Years War: 'Pour ce que plusieurs' and 'A Declaracion of the trew and dewe title of Henry VIII'* (Cambridge: 2006) 29.

[34] See below, Chapter 4, pp. 174–5, for details.

[35] J. Watts, *The Making of Polities: Europe 1300–1500* (Cambridge: 2009) 384, 387.

[36] See below pp. 105–6.

[37] TNA, 12 Edward IV, C 140/41, 39. Martin had two sons, John, who was over twelve in 1472 when his father died, and William.

[38] Devon Record Office, M/T 708.

Ebrington was of little current value when it was given to Lord Wenlock on 12 March 1462, as the tenant, Dame Joyce Beauchamp, was still living.[39]

Fortescue's attempt to save some property for his wife was futile as the same warrant which contained the grant of the reversion of Ebrington to Lord Wenlock also granted him all the family's possessions in Hertfordshire and Middlesex. Wenlock did not retain them permanently, as on 3 February 1468 they were put into the hands of Robert Stillington, bishop of Bath and Wells, and Robert Kirkeham, Keeper of the Rolls of Chancery, both of whom were custodians of other property which the King wished to remove from the original grantee.[40] It could mean that he was becoming disenchanted with Wenlock for his connection with Warwick, but this was unlikely as early as February 1468. Another reason may be found in a grant of land on 1 August 1462 to 'the king's servants' John Fortescue esquire, the son of Sir John's brother Richard, and William Chichely esquire, where 'in consideration of their charges and perils incurred in the king's conflicts and battles', they were given lands to the value of £46. These included 'all lands and possessions in Trewbrigge [Trowbridge], co. Wilts, late of John Fortescue knight, in the king's hands by reason of an act of forfeiture'.[41]

In 1467 Squire Fortescue was granted for life four manors in Devon which had been forfeited by Sir William Cary.[42] Fortescue probably received these benefits for himself and his family because of the proximity he enjoyed to Edward IV as an esquire of the King's body. It could have been at this time that his branch of the family obtained Sir John's former manor of Punsborne in Hertfordshire. In the 1470s Squire Fortescue was appointed sheriff of Cornwall several times and was to distinguish himself in 1473 by successfully besieging the rebellious earl of Oxford at St Michael's Mount, making an important contribution to stabilising the Yorkist regime in the West.[43] By surrendering some of the property of his disgraced uncle into his hands and keeping some in royal custody after 1467, Edward IV was following his favoured policy of conciliating as many influential families as possible. In this case he possibly envisaged that its return might eventually facilitate a reconciliation with Sir John Fortescue. There is no evidence that he maintained

[39] *CPR*, Edward IV, 1461–67, 183.

[40] *Ibid.*, 192.

[41] *CPR*, Edward IV, 1461–67, 212; TNA C 145/323/50, 1468 inquisition into Fortescue's possessions in Wiltshire.

[42] *CPR*, Edward IV, 1467–77, 27.

[43] *Ibid.*, 399–400.

contacts with his family during his exile but it is quite possible that he did so. The comings and goings of French, English, Scots and Burgundian agents and ambassadors in northern Europe and Britain afforded plenty of opportunities for clandestine correspondence. Despite his loyalty to Lancaster, as the months of Yorkist rule stretched into years, prudence might have dictated that some provision be made for the possibility that it would be permanent.[44]

Sir John Fortescue had used the marriage of his daughter Maude to forge ties with the wealthy Sir Robert Corbet, although the original settlement of 1450 allowed for the possibility that, since the bride and groom were both minors, they might subsequently divorce.[45] The Corbets appear to have been as hard-headed as the Fortescues where marriage and property were concerned, for during the reign of Edward IV, when an alliance to a prominent disgraced exile would have been a liability, they arranged that a 'lawfull devorce of marriage is made'. In 1466 it was agreed that the manor of Little Downham, Norfolk, which had passed to Maude's husband when he was twenty, should be held in trust for her to provide for her maintenance.[46] Clermont quoted Blomefield on the affair and added that she retired to the nunnery of Helveston (Elstow/Elnestow) Bedfordshire, where she eventually died.[47]

No information has been discovered about the later years of Fortescue's third child, Elizabeth. Her first husband Edmund Whalesburgh was dead by 1456 and she was married to Thomas Vernon. The Whalesburghs were sufficiently trusted by the Yorkists for Thomas (presumably Elizabeth's father-in-law) to accompany John Fortescue esquire in the assault on the earl of Oxford at St Michael's Mount in 1472/3.[48]

The Fortescue family came quite well out of the potential crisis caused by the disgrace of its most prominent member. The senior branch at Wimpstone remained sufficiently obscure to enjoy its estates undisturbed throughout the civil wars. Henry Fortescue might have died in or soon after 1458, the last year in which he was appointed as a justice of the peace. In 1468 the mayor of Plymouth was pardoned, for, amongst other things, not answering for a debt of £20 owed to Fortescue. When

[44] See below for a discussion of possible contacts between the Lancastrian exiles, Warwick and Edward IV.

[45] See above, pp. 72, 75.

[46] Devon Record Office, 1262 M/TN1. Richard Whyteday was to be responsible for paying her 12 marks a year from the proceeds of the manor.

[47] Clermont, *Works*, 7; Blomefield, *An Essay*, vol. 9, 479; *VCH*, Bedfordshire, vol. 1, 353–8; Elizabeth Hasylden was abbess from 1463 to at least 1473.

[48] See above, p. 77.

in 1473 Margaret Strode, his widow (and by then also the widow of Richard Strode, of Newnham-Strode, Devon), was referred to as the executrix of his will, the documents describe him as a former sheriff of Devon and Cornwall. After his youthful affrays, his later life seems to have been respectable and uncontroversial.[49] The Fortescues of Wood and Fallapit, dynasties Henry had founded through his first and second wives, both heiresses, appear to have lived peacefully under Edward IV.

The Fortescues, later of Punsborne, heirs of Sir John's brother Richard who died for Lancaster in the first battle of St Albans, had lost no time in becoming reliable Yorkists. Sir John's children did not suffer unduly for their father's fall; even the hapless Maud was given a settlement to safeguard her financial security. It is not known where Lady Isabella Fortescue lived after her husband's flight and her loss of the Middlesex and Hertfordshire properties. She could have resided with any of her children or at Norton St Philip. That property does not appear to have been confiscated by the Yorkists and remained in the possession of the Fortescue family until about 1715, when it was sold by Hugh Fortescue, Lord Clinton.[50] Lady Fortescue probably died before her husband's return from exile, since she was deceased by 1473, the date of the inquisition *post mortem* for their son Martin.[51]

Frustrated Hopes

Even in 1464, when both France and Burgundy were at peace with Edward IV, Margaret of Anjou and Sir John Fortescue continued to solicit support for their cause. On 13 December in a series of letters they capitalised on the circumstance that John Butler, titular earl of Ormonde, had taken refuge in Portugal. The Fortescue family's connection with his dynasty went back to the 1420s, when Sir John's brother Henry was Chief Justice of Ireland and had dealings with the Butlers.[52] The Queen could invoke a family tie between Henry VI and King Alphonso V of Portugal as they were both descended from John of Gaunt. She informed him that she was attempting to enlist the Emperor, Henry the Impotent of Castile and the count of Charolais (a Lancastrian through his Portuguese mother) in a grand alliance to provide about 3,000

[49] *CPR*, Edward IV, 1467–77, 109, 327; 'Henry Fortescue', *House of Commons, 1386–1421*, vol. 3, 108–9.

[50] *The Manors of Norton St Philip and Hinton Charterhouse, 1535–1691*, ed. C.J. Brett, Somerset Record Society (Bristol: 2007) xiv.

[51] See above, n. 76.

[52] See above, Chapter 1.

men. It should be led by a 'notable and manly prince or ... capitayne' to invade England, where, Alphonso was assured, the majority of the people were only prevented by fear from rising against the usurper.[53] Besides instructing Ormonde on how he should approach Alphonso, the Queen sent a letter to the King that has not survived. In an endearing note from Fortescue, Ormonde was asked to put in the formal address as no one in Koeur could actually remember the monarch's name! (See Illustration 9.)

Young Edward was also required to show that he was a princeling of learning and dignity by addressing a rather pompous Latin letter, almost certainly drafted by Fortescue or one of the other lawyers, to the unknown King. He praised Alphonso for possessing all the cardinal virtues, to which he added magnanimity (a quality that his family desperately needed to encounter in all their negotiations): 'In you, therefore, most illustrious prince, my best hope resides, who is endowed with justice, prudence, fortitude, temperance, magnanimity and, at the last, all virtue and glory. I approach your might, for now we see no prince in the world so prolific in humanity.'[54] There was much more of the same kind of thing, larded with conventional classical allusions. These honeyed phrases were probably never read by Alphonso, since Scofield remarked that the letter seem to have been intercepted by Louis XI.[55] Prince Edward also sent a letter to Ormonde, 'writen at Seynt Mychael in Barr, with myn awn hand, that ye mey se how gode wrytare I am'. This praised his cousin for his steadfastness against his father's enemies and begged him to do his best for Lancaster in Portugal.[56] Queen Margaret and Fortescue doubtless hoped that this combination of childish innocence and political pressure would be irresistible, for it was the only form of persuasion that they had at their disposal.

Fortescue wrote the last letter that survives amongst those addressed to Ormonde. This provides a good picture of the circumstances of the exiles and the constraints to which their lives were subject. He first thanked Ormonde for the letter they had recently received and expressed their pleasure that he had arrived safely in Oporto. The Queen was sending him instructions separately (although Fortescue had doubtless taken a hand in drawing them up) and a certificate of safe-conduct. He was told he should not trust the good faith of the French king, who was

[53] Clermont, *Works*, 22–8; all correspondence with Ormonde and King Alphonso is taken from BnF fonds fr. Ms 4054, ff. 172–5.

[54] Paris, BnF fonds fr. Ms 4054, f. 172b, trans. Peter Fawcett.

[55] Scofield, *Edward IV*, vol. 1, 370–1.

[56] Paris, BnF fonds fr. Ms 4054, f. 173a.

in contact with the Yorkists. Somerset (Edmund Beaufort, titular duke) had managed to get to Koeur from Brittany and bring six horses with him; Fortescue had visited Paris and returned, 'but this is no verrey surety to you'. After listing the lords and gentlemen who were present at Koeur as he wrote, he advised: 'We buthe alle in grete poverte, but yet the queen susteynethe us in mete and drinke, so as we buthe not in extreme necessite. Her highnesse may do no more to us thanne she dothe. Wherfore I counseille you to spend sparely soche money as ye have, for whanne you come hether ye shulle have need of hit.'[57] This was followed by further advice: if the king of Portugal seemed favourable to their cause Ormonde should stay with him; if he did not, he should not waste his money there but come to Koeur.

The Queen and her advisers seem to have realised that their attempt to forge a grand alliance was unlikely to succeed, and their alternative plans also involved Ormonde, who could be sent off on another mission. Despite the scathing words about Louis XI (which he had probably read when the correspondence was intercepted), Fortescue's recent visit to Paris implied that they still hoped that the King would eventually assist them. Ormonde remained loyal to Lancaster until after the Readeption, when, like Fortescue, he made his peace with Edward IV and had his attainder lifted.[58]

News that Edward had married an English widow, Elizabeth Woodville, was already circulating by October 1464. This brought some comfort to the Lancastrians: Louis XI was affronted since he had offered one of his Savoyard sisters-in-law to Edward, and the conference at St Omer, which was scheduled to discuss an extended truce between France and England, was abandoned. The earl of Warwick, who had not been consulted about Edward's matrimonial plans, was progressively to distance himself from his royal master, although Michael Hicks has questioned whether they caused Warwick serious annoyance.[59] Tony Pollard believed that the marriage in itself may not have led to the breach but its political consequences were profoundly unfavourable for Warwick.[60] On the other hand, the exiles sustained a heavy blow when the death of the second wife of the count of Charolais in 1465 led him to suppress his Lancastrian leanings and negotiate for the hand of Edward IV's sister, Margaret of York. Philip of Burgundy's health was poor and

[57] *Ibid.*, f. 175a.
[58] *ODNB*, 9, 169–70.
[59] Hicks, *Warwick*, 258.
[60] A.J. Pollard, *Warwick the Kingmaker: Politics, Power and Fame* (London: 2007) 58.

he was expected to die soon – the Lancastrians feared that the succession of their erstwhile friend would no longer benefit them.

Another difficulty for the Lancastrians during the middle years of the decade was that their potential supporters on the Continent were split into two camps by the League of the Common Weal. It was an alliance against Louis XI masterminded by Charolais and included the duke of Brittany, Charles, duke of Berry (the king's brother) and Margaret of Anjou's brother, John of Calabria, the duke of Lorraine.[61] Calmette and Périnelle record Margaret of Anjou's presence in Paris in October 1465 and her attempt to reconcile the hostile parties in a joint enterprise to restore her husband to the throne.[62] She was probably accompanied by Fortescue: the French royal accounts for 1465 record a payment to him by Guillaume Varié of 276 livres tournois to allow him to travel to England.[63] No evidence has been found as to whether or not he did so, though with friends and family in the West it would have been quite possible for a visit to go undetected. Meanwhile the League of Common Weal disintegrated. Louis XI made concessions to its members but they were mostly illusory. Edward IV, who had not been involved, had utilised the situation and the possibility that his sister would marry Charolais as bargaining counters, receiving a mendacious promise from the French king that no further aid would be given to the Lancastrians.[64]

The animosity felt by Charolais towards France and the success achieved by Louis in attaching Warwick to his interest was slowly working to the advantage of the Lancastrians. On 14 February 1467, the Milanese ambassador to France reported that John of Calabria, during a probably drunken session at Bourges, condemned Louis to his face for his friendship with Warwick, but he also seems to have hinted that it could be turned to their mutual advantage by bringing the earl into an alliance with his sister.[65] Only a few months later a messenger to the

[61] Kekewich, *The Good King*, 209–15.

[62] Calmette and Périnelle, *Louis XI et l'Angleterre*, 69–70.

[63] Paris, BnF fonds fr. 32511, f. 300a.

[64] Scofield, *Edward IV*, vol. 1, 406.

[65] *Ibid.*, vol. 1, 411; *CSPM*, 117–18, 'As the King persisted in his praise of the earl of Warwick, the duke [John of Calabria] said that as he was so fond of him he ought to try and restore his sister in that kingdom [England] when he would make sure of it as much as he was sure at present or even more so. The King asked what security they would give or if they would offer the queen's son as a hostage should France support another Lancastrian attempt on England. This boy, though only thirteen years of age, already talks of nothing but of cutting off heads or making war, as if he had everything in his hands or was the god of battle or the peaceful occupant of that throne. The King also asked, supposing

Lancastrian outpost of Harlech castle was captured by the Yorkists and during his interrogation mentioned Warwick as one of the Englishmen who was in correspondence with Margaret of Anjou.[66] Neither of these incidents proves that Lancastrian diplomacy had landed such a catch as Warwick as early as 1467, but the fact that similar evidence should come from such different sources implies that formerly entrenched attitudes and interests were already changing. In May the Milanese reported that Louis, fearing that Charolais was about to clinch his match with Margaret of York, had invited Margaret of Anjou to his court. She sent an emissary to the French king at this time and it is likely that Fortescue, who was to be central to subsequent negotiations, was involved. The Milanese also spoke of a French plan to enlist the help of the earl of Warwick in restoring Henry VI to the English throne should King Edward marry his sister to Charolais.[67]

Developments during the next year were to improve the prospects for a restoration of Henry VI. Despite gigantic efforts to retain the friendship of England and prevent the Burgundian marriage, by March 1468 Louis had seen Edward IV successively make alliances with Castille and Brittany and, worst of all, a commercial settlement and marriage treaty with Burgundy.[68] The last English embassy to France, however, had been headed by Warwick, who retained his preference for an alliance with that country, partly because he detested the count of Charolais. Warwick enjoyed a good personal *rapport* with Louis XI and the rumour that both would serve their purposes by taking up the cause of Lancaster began to look like a practical proposition. Jasper Tudor, titular earl of Pembroke, was given some meagre support by Louis at this time. He sailed from Honfleur to Wales with three ships and about fifty men, but his attempt to relieve the Lancastrian garrison at Harlech failed and soon afterwards they surrendered.[69] In October Margaret of Anjou seems to have travelled to Rouen to undertake some kind of expedition – pseudo-Worcester reported wild rumours that she was assembling a

they had promised, if the security would be observed. The duke in a fume said that if his nephew promised at his instance and did not keep his word, they would have to reckon with him.'

66 Ross, *Edward IV*, 118; *Letters and Papers*, ed. J. Stevenson, vol. 2, ii, 788.

67 9 May from Chartres, *CSPM*, 120.

68 Edward was also negotiating for an alliance with Aragon and signed a treaty in October 1468.

69 Scofield, *Edward IV*, vol. 1, 458–9. Jasper Tudor had received a pension from Louis from at least 1465, Paris, BnF fonds fr. 20685, f. 379.

great invasion force.[70] Calmette and Périnelle believed that this was the time when Fortescue submitted four memoirs to the French king; taken together they provided a justification for Lancaster's claim to the throne and a prescription for its restoration. A later hand wrote '1470' at the top of the contemporary abstract in French that survives in the Bibliothèque nationale de France which provides evidence of the contents of the four memoirs.[71] There is reason to believe, however, that the first two memoirs were submitted in the mid-1460s, the third and fourth after May 1468 and before June 1470.[72]

Scofield castigated Edward IV and the Woodvilles for what she believed to be the 'entirely undeserved' treatment of Sir Thomas Cook in 1468 when this wealthy London alderman and former mayor was found guilty of misprision of treason in July; according to Robert Fabyan, he suffered great losses when his properties were sequestered.[73] The evidence and conclusions to be drawn have been discussed by Anne Sutton and Michael Hicks and further light was thrown on the scandal by the assessment of the contents of BL manuscript Additional 48031A, which contains a number of political documents that came from Cook's archives. The evidence they provide leads to Warwick and Fortescue and raises the probability that, as early as 1468, the Lancastrians were in contact with apparently confirmed Yorkists such as Cook and Wenlock.[74]

In June 1468 John Cornelius, a servant of Sir Robert Whittingham, one of the Koeur exiles, was captured in Kent. He was carrying letters from his master and others to various friends in England and under torture implicated Lancastrian 'sympathisers', including a servant of lord Wenlock, John Hawkins. After his arrest it was he who accused Cook, amongst others, of treasonable contact with Margaret of Anjou.

[70] Calmette and Périnelle, *Louis XI et l'Angleterre*, 104; *Letters and Papers*, ed. Stevenson, 2, 792, *Annales*, this is now thought to be a compilation with only a few notes added by William Worcester, *ODNB*, 60, 295.

[71] Paris, BnF fonds fr. Ms 6964, f. 27. The later hand is that of the Abbé Le Grand, who was assembling material for a history of Louis XI in the early eighteenth century. There is also a contemporary copy of the abstracts, Paris, BnF fonds fr. Ms 6975, ff. 108–10, a later hand has dated it '1468'.

[72] Kekewich, 'Lancastrian Court in Exile', 103–4 and translation of the abstract in the appendix, 109–10; see below, pp. 129–33, for a more detailed discussion of the memoirs.

[73] *Great Chronicle of London*, 204–6; Scofield, *Edward IV*, vol. 1, 454–62, quotation at p. 461.

[74] A.F. Sutton, 'Sir Thomas Cook and His 'Troubles': An Investigation', *Guildhall Studies in London History*, 3 (1978) 85–108; M.A. Hicks, 'The Case of Sir Thomas Cook, 1468', *EHR*, 93 (1978) 82–96; *Vale's Book*, *passim*.

None of this directly involved Warwick, although Hawkins had implied that his master, a close ally of the earl, was a Lancastrian sympathiser. Reprisals were still being carried out against some of those identified by Cornelius and Hawkins in November, when another round of arrests was made. According to Ross these were the results of intelligence work carried out in the counties. The two most prominent victims were from families which had been patrons to the Fortescues: Henry Courtenay esquire, brother and heir to the attainted earl of Devon, and Thomas Hungerford, the son of Robert Hungerford, Lord Moleyns, who had been executed in 1464. Ross remarked on the paucity of evidence against the two men and suggested that their condemnation could have been part of a government reaction to rumours of treason.[75] Alternatively it could have been motivated by the ambition of the King's favourites: Warkworth reported a belief that Courtenay's execution was a consequence of Humphrey Stafford's desire to be earl of Devon.[76]

A survey of the contents of BL Additional manuscript 48031A does suggest that, at least in the case of Sir Thomas Cook and his associates, rather more pro-Lancastrian activity could have been taking place by 1468 than Scofield allowed. It would be surprising if any directly incriminating documents survived into the 1480s, when the collection was probably copied, since Cook's goods and papers were ransacked for such evidence when he was accused in 1468 and nothing appears to have been found.[77] Yet a group of documents in the collection is directly linked to Warwick and Fortescue.[78] Some of the Warwick papers date from the first reign of Henry VI, when he was a Yorkist partisan, and the earliest Fortescue document is the *Replicacion*, which was probably written between 1461 and 1463.[79] The latest of the Warwick documents deal with the process by which he and Clarence were alienated from Edward IV, their diplomatic accord with the Lancastrians and the Readeption. Fortescue's *Governance of England*, probably dating from 1471 to 1474, would be the last document in the sequence. These papers could have come into Cook's possession piecemeal by chance between the 1450s and his death in 1478. On the other hand, with the exception of the *Governance*, they might have formed part of a Lancastrian dossier collected by an increasingly sympathetic Cook from the 1460s to his second disgrace

[75] Ross, *Edward IV*, 122–4.

[76] John Warkworth, *A Chronicle of the First Thirteen Years of Edward the Fourth*, ed. J.O. Halliwell (London: 1839) 6.

[77] Scofield, *Edward IV*, vol. 1, 459–60.

[78] *Vale's Book*, 5, for the sympathy shown to Henry VI in the 'Short History'.

[79] See below, p. 165.

in 1471. Watts noted that York's 'broken promises to defend the common weal and broken oaths to obey' Henry VI were repeatedly highlighted and could have been intended for use by the Lancastrians.[80] The final possibility is that they formed part of Warwick's political collection and came into Cook's possession whilst he was a strongly partisan pro-Lancastrian alderman during the Readeption.[81] None of these scenarios proves that Cook was guilty of anti-Yorkist activity as early as 1468, but the fact that he retained so much pro-Lancastrian material in the 1470s is strange: 'Josselyn, an ex-Mayor, and Urswyck the Recorder ... may have had their noses put out of joint by Cook's behaviour on his restoration [in 1470] and have been convinced that he fooled them in 1468.'[82]

Whatever Cook's sympathies may have been, Fortescue was unambiguous in his support of the London alderman in his *De Laudibus Legum Anglie* and declared that Hawkins, at the point of death, rescinded his accusation against him.[83] Cook's espousal of the Lancastrian cause at the Readeption might have been caused by annoyance at the treatment he had suffered from Edward IV's government or it could have been the culmination of a longer allegiance to Lancaster, perhaps including correspondence with the exiles. The hapless Courtenay and Hungerford may also have received communications from their fellow Lancastrians in Koeur.[84] In any case, all the evidence that we possess shows both Margaret of Anjou and Fortescue to have been untiring in their constant pursuit of political support.

Architect of the Readeption

In 1469 the possibility of a Lancastrian restoration became more than a distant, impractical aspiration. The instability of the Yorkist regime was caused not so much by the machinations of the exiles as by the deterioration of relations between King Edward and the earl of Warwick and his ally, the duke of Clarence, Edward's brother. The main source of contention seems to have been the favours that the King poured on Queen Elizabeth's Woodville relatives. These inevitably diminished

80 *Vale's Book*, 35 and n. 138.

81 Fortescue could have passed some of his papers on the succession to Warwick at Angers before the earl departed for England.

82 Sutton, 'Sir Thomas Cook', 105; Hicks, 'Sir Thomas Cook', takes a similar view.

83 Chrimes, *De Laudibus*, 49.

84 The specific charge was that on 21 May 1468 and on other occasions, they conspired to assist Margaret of Anjou to invade England and seize the crown for her husband or son, Scofield, *Edward IV*, vol. 1, 481–2.

the political influence and opportunities to gain more wealth available to Warwick and his Neville relations. The situation was made more dangerous for the King by strong, local, popularly based movements of discontent in the north led by 'Robin of Redesdale' and 'Robin of Holderness'. The former drew on the support of the affinity of the earl and its manifesto contained several of the grievances that had alienated Warwick and Clarence from Edward IV.[85] In July the disaffected magnates crossed to Calais to consolidate their alliance by the marriage of Clarence to Warwick's daughter Isabel. Edward had disapproved of the proposed marriage since it would provide the 'Kingmaker' with an alternative monarch in the shape of Clarence.[86] On their return to England Edward fell into their hands after the defeat of his supporters at Edgecote.

A number of Yorkist noblemen and gentlemen were killed at Edgecote but the conflict seemed to offer no immediate advantage to the Lancastrian exiles. Yet it represented the prelude to two more drastic reversals of fortune, which, against all the odds, were to return Henry VI to the English throne by the end of 1470. Warwick held Edward in tutelage from July 1469 but found that it was impossible to destroy the King's authority without provoking an anarchic reaction. The earl never brought himself to name his son-in-law Clarence as an alternative monarch, realising, apparently, that he did not command sufficient support. By September Edward had recovered his liberty and set about redeploying lands and offices to counteract the disproportionate amount that had fallen to the Nevilles in the preceding months. The nobility had shown no inclination to back Warwick and Clarence, whose actions are characterised as being 'based on nothing more appealing than personal ambition and wounded pride'.[87] By April 1470 it was clear that if they remained in England they would have to submit to Edward IV and rather than do so they fled via Calais (where Wenlock dared not admit them) to France.

The second great reversal of fortune brought real benefits to the Lancastrian exiles, for it was to present them with the chance of recruiting a 'notable and manly ... capitayne' to fight for their cause. The earl of Warwick might seem to have been the least suitable candidate in Christendom and his son-in-law, Clarence, would be an equally unwelcome ally. Yet at some point between May 1468 and July 1470, Fortescue included such a proposal in the fourth of the memoirs concerning the restoration of Henry VI and Anglo-French political and economic

[85] *Vale's Book*, 44–5, 212–15; Hicks, *Warwick*, 270.

[86] Calmette and Périnelle, *Louis XI et l'Angleterre*, 107, 306–8.

[87] Ross, *Edward IV*, 144.

relations that were mentioned in the previous section. The unlikely alliance would be consolidated by the marriage of Warwick's daughter Anne to Edward of Lancaster.[88] The abstract of these memoirs was written in a contemporary hand but the best piece of internal evidence for assigning a date is the reference in the third memoir to the recent parliament in which Edward had promised to invade France in person. This alluded to a speech by the Chancellor, Robert Stillington, bishop of Bath and Wells, delivered on 17 May 1468.[89] The various aspects of the settlement proposed in the document were, in part, agreed at the meeting at Angers between Margaret of Anjou, accompanied by her son and Fortescue, Louis XI and Warwick in late July 1470, so it must have been written before that time. The predicament of Warwick and his friends which was described in the fourth memoir seems to locate it in the period between their flight from England in April 1470 and the meeting at Angers. Fortescue referred to Edward of Lancaster's marriage to 'the' daughter of Warwick in article 1 of the last memoir in the collection. Had he been writing before the other daughter, Isabel Neville, wed Clarence in July 1469, he would surely have used the indefinite article. The underlying assumption of the memoir was that Warwick and his allies were in an unstable and insecure situation and this would not have been known on the Continent until the spring of 1470.

It is suggested below that the first large memoir, 'which states the rights which king Edward claims to have to the English crown and also to the French crown', was in fact both parts of a treatise which survives, the *De Natura Legis Naturae*.[90] The arguments in support of this suggestion will not be rehearsed here, but they include the hypothesis that a preamble or epilogue, tying the treatise specifically to the current situation, would have been attached to the treatise when it was offered to the French king. The second memoir explained briefly the consequences of the conclusions of the first memoir and went on to suggest the means by which a perpetual peace might be made between Henry VI and the king of France. King Edward, who was incapable of establishing a stable peace between England and France, would be satisfied whether he wished it or not.

[88] A. Gross, *The Dissolution of the Lancastrian Kingship: Sir John Fortescue and the Crisis of Monarchy in Fifteenth-Century England* (Stamford: 1996) 75–81.

[89] *RP*, vol. 5, 622–3; *PROME*, vol. 13, 362–4.

[90] See below, Chapter 4, p. 186. Craig Taylor believes that it was a more extended version of some of Fortescue's other tracts on the succession rather than the *De Natura Legis Naturae*, and that it has not survived, 'War, Propaganda and Diplomacy', 83.

The *De Natura* is not the kind of treatise which could be dashed off in a few weeks and is likely to have been composed during the early years of Fortescue's sojourn at Koeur rather than in Scotland. In the second memoir he had found it necessary to suggest a means of placating Edward IV and apparently (although we are reliant on what the abstract tells us) made no reference to any role that Warwick might play in such an accommodation. Edward did not acquire a male heir until November 1470. If Fortescue wrote the memoir in the mid-1460s, a reverse of the settlement imposed on Henry VI by the duke of York in 1460 might have been envisaged. Edward IV could rule on behalf of the ineffectual King Henry for the remainder of his life, but Edward of Lancaster would be proclaimed as his heir. Conversely the plan could have been to recognise the Yorkists as heirs to the throne if the Lancastrian male line failed. In either case a marriage between Prince Edward and one of King Edward's daughters could have smoothed the way to reconciliation. Between 1464 and 1468 such compromises may have seemed the best sort of deals that the Lancastrians could realistically have hoped for. These two memoirs seem not to have been taken seriously by the French government at a time when it was concentrating on reaching a stable settlement with Edward IV, who was also likely to have treated such proposals with scorn.

The third memoir commenced with a useful phrase for dating the last two items: 'Subsequently he has provided another quite brief memoir', implying that the last two items were submitted at a later date than the first two. Edward IV was characterised as a warmonger who could be ejected in favour of Henry VI at minimum expense to France. There were also secret matters that Fortescue did not wish to trust to writing – these he would convey in person to the King or to his deputies. These matters probably concerned the finer points of the diplomatic exchanges which culminated in the agreement at Angers. They might have touched on the difficulty that Fortescue was experiencing in persuading Queen Margaret that she should marry her son to Anne Neville, Warwick's daughter. They could also have included the delicate subject of the transfer of Calais to French sovereignty.

The fourth memoir was described in some detail in the abstract. It occupies the whole of the second page of the document, presumably because its contents were of immediate and practical interest to the French government. The first article dealt with the envisaged accommodation between Margaret of Anjou, her son and the earl of Warwick (it was evidently not politic to mention Clarence by name). The second suggested that means could be found to satisfy Edward IV and achieve a permanent peace between France and England. The third proposed that the English wool Staple could be established in France, in Rouen, Calais (assumed to be French by then) or elsewhere, to the great profit of both countries. The fourth suggested that English merchants in Bordeaux and Bayonne should enjoy similar privileges to those allowed to the Hanse in London. The fifth proposed that if Louis incurred any expenses as a result of Fortescue's plans, he could indemnify himself from the proceeds of the case currently being pursued by Richard Heron in the *parlement* of Paris, provided that Louis was favourable to him.[91] Fortescue's sixth article was a plea that the matters he had divulged should be kept secret in case the enemies of Lancaster used them to their advantage.

The existence of the abstracts implies that, by early 1470, Louis and his chancellor were prepared to take Fortescue's proposals very seriously and needed an *aide memoire* to summarise his compendious prose. This was especially true of the fourth memoir, which contained the terms for an agreement between the Lancastrian and Valois monarchies. Louis XI could be counted on to welcome a *rapprochement* between the former and Warwick, with whom he enjoyed a good relationship. Fortescue doubtless hoped that Edward IV would be eliminated in the course of a Lancastrian restoration but, since he had proved to be a very resilient prince, it was prudent to insert the second article implying that he could be placated. The third article explained Fortescue's anxiety to keep the proposals secret for it seemed to suggest that Calais might be surrendered to France. He did, however, offer a positive advantage to English merchants: had his proposals for the wool Staple and privileged access to Bordeaux and Bayonne been entertained, a small common market might, in essence, have been established over 500 years ago. On the other hand, such a policy was contrary to the sentiments which had been expressed in the *Commodites of England*: in practice, no action was taken in relation to Fortescue's proposals for liberal commercial agreements between England and France.[92]

[91] Chrimes, *De Laudibus*, 132–3 and note, 207–10. Heron was a merchant of the Staple who was suing three Calais merchants for £24,000 in the *parlement* of Paris, claiming that they had confiscated his valuable stock of wool. An alternative account stated that it belonged to the earl of Wiltshire, a Lancastrian, so it had been seized by the staunchly Yorkist merchants of Calais. The case continued for over twenty years, foundering on the problem of whether the *parlement* had jurisdiction over English merchants in Calais. Heron eventually died in penury in sanctuary in Westminster. Chrimes observed: 'It is not easy to see exactly what Fortescue contemplated in this suggestion, but it hardly seems to bode Heron much good', 210.

[92] Hicks, *Warwick*, 296.

An obvious question to ask about the fourth memoir is how far it enjoyed the approval of Margaret of Anjou. Nothing is certain, but it is inconceivable that Fortescue would have contemplated making an agreement with Warwick and Clarence without the Queen's consent. He felt that such an agreement could only be cemented by the marriage to Anne Neville, but Margaret probably regarded such a union as her trump card in the attempt to attach Warwick to the Lancastrian cause, one she hoped that she would not be obliged to play. Equally unwelcome to her was the proposal that Prince Edward should accompany Warwick on his invasion of England.[93]

The anonymous *Manner and guiding between the queen Margaret and her son and the earl of Warwick* and reports from the Milanese ambassador in France indicate that although by the summer of 1470 the Queen would contemplate an alliance with Warwick, she still hoped to withhold the ultimate concession of her son's marriage.[94] Louis seems to have been pessimistic about the outcome of the negotiations: in a letter dated 22 June he urged Jean Bourré, maître des comptes, to persuade Warwick to return to England as soon as possible. The King feared that his presence in France would compromise his chances of remaining at peace with Burgundy. In a letter dated the following day he urged the king of Castille to give no support to his enemy 'Edouard de la Marche' and stated that he had signed treaties for thirty years with his dear cousins the King and Queen of England.[95] No mention was made of Warwick, an indication that diplomacy might have persuaded Margaret to make the ultimate concession between 25 June and 3 July. On the latter day, Louis wrote to Bourré again, saying that Warwick would delay his departure until after he had met Queen Margaret 'ou ilz auront tost fait ou failli'.[96] When she arrived at Amboise on 25 June she was 'very hard and difficult' about the prospect of an alliance with Warwick according to the Milanese ambassador. The marriage was not mentioned in this

[93] *CSPM*, no.184, 136. On 17 May 1470 the Milanese ambassador mentioned the possibility that Prince Edward would accompany Warwick.

[94] *Vale's Book*, 47–8, 215–18.

[95] *Lettres de Louis XI, roi de France*, ed. J. Vaesen and E. Charavay, 11 vols (Paris: 1883–1909) vol. 4, nos 507–8, 511; Paris, BnF fonds fr. 6602, f. 1, 123–5, BnF fonds fr. 6977, f. 170. Hicks, *Warwick*, 289–91, observed how Warwick used the presence of his piratical fleet in French waters to blackmail Louis XI into giving him assistance.

[96] *Lettres de Louis XI*, 4, no. 511, 128–9, Paris, BnF fonds fr. 6602, f. 4, 'when they will either agree or fail'.

report but he said that she distrusted the earl and was unwilling to allow him to accompany her son to England.[97]

Queen Margaret's reluctance to make a settlement with Warwick seems to have been part of an elaborate charade that she had concocted to extract the best possible terms from the earl and Louis XI.[98] Advised by Fortescue, she had learnt painfully over the past years how to negotiate from a weak position and make the most of her circumstances. The letters to Ormonde in 1464 were an example of this, as were her attempts to broker a peace between the factions in the League of the Common Weal.[99] The idea of a deal with Warwick and the marriage of his daughter to Edward of Lancaster seems to have come from her brother John of Calabria and from Fortescue's memoir in the first place. Hicks believed that the *Manner and guiding* was composed for Warwick to show him in a good light to his supporters in England and he attributed the whole scheme for a reconciliation to the earl. But it twice mentioned the intervention of 'the servants of the king of Sicily' (René of Anjou) to promote a settlement and it is probable that it had been discussed by Margaret and her family in the late 1460s when Warwick's increasing alienation from Edward IV became known. Tony Pollard agreed with the authors of the edition of *Vale's Book* that the tough stand attributed to the Queen implies that the *Manner and guiding* was aimed at a Lancastrian audience.[100]

Margaret kept Warwick on his knees begging her pardon for fifteen minutes on 22 July in the cathedral of St Maurice at Angers, but their alliance was a foregone conclusion and Colin Richmond identifies the theatrical element that pervaded the proceedings.[101] To counter the proposal that her son should marry Anne Neville she claimed that Edward IV had offered his eldest daughter as a bride for the Prince. This could simply have been a mendacious piece of bluster but Fortescue had mentioned the possibility of an accommodation with Edward IV, who still lacked a son, in his fourth memoir and this could reflect some tentative dealings between the King and Lancaster.[102] Eventually,

[97] *CSPM*, no. 189, 139–40.

[98] Gross, *Dissolution of the Lancastrian Kingship*, 81.

[99] See above, p. 124.

[100] Pollard, *Warwick*, 69, n. 29.

[101] *Vale's Book*, 47–8.

[102] This possibility is discussed in M.L. Kekewich, 'The Mysterious Dr Makerell: His General Pardon of 27 November 1469', *Much Heaving and Shoving: Late-Medieval Gentry and their Concerns. Essays for Colin Richmond*, ed. M. Aston and R. Horrox (Lavenham: 2005) 45–54.

after persuasion by Louis XI, the counsellors of René of Anjou and, no doubt, Fortescue, who was not mentioned amongst the *dramatis personae*, the Queen assented to the marriage between Prince Edward and Anne Neville and they were betrothed on 25 July.[103] Margaret did manage to substitute Jasper Tudor for her son as the leading Lancastrian who would accompany the invasion of England. The agreement was promulgated with great solemnity in the cathedral at Angers in late July, when Warwick swore on the true cross that in the future he would faithfully serve Henry VI. Louis and his brother, Charles, duke of Guyenne, promised to support Warwick[104] and the Queen undertook to treat Warwick as a faithful follower, 'And for the deedis passed nevur here aftir to make hym reproche.'[105] Warwick would rule England after he first conquered it, Clarence would have the lands he held when he left England, the duchy of York and 'many other'. Anne Neville should remain with Margaret of Anjou and the marriage would not be consummated until her father had conquered all or most of England. The military and financial aid that Louis would grant the expedition was also agreed.[106]

The *Records of the Papal Penitentiary* contain two entries for 17 August 1470. The first requested permission for Anne Neville and Prince Edward to marry even though they were related in the fourth degree of consanguinity. The following entry stated that they had married and begged for absolution and a dispensation to remain married with legitimation of any issue: both requests were granted. Since there is good evidence, cited below, that the pair were married on 28 November, when the union was presumably consummated, it is probably the ceremony of betrothal on 25 July that was referred to in the second papal document. It also stated that the marriage had been consummated, but this seems to have been a formula employed in many of the supplications and it is unlikely that Queen Margaret would have allowed that to happen as early as mid-August, before Warwick had fulfilled his part of the agreement.[107]

[103] Calmette and Périnelle, *Louis XI et l'Angleterre*, 112–14.

[104] Scofield, *Edward IV*, vol. 1, 529–31.

[105] *Vale's Book*, 217.

[106] J.de Wauvrin, *Anchiennes Chroniques d'Angleterre*, ed. Dupont, 3 vols (Paris: 1858–63) vol. 3, 198.

[107] *Supplications from England and Wales in the Registers of the Apostolic Penitentiary, 1410–1503*, ed. P.D. Clarke and P.N.R. Zutschi, Canterbury and York Society, 3 vols (Woodbridge: 2013/14), vol. 2, 1464–92, 23, nos. 1336, 1337. Anne was described as the 'wife' of Prince Edward in the French accounts for their

The agreement at Angers marked the culmination of nine years of diplomatic and military manoeuvres by Margaret of Anjou and her supporters to recover the English crown. It was extraordinary in seeing the reversal of long-held political allegiances, an unlikely marriage contract and the provision of aid by the parsimonious Louis XI on an unprecedented scale. Hicks saw Warwick as the prime mover in the negotiations, and contemporary sources such as the Milanese ambassador and Thomas Basin did not mention Fortescue.[108] Yet his memoirs to the French king did ask for secrecy to be observed and Fortescue's statesmanship, supported by the Queen's Angevin family, must be accorded considerable credit.[109] Until their flight from England Warwick saw his way to renewed power through Clarence. Realising that he had made a poor choice in an alliance that was not welcomed by the English, he would have been receptive to the contents of Fortescue's memoirs, which Louis XI could have shown him at their secret meeting in May 1470.[110] During the next months the policy succeeded better than even the most sanguine supporters of Lancaster and Warwick could have hoped.

Warwick, Clarence, Pembroke and Oxford landed in the West of England in September 1470 and proclaimed their allegiance to Henry VI. Supporters flocked to them and they did not need to fight as Edward IV found himself with a small following in Lincolnshire, menaced by Warwick's brother (the marquis of Montague, who had just changed sides), so he prudently took ship for the Low Countries, hoping for support from his brother-in-law, Charles of Burgundy. This was by no means guaranteed, but the insistence by Louis that Warwick and the Lancastrians, once they had conquered England, should immediately wage war on Burgundy changed its ruler's view of where his interest lay and was to secure help for King Edward. Warwick entered London amidst encouraging signs of popularity, removed a somewhat bedraggled Henry VI from the Tower and set up a government in his name. Parliament was called, although since the records do not survive we cannot

maintenance, September to December, 1470, Calmette and Périnelle, *Louis XI et l'Angleterre*, 125, n. 4, BnF fonds fr. 20685, f. 500b.

[108] Thomas Basin, *Histoire des règnes de Charles VII et de Louis XI*, 4 vols (Paris: 1859) vol. 2, 222–3. He disliked Warwick, describing the earl as, 'ille proditionis artifex' and 'perfidus'.

[109] Kekewich, *The Good King*, 223–6. King René arrived in Tours from Provence, where he normally lived in his old age, on 15 September 1470. He remained in the Loire valley for a year until, presumably, he realised that the Lancastrian cause was hopeless.

[110] Hicks, *Warwick*, 292.

know what, if any, justifications for the re-establishment of Henry VI on the throne were aired.[111] Louis sent him a warm message of support by means of a prestigious embassy that arrived in January 1471. This set in motion a process which was to join England and France in treaties of close alliance and commercial co-operation in the following month.[112]

In the meantime, Margaret of Anjou, her son, Fortescue and most of the Lancastrians who had not accompanied Warwick's expedition were maintained by Louis XI, first at Tours and later at Amboise. On 26 October they paid the price for this luxury: Prince Edward swore that he would support France in a war against Burgundy. There was a remarkable lapse in normal English diplomatic usage: Louis was described as 'king of France'. This was the logical conclusion to the argument that Fortescue had presented in his *De Natura Legis Naturae* concerning the inability of women to pass on the right of succession, but it also symbolised the desperation of the exiles, led by their French Queen, that moved them to dispose of English conquests and claims. By the late autumn it was established that Warwick had carried out the provisions of the agreement of Angers: Edward of Lancaster married Anne Neville at Amboise on 28 November 1470 and on the same day the Prince signed a formal treaty with the French king.[113]

Louis showed his approval of the conquest of England by staging a magnificent reception for the young couple in Paris. Nobly accompanied, they were welcomed by its bishop, members of the university and the provost, their *cortège* passing through streets decorated with tapestries and other hangings. At Christmas Queen Margaret and members of her entourage received gifts of money from the King: Fortescue was given one mark less than the Queen's lady of honour, '49 marcs donnez au Chancellier d'Angleterre, 50 marcs a la Dame d'honneur de la Royne d'Angleterre'.[114] He was still described as 'chancellor' in the royal accounts, although by then it must have been widely known that in England Warwick had reinstated his brother, George Neville, archbishop of York, in that office. The news must have been a disappointment for

[111] M. Hicks, *False, Fleeting Perjur'd Clarence: George, Duke of Clarence 1449–1478* (Gloucester: 1980) 85–7; L. Brown, 'Continuity and Change in the Parliamentary Justifications of the Fifteenth Century Usurpations', *The Fifteenth Century VII: Conflicts, Consequences and the Crown in the Late Middle Ages*, ed. L. Clark (Woodbridge: 2007) 157–73

[112] Scofield, *Edward IV*, 1, 555.

[113] Calmette and Périnelle, *Louis XI et l'Angleterre*, 125–6; BnF Mss fonds fr. 20936, no. 139, 3887, f. 113a–b, an early copy of the treaty; again Louis was described as 'Roy de France'.

[114] BnF fonds fr. 20685, p. 523.

Fortescue but, always the realist, he left no evidence of pique, except possibly in a passage cited below in the *Articles Sent by Edward, Prince of Wales, to the earl Warwick*.

The name of Edward of Lancaster is attached to *The Articles Sent to Warwick*, but they were certainly drafted by Fortescue since they closely resemble parts of his *Governance of England*.[115] They seem to have been written between October 1470 and the end of the year as they addressed some of the problems faced by the new Readeption government. They stressed the need to curb the notorious generosity of Henry VI through the means of a strong council, not dominated by great magnates, and to keep only a small, inexpensive household for the first year of his reign.[116] The underlying anxiety, felt not only by Fortescue but presumably also by the Queen and her son, was that the victorious Warwick would dispense a disproportionate amount of lands and offices to himself and his followers and thus risk alienating Lancastrian support. Fortescue was particularly sharp in suggesting the fate of a chancellor, 'whiche shall fortune tenseale any patente contraye hereto, leese his office and forfaite to the king all his liveloode temporell'.[117]

Warwick received a great deal of good advice, both from Louis XI via his ambassadors and from Fortescue in the *Articles*, but what he most urgently needed to secure the Readeption was money, land and offices. He had very little of these with which he could reward his followers or dispossessed Lancastrians. He could not afford to alienate the Yorkist magnates who had tacitly consented to his coup by appropriating the riches they had enjoyed for the last decade.[118] Pollard believes that he could have returned to England 'armed with Fortescue's remedies', willing to carry out his reforms as they converged with his own ideas, most recently expressed in his proclamation 'for the reformacion ... for the commone wele' that he issued after landing in England.[119] Warwick's commitment to support Louis in a war against Burgundy, however, presented him with a dilemma: it would be unpopular, harming England commercially and financed by extra taxation and this was not a climate in which he could realistically undertake administrative reforms. When the treaties with France were signed in February 1471 the English parliament insisted on modifying the terms and, particularly,

[115] *Vale's Book*, 224.

[116] See below, Chapter 5, pp. 216–20, for a more extensive discussion of the political ideas in this document.

[117] *Vale's Book*, 224.

[118] Ross, *Edward IV*, 155–7; Hicks, *Warwick*, 300–7.

[119] Pollard, *Warwick*, 197; *Vale's Book*, 220.

on withholding the recognition that Louis XI was king of France. One of the treaties established intercourse of merchandise between England and France but it was not couched in the liberal terms that Fortescue had envisaged.[120]

Louis's great diplomatic achievement, which had cost him so much money and effort, was threatened in March, when, with Burgundian support, Edward IV landed in the north of England. It was destroyed in April, on Easter Sunday, when Edward defeated Warwick at Barnet and the earl and his brother Montague were killed during the battle. Clarence had already deserted them and rejoined Edward, so the three military leaders who had made the Readeption possible were no longer available to the Lancastrians. Henry VI passed back into the custody of King Edward.

Margaret of Anjou and her party might have been feted with royal honours over Christmas, but in January they had moved to Dieppe in preparation for the crossing to England. Warwick expected their arrival: in February he had sent Sir John Langstrother, prior of St John's, and others to Dover in the name of King Henry, 'for the fetching of our right dear and most entirely beloved wife, the queen and the prince our son'. A few days later Warwick went to Dover to receive her but had to return empty-handed.[121] Griffiths blamed Louis for delaying Margaret's departure until he had received word that England was committed to war with Burgundy.[122] He was given a misleadingly optimistic account by his ambassadors on their return and sent permission for the Lancastrians to embark at Honfleur on 24 March 1471. Bad weather kept them in port for several more weeks and they only arrived at Weymouth on 14 April, the day of Edward's victory at Barnet.

Clermont stated that, on hearing the bad news, Fortescue advised an immediate return to France.[123] The Queen, however, was persuaded by the martially minded but militarily incompetent titular earl of Devon and titular duke of Somerset that Lancaster could still win without any other support and indeed many followers from the West were rallying to her army. She proceeded with caution, making feints in the direction

[120] Calmette and Périnelle, *Louis XI et l'Angleterre*, 128–33, Wauvrin, *Anchiennes Chroniques*, vol. 3, 58.

[121] Scofield, *Edward IV*, vol. 1, 563–4.

[122] Griffiths, *Henry VI*, 891.

[123] Clermont, *Works*, 37. He cited Rapin for this information, but in Rapin de Thoyras, *History of England* (London: 1751) 75, it was the Queen who proposed that Prince Edward should be sent back to the safety of France; Fortescue was not mentioned.

of Salisbury and Reading, whilst apparently intending to fall back to the comparative safety of Wales, where Jasper Tudor was ensconced. Edward IV managed, nevertheless, to catch up with her small army at Tewkesbury and forced her to a battle on 4 May 1471.

The Lancastrians were outnumbered but, had they remained in their defensive positions, they might have survived the day.[124] Somerset's advance downhill again showed the defective generalship which had been the bane of the Lancastrians since the 1440s. His troops were attacked from the side as well as the front, so they fled, leaving the centre, commanded by the inexperienced Prince, to take the full force of the Yorkist attack. He seems to have been killed in the subsequent rout, although Tudor propaganda credited him with brave words before he was killed in cold blood in the presence of Edward IV after the battle.[125] The Lancastrian left was also defeated and Devon and Wenlock were killed. Other casualties were Fortescue's fellow exiles Sir Robert Whittingham and Sir Edmund Hampden. Fortescue, who was unlikely to have engaged in active combat, was spared, along with his fellow lawyers Makerell and Morton.

Clermont believed that King Edward might have pitied Fortescue's age or that his appetite for slaughter had been satisfied, but this does not explain why warriors like Sir Henry Roos and Thomas Ormonde were also spared.[126] Ross made the credible suggestion that Edward respected those who had remained consistently loyal to Henry VI: severe punishment was reserved for those who like Somerset, Langstrother and Sir Gervase Clifton had broken oaths of allegiance to the house of York.[127] Another explanation for the survival of men like Fortescue and Ormonde could be that other members of their families were loyal Yorkists and the King did not wish to alienate them. A recently discovered reference, discussed below, indicates that Fortescue, either before Tewkesbury or at the time of his capture, might have managed to establish his potential usefulness to the house of York. Margaret of Anjou, the countess of Warwick, and her newly widowed daughter, Anne Neville,

124 Ross, *Edward IV*, 171.

125 Scofield, *Edward IV*, vol. 1, 586–7; R. Fabyan, *The New Chronicles of England and France*, ed. H. Ellis (London: 1811) 662; E. Hall, *Chronicle Containing the History of England during the Reign of Henry IV and Succeeding Monarchs to the End of the Reign of Henry VIII*, ed. H. Ellis (London: 1809) 301.

126 Clermont, *Works*, 38; Warkworth, *Chronicle*, 19.

127 Ross, *Edward IV*, 172–3.

were taken into custody.[128] On the night of Edward's return to London Henry VI died in the Tower, almost certainly murdered by order of the King. If Fortescue went to prison at all, his confinement does not seem to have been harsh or of long duration.

The Elder Statesman

We do not know where Sir John Fortescue was during or after the battle of Tewkesbury on 4 May 1471. He might have accompanied Margaret of Anjou and the other noble women to the 'powre religiows place' where they were captured by the Yorkists, but, if he did, the author of *The Historie of the Arrivall of Edward IV in England* did not think it worth mentioning.[129] An extract from a chronicle of Tewkesbury recorded his capture and implied that he and the other Lancastrian lawyers were with Queen Margaret: 'Thes wer ther taken and presentyd to ye kynge, and pardonyd: ladye Margaret, qwene, ladye Anne, princes, ser John Foskew, chefe Judge of yngland, doctor Makerell, John Throomorton, Mastar Beynton, Mastar Wroghton; all pardonyd.'[130] The preceding list of those killed in the battle was unusually full, which suggests that the anonymous author was in a good position to report what had happened.

A doubt about whether Fortescue was imprisoned after the battle was expressed above. No evidence, beyond the fact that he and some other prominent Lancastrians were spared, has been found about how he spent the months before he was granted a general pardon on 13 October 1471.[131] Clermont filled out the information vacuum with uncharacteristically woolly speculation, based on Campbell, suggesting that once he had refuted his anti-Yorkist polemical works Fortescue retired to spend his remaining years quietly in Gloucestershire.[132] Ebrington would not have been available to him early in the decade, for although

[128] Margaret remained in prison until 1476, when she was ransomed by Louis XI. She lived in impecunious retirement in France until her death in 1482, Kekewich, *The Good King*, 236–7.

[129] *Historie of the Arrivall of Edward IV in England*, ed. J. Bruce (London: 1838) 31, 38; P.W. Hammond, *The Battles of Barnet and Tewkesbury* (Gloucester: 1993) 93–102.

[130] C.L. Kingsford, *English Historical Literature in the Fifteenth Century* (Oxford: 1913) 378.

[131] *CPR*, 1467–77, 296, 'General pardon to John Fortescu, knight, of all offences committed by him before 9 July last.' This should be distinguished from the special pardon that the King granted Fortescue and his fellows immediately after the battle of Tewkesbury and from the later lifting of his attainder.

[132] Clermont, *Works*, 44; Campbell, i, 417.

Sir John Burgh died seized of it on 1 June 1471, Dame Jocosa the tenant presumably remained there until her death.[133] Burgh's death may well have eased the transfer of the reversion back to Fortescue. His attainder was lifted by parliament on 6 October 1473.[134] The final transfer of the property to him in 1474 is discussed below and where he lived until then is unknown.

An entry in the Tellers' Rolls for Easter 1472 in the National Archives shows how quickly Fortescue was welcomed into royal favour and was receiving rewards for his services:

> To John Fortescue, knight, for his attendance on the Lord Treasurer of England [Henry, viscount Bourgchier] for various matters in the interest of the king, sent to him from the Treasurer by his own hand, 40s.[135]

The 'various matters' could refer to Fortescue's writings and his membership of the royal council, which he already enjoyed before he refuted his previous arguments on the succession in his *Declaration upon Certain Writings Late Sent Out of Scotland.*[136] Yet Easter 1472 was early for the Exchequer to be making a payment to a former Lancastrian. If Margaret of Anjou is to be believed, her circle had been in contact with Edward IV with a view to some form of accommodation, and Fortescue and probably Makerell, who was also pardoned, would have been involved. The presence of John Fortescue, an esquire of the royal chamber, Sir John's nephew, at court could have oiled the wheels of secret diplomacy.[137] Sir John had hinted at such a possibility in his memoirs

[133] R. Atkyns, *The Ancient and Present State of Gloucestershire* (London: 1712; repr. in 1974 with an Introduction by B.S. Smith) 425. Burgh was lieutenant to Lord Scales, holding Cherbourg for him in 1443, Griffiths, *Henry VI*, 463, 478; he was a supporter of Edward IV by 1463, when he was appointed sheriff of Salop, *CFR* 1461–71, 122; on March 26 1470 he was sent a commission of array for the defence of the area against Warwick and Clarence. After his death on 1 June 1471, John Leighton esq. held the custody of his lands and property in Wales, Salop, Gloucestershire, Worcestershire and Warwickshire (probably including the reversion of Ebrington) from 22 December 1471, which were in the King's hands on the grounds of the minority of at least one of his daughters who was married to Leighton's son Thomas, *CPR* 1467–77, 219; *CIPM*, C 140/39/61.

[134] *RP*, vol. 6, 69; *PROME*, vol. 14, 140–1.

[135] TNA, E 405 53 Pasch. 1471/2.

[136] See Appendix 2 for a transcript.

[137] In 1475/6 John Fortescue, Esquire of the Body of the King, was admitted to Lincoln's Inn. He was pardoned attendance on all vacations and admitted to repasts for which he gave a quarter of a tun of wine, *Black Books*, vol. 1, 60.

13 King Edward IV, Queen Elizabeth Woodville, Prince Edward, the scribe Haywarde and Anthony Woodville, Lord Rivers presenting his English translation of *The Dicts of the Philosophers*, 1477.

that were presented to Louis XI between 1468 and 1470.[138] By their nature such tentative negotiations would have been secretive but they would explain Fortescue's rapid admission to the Yorkist royal council. His pivotal and successful role in arranging the Readeption would have made him an attractive councillor to Edward IV.

Anthony Gross has raised the possibility that Fortescue had a hand in an anonymous address to parliament in 1474 which was probably delivered by the Chancellor, Thomas Rotherham, bishop of Lincoln. It undertook the difficult task of persuading the Commons to grant a large subsidy to support a war with France only five years after the King had

[138] Kekewich, 'Makerell'.

frittered away a previous subsidy given for the same purpose.[139] The speech contained features that do link it in spirit to the francophobia to be found in passages of Fortescue's *Governance of England*, which was probably given its final form at about the same time.[140] Some of the commercial considerations echo sentiments from the *Commodites of England* and the references to Scipio's wars against Carthage recall Fortescue's use of history to make a political point. As was probably the case with the Lancastrian *Somnium Vigilantis*, it could have been composed by a committee and included recollections of the foreign policy issues raised in the period between the truce of Arras (1435) and the surrender of Maine (1447).[141] If Fortescue did have a hand in writing the speech it would have emanated from the royal council and provided proof of his usefulness to his new master in making the case for war against the duplicitous Louis XI and re-establishing England as a major power in Western Europe.

It was difficult for Edward IV to assemble and motivate an effective fighting force even when operating from strength after his victory over Lancaster. Parliament was wary of granting him subsidies which it knew from experience might be diverted away from their original purpose. They hedged their grants round with stringent conditions and arranged that expenditure would be supervised. Although he did manage to raise adequate finance between 1472 and 1475, Edward realised that much of it would not materialise unless he showed a serious intention to organise a campaign. It might be reassuring that he could count a number of European princes as his supporters, but in practice only the dukes of Brittany and Burgundy were likely to give him any armed assistance. During this difficult period propaganda in favour of the war would have helped considerably in strengthening the resolve of Edward's subjects. If the assumptions made by Gross about the speech to parliament in 1472 and those made below about the *Declaration upon Certain Writings* and

[139] Gross, *Dissolution of the Lancastrian Kingship*, 91–101; *Literae Cantuarienses: The Letter Books of the Monastery of Christ Church Canterbury*, ed. J.B. Sheppard, 3 vols (London: 1887–9) vol. 3, xv–xviii, 274–85.

[140] In this respect I part company with Anthony Gross, who sees the *Governance* as preoccupied with 'peacetime costs and arrangements', *Dissolution of the Lancastrian Kingship*, 102; this reflects a fundamental difference in our approach to dating it. He believes that it existed in more or less its present form by 1460. Whilst agreeing that it incorporates working papers from Fortescue's service to the Lancastrian regime, I maintain that the present structure, anticipated in his *Articles sent to Warwick*, was produced during the early period of the Yorkist restoration.

[141] Gross, *Dissolution of the Lancastrian Kingship*, 95.

the *Governance* are correct, Fortescue may have rendered such services to his new master on no fewer than three occasions between 1471 and 1475.

A number of references have already been made to the *Declaration*; indeed, it is one of the most revealing documents about Fortescue's life, times and capacities to have survived. What was the nature of the service that he was rendering to Edward IV by composing it?[142] Fortescue designed his recantation in the form of a dialogue in English with a 'lerned man' who took him to task for his previous propaganda against the Yorkist claim to the throne. The dynasty had been damaged by his allegations and a detailed refutation of some of the arguments was now required. There were several advantages to this format: Fortescue could pick and choose the parts of his earlier writings that he wished to deny, he could give vent to his feelings at being put in such a position and he could cope with his task by little displays of gentle humour. The details of his refutation will be discussed below in Chapter 4 but the general point to make here is that he reversed his previous position on Edward's claim to the French throne. The works that he wrote in Scotland and France did not just impugn the Yorkist claim to the English throne, they also undermined the Plantagenet claim to the French throne by denying that women could pass on a right to inherit. Edward's invasion of France in 1475 was to be based on that, so a refutation by a senior polemicist such as Fortescue provided an excellent preamble to the campaign.

Was the *Declaration* really going to sway opinion in the same way that Fortescue claimed his original, Lancastrian pamphlets had influenced it against the Yorkist succession? The difficulty he professed to the 'lerned man' (who might have represented his own conscience) in denying some of his former opinions and the way in which he designed the work enabled him to share his anguish at appearing to be a time-server with his readers. His membership of the royal council signals that, even at his advanced age, he was unwilling to relinquish public affairs. Whilst he was Chief Justice he had never enjoyed the power and influence wielded by great noblemen. His ten years of exile had been spent soliciting the support of unwilling European princes until the brief burst of Lancastrian glory from July 1470 to April 1471. During the 1470s his closest friend at court was probably his nephew, who was only an esquire of the bedchamber. In these unpromising circumstances Fortescue's best chance of remaining useful to the King was by his pen: its effectiveness when employed on behalf of Lancaster had been recognised.

[142] BL MS Royal 17 D xv, ff. 311b–326b; Appendix 2.

The importance of the *Declaration* to the process of lifting Fortescue's attainder was spelt out in his petition in October 1473:

> Consideryng Soverayn Lord, that your seid Suppliant lovith so, and tendrith the good of your moost noble astate, that he late by large and clere writyng delyvered unto your Highnes, hath so declared all the maters which were writen in Scotlond and elles where,[143] agen youre right or title, which wrytnges have in eny wise comen unto his knowelege, or that he at eny tyme hath be pryve unto theym; and also hath so clerely disproved all the arguments that hath be made agen the same right and title, that nowe there remayneth no colour or matere of argument to the hurt or infamye of the same right and title, by reason of any such writing, but the same right and title stonden nowe the more clere and open, by that any such writynges have been made agen hem.[144]

The last sentiment may imply that Fortescue did not believe that the Yorkist propagandists had done much of a job in promoting the original claim and that he had rectified their omission. They tended to produce genealogies, some of which included the 'British History' generated by Geoffrey of Monmouth and perpetuated by prophecies. Most were devoid of any argument other than short historical commentaries. The prophecies sometimes appeared separately from the genealogies and were couched in arcane terms that appealed to sentiment and superstition rather than reasoned discourse. A. Allen concluded, however, that although they did not enjoy a wide circulation, they were influential as they appealed to the most powerful sections of society.[145] Fortescue's *Declaration* also made an impact on contemporaries and later generations, for the survival of ten copies (including the one in BL Cotton MS Otho B i which was burnt in the eighteenth century) is an indication of a fairly wide readership.

The record of Sir John Fortescue's attendance at a session of the royal council on 26 November 1474 shows that he remained politically active for at least a year after the reversal of his attainder.[146] He had probably also been occupied since Tewkesbury in preparing the final draft of his advice concerning the future government of the realm, the *Governance*

[143] Another indication that the *De Natura Legis Naturae* was written in Koeur-in-Bar.

[144] *RP*, vol. 6, 69; *PROME*, vol. 14, 141.

[145] A. Allen, 'Yorkist Propaganda: Pedigree, Prophecy and the British History in the Reign of Edward IV', *Patronage, Pedigree and Power in Later Medieval England*, ed. C.D. Ross (Gloucester: 1979) 171–92.

[146] Chrimes, *De Laudibus*, lxvii and n. 7; Scofield, *Edward IV*, vol. 2, 22, n. 1; Signet Rolls, file 1508, no.4671.

of England.[147] Little is known or can be inferred about the remainder of his life. Martin Fortescue died in November 1472: surely the loss of his only son would have been a considerable blow especially as Isabella, Sir John's wife, was already dead.[148] Elizabeth, Martin's widow, kept the manor of Combe by survivorship and took Sir Richard Pomeroy as her second husband. Combe eventually passed to Sir John's grandson John and great grandson George.[149] Fortescue must have been in London a great deal during the early 1470s, engaged in family and political business; he might have stayed at Bosammes Inn, which was still owned by his nephew John in 1487.[150] The property that he had lost in Hertfordshire, Middlesex and Wiltshire could be reclaimed after the reversal of his attainder in October 1473. No evidence has been found that he did so, but since his nephew John was one of the custodians of the Wiltshire holdings and those in Hertfordshire and Middlesex were in the keeping of royal servants, Bishop Stillington and Robert Kirkham, he could have repossessed at least some of them.[151]

Sir John Fortescue had waited a long time to occupy the manor of Ebrington, Gloucestershire, and by 1474 he could finally do so. A letter of attorney dated 16 January 1474 from Sir John directed Thomas Carre to enter the manor and deliver seisin to the bishop of Winchester and other feoffees: 'Let it be known to all by these presents that I, John Fortescue knight, attorn, determine and put in my place my valued attorney Thomas Carre to enter on my behalf my manor of Ebrington in the county of Gloucestershire.'[152] Amongst Fortescue's feoffees the names of past associates occurred, such as the Stonors, fellow exiles like Dr Ralph Makerell and his daughter-in-law's second husband, Sir Richard Pomeroy, in the document that still bears Fortescue's seal.[153] The name 'Benedict Fortescue' also appeared: he was not mentioned in any of Clermont's genealogies so could have been a bastard son or

[147] See below, Chapter 5, pp. 220–35.

[148] See above, p. 121; TNA, Inquisitions Post Mortem, 12 Edward IV, C 140/41, 39.

[149] *CIPM*, Henry VII, ii, 388–90, 10 November 1503. Sir John's direct line has continued and his family was raised in status by the grant of an earldom in the eighteenth century.

[150] See above, Chapter 1, p. 38.

[151] See above, Chapter 3, p. 119, n. 108. Richard Fortescue's branch of the family owned Punsbourne from later in the century.

[152] Devon Record Office, 1262 TG 10. Plummer, *Governance of England*, 43–4, n. 4, questioned whether Sir John Burgh was ever granted Ebrington as Clermont had claimed but see below, Chapter 5, pp. 220–35.

[153] Lady Elizabeth Pomeroy died in 1508, *CIPM*, Henry VII, iii, 324.

grandson of one of the Fortescue brothers.[154] An untimely claim from any of the Corbets could have ruined Sir John's plans so he managed to elicit quitclaims from them. Witnessed by practically the same men who had been named in the letter of attorney, the first was made by Margaret Corbet, the daughter of Guy and an heir of Sir Robert Corbet on 12 January, 1474. The second, by Robert Corbet, squire, her nephew and co-heir and the divorced husband of Maud Fortescue, was made three days later (see Illustration 10).[155]

A few more records of private transactions in Fortescue's last years survive, although it is not clear that he was still living when the later ones were enrolled, since the decease of a feoffee was not necessarily recorded. He was alive when an assize roll was delivered to the Exchequer in February 1476.[156] In the following year he was associated with others in grants of land and rights and the receipt of a licence to alienate land in *mortmain* to Magdalen College, Oxford.[157] In 1477 Edward IV's good friend, William, Lord Hastings, was obliged when together with two bishops and Sir Thomas Billing, the Chief Justice King's Bench, Fortescue acted as a feoffee in a grant of the Hundred of Framland, Leicestershire and its annual farms.[158]

Fortescue seems to have been in London in 1476 when the assize roll was delivered to the Exchequer, but by the middle of the decade he must have been a very old man by the standards of the time, at least in his seventies. His last great treatise the *Governance of England* had been completed and probably offered to the King and his council. He might at last have been content to conform to Clermont's picture: spending a calm and venerable old age withdrawn from political strife. The date of his death is difficult to determine. Clermont quoted a local tradition that he lived to ninety and this seems to have been the basis for the

[154] Clermont had access to the 'Stemmata Fortescuana', written in the late eighteenth century by Mr Inceldon. Enquiries have yielded no information about its present whereabouts but I am grateful to Earl Fortescue for confirming that it is not in his possession. I am also grateful to Hannes Kleineke for a reference to another unknown and possibly illegitimate Fortescue. John Fortescue alias Roos was accused with others of stealing goods from a tailor in the parish of St Anna in Ward, Aldersgate, London, TNA, KB 9/269, March 16, 1452.

[155] *CCR*, Edward IV, 1468–76, 331; Devon Record Office, 1262 M/TG9.

[156] Chrimes, *De Laudibus*, lxvii, n. 9; *Ancient Kalendars and Inventories of the Exchequer*, ed. F. Palgrave, 3 vols (London: 1836) vol. 3, 8.

[157] Chrimes, *De Laudibus*, lxvii, nn.10 and 11; *CPR*, Edward IV, 1476–85, 48.

[158] HMC, *Report on the Manuscripts of the Late Reginald Rawdon Hastings Esq.*, 4 vols (London: 1928–47) vol. 1, 86–7.

14 Tomb of Sir John Fortescue in Ebrington Church, Gloucestershire, *c.*1480. He wears the robes of a Chief Justice.

suggestion of Chrimes that he lived until at least 1479.[159] More recent scholarship, however, has shown that Fortescue was probably born nearer 1400 than 1385/90 and that would take his terminal age down by about a decade. He was buried in Ebrington church, where his tomb with a recumbent figure dressed in the robes of a justice still survives. It probably dates from the time of his interment but the inscriptions are from a later period.

During his long life, Fortescue surpassed his family's ambitions. In the early decades of the fifteenth century his father and brothers progressed steadily up the county hierarchy in Devon (despite several lawless incidents in which Henry and Richard participated), but John junior's career shot ahead of them once he went to London. His appointment as Chief Justice in 1442 must have seemed the pinnacle of his achievement but the volatile and violent 1450s and the high mortality rate amongst royal advisers gave him even greater opportunities: he became the Lancastrian Chancellor in early 1461. This proved to be an empty honour, but it enabled him to occupy a central position in the exiles' subsequent propaganda campaign and the diplomacy that eventually resulted in the brief reinstatement of Henry VI. The defeat at Tewkesbury could well have resulted in Fortescue's shameful death, imprisonment or impecunious obscurity. Instead he regained some of his property and was given a place on Edward IV's council. The prestige he had enjoyed as a diplomat and polemicist probably convinced the King that he was worth employing. We can only speculate on how much influence he enjoyed during his remaining years but his rehabilitation helped to ensure that his lasting claim to greatness, his political and legal treatises, survived and became widely known over the following centuries.

159 Clermont, *Works*, 44; Chrimes, *De Laudibus*, lxvii, n. 13.

Part II
WORKS

CHAPTER 4

The Apologist for Lancaster

The second part of this book discusses the writings of Sir John Fortescue: both those that were issued in an attempt to undermine the claim of the house of York to the throne and the more theoretical works which dealt with wider issues of natural and human law, the origins of the English polity and how it should be governed. References have already been made to some of these works, the *Somnium Vigilantis* in which he may have had a hand and the articles he sent to the French government in the later 1460s in an attempt to engage them with the project to restore the Lancastrians to power. What follows seeks to trace Fortescue's thought from the practicalities of the polemical tracts to the full-scale theory of how England should be governed as it emerged and was developed in the *De Natura Legis Naturae*, the *De Laudibus Legum Anglie* and the *Governance of England.*

The Tracts on the Succession

This chapter discusses the writings of Sir John Fortescue in exile that were intended to undermine the claim that the house of York had a title to the English crown that was superior to Lancaster's. In this first section the four short tracts that can safely be attributed to Fortescue are evaluated and in the second the contents and purpose of the long treatise *De Natura Legis Naturae* are assessed. The latter presents a problem of classification since, whilst the second part deals with the rights of succession in kingdoms in a general way, the first part is a philosophical dissection of the law of nature and how it relates to both divine and human law. Some of Fortescue's most original ideas on sovereignty were aired there for the first time and the treatise is didactic rather than polemical since, as he later stated in the *De Laudibus Legum Anglie*, it was written for the instruction of Prince Edward of Lancaster. These factors might seem to place it more appropriately in Chapter 5 with that treatise, which was also written for Prince Edward. The compromise is to describe the *De Natura's* contents here while the ideas that it contains on good governance will be discussed together with those of the *De Laudibus* and the *Governance of England* in the next chapter.

Fortescue's refutation of his Lancastrian polemical works, the *Declaration upon certain writings sent out of Scotland*, which was written between 1471 and 1473 to secure the lifting of his attainder, is referred to since a number of the arguments he used in his earlier works were discussed and then dismissed.[1] A detailed study on all the works on the succession was published by this author in 1998. This also contains a transcript of *Of the Title of the House of York* and a tabular comparison of its contents with two of Fortescue's other polemical works, the *De Titulo Edwardi Comitis Marchie* (Of the Title of Edward Earl of March) and the *Defensio Juris Domus Lancastrie* (Defence of the Right of the House of Lancaster).[2] His other tract on the succession, the *Replication against the Claim of the duke of York*, is very short and its content and purpose differed from the other three.[3] Only the first part of the *De Natura* contains any thoughts of substance on the issue of good governance but the conclusion to this section will discuss whether any such ideas can be inferred from the shorter polemical works and the *Declaration* that refuted them.

A better understanding of the purpose and origin of Fortescue's works can be achieved through considering the sources that he used. Writers of his time were not meticulous in citing their references and did not necessarily acknowledge everything that had influenced their thinking. Fortescue was no worse than his contemporaries in this respect. On the whole his use of sources was predictable: the Old and New Testaments, classical writers such as Aristotle and Seneca, the works of the Fathers of the Church, along with works on canon and civil law, history and ethics. Many of his citations, however, were not taken directly from his authors but from compilations, a common contemporary practice probably exacerbated in his case by the paucity of available books whilst he was in exile. Two rather surprising books, however, which had only been written a few decades before in early Renaissance Florence, are to be found amongst the generally conventional array of sources: Poggio Bracciolini's translation of the *Library of History* by Diodorus Siculus and the *Isagogue of Moral Discipline* by Leonardo Bruni.

1 See Appendix 2.

2 M.L. Kekewich, '"Thou shalt be under the power of the man": Sir John Fortescue and the Yorkist Succession', *NMS*, 42 (1998) 188–230. See Appendix 1 for Dr Stubbs's English translation of the *De Titulo Edwardi Comitis Marchie*.

3 See *Vale's Book*, 202–3, for the earliest known version of this tract.

Despite the limited range of authorities on which Fortescue could draw, an examination of those he used in his three major treatises, the *De Natura Legis Naturae*, *De Laudibus Legum Anglie* and *Governance of England*, shows a marked difference of emphasis between them.[4] The *De Natura* was generously resourced with many references to the Old and New Testaments, classical writers such as Aristotle and Varro, the Fathers, Scholastics, canon and civil law. The *De Laudibus* contained fewer references and, besides some quotations from the civil law and the Old Testament, favoured secular writers, especially Aristotle. No authority was cited that was not already mentioned in the *De Natura*. The *Governance* is a much shorter treatise than the other two and contained very few references, only eleven in the twenty chapters, and, besides a few biblical and moral citations, favoured historical authorities. What will become clear from the discussion of Fortescue's major treatises is that he used his largely conventional material, as well as the two contemporary works, to draw original and even controversial conclusions.

In answer to one of the duke of York's manifestos in 1450 Henry VI or his advisers warned that popular opinion believed that he would claim what 'ye nother oughte nor as we doughte notthe ye wil not attempte'.[5] Ten years later in the wake of the battle of Northampton, when Henry VI was in his custody, York confirmed those fears by placing a formal claim to the throne before parliament.[6] Fortescue, who was still Chief Justice in October 1460, was less than robust in his response to the challenge.[7] The rebuttals which cascaded from his pen during his exile could be interpreted as a belated compensation for his failure to stand up to York when the claim was first made. This was based on his descent, via the earls of March, from Philippa the daughter of Lionel, duke of Clarence, the third son of Edward III (the second, if only those with issue are counted) as well as from Edmund of Langley, duke of York, the fifth son. The house of Lancaster was descended in the male line from John of Gaunt, the fourth son of Edward III. (See Genealogy of the House of Plantagenet, above.)

The initial objections to the duke of York's title to the throne were not raised by Fortescue but by the Lords in parliament after the justices, king's serjeants and attorney had failed to venture an opinion. Their first

4 See Appendix 4.

5 'You neither ought nor as we doubt not you will not attempt', *Vale's Book*, 186.

6 *Ibid.*, 195–202, a version of the parliamentary record of the exchanges edited to show the Yorkists in a poor light.

7 See above, Chapter 2, pp. 103–5; *RP*, vol. 5, 375–7; Chrimes, *English Constitutional Ideas*, 22–3.

point was that they had all (including York) sworn oaths of loyalty to Henry. Secondly, acts of parliament had confirmed the Lancastrian title to the throne. Thirdly, entails (successions that cannot be bequeathed at pleasure) had been made to royal heirs male and this was proved by chronicles and the records of parliament. Fourthly, if York had wished to press his claim to the throne he should have borne the arms of Lionel of Clarence rather than those of Edmund of Langley. Finally, when Henry IV had taken the throne he had declared that he did so as the heir to Henry III, not as a conqueror. This last could have been an oblique reference to the unfounded libel that Edmund Crouchback, earl of Lancaster, was the oldest son of Henry III who had been passed over for the succession in favour of Edward I on account of his deformity.[8] A short tract alleging this figured amongst the Lancastrian propaganda that was disseminated from Scotland, 1461–63, but Fortescue was to deny responsibility for it in the *Declaration upon certain writings*.[9]

York answered the Lords' objections to his title in writing. As far as his failure to bear Lionel's arms, the swearing of oaths and the entails were concerned his argument was summed up in the epigram, 'though right for a tyme rest and bee put to silence, yit it roteth not ner shall not perish'.[10] The matter of the acts of parliament could easily be dismissed as there had only been one in 1406 and, had the Lancastrian succession been valid, it would not have been necessary to promulgate it. It could have no force against York's right of inheritance 'as it accordeth with Godds lawe, and all naturall lawes'. (Was this a rejoinder to the justices' admission that they could not use the common law to achieve a verdict on the succession?) Finally, the claim made by Henry IV that he was heir to Henry III was simply false, a feeble excuse for his 'unrightwise and violente usurpacion'.[11]

[8] *RP*, vol. 3, 422–3; P. Strohm, *England's Empty Throne: Usurpation and the Language of Legitimation, 1399–1422* (New Haven and London: 1998) 3–5, observes that Edmund was properly called 'Cross-back' in reference to his crusader status rather than 'Crookback' or 'Crouchback'.

[9] Oxford, Bodleian Library MS James 28, pp. 16–17. Henry IV actually claimed the throne on three grounds: inheritance, conquest and election by the people; *RP*, vol. 3, xx; G. Lapsley, 'The Parliamentary Title of Henry IV', *EHR*, 49 (1934) 423–49, 577–606; M. Bennett, 'Edward III's Entail and the Succession to the Crown, 1376–1471, *EHR*, 113 (1998) 580–69; M. Bennett, 'Henry IV, the Royal Succession and the Crisis of 1406', *The Reign of Henry IV, 1403–1413*, ed. G. Dodd and D. Biggs (York: 2008) 9–27; Appendix 2.

[10] *RP*, vol. 5, 377.

[11] *Ibid.*; *Vale's Book*, 199.

The objections made by the Lords to York's claim and the duke's answers seem to have provided part of the framework for Fortescue's subsequent treatises on the subject. This literature mostly survives in incomplete and/or later versions in manuscripts which give little or no evidence about their provenance. This renders any attempt to produce a clear account of these writings subject to many pitfalls. Clermont in his edition of Fortescue's *Works* printed all the parts of the tracts that were then known. Plummer added a few paragraphs to one of them; like Clermont he assumed that the *De Natura* was written in Scotland.[12] The length and scholarly thought in its two parts and the use made of arguments that occurred in the short tracts make it probable that it was the last work in the sequence to be composed.

The surviving short works on the succession are the complete Latin *De Titulo Edwardi Comitis Marchie*[13] and the fragmentary *Defensio Juris Domus Lancastrie*;[14] the English tracts are the fragmentary *Of the Title of the House of York*[15] and the very short *Replication to the Claim of the duke of York*.[16] This last is a slightly expanded version of the question raised about the legitimacy of Philippa, daughter of Lionel of Clarence, which was also touched on in *Of the Title* and the *De Titulo*. The contents of the other three are, as far as can be judged from what remains, very similar to each other. With the exception of the *De Titulo* and the *De Natura*, all of Fortescue's authenticated works which have survived, and one which

[12] Clermont, *Works*, 32, 61, where he firmly stated that the *De Natura* 'has been long since forgotten', 491–518 and supplement 61*–90*; Plummer, *Governance of England*, 77–8, 355–6. See below for a discussion of this view.

[13] In one surviving manuscript, originally Yelverton MS N 69 now London, BL Additional MS 48063, ff. 4–11b. See Appendix 1.

[14] Oxford, Bodleian Library MS James 28, pp. 10–16; University of Kansas, Watson Library MS C 63; in H. Bedford, *The Hereditary Right of the Crown of England Asserted* (London: 1713) appendix, i–iii, the author stated that he copied the extract from Otho B i; L.H. Nelson and C. Nelson, 'A Lost Fragment of the *Defensio Juris Domus Lancastrie*', *Speculum*, 40 (1965) 290–3.

[15] London, BL MSS Cotton Vespasian F ix, f. 122a; Lansdowne 205, f. 137b; Additional 48005, f. 97a–b.

[16] Originally Yelverton MS 35, now London, BL MS Additional 48031A, f. 134a–b; also MSS Harley 543, ff. 163b–164a; 545, f. 136a–b; Hatfield MS 230.4; the copy transcribed by Clermont, 517–18, was formerly Phillips MS 13783, f. 3a. It formed part of the estate of Sir Anthony Wagner, late of the College of Arms, where I was able to view it. It is now owned by a private collector. I am most grateful to Nigel Ramsay for locating it. It lacks the first paragraph plus a long sentence at the beginning of the next one, as does the Hatfield MS, so one of these is likely to have been copied from the other. Both probably date from the late sixteenth century.

has not (the genealogy of the house of Lancaster), are listed in the mid-seventeenth- and early-eighteenth-century catalogues of the Cotton collection.[17] Unfortunately the manuscript in which they were gathered, Otho B i, was destroyed by fire in 1731 but the contents can be reconstructed from several sources, the first a catalogue which was probably compiled in 1638, seven years after Sir Robert Cotton's death.[18]

Otho B i also figures in several later catalogues of the Cotton manuscripts. An entry in a schedule dated 1718 reads: 'B1 Fortescue de legibus Angliae et.cet. Tractatus/10/Folia/120'.[19] The third source is a report after the fire to the committee of 1732 in which the ten items in Otho B i were listed with their folio numbers. They differ little in their details from those listed in the first Cotton catalogue.[20] Fortescue's genealogy of the house of Lancaster, number 5 in Otto B i, is not known to survive. The notes on the commentaries on Julius Caesar and the prophetic verses on England and Scotland (numbers 9 and 10) may have belonged to Fortescue but he was probably not their author. Unlike other contemporary polemicists he never used prophecies to bolster his arguments on the succession, although, in the *Governance* for example, he was not averse to employing the mythical British history of Brut.

[17] C.G.C. Tite, *The Manuscript Library of Sir Robert Cotton* (London: 1994) 38; C.G.C. Tite, *The Early Records of Sir Robert Cotton's Library: Formation, Cataloguing, Use* (London: 2003) 150; Kekewich, '"Thou shalt be under the power of the man"', appendix 2. Colin Tite has recorded fourteen lists of Cotton books dating up to 1674 but many are not complete and in one at least (London, BL Harley 6018, f. 178b) Otho B i had been lent to one of 'divers persons'. C.G.C. Tite, 'The Early Catalogues of the Cottonian Library', *British Library Journal*, 6 (1980) 144–57.

[18] London, BL Additional MSS 36682, B, f. 138b: (1) Fortescue de laudibus legum Angliae; (2) Idem de dominio politico et regali [*The Governance of England*]; (3) Eiudem auctore defensio iuris domus Lancastrie ad Regnum Anglie; (4) Defensio altera per eiusdem [The *Replication*]; (5)Genealogia Domus Lancastriae per eiusdem; (6) Titulus Domus Eboracensis ad regnum Anglie per eiusdem [*Of the Title of the House of York*]; (7) Genealogia Regnum Scotiae a Rege Jacobo 2° usque ad Adam auctore Willielmo Fratours prebendario ecclesio Abberdonensis; (8) Declaratio Johannis Fortescue militis super quibusdam articulis de Jure Ed:° ad regnum Anglie [*The Declaration upon certain writings*]; (9) Notae in Commentarios Julii Caesaris; (10) Versus profetici de Regno Angliae et Scotiae etc.

[19] BL Additional MS 4696, a roll, Dr Bentley's schedule of 1718 of the manuscripts in the Cotton Library.

[20] *A Report from the Committee Appointed to View the Cottonian Library* (London: 1732) 59. Very thorough but contains dispiriting remarks such as 'burnt to a crust'.

It is possible that the Otho B i collection originated from the Fortescue family since Sir Adrian Fortescue, Sir John's great-nephew, certainly had access to a good version of the *Governance of England* in 1532 when he made a copy.[21] Seven years later it must be hoped that there were appreciative purchasers for the 'divers writynges' found in three different chests when his goods were seized for the Crown when he was condemned for high treason.[22] It is unlikely that Sir John Fortescue in the 1470s, rehabilitated as he was and after all his protestations in the *Declaration* that he had not recently seen his polemical works, would have gathered together his respectable Yorkist writings with the Lancastrian tracts that he had disowned. Another member of his family, such as the scholarly Sir Adrian, might have done so. One major work by Fortescue is missing from Otho B i, the *De Natura Legis Naturae*. A simple explanation for this could be that there were never many copies of the manuscript (only one and a half are known to survive) and it was not acquired by Cotton. The *De Titulo Edwardi Comitis Marchie* is also missing. The presence of the *De Laudibus* and the *Governance* could be due to Sir Robert Cotton's practice of binding other works in with an original collection.[23]

An alternative hypothesis is that the Otho B i collection was made by the government of Edward IV, both the damaging propaganda which had come from Scotland and Fortescue's later refutation. In that case the presence of the Lancastrian *De Laudibus* is strange save that it forms a kind of companion treatise of political advice to the *Governance of England*, which, it is argued below, was intended for Edward IV.[24] An indication that the collection could be a dossier on Fortescue's polemical writings on the succession is the presence of the genealogy of the kings of Scotland, which was written by William Fratour, the Scottish canon of Aberdeen, who seems to have collaborated with him in the

[21] Item 7 was by William Fratour and items 9 and 10 were unlikely to have been composed by Fortescue.

[22] Oxford, Bodleian Library MS Digby 145, ff. 133–60; London, BL MS Royal, App. 89, f. 179b; R. Rex, 'Blessed Adrian Fortescue: A Martyr without a Cause?', *Analecta Bollandiana*, 115 (1996) 307–53.

[23] Tite, *Manuscript Library*, 104.

[24] See Chapter 5, pp. 234–5. Sir Robert Cotton could have bound the *De Laudibus* with the other works because they related to Fortescue. As it was the first in the collection this could have been done easily.

enterprise.[25] Otho B i may have contained fifteenth-century originals, later versions or a mixture of the two.[26]

The tracts Fortescue wrote in Scotland must date from between the summer of 1461, when he arrived, and June 1463, when he finally departed for the Continent. A detailed account is given here of the contents of the *De Titulo Edwardi Comitis Marchie* since it is the only complete surviving short tract which deals with the whole question of the English succession and it is likely from what remains of them that the original versions of *Of the Title of the House of York* and the *Defensio Juris Domus Lancastrie* resembled it closely.[27] The last sentence of Fortescue's introduction to the *De Titulo* raises the possibility of a lost work, an 'original book, which treats more at large of these matters in the vulgar tongue'. He could be referring to *Of the Title*, but from what remains it seems unlikely ever to have been very long, although a later hand did write at the end of the last fragment, 'Alia multa hic desunt', implying that originally there was much more.[28] The 'original book' might not have been composed by Fortescue, the 'vulgar tongue' could have been French or another European language or a composition by Fratour or another Scot, but if it was indeed by Fortescue it seems to have been lost. His introduction raises another issue: we know that he expressly disobeyed the injunction by the Lancastrian lords in Scotland, who seem to have taken a hand in the planning of this tract, that he should not defend the Lancastrian title

25 Oxford, Bodleian Library MS James 28, pp.16–17, contains the short piece with English words spelt in the Scottish fashion which makes the allegation about Edmund Crouchback and is unlikely to have been written by Fortescue. It also negates his argument about the undesirability of women passing on the right of succession. Fratour was given a canonry at the Chapel Royal, St Andrews, in 1462, *Calendar of Entries in the Papal Registers relating to Great Britain and Ireland*, vol. 9, *Papal Letters, 1455–64*, ed. J.A. Twemlow (London: 1921) 453–4 and vol. 13, *Papal Letters, 1471–84*, 77, 339–40, 343 (London: 1955).

26 But see Chrimes, *De Laudibus*, lxxix, n. 2. Casley assured Francis Gregor in 1729 that the manuscripts in the volume were in a fifteenth-century hand.

27 Plummer thought that the *De Titulo* was the first of the polemical works, basing his claim on two errors Fortescue made in it which were corrected in other works. The description of Louis XI as 'recently anointed' (15 August 1461) also suggests an early date, 77, n. 1, Appendix I, p. xx. V. Litzen disagreed, 'A War of Roses and Lilies: The Theme of Succession in Sir John Fortescue's Works,' *Annales Academiae Scientiarum Fennicae*, 173 (Helsinki: 1971) 2–73, 26. His grounds were that Plummer had not noticed the reference to a papal letter to Henry VI of November 1461, so the tract must post-date that. Most other commentators have not ventured an opinion on the chronology of the tracts.

28 'Much is missing here', Kekewich, '"Thou shalt be under the power of the man"', 229.

to the throne.[29] He did not explain the reason for the lords' prohibition but it can be inferred that they felt that the case for legitimacy would be weakened by admitting the necessity of defending it. Yet all Fortescue's polemical works were devoted as much to the defence of Lancaster as to questioning the title of York, for the two arguments were inextricably intertwined.

Fortescue briefly stated the Yorkist claim to the English throne in chapter I of the *De Titulo*. It came through two women, Philippa the daughter 'as is asserted' of Lionel, the elder brother of John of Gaunt, duke of Lancaster, both sons of Edward III, and Philippa's granddaughter Anne Mortimer, who was the grandmother of Edward 'sometime Earl of March', the son of Richard, duke of York. Fortescue could not really avoid defending Lancaster, as he pointed out that Henry VI was descended from Henry III in both the male and female lines and by direct male descent from Edward III. The law and custom of England excluded women and their right to pass the succession to their husbands and heirs, but Edward IV owed his claim to two women.[30]

Fortescue then cited the precedent of Edward the Confessor, who, had women enjoyed the right of succession, should have given way to St Margaret of Scotland the daughter (actually his granddaughter, Fortescue was mistaken) of his elder brother, for he would never have committed a sinful act in putting a rightful claim aside. Another precedent was provided by the case of the empress Matilda, since after the death of her father, Henry I, she could not succeed him but the crown passed by election first to a close male relative of the dead king, Stephen, and then to her son, Henry. Having ignored the vicious and protracted civil war that culminated in the settlement, Fortescue provided a biased account of the operation of the English law of inheritance, giving the false impression that women could not inherit their parents' property. This enabled him to proclaim a principle that was to be one of his strongest arguments against the Yorkist claims: 'No one can transfer more right to another person than is known to belong to himself.'[31] This argument was to be used extensively in his philosophical tract on the succession, book I of *De Natura Legis Naturae*, and shows the importance of studying the polemical works for an understanding of the development of Fortescue's ideas.

[29] Appendix 1. Apart from the *Replication*, which is contemporary, all the other titles of the short tracts and of Fortescue's longer works seem to have been assigned by later copyists or editors and this is the case with the *De Titulo*, Kekewich, '"Thou shalt be under the power of man"', 192–5.

[30] See above, Genealogy 2, pp. xxii–iii.

[31] Appendix 1, chapter V.

The delicate matter of the Lancastrian claim to France was dealt with by Fortescue's 'election' argument: Henry V, after concluding a treaty with Charles VI, was recognised as heir after his death by the French 'parliament'. As the exiles in Scotland surveyed their limited options and tried to woo the French king, it would have seemed wise to abandon the actual grounds for the Plantagenet claim to the throne: superior hereditary right. Fortescue continued with bloodcurdling accounts of the problems that could afflict a country ruled by a woman, which could arise either because she did not marry or because she wed an unsuitable man. The possibility that a woman might rule without the guidance of a man was not entertained; indeed, he argued that, 'a woman cannot be a king, nor can the supreme government in temporals [secular powers] over the man devolve upon her'. This led him to quote the phrase from Genesis which was to cause him acute embarrassment when he recanted ten years later: 'Thou shalt be under the power of the man and he shall rule over thee.'[32] These arguments resonate with the opinions Fortescue had expressed about the inferiority of women when he was a serjeant and Chief Justice at Westminster.

Philippa of Clarence was Fortescue's next target, although he did not directly question her legitimacy as he was to do in *Of the Title* and the *Replication*. She was not mentioned in the chronicles as Clarence's daughter, and if the house of York could claim such a prestigious forebear, why was this not recognised in their arms? Even if Edward's family originally possessed the right of succession through Philippa, which they did not, it had devolved by prescription (a period giving lawful title) to the Lancastrian dynasty, which had possessed the crown peacefully for sixty years 'more or less'.[33] St Augustine in his *De Civitate Dei* (quoted in the *Compendium Morale*) cited four proofs of true kingship – divine permission, the approval of the Church, the consent of the people and long possession – and the Lancastrians could claim all those.[34]

Fortescue, and probably those who seem to have been advising him, must have feared that he was on shifting ground concerning ecclesiastical approbation for Henry VI's continued rule. The obsession of Pius II was to marshal the princes of Europe behind him for a crusade against the victorious Turks in Constantinople – other considerations were subordinated to that aim. The Lancastrians, who had been chased from most of

[32] *Ibid.*, x; xx; Genesis 4:16.

[33] The annoying insertion of this phrase undermines the usefulness of the information for dating the tract.

[34] Chrimes discussed the books to which Fortescue may have had access during his exile, *De Laudibus*, lxxxix–xcv; see below, Chapter 5.

England by mid-1461 by a victorious combination of Edward IV and the earl of Warwick, were hardly a promising force for the Pope's purposes. On 11 March 1461, believing Henry still to be in Yorkist custody, he had sent an affectionate but noncommittal letter to him commending him to the care of his legate in England, Francesco Coppini, bishop of Terni, who was proving to be blatantly biased in favour of the Yorkists. The legate was a creature of Francesco Sforza, duke of Milan, an ally of Ferrante of Aragon, king of Naples, who was opposing the attempts of the Angevins, headed by Margaret's brother, John of Calabria, to regain the throne of Naples.[35] So the hapless Lancastrians had to contend with the results of the vicious rivalries in the 'Italian wasp-nest' as well as their own military inadequacies. Constance Head believed that Henry VI never received the supportive letter from the Pope because of the disruption caused to communications after the defeat of the Lancastrians at Towton. Coppini or another agent sent Edward's exposition of his claim to Rome and at the end of March 1462 he received a benign letter from Pius II approving the Yorkist claim and congratulating him on his elevation to the English throne.[36] None of this did Coppini any good since the Pope was furious that he had allowed his devotion to York to overcome his prime function of raising money for a crusade and he ended his days in disgrace in a Roman monastery.

Fortescue's *De Titulo*, which seems to have been intended for an educated and probably clerical audience or recipient, had to make the best of an unpromising array of facts and it has been already been noticed that, as a lawyer, Fortescue could be economical with the truth. In the case of ecclesiastical approbation he seems to have elided the sentiments intended for Henry VI in the letter of March 1461 (such reassuring platitudes would probably have been offered to the gullible king by his clerical advisers) and those that led to the papal condemnation in August 1462 of Coppini, whom Fortescue excoriated as 'that most atrocious legate'.[37] The fact that Edward IV had been crowned and anointed could not prevail against the superior title that Henry was recognised by the Church to possess. Fortescue commented on the sinfulness of the English who had supported Edward in his bid for the throne. He presumably realised that this was not an attractive argument with which to enlist adherents to the Lancastrian cause and it is not found elsewhere in his writings. His next argument was that Edmund, earl of March, had

[35] Kekewich, *The Good King*, 73–5.

[36] *Foedera*, vol. 5, ii, 110; C. Head, 'Pope Pius II and the Wars of the Roses', *Archivum Historiae Pontificiae*, 8 (1970) 139–78.

[37] Appendix 1, p. 279.

only claimed his rightful lands and titles when he succeeded his father in the reign of Henry V, and had paid homage to him and to Henry VI when he came to the throne. Edward and his father, Richard, duke of York, had also recognised Henry as lawful king and sworn oaths of fealty (fidelity) to him.

In the final chapter of the *De Titulo*, despite his introductory self-denying clause, Fortescue could not resist a quick review of the superiority of Henry VI's claim to the English throne, a claim that descended from John of Gaunt, duke of Lancaster in the male line. He praised the manner in which the principle of male descent was applied by his hosts in Scotland. While conceding that kings had sometimes owed their succession to females, he stressed that this only happened when no direct male heirs were available. Although the civil law did allow the inheritance from a deceased father to descend equally to all his sons and their children, this did not apply in the case of succession to the kingdom. The tract ended rather abruptly and one wonders whether it had originally been concluded by an epilogue. From what survives of *Of the Title* and the *Defensio Juris* it seems likely that they would originally have been of similar length to the *De Titulo* and would have differed little in their content from it and from each other, so these tracts are not described in detail here.

The use of Latin and the measured arguments in the *De Titulo* mark it as destined for an educated audience. Queen Margaret arrived in France in April 1462 to enlist the new king, Louis XI, for her cause; Pius II in his *Commentaries* recorded two speeches that she delivered, one to the King and the other to the troops he had gathered to help her reconquer England.[38] Just as the French chancery produced briefing documents for diplomatic negotiations, it is possible that Fortescue and the Lancastrian lords in Scotland intended the *De Titulo* to be an *aide memoire* for the Queen and her followers when she urged the justice of her cause. Fortescue's reference to the 'recent' coronation of Louis XI (18 August 1461) in the final chapter indicates a date later in that year or early in 1462 for its completion. The introduction to the tract, which referred to the opinion of the Lancastrian lords, implies that the design, if not the execution, was in the hands of a committee rather than of Fortescue alone. The space that Pius devoted to Margaret of Anjou in his reminiscences (although, as a supporter of Ferrante's claim to Naples, he did not love her family) indicates that the Lancastrian claim to ecclesiastical approbation in the *De Titulo* might have attracted his

[38] *The Commentaries of Pius II*, ed. L.C. Gabel, trans. F.A. Gragg, 5 vols (Northampton, MA: 1937), book ix, 578–80.

attention. The survival of only one copy of the tract lends credence to the theory that it was produced for a specific purpose and the use of one person or a small group.

The fourth of Fortescue's short polemical works on the succession is less than two pages in length, *The Replication against the claim and title of the duke of York for the crowns of England and France.* The title is likely to be original as it preceded the earliest known copy that came from *John Vale's Book*, a collection that was probably assembled by Lancastrian sympathisers and copied early in the 1480s.[39] The title of '*Replication*', a legal term regularly used at the time for a stage in litigation, might be explained if Fortescue regarded it as the response that he wished he had made in October 1460 when he and the other justices were consulted about York's claim to the throne. There is no internal evidence that can suggest a more precise date than the period of Fortescue's exile in Scotland of two years from the summer of 1461 to mid-1463.

The contents are an expanded version of the doubts about the legitimacy of Philippa of Clarence which were touched on in the other tracts. The purpose was to damn the Yorkist claim by what was described by John Watts as 'a simple but destructive story'.[40] Fortescue also enlarged upon his original argument by describing a vivid and probably mythical scene: the daughters of Edward III went to the Lords in parliament wearing their mantles of state to renounce any right that they had to the crown. This done, they symbolically cast off their mantles and departed in their gowns. In his tracts Fortescue had referred to the entails confining the succession to heirs male: such an entail in 1376 in which Edward III vested the succession in his grandson Richard and then his own sons in order of seniority has been described.[41] The Hatfield and Phillips/Wagner manuscripts of the *Replication* bear a superscription that it was taken 'out of Sir John Fortescue's book of defence of the tytle of the House of Lancaster'. This could refer to Fortescue's other surviving tract in the vernacular, since *Of the Title* contained a version of the allegation of Philippa's bastardy. Or it could mean the 'original book, which treats more at large of these matters in the vulgar tongue' which Fortescue mentioned in the introduction to the *De Titulo* and which, if he was the author, is lost.

Fortescue's *Declaration upon Certain Writings Sent Out of Scotland Against the King's Title to the Realm of England*, his recantation composed

39 *Vale's Book*, 202–3. See above, pp. 127–9.

40 *Ibid.*, 38.

41 M. Bennett, 'Edward III's Entail and the Succession to the Crown, 1376–1471', *EHR*, 113 (1998) 580–607.

between 1471 and 1473 to earn the favour of Edward IV, has since the time of Plummer been taken as a review of his works on the succession (including the *De Natura Legis Naturae*, which is considered below). The tract took the form of a dialogue between Fortescue and a 'lerned man' who pressed him to disown his treasonable opinions. He has been characterised as 'the voice of Yorkist authority, keeping notarial track of the past utterances Fortescue is obliged to withdraw or refute, and making sure that he does so'.[42] The first story referred to in the *Declaration* was that Edmund Crouchback, earl of Lancaster, was the true heir to the throne as the elder son of Henry III. Fortescue energetically denied authorship of the piece and protested that he had never seen it, just as he claimed that he had not 'seen any minute of them [his writings on the succession] sythen I come into Englond'.[43]

By no means all the arguments against the Yorkist succession that appeared in Fortescue's works were refuted in the *Declaration*, but he devoted considerable space to the question of St Margaret of Scotland's failure to inherit England from her grandfather Edmund Ironside. Fortescue alleged that he had been illegitimate and was thus only the half-brother of Edward the Confessor. He chose to leave the kingdom to the Danes, Cnut and his sons, rather than to his Anglo-Saxon family and thus broke the line of succession and destroyed any Scottish claim. No longer dependent on the good will of the Scots royal family, Fortescue could assist the Yorkists in their long-standing antagonism to the house of Stuart.

Fortescue then dealt with his suggestion that Henry V had realised that his claim to the French throne through Queen Isabelle, wife of Edward II, was unsafe. It would have been particularly important to Edward IV in the early 1470s, when he was contemplating a campaign in France to punish Louis XI and revive his own claim to the French throne, that any slur on it should be removed. The 'lerned man' neatly disposed of Fortescue's embarrassing argument by pointing out that the Mortimer earls of March, Philippa of Clarence's descendants and the duke of York, whose mother was Anne Mortimer, were the rightful heirs of Isabelle. Edward IV's claim to France was reinforced, since he had the dynastic right as well as the agreement made between Henry V and Charles VI that the English king should succeed him. So Edward's subjects could fight for him 'in his title for his roialme of ffrance with oute any doute or scrople of counsieaunce'.[44]

42 Strohm, *Politique*, 134.
43 Appendix 2, pp. 287–9
44 *Ibid.*, pp. 294–7.

The contentious argument founded on the Genesis text, 'Eris sub potestate viri ...', had to be addressed and the precise words that Fortescue used to introduce this section merit close attention:

> Lerned man: ye wrote oute of Scotteland oone matier which nedith Right gret and clere declaracion, for it sownyth gretly agen the kynges olde title to his roialme of ffraunce; and so it dydde when it was wryten agenst his title of this londe. Which matier is this, ye wrote that no woman may supremely reigne upon man, ffor God said etc.... And over this ye wrote a boke in laten, be whiche ye entendid to prove the same by many auctorytes, scriptures, and reasons etc.[45]

The first statement could refer to the relatively simple arguments against female rights of succession to be found in the short tracts. The second almost certainly refers to the *De Natura*, with its complex philosophical propositions, and Fortescue did not specifically state that he wrote the book in Scotland. Yet he could not conceal its existence, so took the opportunity to refute some of its arguments. Fortescue did not refer to the *De Laudibus* in the *Declaration* and had not been asked to disown it: we do not know whether the Yorkists were aware of it and it did not deal with the English succession question. Many of the ideas it contained were to be recycled in the *Governance* and were seemingly acceptable to the Yorkists and Fortescue seems to have ignored it in the *Declaration*.

The 'lerned man' claimed that the supposed disadvantage laid on women in Genesis was the worst argument against the inheritance of women in kingdoms that Fortescue had produced. He said that he was very sorry that he had ever written such things, 'or labored upon the makynge of that laten boke' and asked to be excused, since his expertise in the common law did not equip him to pronounce on the succession. The 'lerned man' swept aside these objections, pointing out that advocates were accustomed to argue on either side of a case and were not condemned for doing so. Henry VI was dead, so Fortescue could now, 'honestly and commendably without eny note of blame, argue to ye contrary entent of that ye have doo by fore this tyme, yf ye finde reasons and groundes to do so'.[46] Fortescue then found a reason for rejecting his former opinion: using all the scholastic apparatus at his disposal he argued that women, like men, were under the power of a man – the Pope – but this would not incapacitate them from enjoying the right

[45] *Ibid.*, p. 297.

[46] *Ibid.*, pp. 298–9.

of succession to kingdoms. The 'lerned man' professed himself to be content with this change of heart.

The libel concerning the legitimacy of Philippa of Clarence was one of the most dangerous arguments of the polemical tracts since it could undermine the whole justification for the Yorkist claim. The 'lerned man' excused Fortescue his mistake on the grounds that whilst he was out of England he had no access to the relevant records and he was not an expert in the laws of succession. He obligingly produced an Exchequer account for Norfolk and Suffolk for 42 to 48 Edward III showing that Philippa 'daughter and heir of Lionel and Elizabeth' inherited the manor of Walsingham.[47] The 'lerned man' offered to show Fortescue more such proofs of Philippa's legitimacy but he vehemently declined: 'I pray you, Sir, shew me no moo recordes of this matier ffor this suffysith.' The dry humour which characterised some of Fortescue's pronouncements and exchanges in the law courts and which surfaced in his three longer works is again apparent here.

Several chronicles were then cited by Fortescue to disprove another troublesome allegation, that both King Stephen and Henry II, son of the empress Matilda, had been chosen by election, by the decision of parliament. Rather, Fortescue conceded, she had only been denied her rightful inheritance by the word of the steward of the royal household to which the archbishop of Canterbury gave all too hasty credence, so Stephen was crowned king. Henry II came to England whilst Stephen still lived and they agreed that Henry would inherit the kingdom: there was no election by parliament.

Fortescue concluded the tract by congratulating himself and thanking God (through the mouth of the 'lerned man') that he had so effectively righted the wrongs he had perpetrated in his original writings, since his mistakes had been corrected by the access he now enjoyed to many documents and chronicles. He had not actually addressed all the arguments in the *Declaration* that he had used in his succession polemics, but he probably felt that matters such as entails and oaths of fealty were relatively unimportant once Henry VI and his son were dead.

No indication was given in the *Declaration* of Fortescue's sources, other than Genesis, for his rejection of the claim that women could inherit or pass on the right to kingdoms, but Litzen in 1971 looked to the Continent to suggest what they could have been.[48] Some of Fortescue's arguments seem to have derived from Richard, duke of York's presentation to parliament in October 1460 and the Lords' subsequent

[47] *Ibid.*, p. 304.
[48] Litzen, 'War of Roses', 54–65.

reservations, but the duke had experienced no difficulty in sweeping them aside in his reply.[49] Fortescue evidently realised that he needed to bolster them with some stronger material, and it seems that he did so by utilising a flourishing genre of literature which had been activated in France by the Hundred Years War. These pamphlets and books were produced over a period of more than a century, rejecting the English claim to the throne in tones that ranged from judicious philosophical argument to vituperative polemic.[50] While some relied on chronicles for most of their material others, such as Jean II Juvenal des Ursins, also had access to diplomatic documents from the French chancery.

Litzen identified a close correspondence between passages in *Of the Title*, themselves similar to the other short works, and a French treatise against the English claim to France written in 1464 known as either *La loi salicque* (Litzen) or *Pour ce que plusieurs* (Anstruther, Lewis and Taylor).[51] Craig Taylor has suggested that it was probably written as a briefing document for the French diplomats who were expected to meet their English counterparts at St Omer in 1464, by Guillaume Cousinot II de Montreuil. He had served the French kings as a diplomat and adviser for decades and had visited England several times; he was closely associated with the house of Anjou and had met the exiles both in Scotland and on campaign in northern England. The argument about the unsuitability of women exercising sovereignty was equally useful to the French in rejecting Plantagenet claims to their throne and to the Lancastrians. The Salic Law, which forbade the succession of women in kingdoms, was conveniently developed in fourteenth-century France at the beginning of the Hundred Years War. There is a considerable overlap to be found in some of the material in *Pour ce que* and Fortescue's polemics, but which came first?

Pour ce que includes the Genesis phrase 'Eris sub potestate …' and the conclusions drawn from it about the unsuitability of women for sovereign rule, including 'Nemo potest plus iuris …'. The illegitimacy of Philippa of Clarence, the nature of Henry V's claim to succeed Charles VI and

[49] See above, n. 156.

[50] P.S. Lewis, 'War Propaganda and Historiography in Fifteenth-Century France and England', *Essays in Later Medieval French History* (London and Ronceverte: 1985) 193–213. See also Chapter 3, p. 118, n. 33, above, for more recent work by Craig Taylor. Some of this literature extends well beyond the ending of the Hundred Years War in 1453. No one realised at the time that it had finished and, in any case, the arguments remained relevant to later Anglo-French disputes.

[51] Lewis, 'War Propaganda and Historiography'; *Prétensions des Anglois à la Couronne de France*, ed. R. Anstruther (London: 1847) 1–117; Taylor, *Debating the Hundred Years War*, 1–134.

the Valois right through prescription all recall Fortescue's arguments.[52] Lewis makes the point that the author of *Pour ce que* was employing well-known themes from anti-English polemics: 'That the Lancastrians were usurpers, that the Yorkists were usurpers and that the English were all murderers anyway completed the catalogue of the disabilities of the descendants of Edward III.'[53] But two of its arguments are only to be found in Fortescue's short works: Edward III's recognition that his daughters could not succeed to the throne in the *Replication* and the English common law proviso that land could be entailed to heirs male in the *De Titulo*.[54]

Did the author of *Pour ce que* copy some of these points, including the tale about the illegitimacy of Philippa of Clarence, from Fortescue? He would just about have had time to do so by 1464: Fortescue was in France in 1462 and settled in exile in Bar by the second half of 1463 but there are objections to this hypothesis. The timing was very tight if *Pour ce que* was indeed being produced for the second aborted Diet of St Omer in 1464.[55] If this was the case it would explain the circumspect tones in which the author referred to the respective Yorkist and Lancastrian claims to the English throne, for the main thrust of his rhetoric was that neither had any right to France. The Philippa scandal was mentioned in a catalogue of the criminality and bad fortune of the sons of Edward III, but later, when Edward IV's claim to the English throne came up, her illegitimacy was not urged, stress instead being laid on the incapacity of such a claim to qualify him for the French succession.[56] The French negotiating strategy at the first Diet of St Omer had been to stand firm on the issue of the English claim to their throne but to do a deal with the victorious Yorkist dynasty and perhaps ultimately cement it by marriage.

Another factor which makes it unlikely that *Pour ce que* was copied from Fortescue is the difference in the version of Philippa's situation that it reported, awarding her mother two daughters rather than one, of whom Philippa was not even the elder.[57] No mention was made of Clarence's journey to Italy or remarriage. Given these disparities it is unlikely that these parts were copied from Fortescue or that he himself was their author, a theory toyed with by Litzen.[58] The suggestion that he

52 Taylor, *Debating the Hundred Years War*, 61 and n. 49, 74, 78–83.
53 Lewis, 'War Propaganda and Historiography', 205.
54 Taylor, *Debating the Hundred Years War*, 77–8.
55 Scofield, *Edward IV*, vol. 1, 278.
56 Taylor, *Debating the Hundred Years War*, 76–7.
57 *Ibid.*, 74.
58 Litzen, 'War of Roses', 60.

subsequently made seems more likely, that Fortescue and the author of *Pour ce que* used a common source or sources. Indeed, Fortescue stated in the *Replication* that the story about Philippa 'is plainly founde in the chronicles of France and Seelande'.[59] Given the co-operation between France and Scotland in their mutual hostility to England, it is likely that tracts against the English claims circulated in Edinburgh, as well as in the French court and chancery, and that Fortescue had read some of them. Conversely *Pour ce que* cannot have influenced the content of his short pamphlets since he appears to have composed them all whilst he was in Scotland, before the departure of the Lancastrian exiles in July 1463 and before the French tract was written. The temptation to assign a more precise chronology to Fortescue's tracts has been resisted: the internal evidence, especially that based on papal affairs, is suspect as Fortescue could be economical with the truth when it suited his argument. He seems to have drawn on the tradition of French polemical works on succession for his own tracts but we cannot know whether he and Cousinot saw each other's pamphlets, communicated verbally on the subjects and/or were drawing on a shared source.[60]

Pour ce que appears in three manuscripts with the *Vraie cronique d'Escoce*, a short history of the kings of Scotland in French, almost certainly written by John Ireland, a Scottish adviser to Louis XI.[61] It too could have been intended as briefing material for French diplomats at the time of its composition, 1464. One of its themes is that the Scottish kings rather than the Plantagenets should rule England as they had a superior claim through St Margaret of Scotland, the wife of King Malcolm and granddaughter of the Anglo-Saxon king Edmund Ironside. The Scots had used this claim for centuries to annoy the English, despite the fact that they never had any prospect of making it good. In the hands of the king of France it could be a useful threat to invoke against the English as part of a revival of the 'auld alliance' between Scotland and France. In most of his treatises Fortescue had summarily dismissed any claims through St Margaret to the throne of England since he held that women were incapable of succeeding, but he dealt in more detail with the matter in his *Declaration*. There

[59] *Vale's Book*, 202. Hatfield MS 230.4 has 'Ireland' rather than 'Seelande' [Zeland] (Clermont's text, *Works*, 517, mentions only the chronicles of France). Ireland is mentioned in the text so it would have made sense for the copyist to substitute it for 'Seelande'.

[60] Taylor, *Debating the Hundred Years War*, 24–6.

[61] *Short Scottish Prose Chronicles*, ed. D. Embree, E.D. Kennedy and K. Daly, Latin translations by S. Edgington (Woodbridge: 2012) 27–36, 81–109.

he had to tread delicately since he was devoting considerable space to recanting his former view that women could neither succeed nor pass on the right of succession. Edward IV would not welcome an argument that recognised the rights of the kings of Scotland to his throne, so Fortescue simply declared that Edmund Ironside was the son of a concubine and thus illegitimate. To do so he dealt in detail with the history of Scotland and England in late Anglo-Saxon times, covering similar ground to the *Vraie cronique*. He might have come across such literature in the Scottish and French courts during his visits in the 1460s, or he and John Ireland might both have had access to other English and Scottish histories.

Three of Fortescue's short tracts on the succession seem to have been very close to each other in structure and content, so why was it necessary to produce these separate works and the *Replication*? Fortescue touched on their function in the *Declaration*: 'Lerned man: while ye were in Scoteland ... ther war made many wrytinges, and sent hedyr by which was sawen amonges the peple matier of grete noyse and infamye to ye tytle whiche the kinge oure soveraigne lorde Edward the iiii^{te} hath.'[62] The *Replication* asserted that the crown of England could not descend to a woman and stressed that the female line through which Edward claimed it was vitiated by bastardy. This brief, uncomplicated document in English could easily have been passed from hand to hand or nailed up in public places, 'be it knowen tall wele disposed people': it was an effective piece of propaganda.[63] The survival of six copies (counting the incinerated Otho B i) proves the interest that it held for readers even in the sixteenth and seventeenth centuries.

The fragmentary condition of the *Defensio* and *Of the Title* makes detailed theories about their place in Fortescue's polemical works difficult to sustain. What survives of the latter is straightforward and hard-hitting, likely to appeal to a cross-section of people, including the illiterate, who could hear it read by others. Like the *Defensio* it seems to reflect the content of the *De Titulo* and when complete might have been no longer. Both the Latin works, the *Defensio* and the *De Titulo*, must have been aimed at an educated audience, clerical as well as secular. The latter pamphlet vehemently condemned the activities of Coppini the papal legate and sought to reassure readers that Henry VI, although in exile, still enjoyed papal approval. Fortescue probably knew that this was not the case by the time he wrote it but the Lancastrians were in such

62 Appendix 2, p. 172

63 *Vale's Book*, 202. In this context the account of how William Tailboys circulated a libel against Lord Cromwell is illuminating: see above, Chapter 2, p. 47, n. 17.

a weak position that telling the truth was a luxury they could not afford. From the preamble to the *De Titulo* we know that Fortescue worked to an agenda set to some extent by the exiled lords, and they might have decided that the short Latin *Defensio* had made an inadequate case and could be bettered.[64] If the *De Titulo* was indeed the later of the two perhaps a robust condemnation of the legate (of which no trace survives in the *Defensio*) was required, especially if, as suggested above, it was to be used by Queen Margaret in her 1462 diplomatic offensive in France.

Political ideas were to be the major element in Fortescue's later works so it is timely to enquire whether this was also true of his short polemical tracts. They all dealt vigorously with the specifics of the Yorkist claim to the throne but at least two political themes emerged. They can be found most readily in the complete *De Titulo*: that 'the law and custom of England' must determine the succession and that, in default of a direct male heir, the crown was to be awarded by election. In chapter IV this was the means by which King Stephen was chosen in preference to the empress Matilda and later her son Henry was elected as heir by 'the consent of the lords and people in parliament'. Similarly it was the French 'parliament' that chose Henry V of England as heir to Charles VI of France. None of this adds up to a developed theory of government by consent but it sits well with the preference for political and regal rule (*dominium politicum et regale*) as opposed to regal only rule that Fortescue was to express in the *De Natura Legis Naturae*, the *De laudibus Legum Angliae* and the *Governance of England.* By 1471 he was able to abandon the constraints of the pro-French arguments of his Lancastrian polemical works and produce a robustly English account of good governance. In the *Declaration*, on the other hand, which was written to please Edward IV, he was prepared to sweep aside any role enjoyed by parliament in choosing both Stephen and Henry II. The whole thrust of that, his last work on the succession, was the importance of strengthening the royal authority of Edward IV.

Political and regal rule was to be at the centre of Fortescue's three subsequent treatises on good governance: by establishing a proper law for succession in the *De Natura*, by ruling with regard to the common law of England in the *De Laudibus* and by underpinning royal rule with sound administrative and fiscal practices in the *Governance*. More will be said below about Fortescue's use of the terms, but by 1470 it is clear that the concept constituted for him the key to how England could and should be ruled. By his formula the king retained his prerogative to

[64] Lords were thin on the ground during the Lancastrians' exile in Scotland. This could be a case of Fortescue putting a brave face on an unpromising situation.

govern his realm (regal rule), but a wise ruler recognised the restraints on his power exercised by the laws and customs of the land and took advice from worthy counsellors before making a decision (political rule). These concepts did not clearly emerge in Fortescue's writings until after the dynastic dispute in which he had engaged appeared to have been settled in favour of the Yorkists in the early 1460s.

An element in the exiles' attempts to deal with their woes was to resort to the comforts of religion and philosophy. In 1464 Georges Chastellain dedicated his *Temple de Bocace* to Margaret of Anjou, in which she was exhorted 'to avoid anger and melancholy, to seek peace of heart, attend to virtue, not to dwell on the past and to thwart evil fortune by strength of spirit'.[65] Fortescue may have spent some of his time at Koeur in translating Alain Chartier's French religious meditation, the *Treatise of Hope* (*Traité de l'Espérance*) and his *Four-Part Invective* (*Quadrilogue Invectif*) into English. Clermont was the first to print a fragment of the former work under the title *The Dialogue between Understanding and Faith*. Both he and Plummer were inclined to attribute it to Fortescue.[66] Smith's catalogue of 1718 was the first place where this opinion was recorded, at the time the fragment had only been identified in one manuscript, London, BL MS Cotton Vitellius E x. Subsequently the scholarship of Margaret Blayney has revealed the existence of four fuller copies and the companion piece, the *Quadrilogue Invectif*.[67] All the manuscripts date from the late fifteenth century, but Blayney believed that none of them was the original.

Alain Chartier had been employed at the French court during the early fifteenth century, including the time when the fortunes of the Dauphin/Charles VII and his followers were at a low point. In 1422, just after his parents had agreed with Henry V of England that he would inherit the French throne, Chartier wrote the *Quadrilogue Invectif*, in

[65] George Chastellain, *Le Temple de Bocace*, ed. S. Bliggenstorfer, *Romanica Helvetica* 104 (Berne: 1988) 191; Kekewich, *The Good King*, 208–9; F. Hepburn, 'The Queen in Exile: Representing Margaret of Anjou in Art and Literature', *The Fifteenth Century XI: Concerns and Preoccupations*, ed. L. Clark (Woodbridge: 2012) 61–90.

[66] Clermont, *Works*, 481–90; Plummer, *Governance of England*, 79–80.

[67] London, BL MS Cotton Vitellius E x; Oxford, Bodleian Library MS Rawlinson A 398; Chicago, Newberry Library MS f37, Ry 20; London, Sion College MS L 40.2/E 43; Cambridge, St John's College MS 76 D 1; M.S. Blayney, 'Sir John Fortescue and Alain Chartier's *Traité de l'Espérance*', *MLR*, 48 (1953) 385–90; *Fifteenth-Century English Translations of Alain Chartier's 'Le Traité de l'Espérance' and 'Le Quadrilogue Invectif'*, EETS original series 270, 281, ed. M.S. Blayney (London: 1974, 1980).

which the dreaming author witnessed a distressed lady, France, reproach representatives of the three estates for their cowardice in failing to protect her. The Nobility and Common People argued with one another until the second estate, Clergy, intervened. He pointed out that what Charles needed to succeed was wisdom, wealth and obedience, and the treatise ended on the pessimistic note that he lacked all these assets. The unfinished *Traité de l'Espérance* was started in 1428, and in it in another dream the author was assaulted by Indignation, Distrust and Despair. They awakened Understanding, who brought Faith, Hope and Charity to help him; dialogues between Understanding and Faith and Hope followed. A third between Understanding and Charity was presumably intended to follow.

The regular contacts between Margaret of Anjou, her father King René and the French court could have given Fortescue access to Chartier's works. The desolate theme of the *Traité* might have appealed to a politician still in shock from his loss of goods and status. Chartier had been an outspoken critic of the evils of the court and did not stop short of kings, 'for the sekenesse that cometh from the hede causeth al the membres to be troubled'.[68] The only remedy offered for the injustice of the situation was the comforting thought that the miscreants, including kings, would be punished for their sins in the next world. Blayney discussed whether Fortescue was the author of these translations and concluded that it was a fifty/fifty probability that he was. Evidence of links to his family from two of the manuscripts, the language used and his situation when he would have done the work supports his authorship. Yet she thought that some passages failed to show a secure grasp of the political ideas that were being discussed, surprising if he was the translator.[69] Both works have sufficient political content to appeal to Fortescue, indeed the *Invectif* is not particularly religious. Several references to the tales of bad kings from the Bible were to reappear in the *De Natura* and the *Governance* but the examples are too commonplace to clinch the argument.

It was never likely that the polemical war waged by Fortescue, William Fratour and perhaps other unknown writers would succeed if they were not supported by victory in arms. When in the later 1460s the ambitions of Clarence, the discontent of Warwick and the fears of Louis XI created a new opportunity for the Lancastrians to regain the English throne, Fortescue was ready to throw a very weighty work into the diplomatic scales: this was almost certainly the *De Natura Legis Naturae*.

[68] Clermont, *Works*, 488.

[69] Blayney, *Fifteenth-Century English Translations*, vol. 281, 26–31.

The *De Natura Legis Naturae*

The one argument which figured prominently in Sir John Fortescue's works on the succession which had not been used by the Lords in 1460 was the incapacity of women, because of the frailty of their sex, to succeed to the throne or pass on the right to inheritance. The fact that the custom of England debarred women from the succession was a separate argument and he treated it as such. The suggestion has been discussed above that Fortescue's use of the Genesis text and the inferences he drew from it derived from contemporary and near-contemporary French pamphlets produced to argue against the English claim to their throne. Whilst he was writing his short polemical works in Scotland, Fortescue may have concluded that the exclusion of women was an even bigger and better stick than the other weapons in his rhetorical armoury with which to belabour the victorious Yorkists. Presented in a long, dignified, philosophical treatise it might just induce the Papacy to favour Lancaster in the debate about legitimacy. It could also be persuasive in tempting Louis XI away from the accord he had made with Edward IV at St Omer in 1463. This, it is suggested, was the context for the composition of the *De Natura Legis Naturae* in the mid-1460s whilst Margaret of Anjou, her son and Fortescue were in exile in the castle of Koeur in Bar. The location indicates the initial reason for the composition: Prince Edward needed as he matured a substantial and well-argued rationale for the Lancastrian succession, something which his hapless father notably lacked when called upon to justify the claims of his dynasty in 1460.

Of the three great editors of Fortescue's works, Clermont and Plummer believed that the *De Natura* was composed in Scotland.[70] But in a footnote to his discussion of Fortescue's works Chrimes wrote: 'I must, however, confess that I am not altogether satisfied as to the date of the *De Natura*. It seems to me a very formidable and academic kind of work for him to have composed amidst the plots and alarums in Scotland, where he is supposed to have written it. The evidence for this supposition is not very strong.'[71] Chrimes went on to give his reasons for his doubts which, with others, will be discussed below. P.E. Gill refuted these arguments, suggesting that a reference in the *Declaration* to a 'Latin Boke' written in Scotland settled the matter, ignoring the possibility that the passage

[70] Clermont, *Works*, 32, 61; Plummer, *Governance of England*, 78.

[71] Chrimes, *De Laudibus*, xcii, n. 2.

in question could have occurred in a lost section of the *Defensio Juris Domus Lancastrie*.[72]

Two manuscripts of the *De Natura* are known to survive. The earlier contains only the first book of the treatise, entitled 'Tractatum de Natura Legis Naturae', the later has both books, the second entitled 'Tractatum de Jure Succedendi in Supremis Regnis'.[73] They both start with a preface that refers to two books, indicating that the survival of MS Laud 585 in an apparently complete form does not indicate that it was ever designed to stand alone. The preface of a few paragraphs gives an overview of the contents of the two books. The suspicion arises that, ever the realist, Fortescue knew that it was unlikely that the papal and royal French officials for whom his treatise was intended would read such a long and complex work thoroughly: they might, however, peruse a short preface.

The two books of the *De Natura* differ from each other in content and approach although they were designed to be read in sequence. The first is a philosophical meditation on different kinds of government, regal, political or political and regal, and how the law of nature could determine the question of succession. The second is more practical, describing a trial in an imaginary kingdom, Assyria, where no allegiance was owed by its ruler to an overlord. The king had died and his daughter, her son and the king's brother disputed their right to succeed to the throne before the figure of Justice. This gave Fortescue the opportunity to rehearse the arguments for and against the succession of women and their ability to pass on the right to an heir. He claimed that he wrote to dispel error: 'seeing that under the cloud of this ignorance so many hard-fought wars, so many civil contests, pervading the whole world, have prevailed, not only in the most noble kingdoms of France and England, but in very many other regions also'.[74] By mentioning the succession problem as applying equally in France and England as well as in other countries, he deliberately broadened out the issue to transcend the Lancastrian–Yorkist conflict. This was quite a different approach from that adopted in the short tracts, although it was a logical sequel to the arguments he had employed in them concerning the recognition of the right of Henry

[72] P.E. Gill, 'Politics and Propaganda in Fifteenth-Century England: The Polemical Writings of Sir John Fortescue', *Speculum*, 46 (1971) 333–47.

[73] Book 1, 'Treatise on the Nature of the Law of Nature', Book 2, 'Treatise on the Right of Succession in Sovereign Kingdoms'; Oxford, Bodleian Library MS Laud Misc. 585, pp.1–95, 1460s; London, Lambeth MS 262, ff. 1–102, 1470–1500.

[74] Clermont, *Works*, 191. All quotations from the *De Natura* refer to the English translation by the Right Hon. Chichester Fortescue.

V to inherit the French throne. This could be a sign that the *De Natura* was written during the exile in Bar, when the Lancastrians became ever more desperate as their chances of restoration faded. That desperation culminated in the treaty made between Prince Edward and Louis XI in late 1470, in which their claim to the French throne was quietly dropped.

Fortescue began the first book, 'De Natura Legis Naturae', by arguing that the law of nature was the means by which rightful succession was to be determined and in good scholastic fashion anticipated the objections that could be raised against this claim. The wickedness of the Israelites in asking for a human king when they were ruled by God was robustly condemned in the First Book of Samuel: the prophet warned them that their king would take their best possessions from them. With a playful display of humour Fortescue protested: 'Oh what a battle awaits the author ... Lo! here comes Samuel the leader of the host, and with him the people, more than six hundred thousand of them, saying "We have sinned".'[75] Fortescue had to deal with the apparent disparity between the biblical account of the evils of kingship and his claim that it was in accord with divine and human law, and in doing so he introduced what was to be one of the most important features of his political theory. The judges of Israel, under the guidance of God, had ruled righteously, politically and regally, a form of government commended by St Thomas Aquinas in his *De Regimine Principum ad Regem Cypri*. In fact it was only in the last part of that book, which was probably finished by the pro-republican Ptolemy of Lucca after the death of St Thomas, that political and regal rule was advocated.[76] Fortescue had already established that kings ruled politically as well as regally in England, as they neither made laws nor imposed taxes on their subjects without the consent of the Three Estates.[77] The use of that term rather than 'Parliament' indicates that he intended his treatise primarily for Continental readers.

The use of humanist translations of classical texts was to recur in Fortescue's two later legal and political treatises and they first appeared in the *De Natura*. Rather to the surprise of some commentators, he twice referred to Poggio Bracciolini's translation of Diodorus Siculus, *The Library of History* (*De Priscis Historiis*), which was only completed in 1449.[78] In this case the two short references were only illustrative of

[75] Clermont, *Works*, 202.

[76] *On the Government of Rulers, 'De Regimine Principum': Ptolemy of Lucca with Portions Attributed to Thomas Aquinas*, ed. and trans. J.M. Blythe (Philadelphia: 1997) Introduction, 1–59.

[77] Clermont, *Works*, 205.

[78] *Ibid.*, 197, 276.

his arguments, not essential to them, but he later seems to have used his sources with more confidence. Fortescue might have encountered Poggio whilst he was in England serving Cardinal Beaufort, 1418–22, and was evidently acquainted with at least one of his works. Amongst others, Roberto Weiss, K.H. Vickers and, more recently, Daniel Wakelin have investigated the English scholars and patrons who embraced the scholarship of the Italian Renaissance: some of them would have been known to Fortescue.[79] Another way in which he could later have seen humanist books was through Dr Ralph Makerell, a fellow exile at Koeur with whom he remained in contact for the rest of his life. Makerell was already a doctor of civil law when he took his degree in canon law at Bologna in 1458.[80] He could still have owned humanist works including the Poggio and also Leonardo Bruni's *Isagogue [Introduction] of Moral Discipline* (*Ysagogico Moralis Discipline*, composed 1421–24) and lent them to Fortescue, who used both in the *De Natura* and his *De Laudibus Legum Anglie* but only Diodorus in the *Governance*. Alan Cromartie has, however, pointed out that at this early stage Fortescue would not necessarily have thought of these works as belonging to a distinctive intellectual tradition such as Renaissance humanism.[81]

The objection to linking the institution of monarchy to divine authorisation by means of the law of nature was anticipated by Fortescue: how could regimes with such an origin sometimes be in practice arbitrary and unjust? He severely and humorously interrogated the human 'Law of the king' as if it were a person but he conceded that kings ruling politically would sometimes have to rule regally and vice versa, indeed the powers of the two monarchs were equal. In a sentiment that was to resurface in his later works he observed that the only power that kings ruling regally enjoyed in addition to those held by kings ruling politically was to sin without the control of the law and this was no true liberty for them. He showed, with biblical examples, how regal abuses of power that violated the law of nature had invariably been punished. The law of nature was superior to customary law and was revealed by reason: Justice, law and equity together made up the law of nature. He concluded this part of his argument by reverting to his joke that he was

[79] R. Weiss, *Humanism in England during the Fifteenth Century* (Oxford: 1957); Vickers, *Humphrey, Duke of Gloucester*; D. Wakelin, *Humanism, Reading and English Literature, 1430–1530* (Oxford: 2007).

[80] R.J. Mitchell, 'English Law Students at Bologna in the Fifteenth Century', *EHR*, 52 (1936) 270–87.

[81] A. Cromartie, letter, April 2016.

being assailed by opponents to his idea and hailed the law of nature as superior to all other human laws.

The origin of the law of nature was Fortescue's next topic. It was established at the moment when God created man and gave him dominium over the world. Justice and the law of nature had remained immutable since the Creation, although the first man proved himself incapable by his sin of upholding them. Fortescue went on to explain, with reference to several patristic authorities, the relationship of divine to natural law and their respective functions. The former ruled the spiritual life of humanity whilst the latter guided its temporal concerns.

At the end of the first book Fortescue submitted what he had written to the correction of the Church, a conventional formula, although he was probably aware that he had strayed from his own expertise and comfort zone in the English common law into the realms of the canonists and theologians and was anxious in case he had expressed any heretical opinions. He also, not for the first time, apologised for the great length of his work but it was necessary to establish the legal basis for his argument in the second book, the 'Tractatum de Jure Succedendi in Suppremis Regnis'.

The second book of the *De Natura* started with the establishment of a judge before whom the case concerning succession would be heard. The daughter, grandson and brother of a recently deceased king of Assyria argued over who had the right to the throne. Fortescue avoided any embarrassment that might be caused by asking Justice herself to take the office, explaining that, although her image might be feminine, all the virtues were sexless. At this point Litzen protested against the tedium of the work:

> it is quite a weary task to follow Fortescue's flights of thought through the vindications, which are repeated over and over again, although the sobbing of the daughter and the irony of her son – even the superciliousness of the king's brother – add some human features to the discussion.[82]

Fortescue was, however, adapting the well-tried literary device of a trial, which had been employed since the previous century, as a vehicle for his arguments. The best-known to contemporaries was probably the English translation of the first two books of the *Pilgrimage of the Soul* by the French author Guillaume de Deguileville. In a dream the writer's soul was tried before a court presided over by St Michael but was menaced by Satan: his few good deeds were insufficient and only the intervention

[82] Litzen, 'War of Roses', 34.

of Lady Mercy saved him.[83] The format of a trial would presumably have been congenial to Fortescue with his legal training and long experience of the common law courts of Westminster. Below, an instance of when he actually alluded to that experience in book 2, chapter X is noticed.

In the *De Natura*, the daughter claimed that she should benefit from all just laws of inheritance, including the biblical precedent of the daughters of Zelophelad. Her son protested that her simplicity prevented her from distinguishing between the laws of succession in a kingdom and those for private property. The sphere of women was domestic and, recycling ideas from his shorter tracts, Fortescue claimed that there were many functions such as dispensing justice and waging war for which they were unsuited. These were the kinds of argument that were later to surface in *The First Blast of the Trumpet against the Monstrous Regiment of Women* by John Knox. Although, like Fortescue, he tapped into a well-tried misogynist tradition, there is no evidence that he saw one of the few copies of the *De Natura* that are known to have existed.[84] The daughter's son based his claim on the best of precedents, since Jesus Christ had been, through his parents' lineage, king of the Jews.

The dead king's brother started his speech by supporting the reasons that his great-nephew had given for denying the right of the woman to succeed to the kingdom. He added to these a much more robust account of the physical, mental and moral deficiencies of women which rendered them unsuitable to wield supreme power and supported his tirade with the views of several canonists as well as saints Augustine and Thomas Aquinas. He then showed from the laws of France and England that the woman had no right of inheritance. Fortescue seemed to have forgotten his scenario in chapter X since he wrote as himself in support of his interpretation of the law.[85] The brother followed up the contemporary legal points with a long speech on the succession to the kingdom of Israel proving that Jesus Christ became king of the Jews by divine appointment rather than by any temporal title. He concluded his case by a disarming reference to the costs he had incurred in urging his suit (redolent perhaps of the business transacted in the London courts

[83] Kekewich, 'The Attainder of the Yorkists', 29. If Fortescue had a hand in designing the *Somnium Vigilantis* it would be his second use of the genre.

[84] Numbers 27; Clermont, *Works*, 251–2; J. Dawson, *John Knox* (New Haven and London: 2015) 140–6.

[85] 'These facts are sufficiently well known to the present Writer, who for more than forty years studied and practiced himself in the laws of that realm, and at length discharged for a long time the highest judicial functions of that land', Clermont, *Works*, 261.

rather than in ancient Assyria). In consideration for his closeness in blood to the woman and her son, he was only seeking the award of the kingdom, not his brother's private property.

The three claimants then made their replications to the objections raised by their adversaries. The woman with many sobs and sighs begged the judge for compassion since she was being wronged by her own male kindred. Her defence was twofold: many kingdoms had been ruled by old or sick men or children who could not personally act as warriors and many valiant queens had conducted successful wars in the past. Although Fortescue did not wish the son's arguments to prevail, it was convenient to make him the mouthpiece of several of the misogynist sentiments with which his mother's case would be defeated. He started by denying that he was claiming the kingdom as her heir, proclaiming the principle that had been an integral part of the short succession tracts, 'neminem in alium plus iuris transferre posse, etc.'.[86] He based his case, supported by copious quotations from the scriptures, classical and scholastic authorities, on woman's innate inferiority to man. She was subjected to Adam by divine authority in the Garden of Eden, did not bear God's likeness, had no power of procreation and could never exercise supreme authority over men. To do so would be sinful and the few examples of warlike queens cited were extraordinary phenomena. They could no more create a precedent (and here Fortescue seems to have been deliberately insulting) than Balaam's talking ass would arouse expectations that all asses could speak. He admitted that women could occupy positions of authority in their households or as landholders or nobles, but they would always be subject to a male overlord.

The brother started his replication by reiterating some of the points already made, although he stressed the divine rather than the human origins of his argument. He quoted enthusiastically from Genesis, including the well-tried phrase 'sub viri potestate eris'.[87] In the first part of the work it had been demonstrated that the law of nature was sufficient to settle the dispute, but the brother was anxious to refer it to the divine law. Eve was created with a pleasant subjection to Adam by the natural law, but after she had sinned God put her under a stricter authority by his divine law. Forgetting his assumed identity in his fear that he could be undermining his own case, Fortescue claimed that despite the importance of the divine law, he had devoted the first part of the *De*

[86] *Ibid.*, 268, 'No man can transfer to another a greater right than is adjudged to belong to himself.'

[87] *Ibid.*, 279, 'thou shalt be under the power of thy husband, and he shall rule over thee'.

Natura to proving that the natural law was sufficient for his purpose. In the case of Eve it was her violation of natural law by her disobedience that had led God also to subject her by divine law. The brother then turned to his great-nephew's claim, refuting it by the principle that he could not receive a right from one who did not possess it herself. He then discussed the laws of descent which justified his claim, invoking the natural order of the universe and of inheritance as symbolised by Jacob's ladder, the First Cause and even the English law of attainder. All this took a long time, as Fortescue apologetically recognised in his concluding sentence, for 'whatever is to be great needs no short time to grow'.[88]

The claimants concluded their cases by offering their duplications. In civil or canon law these were the responses made by defendants to the replications to their pleas, another indication of a Continental context for the treatise. The woman was given a very small space and two weak arguments: that Eve's subjection to her husband commenced after the Fall, so it was not part of the law of nature, and that only married women should be under supreme male authority. The son had little difficulty in refuting his mother's arguments by reiterating points made earlier in the first case and by asserting that marriage cannot depress the status of a woman in the second. The pains of childbirth and the dominion that men held over their womenfolk were punishments inflicted by God. He rejected any arguments by his great-uncle that were based on the laws of England or of France, since they could have no influence upon a kingdom that acknowledged no superior. The law of the Empire provided that in the case of wardships males nearest in blood were granted custody, even if they held that relationship through a woman.

The king's brother swiftly demonstrated the contradiction inherent in his great-nephew's two arguments: he could not both reject the alien laws of England and France and then cite with approval those of the Empire. There followed four chapters (LI–LIV) which referred enthusiastically to many provisions in civil law which prohibited sons from inheriting by a right derived from their mothers. This makes astonishing reading when contrasted with the francophobe, anti-civilian sentiments of the *De Laudibus Legum Anglie* and lends further credibility to the theory that the *De Natura* was composed for a continental audience. Finally, the formidable weight of canon law and the misogynist opinions of St Paul on woman were thrown into the balance against the brother's opponents.

[88] *Ibid.*, 300.

The pleas of the claimants were concluded and Justice, who in the course of a long hearing appeared to have changed gender from female to male, made his award in a concluding speech. He began by reiterating some of the points made by the male contenders: many authorities attested to the unfitness of women to rule, the pre-eminence which men exercised over women was compared to the superiority of the soul over the body and the relationship between Jesus Christ and his Church. Judgment was given that the woman and her son were absolutely excluded from the right of succession to the kingdom and it was awarded to the king's brother.

Fortescue then resumed his own voice as the author and submitted his treatise to the Pope. If it were to be circulated amongst the princes of Europe, a former cause of conflict would be removed: 'Peace thus was everywhere so disturbed among men, and the strength of the Church so weakened, that there could scarce be found a prince who was so free from these great perils of war that he could give himself to her defence; and, therefore, the hand of her enemies has grown mighty against her.'[89] This was an astute piece of special pleading, aimed at the wish of Pius II (or his successor) to mount a crusade against the Turks, and exploiting papal frustration at the failure of European monarchs to support it. Fortescue reiterated his central argument that women were incapable of holding or transmitting the right to supreme authority. If they did so it was a sin and long use in a kingdom was not prescription but merely a heap of sins, a sentiment that challenged the duke of York's epigram of 1460, 'though right for a tyme rest and bee put to silence, yit it roteth not ner shall not perish'.

Chrimes characterised the impasse which arose in England in 1460 when the Yorkists claimed the throne: 'In the absence of a direct and competent heir, politics, not law, determined the succession.'[90] Indeed, this was unavoidable when, as the negotiations during that autumn between the King, claimant, Lords and justices made clear, there was no law in England which could authoritatively determine the matter. The Lancastrians got the worst of the political conflict and after a series of short pamphlets, which must have proved little more than an irritant to the Yorkists, Fortescue profited by his time in exile to make the case that a sufficient law did exist to determine the matter. Despite his apologies for the length of the *De Natura*, it was necessary to produce something of weight and conviction, set in the context that he knew best, the pleas and counter-arguments in which he had participated and then presided

[89] *Ibid.*, 331–2.
[90] Chrimes, *Constitutional Ideas*, 22.

over in the king's courts. Common lawyers such as Fortescue were well practised in the formulation of arguments, anticipating and meeting many of the objections which could be raised, supported by a suitable array of learned authorities and deliberately reiterating the main points several times.

The form of the *De Natura* appears to have been unique, but Fortescue was not creating his great treatise out of nothing since a tradition existed in France, as has been noticed above, for the production of literary propaganda to counter English claims to the throne. Activity on the English side was not so effective but Thomas Bekyngton has been credited with a refutation of the Salic Law, *De jure regnum Anglorum ad regnum Franciae*.[91] Amongst other matters it discussed the mode of succession in ancient Persia in a manner that is reminiscent of Fortescue's Assyrian scenario in the *De Natura*.[92] By the early 1460s Yorkist propagandists were applying some of the arguments employed in the Anglo-French debate to England.[93] Both the English and French traditions were available to Fortescue in the construction of what he may have hoped would be the equivalent of a code of law, supported by precedent and learned authority, to make good an embarrassing lacuna in English custom for the royal succession. He departed from his practice in the short tracts (whilst recycling several of their arguments) by avoiding all references to the specific circumstances in England, thus giving the work dignity and status, something he also hoped to achieve by its unusual length.

Some indications have been noted within the two parts of the *De Natura* that it was composed in exile on the Continent, after the argument in England over the succession appeared to have been settled definitively by arms in favour of the Yorkists. The final appeal to the Papacy could equally have been addressed to Pius II up to his death

[91] 'Of the right of the English king to the kingdom of France'; A. Judd, *The Life of Thomas Bekynton* (Chichester: 1961) 39–43; A. Cole, 'Staging Advice in Oxford, New College Manuscript MS 288: On Thomas Chaundler and Thomas Bekyngton', *After Arundel: Religious Writing in Fifteenth-Century England*, ed. V. Gillespie and K. Ghosh (Turnhout: 2011) 245–63.

[92] London, BL MS Harley 4763, ff. 227a–230b. It also contains a near-contemporary copy of an anonymous journal of the English mission to France of 1439. On f. 5a Edward III's address to the Pope justifying his claim to the throne, referred to 'Jus naturale'. E.F. Jacob, 'Sir John Fortescue and the Law of Nature', *BJRL*, 18 (1934) 359–76, traced the use of the concept in the literature generated by the original claim to the French throne made by Edward III.

[93] See Lewis, 'War Propaganda and Historiography', 206–7, for the scanty English literature; S. Anglo, 'The British History in Early Tudor Propaganda', *BJRL*, 44 (1961) 17–48; Taylor, *Debating the Hundred Years War*, *passim*.

in August 1464 or to Paul II after that date. No internal evidence has been found to locate the treatise more precisely in the 1460s (although Fortescue's joke about the signs of the zodiac indicates that the passage was composed in late June or in July)[94] but two other works contain references which suggest that it cannot have been written later than 1468.

The abstract of the four memoirs, the first apparently dating from 1468, presented by Fortescue to the French government which survive in the Bibliothèque nationale in Paris commences with a notice that: 'The Chancellor of England has provided a large memoir which states the rights which king Edward claims to have to the English crown and also to the French crown. In it he demonstrates that the said king Edward can in no way claim the said crowns of France and England.'[95] The probable timing of these memoirs has been discussed above, so if it was indeed the *De Natura* which was referred to it was probably written before the other memoirs.[96] The book sent to the French chancellor was unlikely to have been the original, so more time must be allowed for a presentable copy to be made with a preamble referring specifically to the claims of Edward IV. This would give a realistic time span for the composition of the *De Natura*, if it was written after Fortescue finally left Scotland in the summer of 1463, from late 1463 to 1468.

The other work which refers, this time unambiguously, to the *De Natura* is the *De Laudibus Legum Anglie*. Internal evidence indicates that the latter was completed in late 1470, when at last Henry VI was about to be or had been restored to the English throne. The *De Natura* was mentioned five times, first in chapter IX, in relation to England's political and regal government. 'Fortescue: I think I have discussed this matter sufficiently in a small work, *De Natura Legis Naturae*, which I wrote for your [Edward of Lancaster's] consideration'.[97] We might wonder at the possibly ironic description of 'a small work', yet it was only in the first part of the treatise that the respective merits of political and regal government were discussed so it could be that part that Fortescue had in mind. In chapter XI he reiterated the point he had made in the *De Natura* that a king ruling politically had no less power than one who ruled regally and the next reference, in chapter XIV, repeated the

[94] Clermont, *Works*, 295, 'The sun, which is now shining in Cancer, will not rush suddenly into Capricorn, nor jumping over the Lion will leap into Virgo, until in its successive course it shall have spent a month in Leo.'

[95] Kekewich, 'Lancastrian Court in Exile', appendix 2, 109.

[96] See above, pp. 130–1.

[97] Chrimes, *De Laudibus*, 27.

argument, which was to resurface a few years later in the *Governance of England*. The fourth reference came in chapter XXXIV and made the same point as did the fifth reference in chapter XXXVII. Both dealt with the same theme: the superior merits of political and regal as opposed to regal only dominion.

Fortescue stated in his first reference to the *De Natura* in the *De Laudibus* that he had written it for the consideration of Edward of Lancaster. As Chrimes observed when he first raised doubts about when and where the former was produced, 'Edward had finally left Scotland at the tender age of ten years; but the *De Natura* is scarcely a work for immature minds.'[98] In the same note Chrimes speculated that the work could also have been intended for future use as propaganda. Fortescue must have taken months, if not years, to formulate the complex arguments in the first part and Prince Edward may not have studied it until the late 1460s, when he was regarded as a young adult. All the authorities cited in the *De Laudibus* had already been used in the *De Natura*, another indication that both were written at Koeur.[99] The petition for the reversal of Fortescue's attainder in October 1473 stated that he had contradicted all 'the maters which were writen in Scotland and elles where'.[100] Since the evidence indicates a Scottish provenance for his four short polemics, it must have been the *De Natura* that was written elsewhere.

Of the two copies of the *De Natura* that are known to survive, the earliest is in Oxford, Bodleian Library MS Laud Misc. 585: the script indicates that it could have been written in the 1460s and the hand is that of a French scribe.[101] It contains the first part of the treatise, entitled in the text 'De Natura Legis Naturae'. There is no dedication or other indication of provenance at the beginning and nothing at the end to justify a surmise that it is unfinished. The Preface, however, refers to the contents of the second part as well as of the first. There are a number of annotations in the margins, and unlike the text these were not written in a professional hand. Professor de la Mare believed it to be English rather than French. It looks to me to be similar to the hand which made some of the marginal notes in Bodleian Library MS Rawlinson C 398, a collection of theological and moral works, including Vincent of Beauvais, *Of*

[98] *Ibid.*, xcii–xciii, n. 2.

[99] *Ibid.*, xcii–iii.

[100] *RP*, vol. 6, 69.

[101] I am most grateful to the late Professor Albinia de la Mare for giving me her opinion on this manuscript. It is paginated rather than foliated. See Appendix 3 for details of both surviving manuscripts.

the Moral Institution of a Prince, which belonged to Fortescue and which bears his coat of arms on several folios. Most of the marginal comments in Laud Misc. 585 are brief and conventional, but one at the end of chapter X, p.16, in an only partially legible sentence, indicated that if the reader found the ensuing chapters tedious, he could go directly to the folio designated by a decorative knot device (p. 53) at the end of chapter XXX. If the author of the marginal notes was Fortescue and this manuscript was the original author's text, he seems to have been giving Prince Edward permission to skip twenty out of forty-eight chapters of part I. Part II must have been separately prepared and is now lost.

The other surviving manuscript, London, Lambeth Palace Library MS 262, contains both parts of the *De Natura*. Again, there is no dedication, although the last chapter of part 2 includes an appeal to the Pope, whose name is not given. The content of part 1 does not differ significantly from the Bodleian manuscript and the second part seems to be complete. If the *De Natura* was the 'grant memoire' referred to in the Bibliothèque nationale manuscript, 1468–70, that copy has been either lost or destroyed and it would have contained the second as well as the first part.[102] From the evidence of Fortescue's first memoir, it would also have included some kind of prefatory epistle or an epilogue in which Fortescue laid his treatise before Louis XI and promised enormous benefits if he were to act on it. Another copy was destined for either Pius II or Paul II and it is possible that it is the original of that, which was never dispatched to Rome, or a later copy, which survives in Lambeth.

It looks as if Fortescue wrote the *De Natura* in the mid-1460s, initially for the instruction of Prince Edward, and, if the evidence of *De Laudibus* and the marginal note in MS Laud 585 is to be believed, it was used for that purpose. All Fortescue's references in the *De Laudibus* in which he reminded Prince Edward of his teaching in the earlier work were made to the first book. The second book could have been composed rather later, although the preface of MS Laud 585 makes it clear that Fortescue always intended to write a second, more practical part. It probably occurred to him that such a sophisticated and learned treatise could be put to a wider use as it spelt out the implications of the suitability of the law of nature to determine the succession in supreme kingdoms. He produced a version which was addressed directly to the Pope and probably another adapted for the French king. It was likely to gain a hearing in Paris since its arguments could equally be applied to the English claim to the French throne or to the dispute between

[102] See above, p. 130–1.

Lancaster and York. The second part was cast in the form of a legal case heard before Justice, and the proceedings owed more to the usages of the civil than to the English common law. This seems to have been a deliberate device employed by Fortescue to recommend his argument to the canonists in Rome and the French ministers. His next major work, the *De Laudibus Legum Angliae*, was to tell a very different tale, with its rejection of Continental civil law in favour of English common law and its francophobe sentiments. Yet this apparent lack of consistency had some justification, since the whole argument of the *De Natura* was an attempt to use the ideas of the canonists and civilians in a situation which the common law could not resolve.

Whilst he was in exile Fortescue took upon himself the task of educating the Lancastrian heir to the throne. One of the many things that had been lacking in the mind of Henry VI was a decent intellectual grasp of the way in which his kingship was founded on the laws and customs of England. Part 1 of the *De Natura* demonstrated that good human laws proceeded from divine law and the test of their worth was that they accorded with the law of nature. In case the Prince did not get the point, he lifted some definitions from St Thomas Aquinas and other scholastics to make a distinction between regal only and political and regal government and suggested that the latter was more likely to conform to the law of nature and work for the mutual benefit of the king and his subjects. Fortescue composed a second part to the *De Natura* in which the issue of succession was directly addressed in a manner which would provide the Lancastrians with a convincing case with which to woo prospective supporters on the Continent. Experience may have led him to hope for little from the Papacy but the French king was a more promising source of assistance.

The treatise would also fulfil the expectation of those who were politically aware that whatever was done should conform to the prevailing norms of ethical behaviour. It could provide such a justification for the invasion of England and for Lancaster's abandonment of its claim to the French throne. The way had also been prepared for Fortescue's other great work in exile, the *De Laudibus Legum Anglie*, which was intended to instruct Prince Edward in the fundamentals of the law and government of England, a country that it seemed he was about to rule. But, unlike that treatise and the *Governance of England*, the *De Natura* made no impact on studies of Fortescue's work until the late nineteenth century, when it was finally published by Clermont. The apparent survival of only one and a half manuscripts in England contrasts with the multiple editions of the *De Laudibus* from the mid-sixteenth century and the seven editions of the *Governance*.[103] The length of the treatise and the comparative obscurity of some of its arguments largely account for its unenthusiastic reception by scholars such as Clermont and Litzen.[104] There are, however, signs that the relationship of part I to Fortescue's subsequent treatises and its importance is now being appreciated.[105]

[103] See below, Chapter 6.

[104] Clermont, *Works*, 61, and Litzen, 'War of Roses', 34.

[105] A Japanese translation of the *De Natura* has recently been made by Shinichi Naoe (Tokyo: 2011).

CHAPTER 5

The Adviser to Princes

As a member of King Henry VI's council, even though he would attend only occasionally, Sir John Fortescue was expected to offer advice. During his early years as Chief Justice, it has been suggested above, his low status in relation to the King's inner circle meant that his words were likely to carry little weight and were mostly confined to the technicalities of the law. As time went on the situation changed: the disorderly 1450s, the Crown's chronic shortage of money and the duke of York's ever more determined efforts to wrest power away from Queen Margaret and her followers (several of whom were killed in the process) made Fortescue's position progressively more influential. Apart from the little tract on the *Commodities of England*, which addressed the issue of England's potential wealth just after the loss of Normandy (*c.*1452), none of his political writings seem to have pre-dated the exile of the Lancastrians in 1461. The political element in the *De Natura Legis Naturae* anticipated a number of ideas that were to be found in the *De Laudibus Legum Anglie* (*c.*1470). The *Articles sent by Edward, prince of Wales, to the earl of Warwick concerning the government of England* (1470/1) reads like a blueprint for the *Governance of England*, which also contains much material derived from the *De Laudibus*. This chapter seeks to trace the development of Fortescue's ideas on governance from the short and practical response of the *Commodities* to the thoughtful development of how political and regal rule should determine the law and the administration of England.

Henry VI

The Commodities of England

This little paper was almost certainly written by Sir John Fortescue to lay before King Henry's council between mid-1450 and the summer of 1453, when England had lost Normandy but still expected to retain Guyenne and Gascony. Its informal character, poor presentation, brevity and concentration on the specific issues of England's wealth, security and the importance of the port of Sluys make it look more a collection of notes written in the context of a discussion about raising revenue than a treatise for wider consumption. Many of the government's recent woes had been caused by lack of money, and characteristically Fortescue resorted to his pen to try to remedy the situation. If he was the author it is his earliest work by nearly a decade.

The Commodities has been tentatively attributed to Fortescue by Clermont but Chrimes described his authorship as 'very dubious'.[1] Plummer briefly considered the evidence and believed that it was insufficient to justify an attribution to Fortescue. He did, however, include the only extant copy of the work (the second item in a manuscript which contains a very early version of the *Governance*, possibly dating from the 1470s) in the Fortescue canon.[2] He believed that both items were written in the same hand, but on examination this seems to be unlikely. The preceding treatise is mutilated from the middle of chapter XIX and lacks an ending, making it difficult to offer suggestions about the relationship between the two pieces. After the first four pages the script of *The Commodities* becomes careless and poorly presented, as if the motivation of the scribe had failed. Internal evidence dates the paper from 1450 to 1453, the time when the government was desperately looking for means of raising additional revenue to pay for the war with France. Apart from the possibility that *The Commodities* was work produced for the council, a passage in the *Governance*, which itself may have incorporated papers written by Fortescue from the 1450s, seems to refer to such a work: 'I holde it for undoubted that the peopul of his lande wolde be wele willing to graunte hym a subsidie upon suche commodities of his reaume as biene bifore specified.'[3] This occurs in chapter XI, which deals with the question of gifts and subsidies. No previous reference to such commodities was made in the *Governance* so it is possible that Fortescue had failed to incorporate a working paper on the subject into his final version of the treatise but overlooked this lacuna.

Before the contents of *The Commodities* are considered, it is necessary to discuss an earlier related work, the *Libelle of English Policy*.[4] From

[1] Clermont, *Works*, 547, 'The language in which the excellence of the productions of England is extolled ... so much resembles that of passages in *De Laudibus* and *De Dominio* [*Governance*] that I have little doubt of its origin'; Chrimes, *De Laudibus*, lxxvii.

[2] See Appendix 3; Plummer, *Governance of England*, 80–1; Oxford, Bodleian Library MS Laud Misc. 593, ff. 16r–19v; Clermont, *Works*, 547–54. This edition remains the only printed version of the *Commodities of England*.

[3] *Vale's Book*, 240.

[4] G. Warner, *The Libelle of Englyshe Polycye* (Oxford: 1926).

internal evidence this anonymous verse treatise seems to have been produced in the late 1430s by a writer who was either close to members of the government or was one of them himself. M.M. Postan described him as 'well-informed' and characterised the work as 'saturated' in nationalist sentiments.[5] It is a plea addressed to members of the royal council that recommended two main courses of action: the determined defence of Calais and the creation of a strong English navy to keep the Channel. The first part of the treatise systematically listed the principal countries that traded with England and the commodities which they supplied. When the writer got to the Venetians and Florentines he vehemently condemned the unfavourable terms under which the English did business with them. The characteristically bullionist thought of the times, the desire to retain as much gold and silver within the realm as possible in the belief that it would enrich the country, clearly emerges:

Than these seyde Venccians have in wone
And Florentynes to bere here golde sone
Overe the see into Flaundres ageyne;
And thus they lyve in Flaundres, soothe to sayne ...[6]

The concern shown in the poem about the retention of specie can be explained by the decline in silver and gold stocks throughout Europe in the late fourteenth and fifteenth centuries: bullionism was an understandable reaction from the commercially minded society of the City of London.[7] The later chapters were devoted to various anecdotes, snip-

[5] M.M. Postan, *Medieval Trade and Finance* (Cambridge: 1973) 181, 244. The nature of the *Libelle*'s authorship is indicated by several pieces of internal evidence, e.g., 2, ll. 8–21, the quotation from the emperor Sigismund, could have come from a government source – Warner suggested Lord Hungerford. He names Adam Moleyns, clerk of the council, as the probable author. He belonged to the faction that favoured the policy of making peace with France and Warner sees traces of this in the treatise, xvii, xxxiii, xxxix–xlvi. G.A. Holmes, 'The Libel of English Policy', *EHR*, 76 (1961) 193–216, disagreed, believing it to be the work of an admirer of the duke of Gloucester and thus a supporter of continued war with France. That opinion was shared by the biographer of Adam Moleyns, A.C. Reeves, 'Adam Moleyns, Bishop of Chichester', *Lancastrian Englishmen* (Washington, DC: 1981) 203–63, 209, n.34.

[6] *Libelle*, 22, ll. 428–31.

[7] J.L. Bolton, *Money in the Medieval English Economy, 973–1489* (Manchester: 2012), e.g. a petition by the Commons in 1445 that more halfpennies and farthings should be struck, 239, also 227–9, 232–6, 245–51; R.H. Britnell, *The Commercialisation of English Society, 1000–1500* (Cambridge: 1993) 182–3, made the point that between 1353 and 1467 the availability of gold currency contracted by 18 per cent and that of silver by 64 per cent.

pets of history and a call to subdue the 'wylde Yrishe'. All were brought to bear on the central argument that it was essential to protect English territorial and trading interests.

There can be little doubt that the *Libelle* was known to Fortescue. In the first version of the poem the second stanza of the envoy reads:

> Sythen that it is soothe in verray feythe
> That the wyse lorde baron of Hungerforde
> Hathe thee oversene, and verily he seethe
> Nexte the Gospell: God wotte it was his worde,
> Whanne he thee redde all over in a nyghte.
> Go forthe, trewe booke, and Criste defende thi ryghte.[8]

The close connection between Hungerford and Fortescue, especially in the 1430s when the latter was on his patron's council, and the lawyer's interest in economic affairs, supports the case that he knew the work. The atmosphere of anger and xenophobia which prevailed in England after its desertion by Burgundy at the council of Arras in 1435 is reflected in the *Libelle*.[9] Although Fortescue was perforce to suppress such sentiments in his first writings in exile, the robustly pro-English character of his thought emerged in the *Commodities* and subsequently in the *De Laudibus* and the *Governance of England.*

The end of chapter VI of the *Governance* furnishes evidence that Fortescue supported the wider implications of the recommendations in the *Libelle*. After stressing the importance of keeping Calais he turned to the 'ordinary charge" of maintaining England's sea power:

> It shalbe alwey nescessarye that the kyng have somme floote of shippis upon the see for the repressing of roveres, saving of our merchauntes, our fisheres and dwelleres upon the coostes of our bordores. And that the kyng kepe alwey somme grete and mighty vesselles for breking of an armye, whanne any shalbe made ageinste hym upon the see.[10]

The government of Henry VI had never shown much interest in England's commercial and maritime affairs and it could be argued that this neglect was one of the causes of its economic and military woes

[8] *Libelle*, 57–8, ll. 1149–56.

[9] J.H.A. Munro, 'An Economic Aspect of the Collapse of the Anglo-Burgundian Alliance, 1428–1442', *Bullion Flows and Monetary Policies in England and the Low Countries, 1350–1500* (Aldershot: 1992) 225–44.

[10] *Vale's Book*, 233.

around 1450.[11] The recent *débâcle* with Wenynton had demonstrated the dangerous and expensive consequences of not having a fleet that was directly under royal control. If Fortescue was the author of the *Commodities* it shows him to have gained sufficiently in stature and confidence in the council obliquely to take them to task for one of their many political and military inadequacies.

Internal evidence, the reference to Gascony and Guyenne but to no other English lands in France (apart from Calais), indicates that the *Commodities* was written between 1450 and 1453 before they were reconquered by the French, 'our contre of Gyan, and of Gascowyn; whiche bothe two contreys longythe to oure Soverayne Lorde Kynge ofYnglonde on that other syde the See'. [12] The paper starts with a list of the principal rivers, the first of the seven most precious commodities of England identified by the writer. The names of havens and harbours follow and a description of which stretches of coastline face parts of France, the Low Countries, Norway, Brittany and other areas. The writer explained the object of this exercise: 'And therefore almoner Nations maye have full knowlege of the Reame ofYnglond by the Botayles [boundaries]; lyke as hit ys rehersyd afore that Ynglond ys no lytyll londe but a substauncyall londe, when it abuttythe agenst so many londes of Duche tonge, Frenche tonge and Bretayn tonge also.'[13] The patriotic sentiment concerning the substantial nature of England sounds rather like an attempt to comfort Henry VI and his council after the recent loss of Normandy.

The third commodity of England was the rich soil which sustained the sheep that provided such excellent and plentiful wool. The fourth was the woollen cloth, 'redy made at all tymys to serve the merchaunts of ony two kyngdomys Crystenye or hethynnye'.[14] The fifth commodity was the abundance of tin, lead and sea coal; the sixth 'the grettest treasoure of the worlde', gold and silver ore. Finally, the seventh commodity was that the common people of England are 'the beste fedde, and also the best cledde of any nation crystyn or hethen'. This sentiment, perhaps surprisingly positive in the wake of the recent popular risings,

[11] C. Richmond, 'English Naval Power in the Fifteenth Century', *History*, 52 (1967) 1–15; Rodger, *Safeguard of the Sea*, vol. 1, 146–9; S. Rose, *England's Medieval Navy, 1066–1509: Ships, Men and Warfare* (Barnsley: 2013) 52–3.

[12] Clermont, *Works*, 551.

[13] *Ibid.*

[14] For a recent assessment of the degree to which wool and woollen cloth contributed to national wealth both for individuals and royal taxes, see Susan Rose, *The Wealth of England: The Medieval Wool Trade and Its Political Importance, 1100–1600* (Oxford and Philadelphia: 2018), 132–3, 181–204.

is very reminiscent of passages in the *De Laudibus* and the *Governance*, for example: 'no hamlet, however small, can be found in which there is no knight, esquire, or householder of the sort commonly called a franklin [freeman], well-off in possessions; nor numerous other free tenants, and many yeomen, sufficient in patrimony to make a jury in the form described above'.[15] The author of the *Commodities* enumerated other great advantages enjoyed by the people of England: fish, meat and 'ryght goode ale', the universities of Oxford and Cambridge, the wealth of the bishops and abbeys, the richness of religious shrines and the diversity of the regions ruled by the King.

The writer then turned to the Continent and to an explanation of the importance of the port of Sluys in Flanders for land and sea-borne trade. Its strength lay in the convenience of its situation for trade coming from the north and the south, it was well placed for merchants of Italy and southern Spain who specialised in trading goods from heathen lands such as spices, dates, damask and coral. The principal nations that used Sluys and the goods in which they traded were then listed, finishing with Guyenne, Gascony and Brittany. The paper ended abruptly with a list of goods that were traded by Brittany.

The contents of the first part of the *Commodities* link it to contemporary debates between English and French polemicists about the respective merits of their rival kingdoms. One such account, which might have been written by Charles, duke of Orleans during the 1450s, *Le Debat des heraulx d'armes de France et l'Engleterre*, contains material reminiscent of parts of the *Commodities*.[16] In particular, the English herald listed the riches of England which corresponded quite closely with those enumerated in the *Commodities*, including the capable and prosperous people of the country. This led the editor of *The Debate*, to suggest that it was probably known to Fortescue and that it could have influenced the parts of the *De Laudibus* and *Governance* in which he compared the institutions and political and social condition of the French unfavourably with those of the English.[17] If he was correct in assigning a date in the mid-1450s to the *Debate*, the author of the *Commodities*, almost certainly Fortescue, could not have used it if he wrote the paper between 1450 and 1453. Conversely the informal

[15] Chrimes, *De Laudibus*, 69; *Governance*, chapters III and XII.

[16] I am grateful to Susan Rose for bringing this work to my attention: *England and France in the Fifteenth Century: The Contemporary French Tract entitled 'The Debate between the Heralds of France and England'*, ed. and trans. H. Pyne (London: 1870).

[17] *Ibid.*, xv–xvi.

nature of the *Commodities* makes it unlikely that it would have been available to the French author. The editor may have been correct, however, in supposing that Fortescue knew the work by the time he composed the later treatises. The adversarial, intensely patriotic tone of the *De Laudibus* and the *Governance* recall aspects of the *Debate* and the genre of which it formed a part.

The style and content of the *Commodities*, as well as the similarity of passages to parts of his later works, strongly indicate that Fortescue was its author. It does not read as if it was intended for wide circulation and it is only a few pages long. It starts without preamble or explanation, jumps arbitrarily into the middle of the subject of England's commodities and then to the importance of Sluys and ends without concluding remarks. Indeed, the second part could just as well be called *The Cause that the Merchaunts Makyn to Sluse in Flanders there Grete Repayre*, as that title has as much prominence at the beginning of its opening paragraph in the only manuscript as the *Commodites of England* has at the first. Fortescue might originally have written the two papers at different times and the copyist sought to give them a coherence that they never possessed. Alternatively, both could have been notes compiled for the preparation of a more elaborate work, something like the *Libelle*. The author of the *Commodities* almost certainly drew on that earlier treatise: the discussion of the merchandise that passed through Sluys could have been derived in part from the lists in the *Libelle*.

Fortescue's West Country gentry background, where the sea and shipping were important economic engines of his society, seems to have predisposed him to think about the issues aired in the *Libelle* and *Commodities*. The royal council was to recognise his expertise in 1457, when he was appointed to a commission to investigate the means by which the King could acquire more gold and silver to satisfy his creditors.[18] The *Commodities* does not contain explicit statements of the bullionist/mercantilist policies which informed the *Libelle*. It may, however, be linked to that poem as part of a continuing debate within government circles about how England's commercial interests could best be served at a time when it was losing most of its French lands, was involved in trading conflicts with the Hanse and Burgundy and was experiencing domestic turmoil. Fortescue himself gave a clear account of such debates in his description of the duties of the royal council in the *Articles sent to Warwick* in 1470/1:

[18] *CPR*, 1452–61, 390; Gross, *Dissolution of the Lancastrian Kingship*, 20–1, *passim*.

> for this counsell shall almost contynuelly studye and labour upon the good politike wele of the londe, as to provide that the money be not borne oute of the reaume, and how bolyen may be broughte inne, how merchandizes and commoditees of the londe may kepe theire prices and valure, how estraungeres caste not downe the price of the commoditees growing in the londe, and suche other poyntys of policee.[19]

The *Commodities* is an unprepossessing little document but since, as is very likely, it is the first surviving piece of political and economic advice to have issued from Fortescue's pen, it provides an insight into his thinking on a number of issues nearly ten years before any of his other known works were produced. C.J. Nederman in his study of late medieval and early modern European political thought cites Fortescue as an early example of a thinker who articulated economic nationalism whilst relying on scholastic sources. Nederman concentrates on the ideas to be found in the *De Laudibus* and the *Governance*, where Fortescue linked successful 'political and regal' rule to contented and law-abiding subjects. Nederman does not mention the *Commodites* and is mainly using Fortescue's regular organic metaphors to belabour Liah Greenfeld's contention that early capitalist thought was essentially individualist rather than collectivist.[20] His point is, however, well taken that Fortescue's political thinking concentrated on economic and social factors, rather than the moral/ethical ones that concerned most contemporary writers, whilst he adhered to the essentially medieval organic conception of the political hierarchy. In our own age those contemplating the consequences of Brexit might draw comfort from some of the encouraging sentiments in the *Commodities*, was also written when England seemed to be in danger of losing access to the riches of European trade.

Edward of Lancaster

De Laudibus Legum Anglie

Sir John Fortescue was tutor to Edward of Lancaster and the principal minister of Henry VI and Queen Margaret during their exile. This

[19] *Vale's Book*, 223.

[20] C.J. Nederman, *Lineages of European Political Thought: Explorations along the Medieval/Modern Divide from John of Salisbury to Hegel* (Washington, DC: 2009) 261–76; L. Greenfeld, *The Spirit of Capitalism: Nationalism and Economic Growth* (Cambridge, MA: 2001).

has always been known but, until recent decades, the arresting political theories to be found in the *De Laudibus Legum Anglie* and the later *Governance of England* obscured one of the other purposes for which they were produced: to instruct Prince Edward and Edward IV in the art of good government. Stanley Chrimes, the editor of the former book, which was written between 1468 and 1470, whilst recognising that it was an innovative study of comparative jurisprudence and making a masterly analysis of Fortescue's sources, never placed it in the well-established tradition of books of advice and mirrors for princes that flourished in Western Europe in the late middle ages. For Chrimes, as for many of the nineteenth- and twentieth-century commentators on Fortescue, the main significance of his ideas lay in the perception that he affirmed that monarchy was 'not only limited but parliamentary in character', reflecting 'the constitutional developments that had been taking place since the days of Bracton'. Chrimes stopped short, however, of claiming that parliament could initiate legislation: Fortescue's monarchy was limited only in the sense that it had to observe its own laws.[21]

Translations from Arabic versions of late classical texts made by learned clerics such as Albert the Great and the commentaries of scholars like St Thomas Aquinas in the thirteenth century had put an important corpus of Aristotelian and later works into the mainstream of European thought. Contemporaries would have recognised that Fortescue was acting like Aristotle, the philosopher who reputedly advised the young Alexander the Great, as he attempted to persuade first Edward of Lancaster and then Edward IV to rule wisely. Fortescue was well fitted for the task since not only did he have a fine grasp of English laws and political institutions but he had decades of experience of teaching young lawyers in the London Inns of Court. We know nothing of his early education, but the evidence of his writings shows that he was well aware of the ethical works, based on classical and Arabic texts, such as the *Secreta Secretorum*, the *Dicta Philosophorum* (both translated from Arabic during the 'Twelfth Century Renaissance') and Giles of Rome's *De Regimine Principum*, a product of the early fourteenth century. He had also read more recent French writers like Vincent of Beauvais and Alain Chartier and might even have translated devotional treatises by the latter. By the 1470s a large number of these works were being circulated

[21] Chrimes, *De Laudibus*, Introduction, c–cii. Much of what follows is based on his work; notes record opinions that he expressed and attribute quotations (Bracton was a very influential early thirteenth-century anonymous treatise on the laws and customs of England). Chrimes, *English Constitutional Ideas*, 202–3.

in Britain and Northern Europe and English versions of some of them had also been produced.[22]

Chrimes first published the *De Laudibus Legum Anglie* for Cambridge University Press in 1942. His translation of the original was amended by Shelley Lockwood in 1997, who also included a modern English version of the *Governance* and extracts from Clermont's *De Natura* in her book.[23] Neither the one fifteenth-century manuscript, Cambridge University Library MS Ff 5 22, nor the two sixteenth-century manuscripts of the *De Laudibus* which are known to survive contain any indications of their provenance.[24] Indeed Chrimes found them all to be inferior to the first printed edition, which was made by Edward Whitechurch in about 1546. He surmised that its fuller text was based on the lost original contained in MS Cotton Otho B i, which was destroyed by fire in 1731, and that none of the surviving manuscripts was directly derived from it.[25]

The date of the *De Laudibus* can be assigned with confidence to between 1468 and 1470. It has been suggested above that Fortescue composed the *De Natura* whilst he was in exile in Koeur and that it was written for him by a French scribe; the *De Laudibus* could have been dictated in similar circumstances. In contrast to the difficulty in determining the order and precise purpose of the short tracts there is plenty of internal evidence to locate its inception in Koeur in Bar at a time when Prince Edward was regarded as a young adult and the heir to the English throne. The references to the cases of John Hawkins, a Lancastrian who was executed for treason, and Sir Thomas Cook, who was disgraced and heavily fined on tenuous grounds by Edward IV, mean that part of the work could not have been composed earlier than the second half of 1468. The other limiting events were the departure of the little Lancastrian court from Bar in June 1470, which led to their defeat and destruction at Tewkesbury on 4 May 1471. An additional piece of internal evidence is supplied by the case of Richard Heron, which, Fortescue wrote, had been adjourned in the court of the *parlement* of Paris for ten years. This cannot have been literally true for, as

[22] M.L. Kekewich, 'Books of Advice for Princes in Fifteenth Century England with Particular Reference to 1450–1485', unpublished PhD thesis (Open University: 1987).

[23] Lockwood, *On the Laws and Governance of England.*

[24] London, BL MS Harley 1757 and Oxford, Bodleian Library MS Digby 198.

[25] See Appendix 3 for the argument made by Chrimes.

Chrimes pointed out, the adjournment took place in July 1461, but it does indicate that Fortescue was writing at the very end of the decade.[26]

The reference to Master John Fringe provides another piece of evidence for a date late in the decade or in 1470, since it stated that he was convicted of *lèse majesté* against Prince Edward and executed. Chrimes surmised that this took place in France, since such a crime did not exist in England and the phrase 'iam tarde' implied that it must have happened recently. Four references to 'Fringe' have been found severally describing him as 'gentleman' and 'clerk'. When he was first mentioned he was living in or near Cambridge, 1455–65, and was principal of St Thomas's hostel there, but in the two last references, assuming they applied to the same man, he was a gaolbird and involved in armed robbery. This fits the story told by Fortescue of a man who basely abandoned his clerical status to become a husband and father. We must assume that after 1465 he was no longer able to remain in England and moved to the Continent, where he became embroiled in the Yorkist and Lancastrian plots and counter-plots that were being hatched at the time. None of the references to the continental legal processes can be precisely dated but they indicate that the *De Laudibus* was composed near to the end of the Lancastrian exile.[27]

The fifteenth-century Cambridge manuscript of the work bears no contemporary title of any kind. The title *De Laudibus Legum Anglie* is first known to have been used by the lawyer and printer John Rastell in a reference in his *Liber Assissarum* (Book of Assizes) in 1513, an indication of the early interest that it attracted. Whitechurch called it *De Politica Administratione et Legibus Civilibus Florentissimi Regni Anglie Commentarius*. If he had access to a manuscript from the Fortescue family this title should be taken seriously, but we are unlikely ever to know if he did and may be excused from employing such a long title.[28] John Selden used the *De Laudibus* title in 1616 for the first time in a printed edition. The 1640 list of contents of Otho B i in the Cotton Library called it *De Laudibus* and in David Casley's eighteenth-century catalogue the item was given as *De legibus anglie liber*. Chrimes suggested that Rastell's title gained currency in legal circles but was unknown to printers until Selden's edition made it generally acceptable.

[26] See above, p. 132, n. 91; Chrimes, *De Laudibus*, lxxxvi–vii, 133, 207–10. The Heron case was to drag on for many more years. In 1482 the king's council effectively ended it without granting Heron any compensation.

[27] *Ibid.*, 47, 163–5.

[28] 'Commentary on the Political Administration and Civil Laws of the Most Flourishing Kingdom of England'.

Many of the sources used by Fortescue in the *De Laudibus* also occur in the *De Natura* and *Governance*:[29] he made fifty-two references to the Bible in the *De Laudibus*, eight to civil law and one to canon law. He regularly cited Aristotle and also sometimes used his ideas without attributing them. He did not, however, consult the original treatises and this applies to many of his other quotations from the classics and from St Augustine. The manuscript in the Bodleian Library that bears Fortescue's arms contains amongst other works the *De Morali Institutione Principis* by Vincent of Beauvais and William of Auvergne's *Cur Deus Homo*, which are both referred to in the *De Laudibus*. Additional quotations could have been derived from other treatises in the book.[30] Fortescue used other popular late medieval repositories of wise sayings, versions of the *Auctoritates Aristotelis, Senece, Boecii, Platonis* .... Chrimes did not know precisely which he used and cited several printed editions.[31] He must also have had access to a copy of the *De Regimine Principum* of St Thomas Aquinas and, as was the case of the other works cited above, he used it in all of his three major treatises.[32] Amongst these venerable scholastic works, the recent translations by two Italian humanists, the *De Priscis Historiis* of Diodorus Siculus by Poggio Bracciolini and the *Isagogicum de Philosophia Morali* by Leonardo Bruni, stand out in sharp contrast.[33] Fortescue also made five references to his earlier work, the *De Natura Legis Naturae*.[34]

Chrimes discussed alternative hypotheses as to how Fortescue might have had access to the works he used in the two major treatises that he composed in exile. He could have visited the library of Queen Margaret's father King René of Anjou at Angers or the one in the Benedictine monastery at St Mihiel in Bar. This possibility, however, looks less promising in the light of the investigations carried out by Chrimes, who found none of Fortescue's authorities in René's catalogue and only the Bible and some books of civil law in the surviving records of St Mihiel.[35]

[29] Chrimes, *De Laudibus*, lxxxix–xcv; Clermont, *Works*, 347*–53*; Plummer, 96–100.

[30] Oxford, Bodleian Library MS Rawlinson C 398.

[31] Eighteen of Fortescue's quotations have been found in the edition, *Les Auctoritates Aristotelis. Un florilège medieval. Étude historique et édition critique*, ed. J. Hamesse (Louvain: 1974); see Appendix 4.

[32] See above, Chapter 4, pp. 154–5.

[33] See below, Conclusion, pp. 265–7, for a discussion of Fortescue's use of these works.

[34] Chrimes, *De Laudibus*, chapters IX, XI, XIV, XXXIV, XXXVII.

[35] *Ibid.*, xci, n. 2, xciii, n. 1; A. Lecoy de la Marche, *Le Roi René: sa vie, son administraton, ses travaux artistiques et littéraires*, 2 vols (Paris: 1875) vol. 2, 182–97; J.H. Albanès, 'La bibliothèque du Roi René', *Revue des Sociétés Savants des*

His alternative theory seems in the light of the evidence to be more convincing: that Fortescue carried a small collection of books, perhaps ten to twelve, with him in exile.

Despite the practical difficulties inherent in this proposal it has much to commend it, assuming that Fortescue composed both the *De Natura* and the *De Laudibus* in exile at Koeur and that the *Governance* was given its final form in England in the early 1470s. All he had to do was draw on his own and his fellow exiles' books for the composition of the first two treatises and on his memory for the frequently cited precepts.[36] Many of the references were subsequently recycled in the *Governance* and new ones came from volumes, such as Rawlinson C 398, which he retained on his return to England. This seems to be a more satisfactory explanation for his use of a limited range of authorities than the possibility that he kept visiting European royal and ducal libraries whilst he was engaged in difficult diplomatic exchanges. If he had used some of his fellow exiles' books he did not need to have access to them for his later work as he could recycle his references from the *De Natura*. The type of sources he chose could have been determined to some extent by what was available to him in exile. On the other hand, with the exception of the two Italian translations, they were what a well-educated lawyer of the late middle ages might be expected to use: the Bible, the Fathers and their commentators, books of canon and civil law, the statutes of English law, the works of classical authors like Aristotle and Varro derived from the many compendia that had been made, and histories.

As the best known of Fortescue's works, for the three centuries following his death, the argument of the *De Laudibus* determined the place assigned to him by early commentators in the genesis of English political thought, especially for his contention that political and regal government was superior to regal only rule. Although it had first been aired in the *De Natura*, that work is long and challenging to read and was not available in print until Clermont's edition of 1869. Fortescue gave his exposition of political and regal rule a more central position in the later work and thus identified a crucial and defining feature of English political institutions. The other reason for the popularity of the *De Laudibus* was that it was regarded as an excellent introduction to the common law of England. At several stages in the work, Fortescue gave graphic and very favourable descriptions of the education, careers and

---

Départements, 8 (1875) 301–11; G. Haenel, *Catalogi Librorum Manuscriptorum qui in Bibliothecis Galliae etc. Asservantur* (Leipzig: 1830) 227.

36 His two references to Gratian, for example, were inaccurate, Chrimes, *De Laudibus*, lxxxix.

lives of London lawyers – as an exile he was free to offer ideal accounts at the expense of political realities.[37] He also cited many instances of the superiority of English common law over civil law, whose baleful effects he had observed in French society.

The treatise took the form of a dialogue between Fortescue, who described himself as a 'certain aged knight', Chancellor of the king of England, and Prince Edward of Lancaster and was set in the castle of Koeur in the duchy of Bar. At the beginning Fortescue attempted to divert the Prince from his exclusive pursuit of martial exercises to the study of law:

> I do indeed rejoice, most fair prince, at your noble disposition perceiving as I do with how much eagerness you embrace military exercises, which are fitting for you to take such delight in, not merely because you are a knight but all the more because you are going to be a king. *For the office of a king is to fight the battles of his people and to judge them rightfully*, as you may very clearly learn in I Kings, chapter viii. For that reason, I wish that I had observed you to be devoted to the study of the laws with the same zeal as you are to that of arms, since, as battles are determined by arms, so judgements are by laws.[38]

The Prince objected to this onerous proposition on the grounds that only sacred laws were worthy of study. In the four following chapters of argument drawn from the scriptures, pagan and Christian philosophers, Fortescue wrung from him an agreement to study the law, but with two reservations which effectively set the agenda for the rest of the treatise:

> The chancellor having ceased, the prince began thus, 'You have overcome me, good sir, with your most persuasive discourse, by which you have caused my mind to thirst with no small heat for lessons in the law. Nevertheless, my mind is in two difficulties in the matter, just as a boat in troubled waters knows not whither to direct its bows. One difficulty is that when I recollect how many years students in the curricula of the law devote to their study before they attain to an adequate expertness therein, I fear lest I myself spend the years of my youth in the same way. The second difficulty is whether I shall devote myself to the study of the laws of England or of the civil laws which are renowned throughout the world. For the people should not be governed by any but the best laws; as

[37] J.L. Gillespie, 'Sir John Fortescue's Concept of the Royal Will', *NMS*, 23 (1979) 47–65.

[38] Chrimes, *De Laudibus*, 3, 5.

Aristotle says, *Nature always covets the best.* Hence I should willingly pay heed to your advice in these particulars.'[39]

The first discussion of English law was held in chapter VIII, in which Fortescue reassured the Prince that he should be able to learn enough of its general principles in one year and also have time to maintain his military exercises. Although all the judgments given in the kingdom emanated from the monarchy, Edward (Fortescue seemed to have forgotten that his father Henry VI was still living) would leave their actual delivery to the justices. Fortescue showed his skill as a courtier by observing how well the Prince had mastered the principles of grammar and predicting that the perspicacity of his mind would enable him quickly to attain a similar grasp of the law. Fortescue was to return to the subjects of legal education and the organisation of the system several times in the course of the treatise, but in chapter IX he addressed his other major theme, the superiority of common law over civil law.

The Prince's anxiety about which legal system he should adopt was relieved by the assurance that he had no choice in the matter since England already had one which prevented the monarch from changing it. 'St Thomas, in the book he wrote for the king of Cyprus, *De Regimine Principum*, is considered to have desired that a kingdom be constituted such that the king may not be free to govern his people tyrannically, which only comes to pass when the regal power is restrained by the political law.'[40]

Fortescue's use of the phrase 'is considered' could be crucial here, as commentators have made the point that St Thomas did not sanction his interpretation of the use of political and regal power. One possibility is that he combined other works by St Thomas, notably the *Summa Theologica*, with the *De Regimine*, which was probably completed by the pro-republican Ptolemy of Lucca.[41] The precise interpretation Fortescue put on those elements was his own since it suited the case he was making to the Prince for the superiority of English law that it should be shown to be an integral part of the political organisation of his realm. As Brian Tierney remarked, 'patterns of words (encoding patterns of ideas) often

[39] *Ibid.*, 19, 21.

[40] *Ibid.*, 27.

[41] *Ibid.*, xciv; J.M. Blythe, *Ideal Government and the Mixed Constitution in the Middle Ages* (Princeton: 1992) 39–59, adopted a more nuanced approach to what St Thomas actually meant by political and regal government. The distinction between the two was whether the former was according to the law and the latter absolute. What he lacked, unlike Fortescue, was a formula for an institutional framework that could guarantee a mixed polity.

remain the same for centuries; but, as they are applied to different social and political contexts, they take on new meanings'.[42] The Prince then raised the objection that monarchs ruling politically would be inferior in power to those ruling regally. Fortescue devoted the next two chapters to tracing the origins of political and regal government, using some of the material that had first appeared in the *De Natura* and drew on the same sources, particularly Vincent of Beauvais and Augustine.

The Prince's *resumé* in chapter XIV of what Fortescue had argued and his acceptance of the principles laid down contained ideas that have been of considerable importance to the interpretation of his thought, as it seemed to support the concept of a constitutional monarchy: 'no people ever formed themselves into a kingdom by their own agreement and thought, unless in order to possess safer than before both themselves and their own, which they feared to lose – an expectation which would be disappointed if their king were able to deprive them of their means.'[43]

The Prince then referred to Fortescue's argument in *De Natura* (which was to be repeated in the *Governance*) that the only additional power enjoyed by a king ruling regally was the power to do evil, since he would be acting tyrannically in violating the interests of his subjects. His one remaining query concerned the need to prove the superiority of English law over civil law.

Fortescue replied that the origins of all laws were to be found in the law of nature, customs and statutes.[44] The first applied universally to all systems of law and did not need to be discussed (it had after all been the subject of his previous long treatise), so they could concentrate on the characteristics of English customs and statutes. He claimed optimistically the customs had remained unchanged since before Roman times and that this proved their excellence. Similarly, the statutes of England were good because they did not, as in regal governments, emanate only from the will of the prince but also from assent through the prudent decision of more than 300 nobles and commoners in parliament. The superiority of English law over civil law and its unique suitability for

[42] B. Tierney, *Religion, Law and the Growth of Constitutional Thought, 1150–1650* (Cambridge: 1982) ix.

[43] Chrimes, *De Laudibus*, 35; Lockwood, *On the Laws of Constitutional Government*, 23, n.85 observes that in the *Governance*, chapter II, there is a more explicit distinction between the act of will that incorporates the people and the act of will that 'chooses' the king.

[44] Chrimes, *De Laudibus*, 37; see *The Nature of Customary Law: Legal, Historical and Philosophical Perspectives*, ed. J.B. Murphy and A. Perreau-Saussine (Cambridge: 2007), esp. D. Ibbotson, 'Custom in Medieval Law', 151–75; A. Cromartie, 'The Idea of Common Law as Custom', 203–27.

national needs was demonstrated in the following chapters. The subjects Fortescue addressed included the operation of juries in England and the French practice of extracting confessions through torture. Throughout his account of the merits of the English law he stressed its fairness to the accused and the necessity of avoiding unsafe convictions.

By chapter XXVIII the Prince was prepared to accept that the English common law afforded more protection to the innocent than the Continental civil law. His claim to 'know more certainly what is now done in England than what has been done here in Bar where I at present reside' might have been exaggerated but it supports the probability of regular contacts between the exiles and sympathisers in England.[45] The Prince was surprised that the jury system was not more widely used. Fortescue's reply did not deal in abstract theories of right but instead addressed the socio-economic circumstances in England from a comparative point of view. There was a broad potential base for active participation in the political process in the shires, where knights, esquires and other responsible men of substance were available for service on juries. Their numbers and local standing made it unlikely that they would act corruptly, whilst on the Continent few men had sufficient means to qualify for such work.

Prince Edward still had doubts about how appropriate the common law might be for England since some of his ancestors had attempted to repudiate it and introduce civil law. Fortescue somewhat testily replied, 'You would not wonder, prince, if you considered with an alert mind the cause of this attempt.' He went on to express a central element in his political ideology, '*What pleased the prince has the force of law*. The laws of England do not sanction any such maxim, since the king of that land rules his people not only regally but also politically, and so he is bound by oath at his coronation to the observance of his law.'[46] Some of the Prince's ancestors had not appreciated that these limitations to their power actually guaranteed the security of the monarchy and its subjects. To prove the case Fortescue discussed the results of regal government in France and compared them with the effects of regal and political rule in England.

Fortescue's interest in economic factors, as well as a degree of xenophobia, emerged again in the stress he laid upon the way in which regal government harmed the common people of France. Their sufferings, caused by the heavy taxation and other dues that their kings arbitrarily imposed upon them, were increased by the unjust treatment meted out to those accused of committing crimes. In England, however, the king

[45] Chrimes, *De Laudibus*, 67.

[46] *Ibid.*, 79

could not 'by himself or by his ministers, impose tallages, subsidies, or any other burdens whatever on his subjects, nor change their laws, nor make new ones, without the concession or assent of his whole realm expressed in parliament'.[47] As a result the realm was prosperous and the people lived in comfort and contentment, protected by the law. Fortescue appealed to the Prince to confirm his account of the poverty of the French people from his experience of travelling in that country. No such evidence was available for the very favourable account he gave of the well-being of the English people (many of whom had experienced the ravages of civil war for the past fifteen years). He probably exaggerated their affluence and security for polemical purposes and his memories were those of a nostalgic exile. Another agenda inherent in his argument was his fear that the Prince had been infected by the autocratic ways of the French monarchy, a regime that had delivered a number of humiliating rebuffs to Fortescue and his fellow Lancastrian diplomats during the 1460s.

Prince Edward cut into his mentor's eulogy on the merits of political and regal rule by asking him to revert to his earlier theme of the specific differences between civil and English law, which had been interrupted by his earlier interventions. Fortescue first addressed the civil law practice of allowing the legitimation of bastard children if their parents subsequently married, which was not permitted under English law. The righteous condemnations of the French practice from both Fortescue and the Prince provide an insight into the values of the author. While he normally emerges as pragmatic, worldly and even humorous, in regard to sexual misdemeanours he became positively ascetic in his castigation of 'culpable and mutual lust'.[48]

Two more instances of where the common and civil law differed were then described: how the free or servile status of children was determined and the allocation of guardians to minors. The Prince believed the English practice to be superior in both cases and delivered the well-known eulogy on the benefits of education in a royal or noble household.[49] Ives acidly commented on Fortescue's praise of feudal wardship that 'the English landed classes did everything in their power to avoid so happy a possibility'.[50] Both Fortescue and the Prince were showing signs of fatigue at the relentless accumulation of detailed differences between the two legal systems. A biographical element can be discerned

[47] *Ibid.*, 87.
[48] *Ibid.*, 99.
[49] *Ibid.*, 111.
[50] Ives, *Common Lawyers*, 192.

here, especially if considered in conjunction with the marginal notes probably written by Fortescue in the putative original of the first part of the *De Natura*, Bodleian Library MS Laud 545. He had been concerned with the Prince's education at least since their arrival at Koeur and had realistic expectations of his attention span for legal and philosophical abstractions.

Perhaps it was the need to keep the attention of the Prince, who had expressed an interest in the education of young nobles, that led Fortescue to launch into another rose-tinted account, in this case of the legal training provided by the Inns of Court and the Inns of Chancery.[51] His description of their conduct and cultivation has been extensively used by historians, although some of the details cannot be verified.[52] Yet it is likely that, given his long career based on the Inns, his account was accurate, since much of it can be confirmed by later authorities.[53] C.W. Brooks has also made the point that Fortescue was a student and rising lawyer in Lincoln's Inn earlier in the fifteenth century when the level of litigation in the royal courts was high and his enthusiasm could have been coloured by those memories.[54] During his description of the procedures followed for the appointment of a serjeant-at-law, he made the revealing remark that no advocate in the world enriched himself as much through his office. This perhaps explains the enormous cost to the new serjeant of the gifts and feasting associated with his investiture, £266 13s 4d.[55]

No such display accompanied the appointment of justices, but the subject provided the cue for another of Fortescue's rhapsodies about the legal profession. After spending three hours in court and eating their dinner they

> pass the whole of the rest of the day in studying the laws, reading Holy Scripture and otherwise in contemplation at their pleasure, so that their life seems more contemplative than active. They thus lead a quiet life, free of all worries and worldly cares. Nor was it ever found that any of them

[51] See above, Chapter 1, p. 25, n. 55.

[52] Chrimes, *De Laudibus*, 197–99, n. 23, 200, n. 20. Fortescue omitted practices such as the moots and readings based on the statutes, which, by the fifteenth century, formed an important part of the education of barristers. Perhaps he feared that they would seem onerous to the Prince or beneath his dignity.

[53] See Ives, *Common Lawyers*, *passim*; Baker, *Introduction to English Legal History*, *passim*.

[54] C.W. Brooks, *Lawyers, Litigation and English Society since 1450* (London and Rio Grande: 1998) 79–80.

[55] Chrimes, *De Laudibus*, 123.

> was ever corrupted with gifts or bribes. So we have seen their race so perpetuated by grace that scarcely any of them die without issue, which is like a great and as it were an appropriate benediction of God.[56]

He rejected the role of 'Fortune' in the success of justices' families for it was rather a sign of divine approval. This made an interesting contrast to the ideas of contemporary Italian humanists, of whose works, it has been noticed above, he had some knowledge.[57] They attributed success or failure to Fortune's intervention, although some believed that it could be overcome by prudent conduct. Fortescue's rejection of Fortune might emanate from a purely Christian view that those prospered who led a godly life. An anomaly in the passage was the assumption that justices had free time, although here Fortescue seemed to be in tune with the values of his Italian Renaissance contemporaries, who valued the leisure to study and contemplate (*otium*) over time spent working for worldly objectives (*negotium*). The heavy burdens of Fortescue's work as Chief Justice were discussed above in Chapter 2 and his involvement in politics, family affairs and property and other business can scarcely have left him the amount of leisure he attributed to justices. The evidence of the Paston letters and papers and the Shillingford papers also shows that he accepted gifts and probably also bribes.

Prince Edward had one remaining reservation about the operation of the law in England – its delays. However, Fortescue defended them on the grounds that they could sometimes prevent unjust verdicts being carried out. He cited from his own experience the terrible case of a woman in Salisbury who was over-hastily burnt for murdering her husband and who was posthumously exonerated by the confession of a servant.[58] In his review of criminal justice in the early fifteenth century Edward Powell has produced another defence of the delays in the law – delay motivated litigants to reach peaceful settlements out of court.[59] The consensus amongst legal historians, however, is that the great delays involved in bringing cases to a conclusion drove many plaintiffs

[56] *Ibid.* In an endearing aside Fortescue hoped that when the Prince came to power he would make the justices' robes more ornate for the greater glory of the law and of his realm, 129.

[57] J.G.A. Pocock, *The Machiavellian Moment: Florentine Political Thought and the Atlantic Revolution* (Princeton: 1975) esp. 31–48.

[58] Chrimes, *De Laudibus*, 133–5.

[59] E. Powell, *Kingship, Law and Society: Criminal Justice in the Reign of Henry V* (Oxford: 1989) 273–4.

into Chancery during the fifteenth century and brought about changes in the workings of King's Bench.[60]

The treatise ended with a declaration by Prince Edward that the English common law surpassed all other legal systems. Quotations from Vegetius, the Book of Proverbs and Vincent of Beauvais reinforced the point that the prince who had expert knowledge of the laws of his realm was most likely to rule well. Edward agreed with Fortescue that the discussion should end so that he could start receiving instruction on the general principles of the laws of England, and with conventional piety they concluded by giving thanks to God.

When Prince Edward promised to start studying English law immediately he mentioned his earlier instruction in its form and nature. The passage furnishes evidence for another objective Fortescue had in writing the *De Laudibus*. He hoped that it would be a handbook not only for the Prince but for subsequent kings of England, 'Prince: I surmise that your teaching in this discourse will not be useless to future kings of England, since they cannot enjoy ruling by laws which they do not appreciate.'[61] Written in or just before 1470, it looks more like a summary of what Fortescue had been teaching the Prince for some time than a new initiative that he was launching just when the court at Koeur was about to dissolve in order for its leaders to participate in the process that led to the Readeption of Henry VI. In the chapter on the degree of sergeant-at-law he said that he had explained how it was conferred in earlier discussions and in the penultimate chapter he said that the Prince knew all about the law's delays from his previous instruction. This internal evidence indicates that Fortescue had been attempting to engage the Prince in the study of the broad principles of English law for some time, probably, as the Introduction implied, with limited success. There is a precedent for his use of work for more than one purpose: the *De Natura* was apparently conceived to instruct the Prince but he subsequently intended to lay it before the Papacy and, probably, the king of France.

In 2006 Rosemarie McGerr published an article, 'A Statute Book and a Lancastrian Mirror for Princes', which she later expanded into a book.[62] She suggested that a copy of the *New Statutes of England*, which includes the treatises *Modus Tenendi Parliamentum* and *Tractatus*

[60] See above, Chapter 2, p. 62.

[61] Chrimes, *De Laudibus*, 135, 137.

[62] R. McGerr, 'A Statute Book and Lancastrian Mirror for Princes: The Yale Law School Manuscript of the *Nova statuta Anglie*', *Textual Cultures: Text, Context and Interpretation*, 2 (2006) 6–59; *A Lancastrian Mirror for Princes: The Yale Law School 'New Statutes of England'* (Bloomington and Indianapolis: 2011).

de Senescalsia Angliae, in the Yale Law School Library could have been made for Prince Edward of Lancaster.[63] The arms of England (presumably of Henry VI) and of Margaret of Anjou appear several times in the manuscript but there is no dedication or any other firm evidence for the identity of the early owners. The description of the *Statutes*, which cover the reigns of Edward III to Edward IV, as a 'mirror for a prince' is mainly justified by the preamble, which makes more favourable allusions than were normal to Isabelle, queen of Edward II, the depiction of the kings and offers much external information about Margaret of Anjou and Sir John Fortescue. McGerr suggests that since the book was made in an English workshop it could have been commissioned by Fortescue and recovered by him after his return from exile in 1471. This is an attractive possibility, since the whole thrust of his *De Laudibus*, which certainly could be described as a mirror for Prince Edward, was that he should know and love the laws of England. McGerr concedes that the presence of the arms cannot of itself prove that the *Statutes* were associated with the Prince but it remains a tenable theory.[64] That they constitute a mirror for a prince is dubious.[65]

Fortescue's account of the operation of the English common law in the *De Laudibus* was misleading and over-optimistic and other aspects of the treatise were mendacious: the Inns of Court were scarcely the accustomed resort of the nobility as he claimed. He and his father, country gentlemen, were far more typical of the amateur and professional students to be found there. He also claimed that they were peaceful and harmonious places in which to live and work but evidence from legal cases and the *Black Books* of Lincoln's Inn provides stories of periodic bad behaviour and violence. With so many unsatisfactory features linked to the practice of the common law, how could Fortescue possibly praise it unreservedly in a treatise intended to instruct his master, the future king of England? This question brings us back to the purposes of the treatise: to enthuse the Prince about the laws and political institutions

[63] New Haven, CT, Yale Law School Lillian Goldman Library MSS G +St 11 no. 1.

[64] McGerr, *Lancastrian Mirror for Princes*, 42–4.

[65] Ibid., 47–68, plates 3–5. The figure dressed in fine robes, red and trimmed with ermine, could represent the Chancellor of England. He first appears peeping round the royal canopy in the illustration of Henry IV; he is portrayed full-length with hands extended as if he is offering advice to Henry V and is also shown full-length with hands extended but turned away from Henry VI. This figure, who seems to be a counsellor, offers food for thought and his depiction echoes the kind of playfulness that is sometimes encountered even in Fortescue's most solemn writings.

of England and to promote them above the attractions of the autocratic regime in France. An admission that, in practice, much of the common law was obsolescent and subject to corruption would hardly achieve that purpose.

Shelley Lockwood suggested that the *De Laudibus* was actually a reforming document, taking, for example, the words 'ought to be' that prefaced the description of the operation of juries as entailing an agenda for better, less corrupt practice.[66] Over the previous decade Fortescue had turned himself into an effective and hard-headed polemicist in his tracts on the succession – he knew how to suppress inconvenient truths and to present dubious activities in the best possible light. Had the Lancastrians regained the throne permanently, Fortescue might well have pressed for legal reform, but 1470 was hardly the time to do so. At that time he simply wished to describe English law as favourably as possible. Political reform was certainly on his agenda by then; Tony Pollard commented on the thoroughly reformist argument for the 'good public of the realm' in Fortescue's *Articles sent to the earl of Warwick*, dispatched in the name of Prince Edward when the earl had re-established Lancastrian rule at the end of that year.[67] It sought to implement the political and regal rule discussed in his two great treatises, the *De Natura* and *De Laudibus*, in a very practical fashion by limiting the capacity of Henry VI and his family to rule badly, but a thorough overhaul of the vast fabric of English law was not a project for a new and insecure government to undertake.

Throughout the second half of the 1460s, when he was based at the little court of Koeur, it looks as if Fortescue attempted to give Prince Edward some instruction in the rudiments of English law and political institutions. Probably fearing at the end of the decade that his good work would be submerged by the practical demands of gaining and keeping power, he wrote the *De Laudibus* in the hope that it would confirm what he had already taught the Prince and remain as a handbook for future English rulers. He was not blind to the defects in the common law and may well have wished to reform aspects of it, but a treatise aimed at the heir to the throne on the brink of assuming power was not the occasion for pressing the case. The time for a scheme for political reform came shortly afterwards in the advice that was sent to the victorious earl of Warwick.

Alan Cromartie observed in 'The Common Law, Counsel and Consent in Fortescue's Political Theory' that the whole thrust of Fortescue's advocacy of political and regal government in his three

[66] Lockwood, *On the Laws of Constitutional Government*, xxv.

[67] *Vale's Book*, 222–5; Pollard, *Warwick*, 197. See above, Chapter 3.

main treatises was not to introduce government by popular consent. Rather he suggested that English kings should act politically after taking good counsel from a wise, professional body of counsellors and from parliament.[68] During the first seventeen years when he periodically attended the royal council as Chief Justice, Fortescue had been obliged, as a second-rank royal servant, to watch the prodigal follies of the King and his ministers. Many of these had been destroyed during the fall of Lancaster and for the next decade Fortescue and a few other survivors were the only counsellors to Margaret of Anjou and her son. With the Readeption his opportunity to achieve good governance seemed at last to have come. The view taken in this study is that Fortescue's prince who governed politically would take wise counsel and rule with regard to the laws and customs of the realm, but that it was necessary, if circumstances demanded it, that he should govern regally by resuming the plenitude of power.

Another loyal servant who had been doomed to watch the decline and fall of Lancaster over a period of forty years was George Ashby, formerly a clerk of the signet. Internal evidence for the timing of his 'A Prisoner's Reflections' and the two works that he offered to Prince Edward of Lancaster is not so clear-cut as that available in the *De Laudibus*, but it leads to a similar conclusion.[69] He did not go into exile as far as is known and was imprisoned for a time in 1463. However, like Fortescue he probably wrote his advice for the Prince when it seemed that he would assume power in late 1470 or early 1471. The writer who was eighty when he composed *The Active Policy of a Prince* and its codicil, the *Dicta et Opiniones Diversorum Philosophorum*, was anxious that his master should avoid the many pitfalls that would beset him and succeed:

> In fyndyng sum goode exhortacion
> That myght be to you / gracious and mete,
> Ensuryng youre estate in quiete sete,
> Whiche may never endure but by virtue,
> According to the pleasance of Iesu.[70]

[68] A. Cromartie, 'The Common Law, Counsel and Consent in Fortescue's Political Theory', *The Fifteenth Century IV: Political Culture in Late Medieval Britain*, ed. L. Clark and C. Carpenter (Woodbridge: 2004) 45–67.

[69] Kekewich, 'Books of Advice', 103–38. Other advice about how to rule was offered to Henry VI earlier in his reign before 1450, most notably works by the court poet John Lydgate and the anonymous *Tractatus de Regimine Principum*. For the latter, see *Four English Political Tracts of the Later Middle Ages*, ed. J.P. Genet (London: 1977) 18, 42–173.

[70] *George Ashby's Poems*, ed. M. Bateson (London: 1899) 16.

Ashby adopted a Ciceronian model for his *Active Policy* that divided his advice into three sections: past, present and future. The Prince was told that Prudence could save him from the destruction threatened by vicious and covetous men. The Yorkists would have been Ashby's prime target, but his long experience of government had shown that the greed of royal servants had been one of the weaknesses of Henry VI's rule since he had assumed direct power. After the historic faults of the regime and its opponents, Ashby turned with surprising frankness to the challenges facing the Prince in the present:

> Suche as ye be, so shall ye be taken,
> Youre dedys and werkes shal prove al thing,
> Wele or evyl thei shalbe awaken,
> In chronicles youre Rule rehersyng,
> Either in preisyng either in blaming.[71]

The remainder of the section dealt more conventionally with the virtues normally advocated in 'mirrors for princes'. As he looked to the future Ashby continued to draw on the wise sayings of the philosophers, as he had done in previous sections, to enjoin on the Prince a moral but pragmatic mode of government. Indeed, he had already used so many sayings that the translation of the *Dicta* that he appended was something of a ragbag rather than a faithful, scholarly version. Ashby lacked the ability to convey political realities in the vigorous and intellectually engaging manner that has recommended Fortescue to generations of commentators, but he resembled him in his perception of what had gone wrong and his loyal desire to secure the future of the dynasty.

Fortescue's *De Laudibus* was a carefully argued proposal for a legal and political agenda that would help to save the Prince from the fate that had overtaken his father. The author presumably retained a copy and gave one to the Prince but both of these have disappeared. He omitted to mention it in his *Declaration upon certain writings late sent out of Scotland* which earned his rehabilitation with the Yorkist regime in the early 1470s. It would have been an embarrassing document with its commitment to making Edward of Lancaster a good king. Such copies as existed (and there were probably only a few) could either have been destroyed or hidden. Those that survived were to emerge to enjoy a new life under the Tudors. Fortescue's hopes of moulding a Lancastrian king who would avoid the mistakes of governance that he had been forced to witness during his long years of high office were to die with Prince

[71] *Ibid.*, 20.

Edward at Tewkesbury early in 1471. Yet he did make one last attempt to save the dynasty and its new allies soon after the earl of Warwick achieved the Readeption of Henry VI in England in October 1470.

Henry VI/the earl of Warwick

Articles sent by Edward, prince of Wales, to the earl of Warwick concerning the government of England

Despite the attribution in the title it has always been accepted that this short document, divided into seven articles, was written by Sir John Fortescue since it contains much advice that he later expanded in the *Governance of England*.[72] It occupies a pivotal position between his polemics and advice that were written as a loyal supporter of Lancaster and the last stages of his career when he was a member of Edward IV's council. Devoid of the philosophy and jurisprudence of the *De Natura Legis Naturae* and the *De Laudibus Legum Angliae*, it bears the marks of a hasty composition intended to meet the political challenges posed by the Readeption of Henry VI in October 1470 and was almost certainly written shortly afterwards.

The earl of Warwick was obliged to manage a precarious situation in which the expectations of his followers, loyal Lancastrians, quiescent Yorkists and the unaligned had to be considered; he was also committed by the terms of the treaty with Louis XI to wage an expensive and unpopular war against Burgundy. This was the context of the advice that Fortescue offered to Warwick on behalf of Queen Margaret and Prince Edward. It heralded an era extending from the second reign of Edward IV to the regime of the early Tudors which has sometimes been described as one of a 'New Monarchy'. Efficient conciliar government by professional administrators delivered tightly financed, centralised and authoritarian governance. John Watts, however, saw this in the long term as a 'constitutionalising trend', which would gradually play out over the next century as the monarchy became more reliant on conciliar rule and the law.[73]

The first of the seven *Articles sent to the earl of Warwick* anticipated the clamour that would be made in England by loyal Lancastrians both for rewards for their services and compensation for the losses they had

[72] *Vale's Book*, 50–1, 222–5; London, BL MS Additional 48031A, ff. 146a–8a; MS Harley 543, ff. 172a–173b. It occurs uniquely in these manuscripts.

[73] J. Watts, '"A New Ffundacion of is Crowne": Monarchy in the Age of Henry VII', *The Reign of Henry VII*, ed. B. Thompson (Stamford: 1995) 21–53.

suffered on the King's account. It might be possible to satisfy some, but, when income was scanty, many would be disappointed and become disaffected. It was also important to ensure that the royal livelihood should not be so depleted that the King would be obliged to tax the commons and the Church, 'to his enfamye and the withdrawing from hym of the hertes of his subgiettes'. It would be wise to await the constitution of the royal council, where all requests could be carefully considered on their merits and, depending on the extent of the royal resources, the deserving would be rewarded. This would protect the King, his lords and ministers from recriminations.

The second article dealt with the nature of the new royal council, which was to be radically different from the ones that had advised Henry VI during his first reign. Twelve clerics and twelve laymen who were 'wise and indifferente' were to form the core. They would be joined by four prelates and four lords who would serve only for a year and by the great officers of state such as the Chancellor and Chief Justices who would attend when they were required. The nucleus of twenty-four councillors would hold no other offices. Presumably Fortescue intended that they should be permanent appointees. He did not spell it out but seems to have hoped that ability and honesty rather than exalted rank would be the decisive qualities that would determine the appointment of these men. Such a council would protect the Crown from the evils of household rule and ensure that the King was given the best advice. Nowhere in the treatise did Fortescue use the phrase 'political and regal rule' but it was inherent in much of what he advocated, for example, his description of how the council would operate:

> And that the king do no grete thing towching the rewle of his reaume, nor geve lande, fee, office or benefice, but that firste his intente therinne be communed and disputed in that counseill and that he have herde their advises ther uppon, whiche may in no thing restreyne his power, libertee or prerogatiff.[74]

Any objection that the new council would be too expensive was swiftly met in the third article, where Fortescue claimed that previous ones had been packed with self-seeking magnates who had cost the country dear. The new, professional council would spend its time profitably considering such matters as the prevention of the export of bullion and how its flow into England might be increased. How the value of native commodities might be maintained, how strangers could be prevented

[74] *Vale's Book*, 223. Fortescue does use the phrase 'good politike wele' in article 3 to describe the beneficial results of ruling with the advice of the council.

from lowering their prices and how the law should be upheld and, where necessary, reformed were also fit subjects for the council's consideration of the 'good politike wele of the londe'. All these measures, it was implied, would save money, but the biggest saving would be to refuse large grants to importunate lords. The half of the council that was composed of clerics would also deliver savings, as they need not be paid as much as the lay members. This was the practice in the *parlement* of Paris, which Fortescue quoted with approval.

Article 4 addressed the reality that the King would be obliged to make some grants from his resources, but Fortescue hedged those around with as many safeguards as possible. Before any were made it must be ascertained that the King had sufficient to pay his ordinary charges such as the expenses of his household and administration. Any patents issued in breach of this policy would be annulled. Those patents for grants that were issued must be authorised by parliament or the council, with the exception of patents granted by the King's treasurer, bailiffs and other officers in the course of administering his resources. At that point Fortescue inserted draconian sanctions that were to be employed against any Chancellor who improperly sealed any patent, for he might act only if sanctioned by the council.[75]

Fortescue recommended in article 5 that when the time came for the royal household to be established and financed all its expenses should be paid in advance. He believed that this would make it such an attractive customer that 'the king shall have therby alway the market at his gate' and its costs would be reduced by a quarter. A moral consideration was introduced, in that this policy would benefit the poor and be pleasing to God. Fortescue advised that the Lancastrians should pay their debts promptly as did, he implausibly claimed, other monarchs. He had experienced the hand-to-mouth existence of the English royal household during Henry VI's first reign, culminating in the humiliation on the night of the feast of Epiphany, 6 January 1451, when no victuallers would provide food for the royal table without payment in cash.[76]

In article 6 Fortescue applied the same principle that he had invoked for the members of the royal council to royal servants: none should have another master. If they deserved it, they could be rewarded by offices, normally only one, but in exceptional cases a second might be given, provided that it was run by a deputy who would serve only the one master who served the King. The same concession applied to lay members of

[75] See above, Chapter 3, pp. 137–8.

[76] *Chronique de Mathieu d'Escouchy*, ed. G. du Fresne de Beaucourt, 3 vols (Paris: 1863–4) vol. 1, 303–4.

the council, while the clerics would doubtless be given benefices. In this way the King could reward good service without diminishing his resources or 'livelihood', as Fortescue called it.

The seventh and final article advised the King not to reconstitute his great household for a year, a response to his 'grete povertie', the need to purchase many expensive household goods and the likely costs of regaining his whole realm. If some of his old servants were reinstated, Fortescue wearily predicted, the rest would be jealous, whilst those who were appointed would agitate for the return of their former colleagues. That situation would be very tiresome for the King and 'all thoo that shalbe abowte hym for that yere'. Fortescue undoubtedly assumed that he would be one of the inner circle in the reduced household, probably a royal councillor. The whole document showed great sensitivity to the fragile state of the King. His poor mental health and the ease with which those near him could exert their malign influence had been demonstrated all too well during the last decade of his first reign.

The short piece that follows the *Articles sent to Warwick* in the earliest surviving copy, BL Additional MS 48031A, the *Example what good counsel helpeth*, was not associated with it closely until the publication of *Vale's Book*. Lord Clermont transcribed this paragraph from the sixteenth-century copy made by John Stow, where it had been bound out of sequence between the title he used, *The Governance of the Kingdom of England*, and the beginning of that treatise.[77] The first line reads, 'O what good welthe and properite shulde growe to the reaume of Englande yif suche acounsell be oones perfitely stablisshed and the king guided therby.' It makes good sense if it was referring to the preceding *Articles sent to Warwick*, which Stow had transcribed in another Harley manuscript, 543, with its main argument that a strong council was needed to advise the King.

Fortescue probably thought when he surveyed his handiwork that the *Articles* needed some kind of link with ancient authority to make the innovative thinking it contained respectable and acceptable to his contemporaries. In the *Example* he gave a glowing account of the wisdom of the Senate that had advised the kings of Rome but warned that when they spurned that advice by acting tyrannically the people rose up against them. For many years Rome was then governed 'politikly' by the consuls and the Senate, during which time it ruled successfully. But the consuls eventually fell out with each other and an emperor took power, who, with the advice of the Senate, ruled the whole world. Later emperors,

[77] London, BL MSS Harley 542, f. 125a; Additional 48031A, f. 148b; *Vale's Book*, 51, 225–6. The piece occurs only in these manuscripts.

however, took private counsellors and killed many senators so that their power declined to the present day, when the emperor was weaker than the kings who were formerly his subjects. Similarly, the English kings had once been advised by 'sadde and wele chosen counseilloures' but since they had used private counsellors they had become poor and civil wars had broken out, just as had happened in Roman times. Yet if a wise council, as had been described before, were to be chosen by the English Crown, peace and prosperity would be established in the realm and it would become the mightiest kingdom in the world.

The *Articles sent to Warwick* were a plausible piece of *realpolitik* which recognised that Warwick and the senior Lancastrian representative, Jasper Tudor, earl of Pembroke, would probably welcome restraints upon the foolish generosity of Henry VI, who would be a millstone round their necks while he lived. Relegating him to economical seclusion for at least a year would be a realistic solution to a potential dilemma. The document was a manifesto for reform – the political and regal government that Fortescue had already envisaged in exile in theory in the *De Natura Legis Naturae* and the *De Laudibus Legum Anglie* could take a practical shape in the hands of the Readeption government.

Warwick probably saw Fortescue's *Articles* but, even had he wished to, he never had a chance to implement them. The survival of only one fifteenth-century copy, together with the later one made by John Stow, shows that it was virtually unknown until Plummer published it in the late nineteenth century.[78] The importance of the *Articles* for the development of Fortescue's political ideas, however, is substantial since it encapsulates much of the advice that was to be given shortly afterwards in *The Governance of England.* Central to that treatise was the need for the King to safeguard the integrity of his livelihood, reward his servants in other ways and rule according to the advice of a reformed council and with the sanction of parliament

Edward IV

The Governance of England

The paradox at the heart of the most controversial of Sir John Fortescue's political writings is that it is simultaneously conservative and a manifesto for reform. This has both bedevilled and intrigued commentators over the past 550 years, especially those who expect their political

[78] Plummer, *Governance of England*, 348–53.

authorities to be consistent. In its early days the treatise had no definitive title but was sometimes called *De dominio politico et regale* or *The Governance of England.* Charles Plummer's edition of 1885 gave the latter title a general currency that it has enjoyed ever since.[79] Any analysis of the work and its purpose depends to some extent on the identity of the king for whom it was destined and this has always been a matter of uncertainty and hence dispute amongst commentators. Was it an extended version of the *Articles sent to Warwick*, an earlier attempt to save the Lancastrians from their former mistakes, or was it a wise and measured summary of Fortescue's experience in government offered to his new master, Edward IV?

Three fifteenth-century manuscripts survive and the early sixteenth-century one copied by Sir John's great-nephew, Sir Adrian Fortescue, is also authoritative. These and others from the sixteenth and seventeenth centuries are described in Appendix 3, but the crucial point to be considered here is to whom these four were addressed. The earliest, which probably dates from the 1470s, Oxford, Bodleian Library MS Laud Misc. 593, stops two-thirds of the way through chapter XIX and at least one page has been torn out, so the reference to a king is missing. London, BL MS Cotton Claudius A viii also dates from the 1470s and mentions Edward IV in chapter XIX, although a later inscription at the beginning says that it was written for Henry VI. London, BL MS Additional 48031A was written by John Vale in the mid-1480s and he named Henry VI in chapter XIX. Sir Adrian Fortescue might have had some idea of his great-uncle's intentions and possibly have used his original manuscript when he made a fair copy in 1532 (Oxford Bodleian Library MS Digby 145): he cited Edward IV.[80] The view taken in this study is that the treatise in the form that survives probably incorporates ideas, arguments and even working papers from Henry VI's first reign but dates from the early part of Edward IV's second reign, 1471–75, and was intended for him.

Fortescue had been Chief Justice and periodically a participant in the royal council during the last two decades of Henry VI's reign, when most of the French lands were lost, the administration was virtually bankrupt and some leading magnates became increasingly disaffected. Edward IV's second reign had emerged from a crisis caused by his conflict with

[79] *De dominio politico et regale* in Cotton MS Otho B i, catalogue of *c.*1640 and several others that followed, see above Chpater 4, p. 158, n. 18. The title *The Governance of England* first occurs at the end of the treatise in BL MS Additional 48031 A; *Vale's Book*, 250.

[80] See Appendix 3.

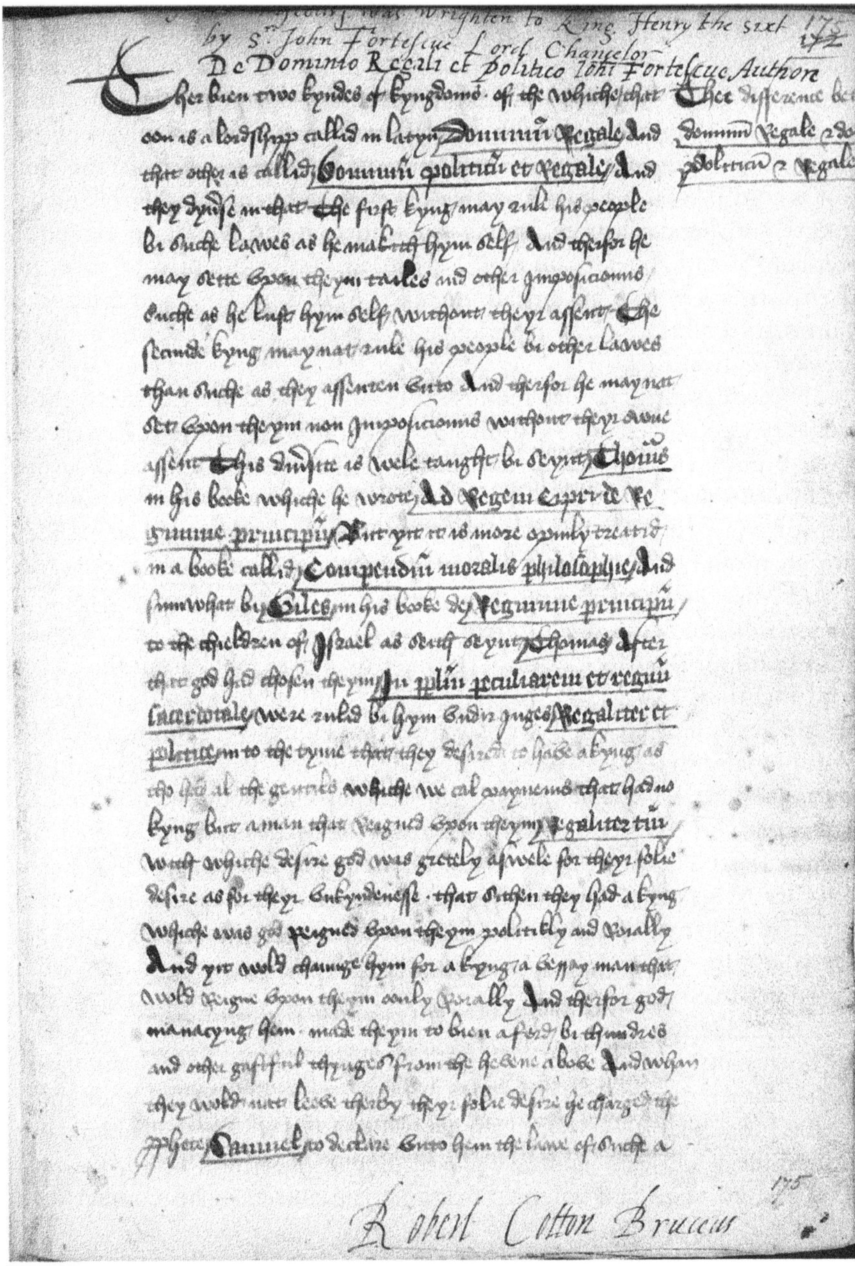

15 First page of the *Governance of England*,
by Sir John Fortescue, British Library
London, BL MS Cotton Claudius A viii, f. 175, early 1470s.

'overmighty subjects' and one of the consequences was to be an invasion of France. The danger was that the costs of this could provoke more unrest, and Fortescue, who had been pardoned and appointed to the council, seems to have offered his experience to alleviate these problems. He might have retained some of his working papers from the Lancastrian council to support his ideas.[81] The reasons for dating the *Governance* to the early 1470s have been discussed in a previous publication, although brief reference will be made to them below, where the question will be principally approached through internal evidence considered in the political context of the time.[82]

Those who read the *Governance* for the first time will find that it is a surprisingly short work occupying respectively fifteen and twenty-two folios in the two earliest complete manuscript versions of the text and twenty-four and forty pages (including footnotes) in the two modern editions.[83] By 1475 it had been divided into twenty chapters and, although some early versions have a slightly different arrangement, the fact that the twenty-chapter version was copied by Sir Adrian Fortescue indicates that it was regarded as definitive by his family.[84]The brevity of the *Governance* in comparison to the tomes on good government that were presented to princes by scholastics such as Vincent of Beauvais and Giles of Rome and the user-friendly way in which it was divided into short chapters with clear headings and highlighted quotations make it look more like a treatise produced to convince the King and council about specific policies rather than a traditional 'mirror for a prince'.[85]

[81] B.P. Woolfe, *The Crown Lands, 1461–1536* (London: 1970) 26, thought that some of the contents of these papers were incorporated in the *Governance.* It has been suggested above that *The Commodities of England* could have been a working paper or papers produced in the 1450s.

[82] *Vale's Book*, 53–66, 250.

[83] London, BL MS Cotton Claudius A viii, ff. 175a–197b and Additional 48031A, ff. 149a–164a; *Vale's Book* (1995) which is the version that appears in London, BL MS Additional 48031A and Lockwood, *On the Laws and Governance of England*, which contains a modernised version of Plummer's edition. He used the incomplete Oxford, Bodleian Library MS Laud Misc. 593 but supplemented it with readings from nine other manuscripts.

[84] London, BL MS Cotton Claudius A viii. John Multon, the stationer responsible for the production of this manuscript, died in 1475; Sir Adrian Fortescue's copy, Oxford, Bodleian Library MS Digby 145, is very close in wording and arrangement to Cotton Claudius A viii. See Appendix 3.

[85] This genre of late medieval literature has received attention in recent decades, early examples are *Four English Political Tracts*, ed. Genet; R.F. Green, *Poets and Princepleasers: Literature and the English Court in the Late Middle Ages* (Toronto: 1980); N. Orme, *From Childhood to Chivalry: The Education of the English*

Despite minor variations that are noted in Appendix 3 and the fact that some manuscripts do not contain the final chapters, the text, which is common to all, contains no substantive differences apart from the name of the king who is mentioned in the longer version.

Fortescue evidently appreciated that his pragmatic advice was more likely to be acceptable if it was presented within a familiar and morally reassuring conceptual framework. To use Quentin Skinner's phrase, he invoked the 'normative vocabulary' of Christian scholarship as it had been used in 'mirrors for princes'.[86] He did not have to look far for his material since he had already used much of it in the *De Natura* and the *De Laudibus*: in the latter work he had based his introduction on it. He had deployed the appeal to ancient authority in the *Articles sent to Warwick* when he tacked on an epilogue, *Example what good counsel helpeth*, demonstrating how the Romans had flourished when they ruled with the advice of the Senate.[87]

Fortescue had used the opposition of two forms of government, regal or regal and political, in his two earlier long treatises, since in both cases it served the particular purposes of his argument. In the *De Natura* he described the origins of regal and political monarchical government in the Old Testament, while in the *De Laudibus* the respective advantages of regal or regal and political government were discussed to urge Edward of Lancaster to prefer the English common law to the Continental civil law. Fortescue needed to show the inherent superiority of English political institutions and how the way in which legislative and executive power was exercised depended on them. This last topic is the central theme of the first two chapters of the *Governance*, which are little more than a reorganisation of the material used in the earlier works. He had referred to all the authorities such as St Thomas Aquinas and Giles of Rome before and recycled most of the quotations.

In chapter II Fortescue invoked the entirely mythical British history which claimed that Brutus, fleeing from the sack of Troy, was chosen by

---

Kings and Aristocracy, 1066–1530 (London: 1984); C.F. Briggs, *Giles of Rome's 'De Regimine Principum': Reading and Writing Politics at Court and University, c.1275–c.1525* (Cambridge: 1999); A. Vanderjagt, 'The Princely Culture of the Valois Dukes of Burgundy', *Princes and Princely Culture, 1450–1650*, ed. M. Gosman, A. Macdonald and A. Vanderjagt, 2 vols (Leiden: 2003) 1, 51–79.

86 Q. Skinner, *Foundations of Modern Political Thought*, 2 vols (Cambridge: 1978) vol. 1, x–xv; C. Carpenter, *The Wars of the Roses: Politics and the Constitution in England, c.1437–1509* (Cambridge: 1997) esp. ch. 1; *The Fifteenth Century IV: Political Culture in Fifteenth-Century Britain*, ed. L. Clark and C. Carpenter (Woodbridge: 2004); Watts, *Henry VI*, 13–80.

87 *Vale's Book*, 50–1, 222–6.

his company to be king and founded a realm that was to be governed politically and regally: 'Thanne he and they made this incorporacion, institucion and oonyng of hem selfe into a reaume to beene reuled and justified bi suche laws as they alle wolde assente unto, whiche lawe therefore is called politicum, and by cause it is mynistred by a king it is called regale.'[88] Fortescue then made an unattributed reference to Poggio Bracciolini's translation of the *De Priscis Historiis* by Diodorus Siculus using the same passages that he had quoted in chapter XV of the *De Laudibus*. In those he noted with approval the political and regal regimes of the ancient kings of Egypt, Saba, Libya and other parts of Africa. Neither Diodorus nor Poggio had used the terms 'political and regal' government but praised regimes which ruled according to long-established laws.[89] In the *Governance* Fortescue went on to contrast regal regimes that had been founded by the power of the prince with political and regal regimes that 'byganne bi the desire and institucion of the people of the same prince'.[90]

The culmination of his argument in chapter III proved that political and regal government made English society fairer, safer and more stable than French society. This led to the conclusion that whilst the king needed sufficient revenue to rule effectively he should not obtain it by oppressing and impoverishing his subjects. The rest of the treatise was devoted to this argument and to offering advice about how revenue could be raised without endangering the stability of the realm. It contained a number of references to England which indicated that it was written there, for example, 'this lande' (twice) and 'IUS POLITICUM ET REGALE under whiche we lyve'.[91]

The dangerous and unjust methods of taxation used by the French king were condemned in chapter IV: 'how much agretter synne is it to take from the pore manne his mete, drinke, clothing and al that he hathe nede of, whiche verile doethe the Frenshe king'.[92] Yet Fortescue conceded in the next chapter that great harm could come from a king's failure to raise adequate revenue. He would succumb to his creditors, lose the elevated status that he should enjoy as king and be pushed to arbitrary and unjust acts to raise money. It is significant that, while in

[88] *Ibid.*, 228.

[89] *The Bibliotheca Historica of Diodorus Siculus translated by John Skelton*, ed. F.M. Salter and H.L.R. Edwards, 2 vols (London: 1956/7) vol. 1, 62–95, 227–8.

[90] *Vale's Book*, 228. See above, Chapter 4, pp. 178–9, and below, Conclusion, for more on Fortescue's use of humanist texts.

[91] *Vale's Book*, 229–30.

[92] *Ibid.*, 230.

the *De Laudibus* Fortescue referred unambiguously to Sir Thomas Cook when making his argument, in the *Governance* the point was so generalised that Edward IV could not be offended.

The next two chapters were devoted to the king's ordinary and extraordinary expenses. The former had been touched on in article 4 of the *Articles to Warwick* and it is likely that this part of the treatise was an expansion of the ideas that Fortescue had developed in exile. His long detachment from the details of government is possibly indicated by the proviso in chapter VI, 'whiche the wryter hereof can now remembre'[93] and a similar sentiment was reiterated in the next chapter. The ordinary expenses included running the household, paying the salaries of the great officers of state, defending Calais and the Marches and carrying out the king's works. Fortescue put the expense of keeping a fleet to defend England, especially her commercial interests, in a separate category as it was funded by the levy of tunnage and poundage but he dwelt on it for several sentences to emphasise its importance.

There was no equivalent in the *Articles to Warwick* for the king's extraordinary expenses, but this is hardly surprising given that they were destined for the government of the penniless and mentally unsound Henry VI, whose prodigality during his first reign had been notorious. Fortescue had prudently recognised that the King should keep a small household and practise rigorous economy, yet this was not advice that would endear him to the luxury-loving Edward IV. The list of extraordinary expenses in the *Governance* therefore included seemly receptions for ambassadors and papal legates, money with which to reward royal servants and pay for new buildings, horses, furs, jewels and the costs of sending out commissions to do justice in the country and of maintaining an army.

In chapter VIII Fortescue somewhat optimistically stated that the King had sufficient income to pay for the ordinary expenses of government. If he could not meet all the extraordinary expenses his subjects were bound to raise the money for them but it should be referred 'to the kingdome, for thoughe his estate be the highest estate temporal in erthe, yit it is an office whiche he mynistreth to his reaulmes defence and justice'.[94] This obligation laid on the people was all the greater since England was ruled by a political and regal regime. The above quotation implied that the King should rely on the consent of parliament when he raised taxation. But Fortescue intended that the obligation should be mutual between the parties. As he had already stated in the *De Laudibus*,

93 *Ibid.*, 232.
94 *Ibid.*, 235.

the King should consult his subjects through parliament and they should meet his reasonable demands.[95] This idea running through both works is probably responsible for many of the arguments and misconceptions that have attended discussions of Fortescue's thinking. The increasingly institutionalised superiority of parliament over the powers of the monarchy which has occurred over the last five centuries has clouded thinking about a system where obligations were no less important for the fact that they were not legally enforceable. A medieval Christian king might violate his coronation oath to uphold the laws and customs of his realm and, if he was strong enough, he would probably get away with it. What he could not avoid was the judgement of God in the world to come or, in Western societies already stirred by Renaissance notions of fame, the verdict of posterity on his tyrannical actions. Fortescue was writing to convince a king and would hardly labour the point, but these consequences were implicit in the work.

'The periles that mowe falle to a kyng by ovur mighti subgiettes', the title of chapter IX, has often been used as an epigram to explain the causes of civil wars in fifteenth-century England. In this part of the treatise Fortescue abandoned the generalised allusions which have tormented commentators and made specific references to recent events. Whilst illustrating the dangers of allowing great magnates to hold wealth that was equivalent to that of their ruler, he referred to the War of the League of the Common Weal (1465), the death of the king of Scotland (1460) and noted that, 'We have also late in our reaume knowen somme of the kinges subgiettes given hym bataill, by occasion that their lyvelode and offices weren the gretteste of the londe, and elles they wolde nat han done soo.'[96] This last could equally well refer to the conflict between the Lancastrians and the Yorkists in the 1450s or the rebellion of the earl of Warwick and the duke of Clarence against Edward IV, 1469–71. The use of the word 'late' makes it more likely that the latter was intended, because events dating between 1460 and 1465 were mentioned. The last example of discord that Fortescue cited was that,

> it may nat be eschewed but that the grete lordis of the lande by reason of newe discentes falling unto hem and by reason also of marriages, purchases and other titles shulne oftyn tymes growe to be gretter thane thei be now, and peradventure some of hem to be of lyvelode and power like a kyng.[97]

[95] Chrimes, *De Laudibus*, 87.
[96] *Vale's Book*, 236.
[97] *Ibid.*, 237.

During the early 1470s the huge Neville inheritance was in the process of being divided acrimoniously between the duke of Clarence in the right of his wife Isabel and Richard, duke of Gloucester who was to marry her sister Anne, the widow of Edward of Lancaster. Fortescue had experienced the ambition of Clarence at close quarters during the diplomatic exchanges in France in the summer of 1470, and probably entertained no illusions that his younger brother would prove more altruistic. Eventually Edward IV seems to have heeded his warning in the first case but not the second.[98]

Chapter X of the *Governance* claimed that it was devoted to the means at the King's disposal for raising revenue. In fact, Fortescue devoted a great deal of it to describing the undesirable measures by which the French king received a high income from taxing his subjects heavily. He warned that if the English king resorted to such devices he would 'have thereof but as had the man that shered his hogge: moche crye and litill wolle'.[99] The example of King Rehoboam gave a further warning that unreasonable taxation could lead to rebellion. A much better alternative was to keep the royal estates and their revenues intact. They could be steadily enlarged since the King was related to many landowners and would, from time to time, inherit more property. The sale of Chirk and Chirk's land, on the border of Wales, had been a great mistake since it had depleted the royal livelihood. That incident had occurred over twenty years before the end of Henry VI's first reign and could be an example of Fortescue using arguments and even council memoranda from his previous, Lancastrian career.[100] Alternatively it could recall a particularly outrageous example of royal improvidence which would still be remembered by some of the recipients of the treatise.

Discussions within the royal council, parliament and amongst the politically active orders of society, dating in some cases from the Lancastrian period, could also be reflected in chapter XI.[101] The subject was resumption, the practice of English kings in the later middle ages of rescinding over-generous gifts to their subjects. Two such major acts had been passed by parliaments during the crisis of Henry VI's reign which

[98] Hicks, *False, Fleeting, Perjur'd Clarence*, 97–104. In 1477 Clarence was arrested after some minor plotting and was put to death in the Tower in the following year on the King's orders.

[99] *Vale's Book*, 238.

[100] Griffiths, *Henry VI*, 385, 397, n. 51.

[101] The title of chapter XI in *Vale's Book* is 'The subsidie that the souldane takith of his subgiettes'; in London, BL MS Cotton Claudius A viii it is 'Here is shewid what off the kynges livelod geven awey mey beste be taken a geyn'.

culminated in Jack Cade's rebellion. Fortescue suggested that if grants of land were to be taken back into royal possession the more deserving of the original recipients could instead be rewarded with money and offices. A sign that this argument had been adapted to the circumstances of Yorkist rule was the concession that some who had given exceptional service should still be given land as befitted a magnificent king. His 'moste worshipfulest bretherne' also deserved to be richly rewarded. This seems to be another reference to Clarence and Gloucester, since one of Henry VI's two half-brothers, Edmund earl of Richmond, had died in 1456. But if a general resumption was not made the people would be obliged to pay more taxes in the future and remain trapped in poverty.

The harm that would be caused by the poverty of the commons was the subject of chapter XII. If they could not afford to buy military equipment their ability either to defeat invaders or defend the King against internal enemies would be impaired, indeed they would be likely to rebel. The epigram in the first sentence is vintage Fortescue:

> For no thing may make his peopul tarise nor make insurreccion but lakke of good or lake of justice, but yit certaynly whan they lakke good they wil arise saying that they lakke justice. Nevertheles yif thei be not pore they will nevur arise nor make insurreccion but yif their prince so leve justice that he geve hym selfe all to tyrannye.[102]

The whole question of whether it was a good idea to keep the commons in poverty and subdued to authority could have been debated in either the Lancastrian or the Yorkist royal council. Several times in this chapter Fortescue dismissed the view that they should be kept in poverty, 'O how unwise is thoppinion of thise men for it may not be mayntened by any reason.'[103] The French were shown in the next short chapter to be inhibited from rising for a different reason, 'cowardise and lakke of hertes'. Fortescue's robust sense of his Englishness emerged again when he proudly made the bizarre claim that more Englishmen were hanged in one year for the courageous acts of robbery and manslaughter than were hanged for such crimes in France in seven years. In Scotland no one was hanged for such crimes in seven years, but only for the cowardly practice of taking goods in the owner's absence.

Fortescue reverted to the subject of resumption in chapter XIV, using it as a basis for making one of the main arguments of the treatise, that a strong council was needed to advise the King. The councillors would

[102] *Vale's Book*, 242.

[103] *Ibid.*, 241.

assist their master in distinguishing between those who deserved to be rewarded after the resumption of their lands had taken place and those who did not. He suggested that such a provision would protect the King from 'inportunyte of suteres' and the indignation of the people who had in the past resented the generosity of the gifts given to his followers. This passage is close to part of article 1 of the *Articles sent to Warwick* and was critical of Edward's first reign, when two Acts of Resumption had been passed, even using the same phrase 'inportunyte of suteres'.[104] Fortescue levelled a new criticism at over-generosity, which was 'no virtue but a spice of prodigalite, and forasmoche it were delapidacion of his crowne'. Even if the resumption meant that some good men were treated unjustly, that was better than hurting the 'goode publique of all the londe'.[105] For once Fortescue abandoned the circumspect tones in which he addressed his new master: the policy he was advocating was too important to be presented in a mealy-mouthed fashion.

The manner in which the council should be reformed to enable it to carry out the heavy load of business planned for it was the subject of chapter XV. Uniquely amongst the early manuscripts, London, BL Additional 48031A is subdivided. 'Shewing in maner the guiding of the kinges counseillours of late yeres' is the title of chapter XVa. The other manuscripts dealt with the material in XVa and XVb in one chapter entitled in London, BL Claudius A viii: 'How the kynges co[unsell] may be chosen and [est]blissed'. Fortescue listed the evils that had affected the efficiency and fairness of the old system: the great lords spiritual and temporal were more preoccupied with their own affairs than with those of the King, no less important member of the council dared to oppose the undesirable consequences of this situation and the magnates could not be trusted to preserve the secrecy of the meetings from their followers. All this sounds like reminiscences from the bad days of Henry VI, although Fortescue was unlikely overtly to remind Edward IV of his participation in the council during the last two decades of that reign.

Chapter XVb is entitled 'How the kinges counsaill maybe electe and establisshed for weele of the king and his reaume'. As a fuller version of *The Articles sent to Warwick*, article 2, it dealt in detail with the way in which the reformed council should be constituted and operate. Twelve laymen and twelve ecclesiastics should be chosen, 'of the wisest and beste disposed that can be founde in all the parties of the lande, and that they biene sworne to counseill the king after a fourme to be divised for their othe, and inespeciall that they shul take noo fee, clothing nor

[104] See Conclusion, p. 264.
[105] *Vale's Book*, 243.

rewardes of any man excepte oonly of the kyng'.[106] Fortescue cited the precedent of the justices of the King's Bench and Common Pleas, who swore such an oath when they were appointed. He envisaged that these councillors would stay permanently in post but if any proved unsatisfactory, in a self-regulating measure, they could be dismissed on the advice of the majority of the council. Four lay peers and four prelates would be invited to join the council for just one year (thus diminishing their effectiveness vis-à-vis the 'professional councillors'). The great officers of state, the Chancellor, the Treasurer and the principal judges would attend when they were needed. Previously the former had been permanent and powerful members of the council whilst the judges had attended only when invited.

One of the principal aims of Fortescue's formula for a new kind of governance was to enable the King to rule economically. The danger that his plans would lead to greater expense was met directly by his protest that kings in the past had lavished gifts on one favourite that totalled more than the projected remuneration for the whole council. This general observation should be compared with the more pointed statement in *The Articles sent to Warwick*, article 3, that, 'ther hath bene gevun in late daies to somme oon lorde temperell much more lyvelode in yerly value than woll paye the wages of alle the newe counseill'.[107] Plain speaking was appropriate for Warwick during the Readeption but not for the victorious Edward IV. It would not be necessary to pay the twelve clerical councillors as much as was to be given to the laymen as the former had no families to support. But if the expense of the proposal was considered too great, the numbers could be reduced to sixteen permanent councillors and the magnates and prelates appointed for a year could be reduced to four.

The last part of this long chapter XV is particularly interesting as it gives Fortescue's view of the proper concerns of royal government. The council should deliberate on how bullion could be brought into the country but not exported and how jewels, plate and money could be 'goten ageyne', how the prices of English goods could be increased, the cost of imports lowered and the navy maintained and expanded. If

[106] *Ibid.*, 244–5.

[107] *Ibid.*, 223–4. There were several candidates for the over-rewarded temporal lord referred to by Fortescue, although the most powerful Lancastrian counsellors such as Suffolk and Somerset had all been killed: Edward IV's rapacious favourites, William Herbert and Humphrey Stafford, had recently been denounced in Warwick's manifestos and the Woodvilles had also incurred popular condemnation.

he was the author of the earlier treatise, *The Commodities of England*, this thinking represents continuity with the ideas he could have aired at the council during the Lancastrian regime. The final subject for the council to debate was 'how the laws may biene amended in suche thinges as they neden reformacioun inne'.[108] The utility of this procedure was that it would enable parliament to deal more quickly with such business. The assumption was that in a well-ordered government legislation would pass without dissent. With a properly planned programme the Commons would not need to reject the royal council's proposals: this was regal and political government *par excellence*. The chapter ended with a suggestion that a book should be kept incorporating the regulations for the conduct of the council.

Chapter XVI is a version of *Example what good counseill helpith* and fulfilled the same function that was suggested above, to associate the *Articles sent to Warwick* with the morally acceptable tradition of 'mirrors for princes'. 'How the Romaynes prospered while they had agrete counseill', unlike the earlier piece, did not praise the republican regime of the Romans but stressed that Julius Caesar and then Augustus had benefited from their Senates' advice so much that they had extended their rule over the whole world. Later emperors declined in power when they despised and brutalised the Senate, as did the Lacedemonians (Spartans) and Athenians when they failed to take good advice. Fortescue's theme of achieving world domination would have resonated well with the policy of Edward IV in the early 1470s and the expectation that he would soon invade France.

Another aspect of the malaise in government that had led to civil war was addressed in chapter XVII: the flaws in the appointment of the royal officials who were essential to the good government throughout the realm. Fortescue, the upwardly mobile lawyer whose family had been office-holders in Devon, showed no more respect for the traditional hierarchy in the counties than he had done for magnates in his recommendations for the makeup of the royal council: 'Somme forster [forester] of the kinges that hathe noone other lyveloode thanne his forstership may bringe moo men into the felde wele arrayed, and namely for shotyng, thane may somme knighte, squier or gentilman of righte grete lyvelode dwelling by hym and having noon office.'[109] He went on to stress how important it was that each man should only be allowed to hold one office, so enabling far more people to work directly for the King. They would be under royal control and their reward would be

[108] *Ibid.*, 246.
[109] *Vale's Book*, 247.

their fees, not land extracted from the royal estate, and the magnates would thus be prevented from giving royal officials posts that would put them under conflicting obligations. The only exceptions should be the King's brothers, whose interests had already been considered in chapter XI, and royal household officials and councillors.[110] Fortescue referred to 'my lorde prince' giving out offices as well as the King. In the early 1470s Edward of York was an infant, but senior members of his household could have exercised those powers on his behalf.

The concern adequately and appropriately to reward household officers and provide for their retirement was also expressed in the following short chapter. Recently corodies (allowances of board and lodging made by monasteries to retired laymen who were often dependants of the founder's family) and pensions had been given to all kinds of importunate petitioners rather than being reserved for royal servants and their families. Fortescue advised that no more should be granted without the sanction of the council, which would achieve considerable savings for the monarchy since the charge would be on the monasteries and not the King.

The subject of chapter XIX was the King's need to build up a large stock of property with which to endow the Crown for perpetuity. It should never be alienated 'withoute thassente of his parliamente', which would not undermine his prerogative since it would strengthen, not weaken his authority. Fortescue had used the same argument in relation to the exercise of political and regal dominion in both the *De Natura* and the *De Laudibus*: the only additional power a tyrant enjoyed was the freedom to sin. Suzanne Marcuzzi has remarked that both kings ruling politically and those ruling regally had the ability to flout the law of nature if they wished.[111] Retribution might well have to wait until the afterlife. Fortescue adopted a somewhat triumphalist mode in this part of the *Governance* by comparing an endowment of the Crown favourably with the foundation of religious institutions like abbeys and colleges:

> This shalbe a collage in the whiche shulne singe and pray for evurmore all the men of Englande, spiritual and temperel, and their songe shalbe suche among other antemes: I blessed be our lord God that hathe sente

[110] *Ibid.*, 248, 'the kinges bretheren mow have ii offices and ... suche men as serven the king aboute his persone or in his counsaill mow have in their contres [counties] aparkership for their disporte whan they come home, or suche another office as they mow wel kepe bi their deputes'.

[111] S. Marcuzzi, 'Sir John Fortescue on Law and Regal Power', unpublished PhD thesis (University of Cambridge: 2011) 199.

king Henry the vith to reigne upon us. He hathe doone more for us thanne evur did king of Englande.[112]

Chapter XX, 'Advertisemente for making of patentes for giftes', represents something of an anti-climax after the high style of the previous chapter and the subject matter would have fitted in better after chapter XVIII, and indeed it has the character of an afterthought. Fortescue had not considered the subject of land granted for the term of the recipient's life which would then revert to the King. The procedure was less harmful to his estate than outright gifts, but it encouraged 'inportune suteres' to ask for such land as soon as it returned to the King. If the grants were to be placed entirely under the control of the council, only truly deserving candidates would receive such gifts and the King would be protected from tiresome solicitations. The experience of successive acts of resumption from the 1450s could be reflected in this advice, especially the failure fully to implement the measure passed during the political turmoil of 1450. The sentiment replicated some of article 1 of the *Articles sent to Warwick*, but a final sentence had been added which does not appear in the earlier treatise: the King might 'leve this order whan hym liste'.[113] This seems to have been adapted to the competent and masterful rule of Edward IV, whereas the whole thrust of the *Articles sent to Warwick* was that the enfeebled Henry should be prevented from taking any initiatives at all.

Indications have been noted above that Fortescue wrote the surviving version of the *Governance* in the early 1470s rather than whilst he was still a servant of the Lancastrians. References to events and people seem to place it in the second reign of Edward IV. The early manuscripts indicate the same conclusion: in London, BL Cotton MS Claudius A viii the king named in chapter XIX was Edward IV. He was also named in the copy made early the next century by Fortescue's great-nephew Sir Adrian Fortescue. Although *John Vale's Book*, written in the 1480s, assumed the king was Henry VI, this could have been a mistake arising from the fact that the greater part of the associated material that preceded it was Lancastrian. The Oxford manuscript, which contains what is probably the earliest copy of the *Governance*, is damaged, so the part of chapter XIX which named a king, infuriatingly, is lost.[114] The scathing terms in which Fortescue referred to lavishing money on

[112] *Vale's Book*, 249. See Appendix 3 for variations in the king named in chapter XIX.

[113] *Ibid.*, 250.

[114] See Appendix 3.

religious foundations at the expense of sound fiscal policy would have been most unwelcome to Henry VI, so the balance tilts further in favour of Edward IV as the recipient.

In the *Governance of England* Fortescue spelt out the implications of political and regal government for the maintenance of royal sovereignty in England. He had already found this political language to be appropriate in his search for a valid law of succession in the *De Natura* and in his description of the English common law as the guarantor of good governance in the *De Laudibus*. He had proposed in the latter that future kings might use it as a handbook to aid their understanding of the law and he may well have regarded the *Governance* as a guide for later rulers to the administration of their realm. In chapter III, after condemning the baleful results of regal only rule, this great apologist for English institutions wrote triumphantly:

> But blessed be God this londe is reuled under a bettir lawe and therefore the peopul therof biene not in suche penurie, disease nor misere nor therby hurte in theire personnes but they bene welthy and have all things necessarie to the sustenaunce of nature. Wherfore they bene mighti and able to resiste their adversaries and enemyes and bete other reaumes that wolde do hem wronge. Loo this is the frute of IUS POLITICUM ET REGALE under whiche we lyve.[115]

For centuries after its composition, the *Governance of England* was known only to some scholars and politicians and it was not as influential as its precursor, the *De Laudibus Legum Anglie*. As the following chapter on the reception of Fortescue's works indicates, this was partly because no printed editions of the former appeared until the early eighteenth century. A further reason was that a large and politically conscious constituency existed to read the *De Laudibus* in the common lawyers of England. The emergence of history as a discipline in the nineteenth century together with two editions of the *Governance* was to change the focus of interest, provoking the debate which has continued ever since about whether the *Governance* contained a programme for a constitutional monarchy, an apologia for an authoritarian one or a nuanced compromise between those extremes.

[115] *Vale's Book*, 229–30.

CHAPTER 6

The Reception and Influence of Sir John Fortescue's Works

The fluctuations in the reputation of Sir John Fortescue as statesman, jurist and political theorist during the centuries since his death reflect changing priorities and values in law and politics. He was already known as an influential judge and politician by 1480; his long career and the interest and relevance of his polemical writings account for this. His family had much to gain by enhancing the reputation of their learned ancestor and were to do so on several occasions during the next four centuries. They took initiatives to spread Fortescue's renown by publishing his works over the following centuries. Their editions and those published by others provide good indicators of the changes in the reception of his works and the consequent fluctuations in his reputation. They are all surveyed in this chapter.

The ideas to be found in Fortescue's political works have sometimes been credited with contributing to the emergence of a 'New Monarchy' under Edward IV and Henry VII when royal finances were prudently managed and professional administrators were preferred as advisers to the traditional nobility. The concept of 'New Monarchy' itself is, however, controversial. K.B. McFarlane would have none of it, suggesting that many of its attributes could be found throughout the later middle ages. Even if it did exist, what evidence is there that Fortescue advocated it and that anyone paid attention to his views during that early period? John Watts suggested in 1995 that Edward IV and Henry VII's reigns did indeed mark 'a new ffundacion' achieved by the kings' managerial skills and the devastating impact of the civil wars on networks of lordship.[1] It has been suggested above that the final year of Henry VI's first reign, 1460, was marked by more prudent management of royal finances and that this can be attributed to the increasing influence of Fortescue over the government.[2] This is a tenable hypothesis but no claim can be made

[1] K.B. McFarlane, *The Nobility of Later Medieval England: The Ford Lectures for 1953 and Related Studies* (Oxford: 1973) 282–7; Watts, 'New Ffundacion'.

[2] See above, Chapter 2, pp. 97-8, n. 214.

that any prince actually read his work after 1470: no evidence has been found of royal ownership or use in any of the surviving manuscripts.[3]

Edward IV and Henry VII certainly proved adept at increasing royal revenue, but the former never showed any inclination to shun his aristocratic companions on his council, even *arrivistes* like the Woodvilles, in favour of the sober lawyers and bureaucrats that Fortescue favoured. Henry VII did indeed employ such professional administrators but there is no evidence that he read or even knew of Fortescue's advice. Fortescue's status as an authority was certainly to grow as the sixteenth century advanced but that was not initially on account of his views on governance.

Fortescue's career remained of interest to lawyers and other educated people during the generations which followed his death. The *Year Books* were initially only available in manuscript but from the mid-sixteenth century a great series of editions was printed by Richard Tottel. They recorded Fortescue's opinions and judgments, together with those of other justices, ensuring his continued renown. The first printed edition of the *De Laudibus Legum Anglie* was published by Edward Whitechurch in 1545/6, when England was in the throes of its first Protestant reformation and at war with France, so its francophobe sentiments would have been welcome to many readers. Twenty-one years later Tottel produced another edition accompanied by an English translation by Robert Mulcaster, who enthused: 'I did not dreame, neither to fynde so rich a treasure in so simple an habite. And because I wished all menne to have parte of my delight, me thought it good to translate it into Englishe forth [out] of Latine.'[4] Seven more editions from the sixteenth until the early seventeenth century by Tottel and Thomas Wight followed. The popularity of the work can be explained by the interest of the text if it is contrasted with the inordinate dryness of the standard legal books of the day. It provided a clear and stimulating introduction to a career in the law and fed xenophobic sentiments about the superiority of the English common law to the French civil law.

The writings of the lawyer Christopher St German (*c.*1460–1540/41), an apologist for Henry VIII's decision to break the ties between the Church of England and Rome, were strongly influenced by Fortescue. The form of his most popular work, *Dialogue between a Doctor of Divinity*

[3] See Appendix 3.

[4] J. Fortescue, *A Learned Commendation of the Politique Laws of England*, written in Latin, translated by Robert Mulcaster (London: 1567) f. 2r. Richard Tottel printed it five times between 1567 and 1578, Thomas Wight printed it in 1598, 1599 and 1609.

and a Student of the Laws of England (originally written in Latin but translated into English and published in 1530) recalled the dialogue between Fortescue and Prince Edward. The advent of the Tudors had made references to the Lancastrian *De Laudibus* politically acceptable. Like its precursor, St German's treatise discussed the common law of England and found it to be superior to others, especially to canon and papal law. St German was strongly anti-clerical and his purpose was not primarily to urge that common law should prevail over civil law (that argument had already been won) but to undermine papal jurisdiction in England. He was a firm believer in the sovereignty of the king in parliament and the wide jurisdiction of the Privy Council and could cite Fortescue as an authority for both.[5] It is unlikely that St German was acting as King Henry's mouthpiece for policies which would have limited his power, but he presumably got away with it as he was perceived primarily as an advocate of the royal religious policy.

Fortescue's family continued to play their part in enhancing his reputation. His great-nephew, Sir Adrian Fortescue (b.*c.*1481), made a fine copy of the *Governance* in his own hand and may have commissioned some of the other early sixteenth-century copies of Fortescue's works which survive. The only known version of the *De Titulo Edwardi Comitis Marchie* contains the devotional initials 'IHS NRI', similar to those on Sir Adrian's copy of the *Governance*.[6] It was a tragedy for Fortescue studies, as well as for Sir Adrian personally, that he was arrested by order of Henry VIII for his continued loyalty to the Church of Rome. His goods were sequestered and he was executed as a traitor in 1539.[7] Three chests full of 'writynges' were taken away and these may well have included works by Sir John that either disappeared or resurfaced later in the hands of antiquaries or as fragments, such as what remains of *Of the title of the House of York*. Had Sir Adrian survived it is possible that a much earlier edition of the *Governance* would have been published. The family was restored to full favour by the 1550s and under Elizabeth I another Sir John Fortescue, the son of Sir Adrian, became Chancellor of the Exchequer. The need for such dynasties to establish their good lineage was noticed above (Chapter 1): this was exemplified by the retrospective

[5] J. Guy, 'Sir Thomas More and Christopher St German: The Battle of the Books', 95–120; 'The King's Council and Political Participation', 121–47, *Reassessing the Henrician Age: Humanism, Politics and Reform, 1500–1550*, ed. A. Fox and J. Guy (Oxford: 1986).

[6] See the Introduction to Appendix 1.

[7] M. Clifton, *Three English Martyrs, Knights of St John: Venerable Thomas Dingley, Blessed Adrian Fortescue, Blessed David Gonson* (Liverpool: 1991) 21–39.

enhancement of the status of their forebears often with the collusion of local historians and heralds on their visitations.

The antiquarianism which both motivated and characterised the heraldic visitations was also the approach adopted by most English writers of history in the sixteenth century. Consciousness of nationhood was increased by the repulse of Philip II of Spain and the expectation that the accession of James VI of Scotland to the English throne would unite all parts of the British archipelago under one monarch. The mood is typified by books such as William Camden's (1551–1632) *Britannia*. Camden was a member of a group of writers and book collectors which included John Stow (1524/5–1605) and the rather younger Sir Robert Cotton (1571–1631) and John Selden (1584–1654). A number of Fortescue's works which survived or are known to have existed passed through the hands of these men. Some they owned, some they borrowed and copied. Their care and the scholarly remarks and the commentaries which they supplied did much to ensure the survival of the greater part of Fortescue's writings and further enhanced his reputation in the process.

Much of the material which John Stow industriously collected was intended to contribute to his *Chronicle of England from Brute to 1580*, later called the *Annales of England* when published in 1592, and his interest seems to have been principally antiquarian. He referred to Fortescue's *De Laudibus* in his *Survey of London*, for example, for evidence that there was originally 'a tenth house of Chancery'.[8] The younger generation, however, had other priorities, 'The work of the sixteenth century antiquaries had been completed and a new, more politically oriented generation was to use the tools supplied to erect buildings never dreamed of by those who first forged them.'[9]

Sir Robert Cotton was one of the new breed who worked towards distinct political goals. His knowledge of Fortescue's work would have confirmed his view that the early seventeenth-century institutions of government did not differ in their essentials from those of the fifteenth century. In the eyes of the political and legal reformers Fortescue had given a perfectly satisfactory account of the proper exercise of royal power and of how the king's councillors and parliament might moderate it. He had also drawn a useful distinction between the king's ordinary expenses, which must be met out of his regular revenue, and his extraordinary expenses. During the parliament of 1610, when the Great

[8] C.A.J. Skeel, 'The Influence of the Writings of Sir John Fortescue', *TRHS*, 10 (1916) 77–114; *ODNB*, 52, 982–6.

[9] F.J. Levy, *Tudor Historical Thought* (San Marino, CA: 1967) 166.

Contract, which would have put royal finances on a secure footing, was under discussion the Chancellor of the Exchequer, Sir Julius Caesar, cited the *Governance* three times.[10] Fortescue could also confirm the conviction of jurists such as Sir Edward Coke (1552–1634) that the common law was the immemorial custom of England and could be used to justify their opposition to what they perceived to be royal encroachments upon it.[11] Coke extended this defence of English rights and customs to the North American colonies in 1606 in the First Charter of Virginia, and other foundational charters followed which institutionalised the protection given by English law, although its precise application remained controversial.[12]

By the late 1620s the dangerous conjunction of expensive wars and an uncompromising young king led to the situation characterised by G.L. Harriss: 'historical and ideological developments led *dominium regale* and *dominium politicum* to oppose each other as rival modes of government instead of being correlative and exchangeable facets of a composite system'.[13] Cotton was caught up in this process and the content of his pamphlets, which appealed to late medieval precedents to justify the use of parliament to curb the royal prerogative, led to his disgrace and the confiscation of his library.[14] He died before the outbreak of the Civil War but the age when antiquarians could make a significant contribution to political debates was passing. There was already evidence of a decreasing respect for the past as an arbiter in politics.[15]

The contribution made by John Selden to the study of Fortescue was apparently motivated both by his scholarly interest in history of the law and the search for precedents. He was a member of a group of poets, lawyers and antiquaries and his interaction with them was facilitated by his membership as a barrister of the Inner Temple, strategically placed

[10] G.L. Harriss, 'Medieval Doctrines in the Debates on Supply, 1610–1629', *Faction and Parliament: Essays on Early Stuart History*, ed. K. Sharpe (Oxford: 1978) 73–103.

[11] J.G.A. Pocock, *The Ancient Constitution and the Feudal Law* (Cambridge: 1987) 57; E. Coke, *Institutes of the Laws of England*, 4 vols (London: 1628).

[12] J.L. Malcolm, 'Magna Carta in America: Entrenched', *Magna Carta: The Foundation of Freedom*, ed. N. Vincent (London: 2014) 120–35. Fortescue did not cite Magna Carta in his works but his emphasis on the laws and customs of the English people made his respect for it clear.

[13] Harriss, 'Medieval Doctrines', 101.

[14] S. Tullis, '*Glanvill* after Glanvill: The Afterlife of a Medieval Legal Treatise,' *Laws, Lawyers and Texts*, 327–59.

[15] K. Sharpe, *Sir Robert Cotton, 1586–1631: History and Politics in Early Modern England* (Oxford: 1979) 250.

between the City of London and the royal court at Westminster.[16] Like Cotton he was one of those who supplied parliament with historical ammunition against the King in the 1620s and he was imprisoned for it. His opinion that law could be reduced to two foundations, either ascertained by custom or established by acts of parliament, effectively excluded the monarchy from the process.[17] He increasingly inclined towards political moderation, however, disliking the extreme measures to which parliament resorted when negotiations with Charles I failed.

Selden did not live to see the Restoration in 1660 but the 1616 edition of the *De Laudibus* and his other scholarly activities in which he offered impartial opinions ultimately rescued his works from the danger of being too closely associated with anti-monarchist thought.[18] In 1616 the Society of Stationers, who held a monopoly for printing common law books, asked Selden to write an introduction and notes to a new edition of Fortescue's *De Laudibus Legum Anglie*. The actual text differed little from Tottel's in the previous century, but it was accompanied by Selden's own edition of Hengham's *Summa Magna* in which he established new standards of meticulous scholarship. As he wrote in his preface, 'divers copies of *Hengham* were examin'd in preparing this, yet could not a perfect one bee extracted from them all. As one helpt another, choise was so made that this might bee the best.'[19] This care was also shown in his work on Fortescue. In July 1616 the Oxford antiquary Dr Thomas Allen wrote to him at the Inner Temple to say that he had acceded to his request to send him a 'lyttle pamphlet'. It partly replicated a printed version that he had (presumably of the *De Laudibus* since no other Fortescue work was then printed) and he hoped that it would prove useful.[20]

There is a paradox to be observed at this stage in the reception of Fortescue's ideas. Generations of historians have worried about what,

16 G.J. Toomer, *John Selden: A Life in Scholarship*, 2 vols (Oxford: 2009) vol. 1, 24.

17 Cromartie, 'The Idea of Common Law', 221 quoting Pocock, *Ancient Constitution*, p.296; D.S. Berkowitz, *John Selden's Formative Years: Politics and Society in Early Seventeenth-Century England* (London and Toronto: 1988) esp. ch. 5.

18 J. Fortescue, *De Laudibus Legum Anglie*, with an Introduction by J. Selden (London: 1616).

19 Toomer, *John Selden*, vol. 1, 187; Ralph Hengham (*c.*1235–1311), Chief Justice Common Pleas/Bench, probably wrote *Hengham Parva* and two consultations, but Paul Brand thinks probably not the *Hengham Magna* on stylistic and other grounds, *ODNB*, 26, 350–1.

20 Oxford, Bodleian Library MS Selden supra 108, f. 110; R.A. Beddard, 'Thomas Allen and John Selden and the 1616 edition of Fortescue's *De Laudibus Legum Anglie*', *Book Collector*, 53, 4 (2004) 533–41.

if any, impact his advice might have had upon his contemporaries, yet much later, throughout the early decades of the seventeenth century, his arguments were a potent force in the debate over the extent of parliament's power to curtail the royal prerogative. The view taken in this book is that while he intended that the king should govern with the advice of wise and honest councillors and with regard to the laws and customs of the realm (*dominium politicum*), if necessary, he could use his royal prerogative to override such restraints by the exercise of his unlimited power (*dominium regale*). Supporters of Parliament under the early Stuarts were influenced by Fortescue and interpreted his work as a defence of parliamentary sovereignty in a fashion diametrically opposed to what appears to have been his original intention in composing his three great treatises.

Fortescue continued to be studied in the late seventeenth century, although by this time he was becoming a vehicle for all manner of bizarre and arcane learning. The *Fortescutus Illustratus* is an example of this genre. It was published in 1663 by Edward Waterhouse (1619–70), described as a 'cock-brain'd man' in Anthony Wood's *Fasti*, and was a massive commentary of mostly irrelevant learning on the *De Laudibus*.[21] The title-page was faced by a large portrait of Waterhouse and proclaimed that it was written for King Henry's son and heir whilst Fortescue loyally attended him in France. It was dedicated to Edward Hyde, earl of Clarendon, the Chancellor, who was clearly meant to be flattered by the implied parallel between himself, recently returned from exile with his master Charles II, and Fortescue at Koeur.[22] This kind of treatment of Fortescue's works marks a departure because his ideas no longer occupied the central ground in constitutional debate. That now belonged to the pragmatic treatises of thinkers such as Thomas Hobbes and John Locke, who had largely set aside arguments based on law and history in favour of reasonable deduction from first principles.[23]Instead Fortescue's still prestigious treatises became the means by which his editors could display their erudition and curry favour with the great.

[21] *ODNB*, 57, 551–2.

[22] Edward Waterhouse, *Fortescutus Illustratus or a Commentary (with large portions of the text) on that Nervous* [Powerful] *Treatise 'De Laudibus Legum Anglie'* (London: 1663).

[23] J.G.A. Pocock, *The Ancient Constitution and the Feudal Law* (Bath: 1974): 'the age in which law was supremely important in determining men's thoughts about the past was succeeded by another in which that importance had been lost', 251.

One of Sir John Fortescue's descendants took the new approach to his works. In the early eighteenth century, John Fortescue Aland of the Inner Temple (1670–1746) brought out the first printed edition of the *Governance of England* with an early version of its title, *The Difference between an Absolute and a Limited Monarchy.*[24] The editor employed the terms 'limited' and 'absolute' monarchy as they would have been more recognisable to eighteenth-century readers than 'dominium politicum et regale'. He used the Bodleian copy made by his ancestor Sir Adrian Fortescue, collating it with Laud Misc. 593 (which he recognised was the earliest version) and Cotton Claudius A viii. He displayed his learning in a long preface in which he traced the history of the common law and of the English language and stressed the importance of knowing Anglo-Saxon. He proved how well he knew that language in a great variety of complicated footnotes which industriously traced the Saxon origins of words used by Fortescue.[25] In his dedication to Sir Thomas Parker, the Lord Chief Justice, he commended:

> The subject of this piece ... the most excellent and curious part of the law, the English constitution. And our Author was so great a lover and vindicator of it, and had so exact a knowledge in all the parts thereof, that I could not but think, that the bringing such a work to light, would not only be acceptable to Your Lordship, but serviceable also to the publick, since it cannot be doubted but that what he lays down, concerning the liberties of the subjects of England, must have the more weight, and stronger influence, when it is considered that it comes from one, who perfectly understood all the points of prerogative.[26]

He went on to praise Sir Thomas Parker in fulsome tones. Like his forebears, Fortescue Aland was successful in advancing his career. His edition was well received, with a second following in 1719 and a third in 1724. He was appointed Solicitor General briefly but his talent seems to have been for scholarship rather than the practice of the law. He was subsequently ennobled as baron Fortescue of Credan.[27]

There had been a distinctly Whiggish tone to Fortescue Aland's remarks in his dedication and introduction: this was to be expected

[24] *The Difference between an Absolute and Limited Monarchy as it more particularly regards the English Constitution by Sir John Fortescue Knight*, ed. John Fortescue Aland (London: 1714).

[25] Toomer describes such etymology as not only useless but 'positively pernicious', *John Selden*, vol.1, 67.

[26] *Difference between an Absolute and a Limited Monarchy*, A3v–4r.

[27] *ODNB*, 1, 558–9.

at a time when the debate over the Hanoverian succession was at its height and no one with any pretensions to advancement could avoid taking sides, and he had made the right choice. Two decades later another publication, Francis Gregor's English edition of the *De Laudibus*, aspired to enlighten the Hanoverian princes (sons of George II), Frederick, prince of Wales and William Augustus, duke of Cumberland. The treatise should be known to princes of the blood and young nobles, for 'unless they are instructed in what is our original constitution, what are the ancient rights and privileges thereof, they can never be able to defend it as they ought'.[28] Gregor was scathing about the quality of earlier editions and about Mulcaster's English translation, which he replaced with one of his own, although he did pay a rather half-hearted tribute to Selden's work. His motives in undertaking the edition seem to have been a combination of genuine scholarly interest and a wish to use the well-known treatise as a means of ingratiating himself with the new dynasty.

The eighteenth and early nineteenth centuries saw a consolidation of Fortescue's reputation as an apologist for the English common law and an advocate of limited monarchy. Yet his treatises were no longer venerated as unique repositories of precedent. In an age where the rule of the monarch in parliament was taken for granted and the greatest political energy was expended in working the party system, much of what he had to say seemed to be stating the obvious. The close personal involvement of the young George III in the governance of Britain and his rejection of the Whig establishment, a policy continued by George IV, gave a new political complexion to the next major commentator on Fortescue.

In 1825, Andrew Amos, a barrister of Lincoln's Inn (1791–1860), brought out a new edition of the *De Laudibus* using Gregor's translation but supplying his own notes. His preface praised Fortescue for 'pursuing a judicious course for securing the future happiness of the English nation, in forming the character of the Heir Apparent to the throne, and acquainting him with the duties of a Patriot King'. But he observed that much had changed for the better since Fortescue's time and that his readers would have to make allowances: 'the reflections which the wisest of our ancestors have transmitted to us often appear to our understandings puerile and ridiculous, the result of contracted or prejudiced views'. Amos's reference to the formation of the character of the heir to the throne so that he might become a 'Patriot King' recalls the ideas of Henry Bolingbroke and the possibility that the monarch could play a

[28] *De Laudibus Legum Anglie*, translated into English by Francis Gregor with the notes by Selden (London: 1737) iv.

more active part in government than had been acceptable in the middle decades of the previous century.[29] In this Amos was behind the times, as political events were soon to overtake such aspirations. As a lawyer he also wanted to use Fortescue as a vehicle to press for the reform of those English legal institutions, 'which are the subject of his panegyric', hoping that Fortescue's remarks 'may be productive of other beneficial effects, if they satisfy the reader, that much of the ancient part of our law requires a serious revisal or amendment'.[30] Amos became the first professor of English law at University College, London in 1829 and was instrumental in bringing about reforms in the criminal law and the legal system in India.[31]

The reform of parliament and the accession of Queen Victoria marked a stage when the powers of the monarchy were unquestionably and permanently curtailed. This tended to restore the prestige of Fortescue's treatises, since there was a genuine interest in legal and scholarly circles in the works of a man who was regarded as the first apologist for the English constitution. John Lingard, for example, wrote of the *De Laudibus* in his *History of England*: 'This treatise is deserving of attention, because it shows what notions prevailed at that time respecting the nature of the English constitution, and the liberties of the subject.'[32] In these sentiments he echoed earlier writers, such as Sir Edward Coke, who had dwelt on the uniquely English character of Fortescue's works.

It was fortunate that Thomas Fortescue, Lord Clermont, had the resources, the industry and a formidable command of scholarly techniques to undertake an edition of the complete works of his ancestor. Clermont printed a number of them separately, but in 1869 he brought out two volumes on Fortescue's life, works and family.[33] The first contains a brief life, illustrated with a number of original documents

[29] *Bolingbroke: Political Writings*, ed. D. Armitage (Cambridge: 1997).

[30] J. Fortescue, *De Laudibus Legum Anglie*, ed. A. Amos Esq. (Cambridge: 1825) viii, xi. The heir to the throne in 1825 was the middle-aged Prince William, who had no legitimate children, and was hardly a likely recipient for such advice, which was intended to form his character.

[31] *ODNB*, 2, 1–2.

[32] J. Lingard, *The History of England from the First Invasion by the Romans to the Accession of William and Mary*, 10 vols (London: 1856) vol. 4, 97, n.

[33] *The Commodities of England* (1863), *De Natura Legis Naturae* (1864) and *The Declaration upon Certain Writings* (1863) are bound together in BL 1502/167, 1, 2, 3, but are separately paginated so could have been originally published apart. The flyleaf of the *De Natura* bears the inscription, 'Sir Thomas Philipps with Lord Clermont's compliments'.

from public records, family archives[34] and foreign libraries. It also includes all Fortescue's works that were known to Lord Clermont: the four tracts on the succession and the *De Natura*, printed for the first time, and provided the latter and the two Latin tracts with translations into English. The notes on the *De Natura* were written by Clermont's brother, Mr Chichester Fortescue, later Lord Carlingford. *The Declaration upon Certain Writings* was also printed for the first time, as was Alain Chartier's fragment, the *Dialogue between Understanding and Faith*, the short *Example what good counsel helpeth* and the *Commodities of England*. The *De Laudibus* was based on the early but incomplete manuscript in Cambridge University Library, collated with the first edition of Edward Whitechurch and accompanied by Gregor's English translation. Clermont printed Fortescue Aland's edition of the *Governance* and also consulted two sixteenth-century copies, the one at Lambeth and Stow's transcript.[35] The last part of volume I contained English translations of some of Fortescue's opinions and judgments taken from the *Year Books*. Volume II traced the history of various branches of the Fortescue family, including the French, from the middle ages to the nineteenth century.

Despite his modest disclaimers in his preface, Clermont provided an excellent account of Fortescue's life and works, one that has been the starting point for most subsequent commentators. His motives seem to have been primarily altruistic. His autograph letters accompanying the donations are still attached to the copies in the London Library ('if you do not object to add two heavy volumes to your library, June 1872') and the Society of Antiquaries show him personally distributing the limited number of copies of his privately printed work. His political alignment is not as evident as that of some of the earlier editors, although it can be discerned from time to time. At the end of his account of Fortescue's life, for example, he quoted approvingly from a long passage by Lord Campbell, '[Fortescue] to whose explanations and praises of our free constitution, we are in no small degree indebted for the resistance to oppressive rule, which has distinguished the people of England.'[36] In this respect Clermont seems to have been in sympathy with the prevailing contemporary view of Fortescue as an early apologist for constitutional monarchy. His editions marked the last of a number of occasions when a member of the Fortescue family

[34] Now deposited in Devon County Record Office.

[35] See Appendix 3.

[36] Clermont, *Works*, 50, quoted from J. Campbell, *Lives of the Lord Chancellors*, 10 vols (London: 1845–7) vol. 1, 371, 6ff.

was proactive in enhancing Sir John's reputation as a jurist and political thinker.

Fifteen years after the appearance of Clermont's edition of Fortescue's *Works* Charles Plummer brought out a completely new edition of the *Governance*. It was accompanied by a long introduction to Fortescue's life, times and works, scholarly notes and several appendices in which he published for the first time fragments from the tracts on the succession (which were unknown to Clermont) and the *Articles sent to Warwick*. He found the short *Twenty-two Righteousnesses belonging to a king* 'commonplace and poor', unworthy of Fortescue.[37] Clermont had printed it as one of his works although it was not clearly connected to any of the others and it occurs only in *John Vale's Book* and Stow's copy. It is a translation of part of the anonymous seventh-century Latin *De xii abusivis saeculi* (The Twelve Abuses of this World) and is indeed unlikely to have been written by Fortescue.[38]

Plummer based his edition on Oxford, Bodleian Library Laud Misc. 593 but recorded variant readings from the other nine manuscripts that were known to him and relied on Cotton Claudius A viii to provide the final chapter and a half.[39] His work is the first to be recognisable to modern historians as an attempt to relate Fortescue's thought to the political circumstances of his time. Plummer touched on such questions as 'bastard feudalism', a concept that he initiated, and the 'New Monarchy'[40] and was not prepared to define Fortescue's ideas in the simplistic terms used by his predecessors:

> The point in which he shows most boldness and originality is his scheme for the reorganisation of the Privy Council. In this, and in his proposals for permanently endowing the crown and reducing the power of the nobles, he certainly prepares the way, however unconsciously, for what it is the fashion to call the New Monarchy. I am therefore unable to regard Fortescue's scheme of reform, as Dr Stubbs apparently does, as being in the main an exhortation to Edward IV to revert to the Lancastrian system of government.[41] I would rather say that Fortescue, while remaining true

[37] Plummer, *Governance of England*, 81.

[38] BL MS Additional 48031A, ff. 164b–165a; MS Harley 542, ff. 139b–140a; *Vale's Book*, 251–3.

[39] See Appendix 3.

[40] The term was first coined by a contemporary of Bishop Stubbs, J.R. Green, *A Short History of the English People*, ed. R. Hudson (London: 1992) 291–307. The first edition was published in 1874, giving Plummer plenty of time to absorb it.

[41] W. Stubbs, *The Constitutional History of England*, 3 vols (Oxford: 1878) vol. 3, 240–7.

to the great constitutional principles which he had previously enunciated, urges the king to avoid the main weaknesses of Lancastrian rule, its unsound finance, its subserviency to aristocratic influence, its lack of 'governance' and justice.[42]

'Bastard feudalism' was in Plummer's view one of the defining evils of the reign of Henry VI:

> In place of the primitive relation of a lord to his tenants, [it] surrounded the great man with a horde of retainers, who wore his livery and fought his battles ... while he in turn maintained their quarrels and shielded their crimes from punishment. This evil, as we shall see, reached its greatest height during the Lancastrian period.[43]

'Bastard feudalism' has proved to be a useful shorthand term for the way in which some English magnates exercised their power in the later middle ages. McFarlane in an essay devoted to the subject believed that under strong kings like Henry V and Henry VII retinues of paid retainers did not present too much of a problem. Under a weak king such as Henry VI their existence played a major part in the outbursts of civil war in the 1450s.[44] Because Plummer coined the term in the introduction to his edition of the *Governance*, Fortescue is perhaps too readily associated with the idea. For him the dysfunctional 'overmighty subjects' posed a threat principally because some of them could equal the king in wealth. Social unrest from the bottom came when the commons were kept in poverty by heavy taxation – again economic factors were uppermost in his thinking. The nearest Fortescue really came to discussing 'bastard feudalism' was when he said that those employed by the Crown should not have any other posts since their loyalties would then be split and those who did not deserve the gifts they had received should be subject to acts of resumption. He never spelt out the implications of excluding most of the nobility from the royal council, but that too would have tended to weaken their power in the counties as well as at Westminster.

Plummer set out the agenda for interpreters of Fortescue's political ideas for almost a century: they could either support the 'Lancastrian constitutionalist' argument which had been made most ambitiously by Bishop Stubbs in the late nineteenth century, or see Fortescue as an apologist for a ruthless bureaucratic 'New Monarchy', initiated tentatively

[42] Plummer, *Governance of England*, 87.

[43] *Ibid.*, 15–16.

[44] K.B. McFarlane, *England in the Fifteenth Century: Collected Essays* (London: 1981) 23–43.

by Edward IV and subsequently followed through by the early Tudors. Stubbs interpreted Fortescue's writings in a resolutely constitutionalist light: all the Lancastrian monarchs had ruled with parliamentary consent and, after the unfortunate breakdown of authority 1449–1451, sought to return to that happy situation. The system advocated in the *Governance* was a mere restoration of what had been 'in use under the Lancastrian kings.'[45] No more editions of Fortescue's works were to appear for over fifty-five years.

Early in the twentieth century W.S. Holdsworth suggested that Fortescue's exile gave him the opportunity to reflect from the outside on the condition of his country. The comparative approach was another facet of his writings that had not previously been appreciated. Holdsworth went on to give a balanced account of the issues addressed in the treatise: 'He was not a man to exalt unduly the powers of the king and Council at the expense of Parliament; but it is clear that he did not consider that the medieval legislation had impaired the powers of the Council to exercise a wide jurisdiction to deal with the prevalent disorder.'[46] F.W. Maitland, in the course of a series of lectures delivered a few years later, adhered to the predominant view of Fortescue as an advocate of constitutional monarchy. But he also associated his ideas with the emergence of the 'New Monarchy' which he attributed to the capacity of Edward IV and Henry VII to work within 'the legal limits of royal power erected in earlier centuries' by managing parliamentary institutions to carry out their wishes. Maitland emphasised the specifically English characteristics of the common law which Fortescue had defined: the variety of actions available to litigants, the jury, emphasis on case law and precedent and a higher legal profession which was well educated at the Inns of Court. Henry II safeguarded these excellent features by establishing permanent courts of professional judges at Westminster as well as sending itinerant judges throughout the land. Henry VII found that he could use parliament rather than civil law to achieve the strong government he desired.[47]

The advent of S.B. Chrimes to the field of late medieval studies threw a new and penetrating light onto Fortescue's works. In his *English Constitutional Ideas in the Fifteenth Century* (1936) he gave an account of the origin of Fortescue's ideas and of how they should be interpreted in terms that would be recognisable to his contemporaries. He

[45] Stubbs, *Constitutional History*, vol. 3, 194, 240–7.

[46] Holdsworth, *History of English Law*, vol. 1, 491, 2, 568–71.

[47] J.G.H. Hudson, *F.W. Maitland and the Englishness of English Law*, Selden Society (London: 2007) 3–31.

concluded that, 'His originality lay not in any exceptional constitutional enlightenment nor in liberal sentiments, but in his attempt to array bare constitutional facts in the imposing raiment of political theory.' In 1932 C.H. McIlwain had published his *Growth of Political Thought in the West* and this seems to have influenced the thinking of Chrimes about the central issue of what precisely Fortescue meant by 'dominium politicum et regale'. McIlwain thought that most commentators had been led to impute a theory of constitutional government to him because they misunderstood the feudal concept of 'dominium'. The English monarchy was limited by precedent but it was not controlled by any force beyond itself.[48] Chrimes argued that, far from advocating new limitations on the power of the monarchy, if it had been carried out, 'Fortescue's scheme of reform would have involved the atrophy of English constitutional development.' Eric Ives was later to give support to this view of Fortescue's theories when he pointed out that the common law was the king's law administered by judges holding office at his pleasure, it was tender towards his rights and responsive to his wishes. The dictum, 'ea interpretacio sequenda sit que pro rege fecit', gave authority to the prince: although some would object that it fell short of the authoritarian civil law principle, 'quod principi placuit legis habet vigorem'.[49]

In 1942 Chrimes brought out a new edition of the *De Laudibus* accompanied by his own English translation, introduction, notes and appendices and a general introduction by H.D. Hazeltine, editor of the series (Cambridge Studies in English Legal History), which drew together for historians of the second half of the twentieth century the current knowledge of Fortescue's life and works. It was even more impressive in that it was completed and printed during the Second World War and something of the prevailing ethos can be found in the editor's final patriotic encomium, written in a very different tone to his earlier, dispassionate, analytical study of Fortescue's thought:

> The force of Fortescue's personality overcomes the years; we recognise in it the authentic voice of English character. Sometimes, moreover, it brings to us over the five hundred years a message, of warning and of comfort, that even now, as ever, we can ill afford to forget. '*Sed libertas*

[48] C.H. McIlwain, *The Growth of Political Thought in the West: From the Greeks to the End of the Middle Ages* (New York: 1968) 354–63.

[49] 'That interpretation should be followed that favours the king', 'what pleases the prince has the force of law', Ives, *Common Lawyers*, 193; Chrimes, *English Constitutional Ideas*, 300–32, quotations at 324, 332; Vale's *Book*, 65–6.

a Deo hominis est indita nature. Quare ipsa ab homine sublata semper redire desiderat.'[50]

Forty-five years were to pass before the need was felt for new editions of any of Fortescue's works, although, with accessible copies of Plummer's *Governance* and Chrimes's *De Laudibus*, scholars were able to speculate at large on the meaning of his ideas, particularly of *dominium politicum et regale*. Most were still engaging, in ever more sophisticated terms, with the issue of whether Fortescue was advocating a limited monarchy.[51] J.P. Genet, who believed that the *Governance* was written for Warwick's restoration of Henry VI and later revised for Edward IV, inclined to the McIlwain school in discussing the meaning of Fortescue's political and regal government: a people agreed to obey a prince provided that he would safeguard their goods. This worked well in England, where a flourishing gentry were sustained by a prosperous economy which underpinned the socio-political fabric of the country. This polity was contrasted favourably with the abject condition of the peasantry in France.[52] A.L. Brown, however, pointed out Fortescue's failure to reconcile the power of a divinely appointed monarchy with its obligation to protect the goods and security of its subjects.[53] Some of these variant views can be attributed to the fact that Fortescue, like other contemporary writers, did not always feel the need to be totally consistent. It was noticed above in Chapter 5, for example, that the similar advice offered to Warwick/Henry VI (*Articles sent to Warwick)* and to Edward IV (*Governance*) was altered in some cases to suit the very different political circumstances in which the two treatises were written.

Some scholars have cast original light on Fortescue studies: G.L. Harriss stressed Fortescue's view of the 'collegiality' of Crown and subjects as the essence of the English political system as it was exemplified

[50] Chrimes, *De Laudibus,* cviii, 104–5, 'But freedom was instilled into human nature by God. Hence freedom taken away from man always desires to return.'

[51] R.W.K. Hinton, 'English Constitutional Theories from Sir John Fortescue to Sir John Eliot', *EHR*, 75 (1960) 410–25; Gillespie, 'Sir John Fortescue's Concept of the Royal Will'; J.H. Burns, 'Fortescue and the Political Theory of *dominium*', *Historical Journal*, 28 (1985) 777–97, who wearily remarked that *dominium politicum et regale* had been so much discussed that it seemed threadbare but it was still an unavoidable topic for analysis; N. Doe, 'Fifteenth Century Concepts of Law: Fortescue and Pecock', *History of Political Thought*, 10 (1989) 257–80.

[52] J.P. Genet, 'Les idées sociales de Sir John Fortescue', *Économies et sociétés au Moyen Âge: Mélanges offerts à Edouard Perroy* (Paris: 1973) 446–61.

[53] A.L. Brown, *The Governance of Late Medieval England, 1272–1461* (London: 1989) esp. ch. 1.

in chapter XIX of the *Governance*.[54] Veikko Litzen took a European perspective in 1971 when he engaged with a previously neglected aspect of Fortescue's writings, the question of the English and French successions and how Fortescue's tracts and French polemics might have interacted, a subject more recently pursued in the publications of Craig Taylor.[55] Anthony Gross also looked at the European dimension in 1996 when he analysed the French Chancery's memoranda on Fortescue's writings. His book on *The Dissolution of the Lancastrian Kingship* made the important point that Fortescue is 'easily misjudged as a detached constitutional theorist, [he] is best understood as a pragmatic political polemicist'. He subjected Fortescue's career and thought to the most extensive scrutiny that it had received since the work of Chrimes. It sits very well with the new approach to political ideas discussed in the following paragraphs, an approach that is also taken in this study.[56]

The most significant development during recent decades has been the advent of Quentin Skinner and those who use similar methodologies to examine political ideas and the language used to express them in the context of their contemporary value systems. Skinner considered Fortescue's rejection of the Roman civil code in the *De Laudibus* as a continuation of an English brand of xenophobia, first manifested by Bracton two centuries earlier, on the grounds that it was alien to the perception of the 'political' nature of England's government, as were the canon law and the papal claims it incorporated.[57] The attraction of Skinner's approach to historians is that it releases them from the obligation to confine themselves to 'canonic' texts. The writings of Fortescue can be studied far more satisfactorily if his short polemical works and associated speeches, tracts and poems can be considered. When placed in their political and ideological environment they can do rather more than simply to enable the commentator to analyse the philosophical significance of the text.

One of Fortescue's most important contributions to the development of political ideas was his use of language. Maurizio Viroli has discussed how the civic humanists of fifteenth-century Italy drew on the traditions

[54] G.L. Harriss, 'The King and His Subjects', *Fifteenth Century Attitudes: Perceptions of Society in Late Medieval England*, ed. R. Horrox (Cambridge: 1994) 13–28.

[55] See references and discussion in Chapter 4, pp. 169–72.

[56] Gross, *Dissolution of the Lancastrian Kingship*, 62 and *passim*. Despite our agreement on many aspects of Fortescue's work, it should be noted that Anthony Gross and the author have been arguing amicably about the authorship of the *Somnium Vigilantis* and the king for whom the *Governance* was destined for over two decades.

[57] Skinner, *Foundations*, vol. 2, 54–6.

of the political virtues (often identified as the Cardinal Virtues of Justice, Prudence, Fortitude and Temperance), civil law and the writings of Aristotle and his commentators to equate politics with civic philosophy.[58] Fortescue's use of the term *dominium politicum et regale* and its variants in his three major treatises was ambiguous but it provided subsequent writers with a means of holding a sophisticated debate about the proper location of sovereignty. He contributed to an 'indispensable linguistic resource which is the refinement of a language of practical politics'.[59]

The 1990s, responding perhaps to the energy that had been injected into the study of political ideas by the work of Skinner and like-minded commentators, saw a resurgence in studies of Fortescue underpinned by new editions of his works. In 1992 a symposium on Fortescue was organised by Anthony Gross at the University of Kent, at which the speakers were Gross, Shelley Lockwood and the author of this book. In 1995 *The Politics of Fifteenth-Century England: John Vale's Book*, edited by the author, Colin Richmond, Anne Sutton, Livia Visser-Fuchs and John Watts, appeared, followed in 1996 by Shelley Lockwood's *On the Laws and Governance of England.* The former contained a calendar of a number of fifteenth-century political manifestos, a short history, letters and so forth, as well as an early version of Fortescue's *Governance*, his *Articles sent to Warwick*, *Example what good counsel helpeth* and the *Replication against the claim and title of the duke of York*, all copied in the early 1480s. Lockwood's edition of the *Governance* and *De Laudibus*, both in modern English, made two of Fortescue's major works accessible to a wider readership than had before been possible.

A few years earlier Christine Carpenter had taken issue with McFarlane's view, also voiced by J.R. Lander, that English politics were primarily motivated by self-interest, particularly the acquisition of property and patronage. She suggested that the magnates and gentry realised that their individual concerns might often best be served by pursuing

[58] M. Viroli, *From Politics to Reason of State: The Acquisition and Transformation of the Language of Politics, 1250–1600* (Cambridge: 1992) 71. For the early fifteenth-century Florentine chancellors, Coluccio Salutati and Leonardo Bruni, Aristotle's political thought provided a philosophy of civic life – a republic governed by measure and proportion which was reflected in the lives of its citizens whose virtue was ensured by good laws.

[59] Strohm, *Politique*, 18; concentrating on the early Lancastrian period, Jenni Nuttall discusses how the deposition of Richard II and usurpation of Henry IV in 1399 led to the development of a political language to describe those events, *The Creation of Lancastrian Kingship: Literature, Language and Politics in Late Medieval England* (Cambridge: 2007).

collective aspirations.[60] John Watts read the *De Laudibus* and the *Governance* against the background of the English civil wars and the search by the political nation for a safe authorization for the exercise of political power. He saw the latter in the creation of a richly endowed monarchy and a council where career bureaucrats predominated:

> [K]ing and nobility, head and limbs of the old body politic, were essentially removed from power: the former had little choice but to endorse the views of his council and parliament; the latter were to become wealthy nonentities, enjoying their lands in peaceful obscurity, but ever-threatened by the accidents of heredity and the king's 'feudal' prerogatives.[61]

In his following paragraph Watts recognised that Fortescue had taken a step back from 'the enormity of what he was suggesting' in the well-known final sentence of the *Governance*, 'And yit he may leve this order whan hym liste.'[62]Fortescue had come to his revolutionary view of how royal authority should be exercised by his experience of the dangerous instability of his time but he had to recognise that his solution was not actually compatible with the political reality of the prerogative.

Alan Cromartie's work has consolidated many of the more recent discussions. Like Gross he recognised that it was unrealistic to expect total consistency from one whose former career had been dedicated to the flexible interpretation of the law.[63] Fortescue like other lawyers used the term 'reason' as a justification for modifying the law when it was unsatisfactory. The equitable (the use of 'reason') interpretation of the common law was a characteristic of the Court of Chancery. Fortescue had taken many of his arguments from civil and canon law in the *De Natura* but then roundly condemned both systems in the *De Laudibus*. Cromartie cut the Gordian knot by suggesting that Fortescue's monarch possessed the absolute power to decide when and how he would take counsel and when he could suspend normal rights and laws for the greater good, but he still regarded a professional royal council as the best body for making such judgements. When Fortescue referred to 'assent' he meant that the

[60] McFarlane, *Nobility*, *passim*; J.R. Lander, *Conflict and Stability in Fifteenth-Century England* (London: 1969) *passim*; Carpenter, *Locality and Polity*, 6–8.

[61] Watts, *Henry VI*, 49–50; Watts, 'New ffundaccion'; Shelley Lockwood's Introduction to the *Laws and Governance of England* coincides with this view.

[62] *Vale's Book*, 250.

[63] Gross, *Dissolution of the Lancastrian Kingship*, 89–90; A. Cromartie, 'Common Law, Counsel and Consent in Fortescue's Political Thought', *The Fifteenth Century IV: Political Culture in Late Medieval Britain*, ed. L. Clark and C. Carpenter (Woodbridge: 2004) 45–67; Cromartie, *Constitutionalist Revolution*, ch. 1.

ruler was prepared to take advice rather than to seek popular consent to his laws. Paul Strohm's *Politique* (2006) portrayed Fortescue as a writer enjoying, with others, a pre-Machiavellian moment producing texts that were informed, unsentimental and keenly concerned with political practice in the world.[64] His cover illustration encapsulated the view that a worldly minded prince who consulted properly within his realm and who allied himself to 'reason' could defeat arbitrary Fortune and by this 'politique' behaviour secure himself in power.[65]

In 2011 Suzanne Marcuzzi completed a PhD thesis in Cambridge in which she undertook a thorough reassessment of Fortescue's political theory, tackling the intractable problems of what exactly he meant by 'political and regal dominium' and the concept of 'assent'. She incorporated a great deal of work on his first treatise, the *De Natura*, into her study and this has been beneficial in producing a more rounded account of his ideas than has often been the case. She suggests that the 'medieval conception of a well-ordered universe in which everything naturally strives towards the ends given by God is central to Fortescue's theory'. This leads to the conclusion that neither liberty nor law were of paramount importance, but rather the need to uphold the natural order of the universe with each social group performing its function. For this to happen, the unfettered authority of the king was essential, whether he was presiding over a 'political and regal' or only 'regal' regime. Just laws and good government were identified in terms of the ends they sought, not the means by which they were created or enforced.[66] The present writer takes a more pragmatic approach: Fortescue's *De Laudibus* and *Governance* were inseparable from their political context and his need to ensure the means by which stability could be achieved, that is through the exercise of the royal will to take counsel and uphold good laws and sound administrative and fiscal provisions.

M.R.L.L. Kelly's 'Sir John Fortescue and the Political Dominion' (2014) took a different view of the problem of interpreting political and regal rule.[67] In both the *De Laudibus* and the *Governance* Fortescue was

64 Strohm, *Politique*, *passim*; for the illustration in BL MS Harley 7353, J. Hughes, *Arthurian Myths and Alchemy: The Kingship of Edward IV* (Stroud: 2002) 83–5.

65 BL MS Harley 7353, a Yorkist genealogical roll. It shows Edward IV surmounting Fortune's Wheel watched by members of the nobility and clergy. A figure of Reason dressed as a judge in crimson and a silk coif inserts a spoke which prevents it from turning to displace him.

66 Marcuzzi, 'Fortescue on Law and Regal Power', 223, 227–31.

67 M.R.L.L. Kelly, 'Sir John Fortescue and the Political Dominium: The People, the Common Weal and the King', *Constitutions and the Classics: Patterns of Constitutional Thought from Fortescue to Bentham*, ed. D. Galliga (Oxford: 2014) 51–85.

constructing a norm of what good governance should be. There was a clear distinction between English kings, who took the coronation oath which put them under an obligation to the people to rule politically, and some foreign regal rulers, who did not take such an oath. She made the point that during his turbulent times, in contrast to what Machiavelli was soon to advise, Fortescue 'firmly placed the development of the English constitution on the path of law, not arms, to the great benefit of the English-speaking peoples ever since'.[68]

Interpretations of Fortescue will and should continue to reflect the political preoccupations and priorities of writers' own times. This chapter has shown how increased interest, knowledge and debates about his ideas have often arisen from scholarship devoted to producing new editions of his works. The *De Natura Legis Naturae* has only once been published, nearly 150 ago, and was often shunned for being unconscionably tedious, but recent studies have shown how important it is to the development of Fortescue's thinking in anticipating ideas that were later repeated in his two other great treatises. A new edition would be welcome to stand beside those of Plummer and Chrimes and the scholars who have engaged with and extended their work.

[68] *Ibid.*, 84.

Conclusion

To conclude this study of Sir John Fortescue and the governance of England several topics will be considered that throw light on his character, in so far as it can be recovered, the ideological, cultural and political climate in which he worked, the impact this had upon his thought and the claim made by Chrimes that he was 'the authentic voice of English character'.[1]

It is possible to get some idea of Fortescue's character both from his writings and from the documents which record his career and business dealings. He was able, flexible, hard-working and hard-headed; professionally and politically he acted pragmatically. He seems to have been conventionally religious and was anxious that what he wrote on the succession question should not violate canon law: he may have translated at least part of Alain Chartier's *Treatise of Hope*. His relationships with female members of his family seem to have been determined by profit and loss rather than by affection. Both his marriages were arranged with heiresses in areas where he aspired to build up his career prospects. His daughter Maud was the victim of a marriage which he saw as a means of aggrandising his family, but his attitudes in this respect were typical of his time. Fortescue was sociable, liking wine, good dinners and the company to be found at the Inns of Court. The Inns were crucial to the preservation of the English character of the common law:

> These unique institutions, thoroughly entrenched in English social life, helped preserve English law from Romanising influences, since the lawyers who dominated the Commons as well as the courts had received their legal education not in the universities where civil law was taught, but in the Inns where the common law was nourished.[2]

[1] Chrimes, *De Laudibus*, cviii, 104–5.

[2] H. Potter, *Law, Liberty and the Constitution: A Brief History of the Common Law* (Woodbridge: 2015) 90.

The *Year Books* testify that the exchanges between the justices and sergeants in the common law courts were sometimes humorous and a few of Fortescue's judgments seem distinctly light-hearted, a side of his character that his writings, including the *De Natura*, also show. His major works were produced in a pressurised atmosphere: the defeat of Lancaster 1460–3 obliged him to issue ever more elaborate justifications for a usurpation that took place sixty years earlier. As a lawyer this kind of pleading was not totally foreign to him but together with his fellow justices he had already protested their unfitness for such a task in October 1460. The imminent reinstatement of his masters in 1470 brought forth the *De Laudibus*, where we can see the man more clearly than in any of his previous works. His scenario of a dialogue with Prince Edward at Koeur reports exchanges that could have actually occurred over several years. Although cleaned up, over-optimistic about the value of the common law and with a satisfactory outcome the treatise gave a convincing picture of a work-shy teenager and a deferential but testy tutor who doggedly attempted to engage a future ruler with the laws of England and their political significance. His humiliation as an impoverished and powerless exile forced to sue the French king for support may have finally been revenged in the francophobe sentiments that he expressed in the *De Laudibus*. It was a risky strategy to employ at a time when the Lancastrians were still dependent on the good will of Louis XI and it seems probable that Fortescue's views were genuine, harking back to the early decades of the century when he and his family were caught up in the heady atmosphere of the Normandy campaigns. Fortescue's scorn for the French mode of government and the economic hardships it entailed for many of the population was repeated in the *Governance*, timely sentiments when Edward IV was planning an invasion of France.

The *Declaration upon certain writings late sent out of Scotland* was the product of external pressures from the Yorkist regime and not a tract that Fortescue would have chosen to write, as he protested several times. The 'Lerned Man' personified those pressures and kept him relentlessly to his task of disowning his former polemics, although Fortescue could not resist mocking him for the weight of historical precedents with which he plied him. The *Governance* probably incorporated working papers from his career as a servant of the house of Lancaster as well as ideas from his earlier major treatises and a new model for royal administration. In it he seems to have at last been free to write what he truly believed, motivated by the same sense of duty that had kept him loyal to Henry VI for so long. This is why his ideas, at last expressed with honesty and with few concessions to Christian ethics in a clear, eloquent style, have continued to engage his readers.

From aspects of the intellectual and ideological climate in northern Europe and England in the fifteenth century that could be explored for their influence on Fortescue's thought, three themes seem to be particularly productive: the tradition of 'mirrors for princes', the ideas that engaged the politically active during the reigns of Henry VI and Edward IV and the impact of Italian humanism. These sources of influence may seem to be varied and even contradictory but such a judgement could stand as a verdict on the corpus of Fortescue's work itself. Indeed, much of its interest lies in its complexity and the apparent incompatibility of some of his ideas with each other. One aspect of the matter to be borne in mind is that his extraordinarily long career could quite reasonably have led him to form different conclusions as social and political circumstances changed around him: self-interest was probably also a factor. There are signs, for example, in the *De Natura*, which was written abroad in exile in the 1460s, that he respected the Continental civil law despite the fact that it was unlikely to promote the political and regal rule that he favoured. When he was in the process of quitting France as he completed the *De Laudibus* and under Edward IV when he seems to have written the *Governance*, he compared civil law unfavourably with common law and condemned the misery that the former fostered in France.

The influence of the tradition of the 'mirrors for princes' on Fortescue's advice to rulers has been noticed above in Chapter 5. This stage in the development of ideas about good government in the late middle ages was not taken seriously until the late twentieth century.[3] A convincing case for its importance has been made by John Watts in his *Henry VI and the Politics of Kingship* and other publications. He reiterated Quentin Skinner's contention that, whatever a ruler's private views or preferences might be, his public use of power was required to accord with the moral code as it was purveyed by Christian doctrine, the law and by ethical works such as 'mirrors for princes'.[4] The most compelling evidence that Fortescue wished his readers to identify his work as part of this genre is to be found at the beginning of the *De Laudibus*. His scenario enabled him to advise Edward of Lancaster that his excessive practice of the cardinal virtue of Fortitude in his use of arms was endangering his chance of acquiring a grasp of the other essential kingly virtue of

[3] A pioneering exception was L.K. Born, 'The Perfect Prince: A Study in Thirteenth- and Fourteenth-Century Ideals', *Speculum*, 3 (1928) 470–504, then in the 1980s, Green, *Poets and Princepleasers*; Orme, *From Childhood to Chivalry*; Kekewich, 'Books of Advice'.

[4] Watts, *Henry VI*, 6–9.

Justice. The rest of the treatise was an encomium to the excellent justice provided by the common law and to the political and regal form of government in England which it safeguarded. Very little of this would have been familiar to readers of 'mirrors for princes', so it was part of Fortescue's lawyer's craft to lead his readers via known moral sentiments to new and often harsh political realities.

The *Governance* did not directly assume a princely reader until the penultimate chapter XIX and yet much of the advice would have been immediately recognisable as ingredients of scholastic 'mirrors for princes'. Fortescue deliberately invoked the model in the first two chapters by citing well-known authorities on princely rule such as St Thomas Aquinas and Giles of Rome, as well as biblical quotations. The whole thrust of his advice – that a king should deal justly with his subjects by avoiding heavy taxation and living of his own, assisted by a wise and honest council – was what princes in Western Europe had been told by writers and preachers for several hundred years. What would have been less familiar to his readers (and some of these features are also to be found in the *De Laudibus*) was the extensive use of modern as opposed to ancient illustrations of his points, the detailed recommendations for reform, the scathing condemnation of past malpractice and, most notable of all, the absence of the justification of Christian morality for much of what was suggested. Taken together the treatises are the first major example in England of the theoretical 'desacralization of political authority'.[5] Religion seemed to reappear as a factor in government policy in chapter XIX of the *Governance*, but what Fortescue was actually saying was something quite different: that it was much better to put the Crown on a secure financial basis than to waste money (*pace* Henry VI) on abbeys, hospitals and other religious foundations.

The question arises of whether Fortescue used the language of 'mirrors for princes' because he genuinely regarded his works as products of a long scholastic literary tradition. Or was he cynically manipulating well-known and acceptable ideas as a cover for his *realpolitik*, as Machiavelli was later to do in his *Prince* and *Discourses*?[6] It is suggested here that Fortescue had been a prominent public figure for nearly four decades who attracted both friendly comment as well as condemnation but he was never singled out for any notable acts hostile to Christian ethical standards for which his enemies might well have castigated him. Records of his property transactions survive (but not his will) and had

[5] M.S. Kempsall, *The Common Good in Late Medieval Thought* (Oxford: 1999) 25.

[6] N. Machiavelli, *The Prince*, ed. M.L. Kekewich, trans. C.E. Detmold (Ware: 1997) xii–xx.

he chosen to devote more than the modest gifts to good works that are known the fact would have emerged.[7] A legitimate conclusion to draw is that while his writings show him to have been conventionally pious there is nothing to indicate that he was either unusually religious or sufficiently godless to attract comment. This leads to the assumption that he was sincere in the moral justifications which he rather sparingly produced for his advice and that he set them in a conventional format to make his main, secular concerns more acceptable. As Judith Ferster wrote of 'mirrors for princes', the 'tradition was an integral part of political thought, supplying ways of perceiving sociopolitical processes and a repertoire of roles actors could appropriate'.[8]

The evidence of Fortescue's writings and his not excessively generous religious gifts indicate that he met the expectations of the Christian society in which he lived but felt no need to exceed them. On the other hand, his tracts and treatises show him to have been responsive to some of the most innovatory elements in contemporary thinking. These did not derive from learned treatises such as the anonymous mid-fifteenth-century *De Regimine Principum*, which was probably written by a cleric, or George Ashby's poem *The Active Policy of a Prince* (although the latter may well have been known to Fortescue).[9] It was experience from his own public career as a senior lawyer and close observation of the activities of the royal council and parliament that led Fortescue to form his critical attitude towards aspects of royal governance. This linked him to ideas which derived from the public discourse of political songs and poems, parliamentary debates and popular manifestos which were characteristic of the turbulent reign of Richard II and which re-emerged in the decade that led up to Jack Cade's revolt and the parliamentary criticism of Henry VI's advisers that accompanied it. Some of the contents of later articles, such as those issued by the partisans of 'Robin of Redesdale', also found their way into Fortescue's *Articles* and *Governance*.

The fact that Fortescue was one of the royal officials singled out for condemnation by insurgent opinion in 1450 might seem to have distanced him from reformist programmes. Yet the criticisms of the government of Henry VI which were made by the successive parliaments of 1449 and 1451 principally emanated from the order of society

[7] See above, Chapter 2, p. 70, nn. 98, 99.

[8] J. Ferster, *Fictions of Advice: The Literature and Politics of Counsel in Late Medieval England* (Philadelphia: 1996) 176.

[9] See above, Chapter 5, pp. 214–15.

to which he belonged, the gentry.[10] The dangerous combination of the loss of the French territories, the blow this delivered to national pride and the perception that royal counsellors of questionable origin were responsible for these disasters, disposed them to withhold co-operation until the regime undertook some reforms. Two acts of resumption were passed and although their efficacy was limited by the many exemptions to their provisions that were granted, they did restore some semblance of order to royal finances after the collapse of 1450. This was the policy, but without the extensive exemptions which threatened to undermine it, that was recommended by Fortescue in chapter XIV of the *Governance*.

Some of Fortescue's policies for securing a sound financial basis for the royal government may have coincided with similar demands by Cade's rebels, but their main cure for its malaise, the appointment of great lords to be the King's principal councillors, was diametrically opposed to his ideas.[11] In Fortescue's small, professional council the four temporal and four spiritual lords were to be a minority and were chosen by the king for only a year at a time. This was intended to vest real power in the sixteen remaining non-noble councillors, who presumably were permanent, although he did not spell it out. This was certainly implied, 'as whan a counseillour dieth, how a newe counseillour maybe choosen ... mowbe conveyed be leyser'.[12] It was not the absence of great lords and prelates (unreliable powers who would put their own interests before the common good) that Fortescue believed had been wrong with governance in the 1440s and 1450s, but the malign influence of those who did attend, lack of commitment to the royal government and the readiness of councillors of all stations to line their own pockets. His solution was unlikely to fire the popular imagination, but the combination of a few lords who could be summarily removed with a professional corps of councillors entirely dependent on the king was to prove effective as it developed under the Tudors.

One aspect of government which was singled out by the rebels in 1450 for particular condemnation was the operation of the court of King's Bench in Kent. Yet more generally they seemed content to observe the rule of English law, and in this respect both Fortescue and the rebels supported the traditional legal framework:

[10] B.P. Wolffe, 'Acts of Resumption in the Lancastrian Parliaments, 1399–1456', *EHR*, 73 (1958) 583–613.

[11] *Vale's Book*, 204, 206.

[12] *Ibid.*, 246.

> And the peopull so enpeched or endited thoughe it be untrewe may nat be commytted to the lawe for here delyveraunce but holde still in prisoun. the fals progenye and affinite of the duc of Suffolke, the whiche bene openly knowen, and they to be punisshed after the custum and lawe of this lande.[13]

The *De Laudibus* was a prolonged eulogy to the superior merits of the English common law, which promoted through political and regal government contented, robust and obedient subjects, in contrast to French society burdened with a regal regime and its partner, civil law. Despite Shelley Lockwood's claim to the contrary, Fortescue did not recommend reforms to the law in either the *De Laudibus* or the *Governance*, although, whilst Chief Justice, he had been prepared to take practical measures to change or outflank the common law when it was dysfunctional.[14] Cade's rebels were also prepared to accept the status quo, they did not seek to change the law but rather to ensure that it was properly enforced.

Despite the fact that Fortescue was in exile between 1461 and 1471, the growing popular disillusionment with the rule of Edward IV and the literature that it produced seems to be reflected in the *Governance*. This is hardly surprising, since the origin of much of the advice can be traced back to the demands for prudent financial management made by the Commons and the rebels, 1449–51. Some of these in turn were recycled by the Yorkists in their manifestos of 1459–60 just before the regime changed.[15] When Warwick and Clarence commenced their open leadership of popular opposition to the Crown in 1469 they utilised this tradition, which was most notably reconciled with the needs of the new decade in the articles and petition of Robin of Redesdale.[16] After the inevitable call for the punishment of 'sedicious persones', in this case the Woodvilles and other royal favourites such as Humphrey Stafford and William Herbert, it proceeded to demand that the King should take the advice of his lay and spiritual lords to establish, 'sufficiente of lyvelod and possessions by the whiche he and all his heires aftir hym may mayntene and kepe theire moste honourable estate with all other ordynary charges necessarye to be had in this lande'.[17]

[13] *Ibid.*, 'The complaints of the commons of Kent', 204; 'Articles of the Captain of Kent', 206.

[14] See above, Chapter 2, p. 64, n. 74.

[15] *Vale's Book*, 'Articles of the commons of Kent at the coming of the Yorkist lords from Calais, 1460', 210–12.

[16] *Ibid.*, 212–15.

[17] *Ibid.*, 215.

The first of the demands in the Redesdale manifesto was to reappear in articles 1 and 4 in Fortescue's *Articles sent to the earl of Warwick* and in the *Governance*, especially in chapter X. A small, loyal and efficient royal council was to be the means by which fiscal prudence was to be achieved. Tunnage and poundage was mentioned in the manifesto, with the proviso that it should only be used for defending the sea, and chapter VI of the *Governance* defended the necessity of keeping it for the same purpose. Although it had been instituted as a tax for purely maritime expenses in the fourteenth century, it had become part of regular taxation by the 1390s.[18] The rebels of 1469 cited it as just another instance of the extortion of Edward IV's advisers, but Fortescue, ever preoccupied with commercial prosperity, was anxious that it should be used to protect trade.[19] The tax was probably not mentioned in earlier manifestos because, whilst England and France were almost permanently at war with each other, the government had been fully justified in levying it.

In 2011 Guy Lurie suggested another source of ideas in the *Governance*, the acts of resumption passed during the reign of Edward IV.[20] This is surprising as the first two in 1461 and 1463 were principally aimed at Lancastrians and their sympathisers. The third act was passed in 1467, when the King was getting wind of opposition nearer to home, and the last in 1473, when Fortescue had been rehabilitated and sat on the royal council. He approved of the principle of resumption, although the last act might have been passed after he had completed the *Governance*. Another of Lurie's ideas is less convincing, that after his pardon, representing 'a personification of the English system of law, Sir John Fortescue sat from then on by the side of Edward IV'.[21] The scanty records of Fortescue's life after his return to England, apart from his own writings and much supposition, do not indicate that the old statesman enjoyed such an important and prominent position.

The underlying assumption made by the gentry in parliament and by their leaders in both the Lancastrian and early Yorkist periods was that the laws and customs of the realm were sound. It was widely believed that a few decades previously monarchs had ruled wisely, employed suitable advisers, made prudent financial decisions and avoided the excessive taxation of their subjects. All that critics of the government asked was that a return should be made to the good old days. The long

18 Brown, *Governance of Late Medieval England*, 69.

19 *Vale's Book*, 215.

20 G. Lurie, 'Sir John Fortescue's Legal Prestige', *History of Political Thought*, 32 (2011) 293–315.

21 *Ibid.*, 315.

reign of Edward III and the short reign of Henry V were usually cited as examples of good governance. Fortescue in the *Articles sent to Warwick* and the *Governance* was being more innovatory than other critics of the status quo. At the beginning of *Example what good counsel helpeth* he exclaimed, 'O what good welthe and prosperite shulde growe to the reaume of Englande yif suche acounsell be oones perfitely stablisshed and the king guided therby.'[22] Fortescue went on to show how the Romans had prospered under the rule of the Senate, which he equated to the royal council. The same idea was repeated in the *Governance*, chapter XVI, and widened to include the ancient Greeks, although he was vague about how their council functioned. The assumption in both works was that he was not recommending a return to traditional English royal government but a new departure.

The use of classical precedent for the authorisation of Fortescue's plan raises the question about a third possible source of influence on his thinking. Could he, in addition to deriving the form of the *De Laudibus* and *Governance* from the scholastic 'mirrors for princes' and some ideas from contemporary political programmes, also have taken his view of the proper administrative and legal structures of government from Italian humanist writers?

In his study *Humanism in England in the Fifteenth Century*, Roberto Weiss observed, 'Even a conservative like Sir John Fortescue is found quoting Bruni's *Isagogicon* and Poggio's version of Diodorus in his *De Natura Legis Naturae* and *De Laudibus Legum Anglie*.'[23] Fortescue also referred to Poggio's version of Diodorus Siculus in chapter II of the *Governance* without naming the translator. A. B. Ferguson took a broader view than Weiss of Fortescue's relationship with the social and intellectual changes that were taking place in Europe:

> Fortescue's mind laboured in a curiously deceptive light shed on the one hand from the traditions of scholastic thought and on the other from the rapidly maturing realities of Renaissance life. It was a time when, for the best of practical reasons, men of insight were making new approaches to these realities while still working with a theoretical apparatus inherited from an earlier era. To concentrate exclusively on the latter is, therefore, to run the risk of misinterpretation.[24]

[22] *Vale's Book*, 225.

[23] Weiss, *Humanism in England*, 178, n. 2.

[24] A.B. Ferguson, 'Fortescue and the Renaissance: A Study in Transition', *Studies in the Renaissance*, 6 (1959) 175–94.

Ferguson's article gave due weight to the limitations that the scholastic 'theoretical apparatus' set on Fortescue's capacity for innovative thought. Ferguson also believed that he gave little attention to statecraft, a skill which would have aligned him to the Italian and French political thinkers of the late fifteenth and sixteenth centuries. He did, however, recognise that Fortescue's grasp of *realpolitik*, history and the importance of social conditioning anticipated an approach that was to be characteristic of Renaissance theorists.

The references made by Fortescue to works by Poggio Bracciolini and Leonardo Bruni, when noted all, have sometimes been dismissed as superficial window dressing. Chrimes, for example, thought that whilst his citations had literary interest they were in no way fundamental to his doctrines.[25] More recently Wakelin has characterised humanist debate as 'an otiose show of rhetoric or, worse, a screen for flattery or political control'.[26] In a later publication he has observed that humanist influence was, in fact, quite widely disseminated in England from the fifteenth century. It may be found in literature, architecture, tapestries and so on, well beyond the small circle of those who have been defined as classical scholars.[27]

Fortescue used a passage from Leonardo Bruni's *Isagogue* to draw together and thus clinch an important argument in the *De Laudibus* by stating that only the acquisition of virtue could secure true happiness.[28] Flattery seems to have been far from his mind as he doggedly pursued the idea that featured in all three of his major treatises, using the same passage from Poggio/Diodorus to support the superior merits of political and regal government over regimes ruled only regally, a central plank in his argument:

> The king of Scottys regneth upon his people by this lawe that is to wete REGIMINE POLITICE ET REGALI. And as Diodorus seithe in his booke DE PRISTIS [*sic*] HISTORIIS, the reaume of Egipte ys reuled by the same lawe, and therefore the king there of chaungeth nat his laws withoute assente of his peopull. And in like forme as he seithe ys reuled the kyngdome of Saba in felici Arabia, and the lande of Lubye and also the more parte of alle the reaumes of Awfrik, whiche maner of reule and lordship the seide Diodorus in that boke praysithe gretly. For it is not

[25] Chrimes, *De Laudibus*, xc.

[26] Wakelin, *Humanism, Reading and English Literature*, 168.

[27] D. Wakelin, 'England: Humanism Beyond Weiss', *Humanism in Fifteenth Century Europe*, ed. D. Rundle (Oxford: 2012) 265–305.

[28] Chrimes, *De Laudibus*, 11.

> oonly good for the prince that may therby the more surely do justice thanne by his owne arbitermente, but it is also good for his peopull that receyve therby suche justice as they desire hem selfe.[29]

In his use of ancient texts to support his advice Fortescue showed himself to be open to the newest intellectual influences, but he approached them with reservations, a characteristic that was to define French humanist scholars in the following century.[30] While the study of their national history depended on the humanist approach to classical and medieval sources, writers such as Guillaume Budé, François Badouin and François Hotman refused to be bound by the Italian reverence for the works of ancient Rome. Like their government they were concerned to assert Gallican liberties in the face of long-standing claims to hegemony made by the papal curia. A mythical Trojan hero, Francus, was believed to have been the progenitor of the Frankish peoples from whom the French were descended, thus neatly upstaging the later Roman occupation and influence on their culture. The *Digest* of the emperor Justinian was attacked, mainly on the grounds that it had been badly edited by his jurist Tribonian, and the indigenous character of French law was asserted.[31] Etienne Pasquier, a humanist legist, was led in the late sixteenth century, 'to revise the conventional Italianate view of the revival of learning, believing as he did that, in France at least, "good letters" made their appearance in the twelfth century'.[32]

Much of this has a familiar ring. Fortescue, while giving due weight to historical precedent drawn from the Bible, the Fathers of the Church, the scholastics and ancient Rome, had at the same time a robust faith in English traditions and institutions. His polemical tracts and the *De Natura* drew liberally on civil and canon law and on the philosophy of the schools for his purpose of justifying his claim that women could not succeed to kingdoms or pass on the right to do so, but he changed his strategy in the *De Laudibus*. He moved from a tacit acceptance of the civil law that was derived from practice in ancient Rome and instead urged the superior merits of indigenous common law. Fortescue's heavy

[29] *Vale's Book*, *Governance*, 228.

[30] D.R. Kelley, *Foundations of Modern Historical Scholarship: Language, Law and History in the French Renaissance* (New York and London: 1970); *History, Law and the Human Sciences: Medieval and Renaissance Perspectives* (London: 1984); *The Human Measure: Social Thought in the Western Legal Tradition* (Cambridge, MA: 1990).

[31] F. Hotman, *Antitribonianus sive dissertatio de studio legum*, ed. G. Beyer (Lipsiae: 1704).

[32] Kelley, *Foundations*, 299.

reliance on civil and canon law sources in the *De Natura* contrasts with his scanty use of any authorities in the *Governance*.[33] He traced the origins of English political society to the Trojan Brut, avoiding, like the French humanists half a century later, dependence on classical models for his nation's laws and customs.[34]

English jurists since the time of Glanvill and Bracton had been urging the unique character and advantages of their common law, so Fortescue was not making a new claim in his *De Laudibus*. What was a novelty, however, was the direct link he made between the nature of English law and the political institutions it underpinned. He went on to draw unfavourable comparisons with Continental modes of government, especially the French, claiming that the latter led to poverty and tyranny. He praised the English mixed constitution, 'political and regal government', where the royal prerogative was balanced by the prince's willingness to observe the laws and customs of the land, to take good advice from his council and allow parliament to validate new laws. Fortescue's programme of reform in the *Governance* was actually an admission that political and regal governance had not been functioning smoothly in previous decades: his former master Henry VI had lost his throne under that system. So where did that leave his apology for English laws and customs?

Only a few decades after his death the *De Laudibus* was increasingly read and venerated in legal and political circles. England and France were frequently hostile to each other throughout the Tudor period and the book told the English exactly what they wished to hear. In the following century, as has been suggested in the previous chapter, both parliamentarians and royalists could find what they wanted in the book concerning 'political and regal' government. The *Governance* was not published until the early eighteenth century, and it was more than a century later when commentators started to interpret it as a programme for constitutional government and to congratulate themselves that it was English. The political circumstances in which it was produced were not regarded as particularly relevant to its content.

The Introduction suggested that Fortescue's writings on English society, law and government are timely in the early twenty-first century, when a debate is being held about the nature of the national character. Andrea Ruddick wrote persuasively in 2013 about the emergence of a consciousness of English nationality during the 'long' fourteenth

[33] Appendix 4.

[34] Chrimes, *De Laudibus*, 33; *Vale's Book*, 228; T.D. Kendrick, *British Antiquity* (London and New York: 1970) esp. chs 1 and 2.

century, fostered by the early stages of the Hundred Years War, the increasing use of English and the cultural heritage that it produced. Krishnan Kumar, writing ten years earlier, however, would have had none of this, since for him 'Englishness' only briefly emerged in the late nineteenth century and revived when devolution and independence within the British archipelago became live issues.[35] Ruddick's interpretation is underpinned by Mark Ormrod's study of the significance of the 1362 Statute of Pleading, by which English rather than French was to become the compulsory language of oral communication in all royal and seigneural courts. It was

> not solely or even principally about proper access to justice but rather about the reinforcement of a particular sense of political and cultural identity ... [and] may represent a particular desire to demonstrate that the English could at once emulate and distance themselves from the French by using their own vernacular in their own courts.[36]

A child of the late fourteenth and early fifteenth centuries and raised in a community that was deeply involved in the Hundred Years War, Fortescue enthusiastically embraced his country's English laws and customs.

Fortescue was almost certainly the author of the *Commodities of England* and dwelt in that little paper on the distinctive topography and products of the country. He rejoiced in its fertility and prosperity, which underpinned the sterling qualities of its people. Twice in the *Governance* he stressed the special status of the country as an island and the resulting need to be self-sufficient and encourage martial exercises: 'we biene an ielande and as it is saide before, we may not sone have socour of any other reaume, wherefore we shulde biene a praye to alle oure enemyes but yif we [be?] mighty of oure selfe'.[37] Many similar pro-English sentiments from Fortescue's major works have been quoted throughout this study.

Respect for legal and political institutions that ensure peace and security and a desire that every citizen should be treated fairly are often seen as specifically English values. All these are to be found in Fortescue's

[35] Ruddick, *English Identity*; K. Kumar, *The Making of English National Identity* (Cambridge: 2013).

[36] W.M. Ormrod, 'The Use of English: Language, Law and Political Culture in Fourteenth Century England, *Speculum*, 78 (2003) 750–87, 781. See also J.P. Genet, 'Empire and the English Identity: Reflections on the King of England's *Dominium*', *The Plantagenet Empire*, ed. P. Crooks, D. Green and W.M. Ormrod, Harlaxton Medieval Studies 26 (Donington: 2016) 35–48.

[37] *Vale's Book*, 240.

writings, and the influence that he has exercised over lawyers, historians and political thinkers for much of the last 500 years justifies the claim that he defined these aspects of Englishness for following generations and did so in a persuasive and accessible manner. Yet he never mentioned Magna Carta, for many people today the touchstone of English liberties. Taking issue with Andrew Blick in his desire for a written constitution, Linda Colley has recently made the point that, 'in England and Wales a powerful influence has also been exerted by the common law, which is essentially based on a series of precedents and judicial decisions, not on a written code'.[38] Fortescue with his great knowledge of the statutes of the realm and of legal precedent would have had no particular reason to privilege one of the many charters that dealt with the rights and duties of the subject. For him the whole body of the laws and customs underpinned the good governance of England, which, in any case, had been a 'political and regal' realm long before Magna Carta.

This study of Fortescue's career in its political context leads to the conclusion that he recognised the insoluble nature of the problem concerning the implementation of royal authority during the long years of Henry VI's mature reign. During his exile in the 1460s it must have seemed that history was repeating itself under Edward IV, surrounded by the parvenu Woodvilles and other favourites who were condemned by a section of the nobility led by his own brother and the overmighty Warwick. Early in the following decade, when Fortescue again had the opportunity to advise a prince, the wealth and power of the treacherous Clarence and his younger brother, Gloucester, gave cause for alarm. The remedies for such evils offered first to Edward of Lancaster in the *De Laudibus* and the *Advice sent to Warwick* and then to Edward IV in the *Governance* stressed the centrality of Fortescue's own former sources of experience and influence: the gentry's role in the political nation, the law, economic prosperity and the work of professionals within the royal government.

[38] L. Colley, review of A. Blick, *Beyond Magna Carta: A Constitution for the United Kingdom* (London: 2015), *TLS*, 18 September 2015, 4.

APPENDIX I

Of the Title of Edward Earl of March (De Titulo Edwardi Comitis Marchie)

From a unique manuscript formerly Yelverton N 69, now London, BL Additional MS 48063, ff. 4a–11b. The script is in a fine cursive humanist hand probably of the early sixteenth century. There are two watermarks, one almost obscured by the script, the other a large decorated pot and was a kind of mark widely used in Europe in the later middle ages and early modern period but no exact parallel has been identified. At the top of f. 4a in the left-hand margin the devotional initials 'IHS. N.R.I.' occur. A similar inscription is to be found in Oxford, Bodleian Library MS Digby 145, in the copy of the *Governance* made by Sir Adrian Fortescue in 1532. The tract was translated from Latin into English by Bishop William Stubbs and inserted into the edition by Thomas Fortescue, Lord Clermont, *A History of the Fortescue Family in all its Branches*, 2 vols (London: 1869) vol. 1, *Works*, 61*–90*.

Introduction

Whereas, at the instigation of the enemy of the human race, after that in mad rage not a few of the nobles of the realm of England have been extinguished through intestine wars, dissensions and divisions have arisen about the right of the king's majesty to the crown of England, a certain knight of no mean prudence and valour, noble and most experienced in the laws, persevering in his fidelity to the Most Christian King of England, Henry VI, in the manner of one in exile among the Scots, has thought it in the highest degree opportune and necessary that a remedy should be applied to these dissensions.

And whilst by the assistance or advice of his illustrious lords (those especially whom the royal blood so gracefully adorns and ennobles), he dares not discuss the true, just, and undoubted title of the most illustrious and most Christian King Henry aforesaid to the crown of England, or to debate it, or to declare it strongest, or, as he could do, to demonstrate it to be most true and most undoubted, being rightly forbidden to do the same under the heaviest penalty; he thinks nevertheless, that he may assist those who have mistaken and are in error, if he can demonstrate by inevitable reasons that the pretended title of Edward sometime Earl of March is untrue, and that Edward himself is not the lawful king of England, but only a usurper of the royal dignity; and if by his means the faithful possess this book, not so short as useful to the increase, constancy, and defence of their fidelity; if also he removes the stumbling-block of offence out of the way of the simple little ones, by making manifest the truth to those who before were ignorant of the right and truth of the matter; and if, moreover, the assailants of the recognised truth acknowledge that their falsity has been utterly defeated; which indeed they will see more openly and more evidently if they read through that original book, which treats more at large of these matters in the vulgar tongue.

Chapter I. Here follows the descent of the said Edward, by which he pretends a title to the crown of England.

Edward himself was son of Richard, the son of Anne, the daughter of Roger, the son of Philippa the daughter, as is asserted, of Lionel the elder brother of John of Gaunt the father of King Henry IV, from whom came Henry V, from whom came Henry VI; and as the next legitimate heir of Richard II sometime King of England son of Edward first-born son of Edward III King of England and father of the said Lionel and John, he asserts his pretended right to the crown of England.

Chapter II. Objection is raised to this pretended title.

From the allegations of Edward himself these things are clear; our most Christian King Henry VI is the true heir of Edmund son of Henry III on the female side, that is through the lady Blanche wife of John of Gaunt and mother of Henry IV; our said king (not alone but with his lawful son Edward Prince of Wales) descends by the direct line, by the male sex from the said Henry III, through Edward I and Edward II, and Edward III kings of England; he is also the nearest in the line of consanguinity to the said sometime Richard II among all now living, and is nearer to him than this Edward now usurping by two degrees: as is clear upon examination. Seeing, however, that the right which Edward now usurping pretends is derived to him through two women, that is to say Anne and Philippa, it is certain by the law and custom of England, and shall be manifest that women, or their husbands on pretext of title of their wives, or the children of the same, have always been excluded from all right of succeeding to royalty, and are to be for ever whilst the same law and custom continue, duly, justly, and legitimately excluded; and that the nearer male descending by the male line ought on the death of a king to succeed in the right of the kingdom.

Chapter III. This is declared by several examples.

Whereof one from the history of the English, is taken from the things which were done and approved before the Conquest: that is to say in what manner the Holy King Edward the Confessor succeeded his elder brother Edmund Ironside in the kingdom of England, in the life of Saint Margaret who was given to wife to Malcolm King of Scotland; which Margaret was the daughter of the aforesaid King Edmund. And if it had been fair and just that through a woman the right of the crown of England should devolve on her husband or her lawful son, Malcolm King of Scotland, and after him his sons up to this time kings of Scotland, according to their lawful succession through that Margaret daughter of Edward son of the said king Edmund, ought, as true and lawful heirs of England, to have had successively a true title to the crown of England, and to have been invested with the diadem of the kingdom of England, to the exclusion of Saint Edward the younger brother of the said King Edmund; and then it would follow that men ought to say that Saint Edward forced himself into the royal throne, and as an intruder into and usurper of the kingdom reigned unrighteously over the English, and contrary to the rights or custom of England by violence and tyranny through his whole life from the time when he began to reign occupied the right of another person; and what would be still worse, procured, as much as he was able for another, that he after his death should likewise occupy the right of the other; since in his lifetime he effectually willed that William Duke of Normandy should succeed him in the kingdom of England, and ordained to the prejudice, if the said Margaret had been heir, of the lawful heirs descending from the said King Edmund through Margaret wife of Malcolm; but to think this or say it is wicked; wherefore also that is not true from which such conclusions follow.

Chapter IV. A second example from the Acts of the English after the Conquest.

Again, the only child of Henry I, king of England, called Matilda, given to wife first to the Emperor and after his death married to the count of Anjou, bore to the same count a son by name Henry. This Matilda, on the death of her father King Henry, succeeded him peacefully in the duchy of Normandy; yet did not she, as neither did her son Henry succeed to his grandfather Henry I in the kingdom of England immediately, since law and custom withstood, because that to women, their husbands or children on the pretext of the title of the woman, succession to the right of the kingdom and crown is, as is aforesaid, precluded; and she with all diligence and labour went to no small costs in all things in order that the English might receive her son Henry, as being the next of the blood of Henry I, to be king; which thing they would not have him do even by way of election, lest he should have said that he was entitled to the crown of England in the right of a woman; and if they could obtain no heir by the male line they would receive any descendant rather than by the title of a woman, on account of the inconveniences which would follow therefrom; by right of election therefore and not otherwise, by common assent of lords and people, they received as their king Stephen count of Blois, son of the sister of the said Henry I, who reigned eighteen years and more, that is to say, even to the end of his life: which Stephen, however, when his two sons were dead, with the consent of the lords and people called together by him freely in parliament, enact and ordain that after he himself was dead Henry the son of the Empress should succeed him, not by the title of his mother, which was no title at all, but by the election of the barons and people in parliament, to the end that, not by right of succession but by authority of Parliament, he and his sons his successors being males should reign for ever, lest by any means, contrary to the laws and custom of England, they should entitle any one to the right of the crown of England through a woman.

Chapter V. The same is confirmed by the law of England in like case.

Again, by the laws of the kingdom of England, if any possession, portion of land, or tenement be given to any man and the male heirs descending from him; given that he to such demesne is thus given had two sons, whereof the elder had a daughter, and she a son; then when the man was dead to whom such portion of land or tenement was given, as aforesaid, and the first-born son and his daughter were also dead, the son of the woman being alive, the younger son of the man to whom the demesne was so given shall be heir of that demesne, and the males descending from him and not the son of the woman, for as much as the woman can have no right in such inheritance, and according to the laws 'No one can transfer more right to another person than is known to belong to himself.'

Chapter VI. It is confirmed also by the like right in the kingdom of France, and of Spain also, the kings whereof, like the kings of England, were from ancient times anointed.

Again, in the kingdom of France, if any one were entitled to royalty through a woman, the right to the crown of France would have at one time descended to the king of Navarre, and at another time by a like title to the Count of Flanders, and afterwards by like right to the King of England, as clearly appears to anyone who reads the chronicles of France. By this manner of title certain Kings of England have for a long time claimed such a right to the crown of France, even to the times of Henry V, who having found out clearly that no right could have devolved from a woman upon him by the title of the woman, did, in the presence of Charles King of France and the nobles of the kingdom, touching the Holy Gospels, swear that he would by no means, during the life of the aforesaid Charles, cause himself to be called, or proclaim himself King of France, so far as it lay in his power, being content with the name of only Regent of France and heir of the aforesaid Charles to the crown of France; who, having married the daughter of the aforesaid king, was, by authority of the Parliament, made and selected heir of Charles to the crown of France, to succeed him lawfully in the kingdom of France; by virtue of which title, and not by virtue of descent from a woman of the house of France, our most Christian King Henry VI was after the death of his father Henry V, and of the aforesaid Charles, anointed King of France at Paris, and solemnly crowned.

In like manner, also, the Duke of Lancaster and the Duke of York, who married the daughters of Peter sometime King of Spain, would have had a right to the crown of Spain, if through women any right accrued to their husbands or their children to the royalty of that kingdom.

Chapter VII. Inconveniences which would follow on the opposite supposition.

Again, if through a woman any right to the royalty of England should accrue to the husband of the woman or to her children, many inconveniences would follow which are recited in the original, of which a few are inserted here: because, given that failing a son to the King of England, he had several daughters, through them or their children or husbands there would be made a division of the monarchy into several kingdoms. Again, if an emperor or a king had at the time of his death an only child, a female of the age of three days, so great a kingdom would thus be destitute of king or emperor, at least until the female child were seven years old; since a woman cannot be a king, nor can the supreme government in temporals over the man devolve upon her by any means, seeing that the Lord said to her, 'Thou shalt be under the power of the man and he shall rule over thee'. After the said age of seven years, indeed, it is lawful for such woman to contract marriage; which being contracted and solemnly published in the face of the church as the laws will in like cases, still such husband will from such solemn contract be able to be called truly neither king or not-king, until such woman have come to full age; and so all the meantime the kingdom would stand in suspense without a supreme governor, and the commonwealth would be endangered; besides many other inconveniences which may follow. Or if, through such marriage, such husband should in such kingdom be entitled and should be truly king through such woman, then when the woman should have come to full age, and should be unwilling to abide by her former contract, but should have contracted with another and have been carnally known by him, by the mere such caprice of a woman is lost to the first espoused the right to the royalty; and so he who was before not-king becomes king, and he who was before king becomes without his own fault not-king; which things seem absurd, most especially if we speak of anointed kings, such as are the kings of England, France, and Spain, which three only, as is aforesaid, were anciently anointed. Supposing that such a woman should be unwilling to be married up to the thirtieth or fortieth year of her age, during all that time the kingdom would be destitute of a king; but if the inhabitants of the kingdom should in the meantime have taken another person for their king, she afterwards having married and having a son, the first elected by the people will have to give way to the person espoused of the woman, or to his son, which is ridiculous. Again supposing the king the husband of such woman to die, the kingdom would in the meanwhile wait without a supreme governor through the time of her widowhood, perhaps for the space of ten or twenty years or more at the will of the woman. Again, if the woman should live in chastity, the kingdom would be without a king all her lifetime, and from this the commonweal of the kingdom would be imperilled. Again, since compulsion is contrary to the nature of a contract by divine law as well as human, the woman may freely take to herself any husband out of a choice; who by knowing her will render such matrimony consummate and indissoluble, and so such woman might take to herself as a husband some man vile in race and of the lowest degree in virtue, a slave or serf of any inhabitant of the kingdom, making a slave lord supreme of the kingdom: or she might be espoused to some one who was always at enmity with the inhabitants of such kingdom, to its perpetual overthrow: or to some duke, or count, or king of another kingdom, who would carry off the all revenues of such kingdom to himself, and there spend them to the impoverishment and loss and intolerable damage of such kingdom.

Chapter VIII. Showing Argument against the aforesaid pretended title, that Philippa was not the daughter of Lionel.

Again, in the chronicles and histories of England is made express, plain, and special mention of all the children of all the sons of Edward III, sometime King of England, father of the said Lionel, that is to say, who, how many, and of what sex they were: but of the issue of Lionel himself, who was Duke of Clarence, that is, of this Philippa, no mention is made: nay, they are silent even about the succession of Lionel, as if he had died without issue or children; which they would not have been if he had regarded Philippa as his lawful daughter and heir. Whereof it may be regarded as a confirmation that neither Edward now usurping, nor any progenitor of his, descending as they say from the aforesaid Philippa, has had the name of the said duke, or has succeeded in the duchy of Clarence, or bears or bear the royal arms (of Anne) with a difference added as that Duke of Clarence did, but only the arms (of Anne) of March and Ulster; none of which, however, they would have omitted, since, in consideration of the splendour of their origin and honour of nobility, they would have set no slight value on such and so great bearings; as the rest of the lords who descended through women from the said King Edward III have none of them omitted such bearings; if this Edward now usurping, and his forefathers had been lawful successors of so great a duke in his right through a woman heiress of Lionel. Also, if this Philippa had been the daughter and sole issue of so great a duke so near to the royal stock, it is probable that she would not have been given in marriage to so mean a person, especially descending from marked and corrupted blood, that is, from Roger Mortimer, who for the crime of high treason committed against King Edward the father of the said Lionel, was openly and judicially convicted.

Chapter IX. Argument proving that lapse of such right, if he could have had any, had been made by legitimate prescription.

Again, taking to be true what is not true – namely, that Edward now claiming the kingdom could have had in right of women any title to the crown of England, so that there had been no custom or law excluding women from such title, which, however, is not admitted, Edward Earl of March nevertheless can now have no right from such descent. For if he could have had any from his parents descending from Philippa, through whom he challenges such right in the kingdom, abandonment of such right has occurred in several ways. First, by lawful prescription: for Henry VI our most Christian King, his father Henry V, and his grandfather Henry IV, have been continuously for sixty years, more or less, in peaceable possession of the kingdom and crown of England, and have reigned as kings of England in their times peaceably and quietly, and have borne the sceptre, and received unction and the insignia of royalty, and each in his time has reigned so in quiet and borne the sceptre, and received the unction and the insignia of royalty, and has used the same, the successive progenitors of Edward now usurping being present, not contradicting, but silently and expressly consenting, and in nothing reclaiming; although some of the progenitors of this Edward have conspired sometimes secretly against their kings, and attempted to make treasons contrary to their fealty, incurring the charge of high treason. Since then lawful prescription is a title sufficient to extinguish a right before acquired, if Edward could have had any title from the said Philippa, which he never had, he would be by lawful prescription sufficiently excluded from such right.

Chapter X. Confirmation taken from Augustine 'de Civitate Dei', as it is quoted in the book which is called 'Compendium Morale'.

With this Augustine well agrees, saying that there are four things which approve the title of any king, and confirm and establish him in any kingdom; which are Divine permission, Ecclesiastical approbation, Consent of the people, and Possession for a long time continued, and of these four none is lacking in our most Christian King Henry. For by the entire consent of the all nobles and commons of the kingdom, Henry the present king, and Henry V his father, and Henry IV his grandfather have been for so long time in peaceable possession of the kingdom and crown of England as suffices to the lawful prescription of the kingdom, and is such a length of time as is required according to the dictum of Augustine, and suffices.

So far as regards ecclesiastical approbation it is clear; for without any interruption or contradiction the ambassadors of the said kings of England and their lawful proctors have been admitted and approved in the council of Constance and of Basle, and in the court of Rome generally. All the popes also for sixty years more or less have transmitted to those three in succession, and to each of them as true and lawful kings of England apostolic letters, and bulls as well of grace as of common justice; have confirmed archbishops and bishops of England at the petitions and desires of those kings, and of each of them, and ordered them to be consecrated. In all which bulls or briefs apostolic they have called them kings, and each of them king of England, and have confirmed it by their writing; and now lately, since the recognition by the present Pope Pius of the usurpation of the said Edward, in a certain bull of his transmitted by the most holy Pope to our most Christian King Henry, that is to say , at the end of November A.D. 1461, owing to the possession and right of his father and grandfather, that is to say, Henry V and Henry IV, the Pope approves the title of the most Christian King Henry VI, calling him his dearest son the king of England, and those who rose up against him his enemies, and those who died in his cause at Northampton faithful; he disproves also the temerity of that most atrocious legate, as well for the assistance and counsel which he furnished to the king's enemies as for raising the standard of the church against him and the army of his faithful, and contrary to the will of the same most holy Pope, as he himself writes to the king's highness, abusing the power committed to him by unjustly promulgating sentence of excommunication against those who were faithful to the same king's highness, and forbidding due burial to the king's faithful fighting in just cause, and while so fighting dying valiantly. Moreover, the Pope promises in the same letter to the king, as soon as it shall happen that that most wicked legate shall be recalled, so to correct and punish him according to his demerits, and according to the demands of his offences, that he shall be an example for the future to others, lest so hereafter against the rights and the will of the supreme Pontiff, whether his own or of his successor in the same apostolic see, any in like manner abuse the power of Peter. Also the most holy Pope counsels, and under apostolic benediction enjoins on the same our most Christian King Henry to contend manfully for his right, not secluding from him the benefit of his right, that is to say, that all Englishmen and others lawfully subject to his rule bearing arms against him, rising up against him, and rebelling, should be, until they have returned to their true obedience, held as excommunicated. Also, that the most Christian and most pious soldier of Christ our King Henry has reigned by one God from whom is all power in heaven and in earth both accepting and approving his reigning appears from these things which follow:– First, that when there was lacking to him all pleasure of ruling, all desire of reigning, and all power of desiring the same, in the first year of his age, God had set him most graciously on the throne of his father and grandfather; whom after the seventh year of his age, with the consent of all the people, He ordained to be solemnly crowned and anointed, not with common holy oil, but with oil fore-ordained by the

Lord to anoint him therewith, which his kind patroness the most blessed Virgin Mary delivered to Saint Thomas Archbishop of Canterbury in the phial, which even until now is most carefully preserved in the keeping of the same most Christian King Henry, saying to him: 'The Kings of England who shall be anointed with this oil shall be gentle and shall be champions of the church'; by virtue of which unction due to him through the touch of his most pure hands uncontaminated by any stain, such as the blood of homicide or the hunger of luxury, those sick of the king's evil of whom physicians have despaired do even to this day receive by the gift of the Lord the desired health, to the praise of Almighty God, of whose grace comes the grace of healings, to the strengthening in fidelity to the king of all who behold and assist, and to the confirmation by the Lord's approval of his most undoubted title. But if it be objected that such virtue in the healing of those sick of the said disease, since it follows the royal anointing of the hands, accompanied as regularly the touch of the hands of Edward as that of our most Christian King Henry; whence, because such curing of the sick with consecrated oil regularly works such works of healing, it will approve the title of either, or of none of them: in answer to this it is said, that our one God works not such works of healing regularly by any mortal man who is anointed with such consecrated oil, as being by such holy unction ordained to be the Lord's Christ or the Lord's anointed, which none is except he who is duly, regularly, and lawfully anointed. That this may be clearly understood, it must be remarked that, as in the sacramental anointing of any one in his ordination to be a priest anointed of the Lord, among other things three are required of necessity, that is to say, a due minister, that is, the bishop with intention; a due form of ordination and unction; and due matter, that is, a person fit to receive such order and unction; (on account of the lack of the third of which, a woman is neither made, by one believing her to be a man, a priest by reason of the anointing which she has received from the bishop, nor confirmed as a Christ of the Lord or the Lord's anointed); so in the royal unction is required of necessity, among other things, a person due and fit of right to receive duly such benediction and unction; that is to say, such a man as has among other things a just title to the crown which he receives or to the kingdom over which he is anointed, that is, a liege people duly, lawfully, and of right subjected to him; which Edward has not in the kingdom of England, since he himself and all the inhabitants of the kingdom of England have been and are still subject to our most Christian King Henry; from which subjection or due service they cannot revolt or be absolved on their own authority or on that of all those together who are so subjected to him by any means. For if such unction and coronation by the Bishop of Canterbury sufficed to ordain any one to be a king anointed of the Lord, or the Lord's Christ, then he, at the clamour of insurgents in Kent, might at will ordain one other of them as king, even ordain at their pleasure as many and as great anointeds of the Lord, or Christs of the Lord; which is ridiculous. It remains therefore that, for the lack of a due title to the crown of England, Edward now usurping will be in no wise by that unction and coronation ordained to be anointed of the Lord or a Christ of the Lord.

Chapter XI. Argument showing that it cannot be truly said that Edward is chosen by the Lord to be King of England by a private and secret disposition of the Lord.

Besides by no one is it doubted that such a king reigns duly by God, who according to the law or laudable custom of his kingdom, the law of God or of the church not opposing, is duly anointed, crowned, and holds the sceptre of such kingdom. This is manifest; for, in the law of Christ the Lord is not wont to assign any one's kingdom regularly in any other way: and therefore as after the Lord in the Old Testament by a law published immediately by himself formed the kingdom of Judah in the hand of David, entitling the kingdom to him and his lawful sons, saying, 'Of the fruit of thy body will I set upon thy seat', it was not allowed to the people of Judah, on account of any fault of the sons of David, to transfer the kingdom of Judah from his seed to strange blood; so neither is it allowed to the inhabitants of England or of any other kingdom to transfer the kingdom thereof from the incumbent for the time reigning according to the law, or laudable custom of such kingdom, to another person, and chiefly on pretext of a private disposition or election by God of another person, provided such election or disposition by God does not make itself known openly by manifest, certain, and authentic revelation. The force of this reason lies in this, that the law or laudable custom of any kingdom not contravening the law of God or the Church, is a law published mediately by the Lord and approved, which, by those who have from Him power to make law, is made and approved. It is clear by both arguments that there is no parallel between our most Christian King Henry and the usurper Edward on the one side, and the holy man David and Saul on the other: first because the kingdom of Judah was never confirmed by any law to Saul and his lawful sons, nor did he obtain the kingdom of Judah by hereditary right as our most Christian King Henry obtained the kingdom of England by hereditary title: secondly, because when Saul for his sins was rejected the virtuous David was promoted to the kingdom of the Jews; whereas such comparison would be transverse between the most Christian King Henry, pious, continent, and honestly living, and Edward the usurper of the kingdom of England.

Chapter XII. Incidental argument showing the enormous offence of the inhabitants of England who assisted the usurper Edward.

Moreover, even if this Edward had wished to rise up on his just title, as he says, against his king that he might cast him down and turn him out of his kingdom; – then all the liege men subject of right to King Henry rising up with Edward contrary to their fealty to the king had offended inexcusably against the Lord, and their king himself. For in the case that our most Christian King Henry had held the sceptre of the kingdom unrighteously, as he has held it most righteously, he alone would have sinned in this, and all his liege men fighting for him according to the fealty by which they were bound to him, that they should defend their lord against his enemies, would have fought virtuously and laudably, and would have contended meritoriously, as it is taken by Augustine against the Manichees, and inserted in the Canon XXIII; Question I. '*Quid culpatur in bello*'.

Chapter XIII. Argument founded upon that principle of law that by renunciation and contrary act lapse of right is made.

Moreover after the death of Roger Earl of March, from whom the aforesaid intruding Edward pretends his title, Edmund his son who succeeded him in the earldom of March, in the chancery of King Henry V, as the custom is of heirs after the death of their predecessors, sued out and prayed livery and possession of the earldom of March, and so received his lands from the hands of the king as from his true natural king and chief lord; – and for them as son and heir of the said Earl Roger did liege homage and fealty to Henry V, and by word and deed confessed, recognised, and approved the said Henry for his true, righteous and natural lord. And afterwards in certain indentures consigned as well with the seal of arms as with the sign manual of the said Edmund, by which he was retained as a paid soldier with the aforesaid King Henry V in his war in his Duchy of Normandy, he named, affirmed, and recognised him to be King of England, and his supreme and liege lord, and remained during his life his liege and faithful subject. And the same Edmund Earl of March after the death of Henry V did like liege homage and fealty to Henry VI in his most tender age, as to his king and the true heir of

Henry V. Which Edmund also dying without children, the earldom of March came down by hereditary right to Richard father of the intruder Edward, who in all respects did, for the same possession and delivery of the same earldom, fulfil, as Edmund had before done, what was of right by custom of the Court of Chancery. Which Richard also having been made lieutenant of Henry VI first in France and afterwards in Ireland, did, by his writs indented and sealed with his seal of arms and subscribed by his own hand, promise to the same king faithfully, according to the form and effect of the agreement, to serve him as his subject and true liegeman; and in both writings named him, by word and deed recognised and approved him as his supreme and chief lord and King of England.

Moreover, the same Richard in the time of a certain sickness of Henry VI, himself being ordained by the authority of Parliament Protector of England during the king's sickness, did, by his writings in that very parliament and after it, frequently recognise, confess, and as well in writing as by word and deed approve him for his true chief and supreme lord and his king.

Chapter XIV. Argument proving that by abjuration he was excluded from his right, if he could have had any.

Also, Richard, father of Edward the usurper, oftentimes swore on the holy Gospels of God and upon the Lord's Body seen and taken, that he would always be a faithful liegeman of Henry VI, King of England, and that always to the best of his ability he would aid him in all things which pertain to the honour and glory of the dignity and right and name royal; in which oath is contained an express abjuration of the contrary, and an exclusion of the pretended right to the crown. A like oath the intruder Edward took in the presence of the Archbishop of Canterbury, and of the clergy then convoked to the church of S. Paul London. For he took a corporal oath, touching the cross of Canterbury, that he would honour our most Christian King Henry as his king, and would obey him as his true chief, liege, and supreme lord during the life of the aforesaid King Henry and his own, and would defend him as his true king against all men living: and in the parliament held at Westminster he promised to observe the same, and bound himself of his own accord, besides oaths at several times taken on the occasions of his creation as knight and afterwards as Earl of March, on which occasions, as is the custom, he swore concerning the keeping of fealty to our king Henry, and defending him against all opposed to him.

By these arguments and reasons insoluble as the earth, militating chiefly against the pretension of the usurper Edward, as well by the removal of objections, it is inferred that our most dread King Henry VI by a just, clear and undoubted title, is the true and right King of England, and ought to reign over the English by every right natural, divine, and human; and that to the said usurper Edward or his progenitors no right to the crown of England has belonged or ought to belong; to the wider declaring whereof, and chiefly to the most especial declaring of the undoubted title of our King Henry to the crown of England, there are not wanting reasons most strongly grounded upon right divine and human, which, the Lord willing, at the best hour in which all the adversaries of our king will not be able to resist him will become clearly known; with the true letter apostolic speaking more fully of the aforesaid sent by the present Pope Pius into Scotland to our most Christian King Henry; and with a true copy or transcript of the bulls sent to Lewis the king's cousin in France lately anointed [18 August 1461], in which he exhorts him, under the blessing of Almighty God, by papal authority to the help of the most Christian King Henry, to the overthrow and final confusion of his enemies, and to the lasting continuance of himself on the throne of his father, to the honour of our Lord Jesus Christ, to whom be honour and glory for ever and ever. Amen.

It is to be remembered that Henry IV was the nearest male heir on his father's side to Henry III sometime King of England; that is to say, he was the son of John, son of King Edward, son of Edward, son of Edward son of the aforesaid King Henry. And the same Henry IV was, on his mother's side, nearest of blood to the same Henry III, that is to say, he was son of Blanche, daughter of Henry, son of Edmund vulgarly called Edmund Crookback, son of the afore-named Henry III; so by that line the aforesaid Henry IV could by no means have been King of England, because that kingdom is heritable by male heirs, descending through males, as is above noted , and was inherited by such heirs from all time, and not by others: and, moreover, the same Henry IV sometime King of England was nearest male heir to Richard II sometime King of England, and the nearest to him in line of consanguinity among all men then living: for he was the son of the uncle of King Richard, that is, son of John brother of Edward father of the aforesaid King Richard. For although it so be, that before these times there were taken for kings of Scotland certain of the royal stock of Scotland, descending therefrom through a woman or through women; for example, when the line of the males descending lineally from Malcolm was determined, Balliol, who descended from the elder daughter of David son of Henry son of David Canmor once King of Scotland, was taken and crowned King of

Scotland; and in like manner after him another, namely, Stewart, who descended from the aforesaid Bruce by a woman daughter of the said Bruce, when to him in like manner failed heir descending lineally from him, obtained the supreme kingdom of the Scots; yet never, whilst any male whatsoever was alive descending lineally from the stock of the king by the male sex, has anyone descending by a woman been taken for king, reigning peaceably; nor would it have been fitting to be so; for if it were so, any person, vile by race, and of the lowest degree in virtue, ignoble on the father's side might be [raised] to be king whilst there was living a male heir descending from that noble royal origin who had preserved in himself the noble precedence of kings, their blood and name together, which would appear absurd and far alien from right reason. In chronicles therefore it is very seldom found that the noble succession of male heirs lineally descending through the male sex being contemned, a succession of women has reigned. Moreover, although it be so according to the civil laws which hold that the inheritance of a dead father should be divided among his sons according to equal portions; nevertheless, according to the same laws, the right of the kingdom [or] its royalties belong to the elder son; whence it appears that the rights are not similar in the case of the royalty and private possession.

THE END

APPENDIX 2

The Declaration upon certain writings late sent out of Scotland

London, BL MS Royal 17 D xv, ff. 311b–326b

This copy from the shop of the stationer John Multon dates from the early 1470s and is thus chronologically close to the original, which must have been composed between Fortescue's pardon in October 1471 and the reversal of his attainder in October 1473. Professionally written, with calligraphic flourishes, sometimes containing caricature heads in the capital letters which adorn opening sentences of each section, it was, however, carelessly copied and there are a number of corrections, mistakes and omissions. It also contains Geoffrey Chaucer's *Canterbury Tales*, ff. 1a–302a; the *Somnium Vigilantis*, ff. 302a–310b; the *Balet of the Kyng*, ff. 327a–332b and the *Book of Nurture*, ff. 333a–348b. Mistakes in the *Declaration* have been made good in square brackets from BL MS Harley 1757, which was probably written by Robert Glover, Somerset Herald, 1570–88, during the reign of Elizabeth I, ff. 188a–195b; it also contains a fragment of the same work, ff. 204a–207b. Other copies consulted are: BL MS Harley 537, ff. 1a–8b, late sixteenth century, incomplete; two other copies in the BL are MSS Additional 48020, ff. 1a–18b, late sixteenth century (formerly MS Yelverton 21) and 48079, ff. 11a–29b, early seventeenth century (formerly MS Yelverton 86). It is possible that these four manuscripts were copied from a different version from that one used by the Multon shop. They all omit the heading, 'How Edmond Irensyde gave this lond to the danes'. None of them contain the error made in the Multon version on f. 312b, in which Blanche of Lancaster is described as the daughter of 'king' rather than 'duke' Henry. Their original could have been Cotton MS Otho B i, since Harley 1757, probably the earliest in this sequence, also contains a complete *Governance*, ff. 196a–203b, and a complete *De Laudibus*, ff. 208a–226a. Other copies of the *Declaration* are London, MS Lambeth 262, ff. 129b–140b; Norfolk, Holkham MS the earl of Leicester; Oxford, Bodleian MS Digby 198, ff. 76a–90a; San Marino, CA, Huntingdon Library MS Ellesmere 1131, ff. 31b–40a; Keswick Hall, near Norwich, John Henry Gurney Esq. no. xxii, ff. 37–9.

The original spelling has been largely retained, apart from thorns, 'y's which are read as 'g's, the removal of double 'f's and some minimal modern punctuation. The use of capital letters has been adopted. The Latin translation by Mary Ruskin is put between square brackets.

The declaracion made by John Fortescu, knight, upon certayn wrytinges sent oute of Scotteland agenst the kinges title of the Roialme of Englond

[red in margin] The introduccion of the matier

A lernid man in the lawe of this lande come late to ['s' deleted] the same sir John Fortescu sayinge iin this wise. Sir, while ye were in Scotelande with Henry somtyme ['king' inserted] of this lande, in dede though he were not so in right, there ware made there [first 'e' inserted] many wrytinges and sent hedyr by which was sawen amonges the peple matier of grete noyse and infamye to ye tytle whiche the kynge oure soveraigne lorde, Edward the iiii^{te}, hath and thoo hadde to reigne upon us. And truly Syr, the conceyvinge and endytynge of thoo wrytinges have be ascribed to you in the opynion of the people, considerynge that ye were the chief councellor to ye said late kyng. For whiche cause hit is thought to many right wyse men and also to me and other of your frendis that it is nowe your dutee and also ye beth bounde in conscience to declare your selfe herein. And also the qualites and effectes of all such wrytinges was ye were thoo pryve unto ['in' inserted] such wyse as thay turne not hereafter to ye kinges harme, and that ye doo this by wryting such as may come to the knowlache of the people also clerely as dyde the sayd wrytinges sent oute of Scoteland. Of whiche many yete remaynen in the handes of full evyll dysposed people that pryvely rowne and reden thaym to the kynges dyshonour and disclaundre of his said title. Wher unto Fortescu sayd in ye forme that foloith.

[red in margin] Fortescu agreith him to make such declaracion as is desyred

My verray good and tru frende, I thanke you hertely of yor sadde and faithfull councell, which I shall folow also ferre as shalbe possyble to me, for I know undoubtedly that it reason I do as ye move me. But yit is so that ther were many such wrytinges made in Scotelande of which sum were made by other men than by me wherunto I was never pryve. But yet the bryngers of thame unto this lande said they were of my makyng hopynge tharby that thay shulde been the more favoured. There were also other wrytinges made therby ye said late kynges councell and sent hedyr to whiche I was not well willynge but [f. 312a] yet thay passed by the more partie of that counceill. And over this there were made wrytinges there some by myne assente and some by my selfe. In all such wrytinges it shall nede that my declaracions were dyvers according ['to my' omitted] mertes in makinge of them. Neverthelesse I wollde fayne in all thoo wrytinges declare the effectes of thayme after my reason and lernynge yf I myght have the copyes and doubles of thayme ['which I have not, nor have seen any minute of them' omitted] sythen I come into Englande. And therfor I pray you hertely to gete me some of the sayd wrytinges or copies of theym yf ye can do so. And els that ye woll declare to me suche of the matiers as ye can now remembre. Wherunto the said lernyd man tho said in this wyse.

The lerned man

[red in margin] This article concernyth Edmond Crochebake

Syr, I have none of the said wrytinges nor yet any sayd copy of theym, but yit I remembre me well of dyvers maters wryten in some of thayme of whiche oone mater is this: kynge Henry the thirde hadd two sonnes of which the elder, as the wryting saith, was called Edmunde, and ye yonger Edwarde. And because that Edmunde hadde a grete difformyte in his bak, he was called Edmunde Crochebak. And by that cause the kynge wold not that he shulde be kynge of Englande after hym, but wolde tharfore that his yonger sonne shulde succede him in his realme. And by that cause made the said Edmunde erle of Lancastre, Leycestre and Derby, and caused his sonne called Thomas of Lancastre to be erle of Lyncoln by maryage and gaffe to him ye erledome of Hountyngdon and many other gret lordshippes, and made the countee of Lancastre to be a countee [f. 312b] palatyn to thentent that his said older sonne shulde be the lesse in the daunger of his yonger broder when he were kynge. Of which Edmunde was afterwarde descended Blaunche, doughter to kynge ['to kynge' repeated, this is incorrect; the text should read 'doughter to Henry the fyrste duk, etc.'] Henry the fyrste duk of Lancastre, sonne to Henry, seconde sonne to ye said Edmunde. For the forsaid Thomas dyed with oute issue, which Blaunche was afterwarde wedded to John the thirde sonne to kynge Edwarde the thirde. Which John and Blaunche hadde issue Henry afterwarde kynge of England, called kynge Henry the fourth. Which hadde issue kyng Henry the fyfte and he had issue kynge Henry the vi[th], which by this meane was nexte heire to kynge Henry the thyrde. Syr, was this your wrytinge?

Fortescu

[red in margin] The answer to the forsayd article

For sothe Syr, nay nor I was never ascentynge to the wrytyng therof and yit I was gretely desired by my felowys in Scotelande to have made this wrytinge or other lyke therto. But I wolde not do it be cause I knew veryly that it was untrue, as it apperith undoutedly by a cronycle called the Cronicle of Saynt Albanes, in the whiche the wryter as me thought kept an ordre and a rule infallible, for he wrote every moneth and what the kinge didd in every grete mater in that moneth, and what ambassatours or other new thinges come unto hym; so as by lyklinesse he might not erre in his cronicling. By whiche cronicle hit apperith in what day and monith Edwarde sonne to kynge Henry the thyrde was borne, and howe in the next yere after that at a day and place specyfied in the same cronicle, the quene was delyvered of a doughter, and in an other yere after that, of an other doughter, and tellith there names and how after the byrth of tho twoo [f. 313a] doughters she was delyvered of the said Edmunde. By which cronicle hit is clerly shewyd that the said Edwarde was iiii or v yere elder than his forsayd broder Edmunde. And in the cronicle called Flores Cronicarum, whiche is holde of grete auctorite than eny other cronicle wryten in this lande, the same Edwarde is ofte tymes callyd *Edwarde Primogenitus Regis Anglie.* Wherthorought and by many reasons whiche I now leve for schortenesse I was indubitably lerned that the said Edwarde was the elder brother. Wherfor I wolde not assent to that wrytinge made in Scotelande nor se hit, but I said to thaym that moved it that it was untrue.

The lerned man

[red in margin] The lerned man agreeith him welle to the said declaracion

Truly Syr, than said this lerned man, I am right glade that I have harde you say thus, for by this declaracion the kinges title shalbe more clere in the oppynion of knowledge of the people in that matier than it shulde have bene yf the said untrue wrytinges hadd never be made. And therfor I now desyre to have communycacion with you upon such other maters as I remembre were also wryten oute of Scotlande. Trustynge that after your declaracion made in ['tyme' erased] theym, thay shalle also turne unto the kinges good, how be it thay were not made to that entent.

Item the lerned man

[red in margin] This article concernith Edmonde Irensyde

Syr, ye wrote in Scoteland that the kynge our soverayne [f. 313b] lord claymeth this reialme by discent from ii women, which reialme is not inherytable by any woman, as ye said. And in proffe of your entent ye wrote howe Edmunde Irensyde, elder brother to saynt Edwarde the Confessour hadd issue a sonne, which hadd issue a doughtere, weddyde to Malcolyne, kynge of Scotthies, now canonized and called saynt Margarete, of which kynge and margarete have been sithen dyscendide all the kynges of Scoottes. Whiche not withstondynge after the dethe of the said Edmunde, saynte Edwarde reyned in this londe peseably all the lyffe of the said saint Margarete, with oute eny clayme made uppon him by hyr or by her husbande, and with outen that eny of ther heires have claymed this londe at any tyme sithen. Whiche clayme thay wold have yf it hade bene inheritable by eny woman or by the issue of a woman. And also saint Edwarde that was so rightwos and tharfor is now a saynt canonized, wolde not have kepe this londe from the doughter of the sonne of his elder brother yf she ought to have hadde it by inherytaunce. Syr this wrytynge importith two thinges: oone is evidence that the corone of this londe is not inheritable by a woman; the secunde is that if it be inheritable by awoman than ye kynge of Scottes oughte to have it. How sore thes ii maters bene a gene the kynge and his title your reason felith well y nough, and therfor thay nedyne right playne and open declaracion where in I wold fayne here you.

Fortescu

[red in margin] Here is dispro['ved' omitted] the fyrst poynt that the forsayd article importhe

My frend the fyrste poynt whiche ye saye that the ['kinge' deleted] forsayd wrytinges importith and shulde be evidence that the corone of this londe is not inheritable by a woman, may not make eny suche evidence. For hit apperith in the cronicules of this londe [f. 314a] and specially in Poliocoronicon the vi[te] boke in the xxviii[ti] chaptre that Edgare Adelynge, brother to saint Margarite, was one lyve and in Englonde at the tyme of the dethe of saynt Edwarde and longe after, wherfor saint

Margarete in the lyfe of the said sainte Edwarde might have hadd no title to the corone though it had been discendable to heires females. Wherfor here noun clayme or the possession of saint Edwarde proven noo thing or makine eny ['thinge' erased] evidence for the right of succession yf women in this roialme or in any other.

Fortescu

[red in margin] And here is disproved the secund poynt of the same article

And as to the secunde poynte whiche ye saye that the forsaid wryting importeth, that is to say, if this londe be inherytable be woman, than the kinge of Scottes shuld have right therto. That mater may be clerely dysprovede be many reasons of which oone is this: the sayd Edmunde Irenesyde was a basterd, goten by kynge Ethelrede, otherwyse called Adelrede, uppon his concupyne called Algeva, doughter to oone Egelrede, longe tyme be fore that the said Ethelrede was wedded to Emme, doughter of Richard duke of Normandy, by whom he hadd issue saynte Edwarde the Confessour, as it clerely apperith, also well by the cronicles wryten by Petrus Pictavencis and by frere Nycholl Tryvet, whiche I have seen and radd sythen I come into this londe as by other cronicles of which I am late enformed and hope to se thayme a gene within a fewe days. Wherfore the children discendid of ye sayd Edmunde Irensyde may not by any lawe inherete the roialme of Englond or eny other lande as herres to the said Ethelrede or to any of his auncestries. And thought he hadd bene mulier [legitimate] as he was not, yet the kynge of Scottes may not clayme this roialme by reason [f. 314b] of him, as it shalle clerely appere by the reasons that foloyne.

Fortescu

[red in margin] How Edmond Irensyde gave this lond to the danes

Fyrste it was so that after many batels hadde be twene kinge Knoght and Edmunde Irensyde, thay accorded to determe ther werre by a singuler baytale called duellum of thaym selfe. In which batelle when thay wer booth werry, accorde toke be twene tham, that this lond shuld be departed be twene them bothe for terme of thayre lyves, and he that outlyved shulde than have the hole to him and to his heires for evermore. By force of whiche accorde thay bothe kepte and occupied this londe in coomon alle the lyfe of the sayd Edmunde Irenside. After whoos dethe kynge Knoght kepte and occupied the same lande sole as kinge tharof by force of the sayd accorde. And hadd issue Harolde Harefote and Harolde Hardknoght, and died peasibly seased tharof, aftere whos dethe, his said ii sonnes hadd and enjoyued this lande peasabely oone after that other alle the days of thaire lyves, and died with oute issue. Wherfor this lande was than with outen eny kynge, by which occasion thay drove hens alle ye danes and chose saint Edwarde, tho beynge in Normandy with his moders kynne, to be thaire kynge. And than sent for him and made him kynge of Englande, which astate he contynued peasably all the deys of his lyfe. What ryght than might have remayned in thissue of Edmonde Irensyde, though he had been mulier, sethen he hadde graunted his roialme to the daynes in fee for evermore, be force wherof thay kepte and enjoyued peasibely iii generacions, and than loste it for defaute of heires? How than might eny of thissue of Edmunde Irensyde, m̃ales or females, clayme this londe, whiche the same Edmunde had goven [f. 315a] to the daynes, which by force tharofe and also by conquest kepte peasably into thare fourthe generacione? Suffysith not than this mater to exclude and barre the Scottes yf thay wold clayme this londe by the heires of Edmonde Irenside, by whom daynes have grete colour to clayme it than they? And yet they have no maner of ryght tharto as it shalle well appere by a matier that hereafter shall folow. Butt yet I shall shew fyrste a nother mater by which ye heires of the said Edmond beth excludid and barrable to clayme this lond as cousins to saint Edwarde, though he hadd be mulier, which is this.

Fortescu

[red in margin] The seconde argument made agenst the heires of Edmonde Irensyde

The lawe of Englond is such that if a man havinge a brother of halfe blode be seased of any londe in fee simple, and dye with out issue, that lond shall never discende to his said brother nor to his issue, but it shall rather eschete to the lorde of whom it is holde, that is straunge to that blode and to his heires for evermore. Than sethen Edmond Irenside, though he hadd been mulier, and saint Edwarde were brotherne but of halfe blode, that is to say Edmunde was issue to the forsayd Alysone [previously spelt 'Algeva'] and saynt ['Edww' erased] Edwarde was issue to Emma, doughter to the duke of Normandy, the said Edmonde nor eny of his issue might never succede nor bee heire to saynte Edward. Which mater he well consideryng and that he hadd none other kynne which ought to enherete his roialme after him, willyd that William duke of Normandy, his next cosynne in his moders side, might succede him in his roialme of Englonde. Wherunto Harold, sonne of erle Godwyn and the gretteste lord of Englonde, and also the more parte of all the lordis spirituelx and temporalx [f. 315b] of this londe were welle aggreyd and promytted that it shallbe so; and the same Harolde made lyke promys in Normandy to the duc him selfe. But yet after the dethe of saint Edwarde, he abated and ocupyed this roialme hym selfe as kynge tharof. For whiche cause the said duc of Normandye come over with a grete hooste and conquered this londe. Buth not all ['then' in other versions instead of 'all'] the heires of Edmonde Irensyde though he hadd be mulier [legitimate], but yet half a brother of saynt Edwarde, barred for evermore by the lawe of Englonde to clayme this roialme or any londe as heire to saynt Edwarde, to whom theire auncestre was brother but of half bloode.

Fortescu

[red in margin] The thyrd argument made agenst the forsayd heyres

Item, it is wryten in the boke of Judicum the xithchapitre that Iepte sumtyme jugge and gouvernour of the children of Israell iustyfied thar possession in certayn landis, whiche thay hadd goten by conqueste of the children of man ['amon' written above, 'amon' also in margin, 'Amon' in other versions], by cause thay hadd kepte and occupyed the same landes peasably after thaire conquest by the space of iii c yere. How moche more lawfully than may the kynge our soverane lorde, whos progenitours and him self bona fide have been peasably possessed of this londe more than iiii c yeres, justyfie his possession tharin agen the forsayd daynes and scottes yf thay wold clayme hit by any title grawen to thaym by Edmunde Irensyde or eny other man be fore the conqueste? And in lykewyse a gen the Saxones, Romayns and Brytons, which in olde days have been lordes here, the possession truly of cccc yeres excedith grettely the title of prescripcione used in eny roialme of the worlde. And yet is prescripcion oone of the strengest titles auctoryzed by any lawe. Is not nowe the [f. 316a] forsayd wrytinge made in Scottelande concernynge Edmonde Irensyde, though he hadd be mulyer, clerely provede of noone effecte and that it maketh noon evydence a gen the kyng our soverane lorde? But that the kynges title by occasion of that and by reason of this declaracion is more clere and shalbe more openly knowen than it shuld have been if that wrytinge hadd never be made, wherthorow it turneth all to the kinges good though the utterer tharof ment not that it shuld have doone.

The lerned man

[red in margin] The consyderacion which ledde kinge Henry to make acorde with Fraunce

Sir than said this lerned man, ye wrote also while ye were in Scottelande that kinge Henry the v[ti] , beinge lerned by wyse and connyng men that he might not have the roialme of Fraunce by the title of a woman, that is to sainge by the title of quene Isabell that was doughter to the kynge of Fraunce and syster to iii kinges that reyned ther after the deth of hir fader, lefte for that cause that title and clayme and also the stile and name of kynge of fraunce, whiche ['he' omitted] hadd used many yeres byfore. And accorded with Charles the kynge of Fraunce to wedde his doughter Kateryn, and dide soo and apon the treaty of that maryage accorde, toke betwene kynges by thassent and counsell of the more partie of the Doseperes [great nobles] and iii estates of that londe, that the said kynge Charles shuld have and enjoy peasably ye roialme ['kynge' deleted] of Fraunce, with the dignite, stile and name of ['of' repeated] kinge of fraunce, all the dais of his lyffe. And after his decesse the roialme of fraunce shuld remayne and goo to the said kinge Henry and to his heires, kynges of Englonde for evermore. And that the same kynge Henry and his heires shuld [f. 316b] be regentes of fraunce and called heres et regens regni Francie all the lyffe of the sayd kynge Charles. Whiche accorde and all thynges conteyned in hit was affermed and made sure aswell by the iii astates of Fraunce with thassent of the mooste partie of the Dousepers as by a parlament holden in Englonde the ix[th] yere of the said king Henry. By force and cause of whiche accorde the same kynge Henry loste the name and stile of kynge of Fraunce in all his wrytinges and was called Rex Anglie heres et regens regni Francie in his patentes, and wryteth all the dais of his lyffe, and so was his sonne called after him all the lyfe of the said kynge Charles. After whos deth the same sonne was in Parys crouned kynge of Fraunce, beynge ther present the more partie if the lordes of Fraunce that were not at werre with the said kynge and Charles the day of his dethe, which lordes all assented to that coronacion. By which wrytynge ye entended to prove ii thinges, oon is this that kynge Henry the v[te] understode that ye roialme of Fraunce was not inherytable by the title of a woman. The secunde is that Henry sonne to the said kynge hadd right to ['to' repeated] the roialme of Fraunce by reasonne of that accorde and not oure soferayne lorde kynge Edwarde the fourth.

The lerned man

[red in margin] The distroccione of the fyrste poynte of that consideracion

Syr, me thinketh that your said wrytinge may not prove any of thes said ii poyntes. For as to the fyrste poynt, the levyinge of kyng Henry the v[te] in title of the roialme of Fraunce may not prove it nor by evidence to the profe of hit. For he was not next heire to the forsaid quene Ysabell, by whom we thoo hadd our title to Fraunce, for Edmunde at that tyme erle of Marche, was next heire to the said quene Isabell. That is to saynge he was sonne to Roger, sonne to Phillipp, doughter to Lyonell, sonne to kynge [f. 317a] Edward the iii[de] sonne to the forsayd quene Isabell. For which cause the said Roger, fader to Edmond, was proclaymed heire apparaunt to kynge Richard in his parlament holden at Westmynster the xii[th] yere of his reynge. To which Roger and all so to Edmonde the kynge our soverayne lorde is next heire, for he is sonne to Anne, doughter to the said Roger, and also suster to the said Edmond, late erle of Marche, which is dede with oute issue of his body. And the forsayd kynge Henry the v[te] was sonne to Henry, sonne of Johne, yonger brother of the forsayd Lyonell, in which case he myght not be heire to quene Isabell. And by the consequens tharof he might not have hadd the roialme of Fraunce alle the while ther wer any issue of the said Lyonell onlyve. By the whiche consideracion he lefte the name and style of kynge of Fraunce and made the said treatie, and not by the consideracion whiche ye imagyned on your said wryting for els he hadd had no colour of title to that roialme. And therfor, Syr, me thinketh that now ye forsaid fyrste poynt is clerlye dysprovede.

The lerned man

[red in margin] The distroccion of the ii poynte of the same consyderacion

And as to the seconde poynt of the same consideracion, ye knowe welle how that accorde and title that greve tharby was goten by the costes, charges and aventures of this londe fore the good and profytte tharof, which I wotte welle hath coste this londe cc ml li and more. And sythen kynge Henry the v[te] is now dede with oute issue, the title and right that grewe by that accorde is now holyche and oonely unto the kynge our soverayne lorde, whiche is indubytable his next heire masle. So that now he hath [f. 317b] title and right to ye roialme of Fraunce, as well the title that growe of that accorde, as by his olde tytle whiche he and his progenitours, heires to the forsayd quene Isabell, have longe hadd.

And which his forsaid noble auncestree Edmond, erle of Marche, hadd by for the said ['thes' deleted] accorde, and at the tyme of the makynge tharof. And his heires alway sythen have hadde, as well in ['the' inserted, 'his' deleted] lyves of the sayd kynge Charles, kynge Henry v the^{te} and of his sonne, as sythen not excludede by the forsaid accorde to have and clayme it as next heires too quene Isabell. So that in the lyfe of said Henry, sonne to kynge Henry the v^{te}, the kynge our soverayne lorde hadd as verely right to the roialme of Fraunce and shuld have hadd agen the same sonne yf he hadd been inpossession of that roialme, as he now hath agene kynge Lowys, which occupyeth thee same roialme, and as his noble progenytours have hadd agene the auncestryes of the same Lowis, the forsaid accorde notwithstondynge. Neverthelesse his highnes hath now bothe titles, that is to saynge his auncien title auncetrell, as next heire to quene Ysabell, and this new title that was gotene by the forsaid accorde. Is not nowe the forsaid secunde poynte as clerely dysproved as the fyrste, so that by the forsayd latter mater wryten oute of Scottelande thaire remayneth no more maner evydence agene the kynge nor his title?

Fortescu

[red in margin] Why kynge Henryis councell wrote agene the succession of women in kyngedomes

Syr ye have so clerly declared theffectes of the forsaid laste wrytinges that it ['s' deleted] now nedith not more declaracion made by me, and I am [Harley 537 ends here] right gladd to here of youe and to undyrstonde by your saynge. How grete nede the councell [f. 318a] of the laste kynge Henry hadd to wryte agene the title of the enherytaunce of women in kyngdoms, for els by that title the kyng, our soverayne lorde, myght have distroyd inevitably the title whiche the sayd late kynge hadd on the roialme of Fraunce by force of the forsayd accorde, as ye have clerely schewed. Also by that title the kynge oure soverayne lorde was undoutably inherytable to the roialme of Englond by fore the same kynge Henry, consyderynge that he is descended of Lyonell, the older brother, and the same Henry was descended of Johne, the yonger brother, as is be fore openly declared. O howe good lorde is good [God] to the kynge oure soverayne lorde, that now hathe geven him thies bothe titles, wherethorow his subgettes may fight for him in his title for his roialme of Fraunce with oute any doute or scrople of counscieaunce. For by syde his auncien title, that roialme is now also clerely sure to him and to his heires by the said accorde as all the councell of bothe roialmes coude or yet canne make it.

The lerned man

[red in margin] Here is desyred a declaracion a gen the boke of Laten and other wrytinges made in Scotelande

Than sayd the lerned man truly, Syr, me thyneth youe well desposed in all thees maters hiderto for in all wrytinges made by your self ye have confessed the trouthe and declared the cause why ye wrote so, wherin I cane assigne no defaulte ['in' inserted] you. And in thoo thinges that were wryten [a separate'y' deleted] by other men agenste your wylle, ye have declared the qualites and merytes of thaym bothe truly and planely to the kynges good and honour as me thynketh, [f. 318b] for whiche ye be worthy right grete thanke. But yet Syr, ye wrote oute of Scotteland oone matier which nedith right gret and clere declaracion, for it sownyth gretly agen the kynges olde title to his roialme of Fraunce, and so it dydde when it was wryten agenst his title of this londe. Which matier is this, ye wrote that no woman may suppremely reigne upon man, for Gode said to the fyrste woman thise wordes: *Eris sub potestate viri et ipse dominabitur tui* [Thou shall be under the power of man and he shall rule over you]. Which wordes said to hire was said to all the kynd of woman, as the wordes tho said by Gode to the fyrst man were sayd to all man kynde. And ovir this ye wrote a boke in laten be whiche ye entendid to prove the same by many auctorytes, scriptures and reasons, wherin yf ye so declare your selfe and the matiers of that boke as ye kynge be not harmed by theyme, ye than acquyte you well and do tharin to his highnesse right acceptable and lovynge service.

Fortescu

[red in margin] Fortescu dredith that the declaracion which is desyred of him wold be to his infame

I wolde fayne ['fayne' repeated]do as ye move me God knowyth, and am right sory that ever I wrote so or labored upon the makygne of that laten boke. But yet the werke to whiche ye now desyre me were more conveny-ent to another mans pen than to myn, for I have wryten so much tharin to another entent as ye know welle, that yf now I do as ye meve me, my werke tharin wyll soune so lyke dowblenesse that in the oppynyone of the people and namely of simple men, I may tharby fall into infame of dowblenesse. And yf it be doon by a nother man, he may have no hurte be it but he shall have right grete worshipp yf he ['do' inserted] it coonyngly wher [f. 319a] for I wold be right gladd and helpe him tharin in alle that I coude and honestely might do. Also Syr, sithen thies maters to whiche ye stere me concernen the right of succession in kyngedoms, whiche is the grettest matier temperall in all the worlde, they oughten to be tre['d' erased]ted and declared by the mooste profounde and grettest lerned men that can be goten tharto and not by men of my simplenesse that have not moche labored or studyed in any faculte excepte the lawes of this londe, in which the studientes lerne full lytell of the right of succession of kyngdomes. And also yf any thinge be wrtyen herein which may resonably be disproved shalle fortefye and helpe the oppynyon of all theym that have wryten to the contrary entent. Wherfore I drede me sore to wryte herin knowynge myne insuffyciente tharto. And that if it be not sufficiente, men wolle say that I made it suche for to strengthen tharby my rather ['earlier'] wrytynges. *Et sic erit novissimus error pejor priore* [And thus the newest error will be worse than the previous one]. Wherfor me thinketh the kynges highnesse wolde be moved to comytte this werke to such as beth more able and more profe tharto than I.

The lerned man

[red in margin] The wrytinge that now is desyred may never be unworshippfull

Youre wysdome Syr conceyveth well how sergeauntes and advocates that been right worshipfull men arguen dayly to prove the titles of thayr clyantes, and after that in a lyke case for a nother clyant thay arguen to the contrary entent and beth not for that ['and o' deleted] nor ought to be blaymed. So also doone the jugges in maters of gret diffyculte wherin thay beth also indifferent, [f. 319b] as thay be for such disputacion ys to thayme beste meane to finde the right on every doughtous case. Gracian also, that compyled the booke of the lawe cannon called decrees, in all his questyons whiche he maketh in the case which he puttith there, called causes, disputith for eithur partie of every questione. Thus doth saynt Thomas in Secunda Secunde and in all his bokes, where as he asketh eny questions, and thus doone all the clarkes that determyn eny materis on scoles. For this ordre is no doublenesse but argument and proof of coonynge and vertue. And sithen your wrytynges, whiche ye have made in thee matiers, in the whiche I now move you were but argumentes, and ye no jugge but a parcyall man, servaunt to him for whos favour ye made the argumentes. And his cause is now expired and he deed, ye may nowe honestly and commendably withoute eny note of blame, argue to ye contrary entent of that ye have doo by fore this tyme yf ye finde reasons and groundes to do so. And also ye ben nowe bounde in consciance and by right to do so, consyderyng that ye be the kynges liege man and of his councell, and founde in his noble grace also grete clemence and favours as ever dyd man sithen he fyrst reyned upon us. And ['And' repeated] peraventur your olde argumentes and wrytynges mowe els turne and be occasion to his harme or to the infame of the title be which he reigneth apon us, which I am right sure ye wold not were so. And Syr yf ye wryte as I mowe you to do and than it fortune your wrytynge to be not of suche effecte as ye entende, which thinge me thynketh ye drede gretly, the kynge shall not be harmede tharby, for his highnesse may than make other notable and connynge men to make better wrytinge tharin, wherin thay shalle fynde lesse diffyculte whan thay have seen your wrytinges.

Fortescu

[f. 320 a] [red in margin] A woman is under the power of man while she is under the Pope

Syr youre reasons and motyves beth so gret that yf I do not as ye move me, I dred that men shall holde me selfewylly, and tharfor I wolle assay and do as ye desyre me. The matier which ye say I wrote and is so gretly agenst the kynge is this, I wrote how that me semyd no woman ought soveranly or supprimely reynge upon man, which matiers I pretended to prove by the juggementes which God gave uppon the firste woman whenne sche had synned saynge to here thise wordes: *Eris sub potestate viri et ipse dominabitur tui* whiche been wrytten in the boke of Genesis the thirde chapitre and beth such in Englyshe: Thou shalt be under the power of man and he shall be thy lorde. Which wordes spoken to that woman was as I thoo wrote, spoken to all kynde of woman, as the wordes tho spoken tho by God to ye firste man was said to all mankynde. This matier ye now desyre that I woll so declare and also the matiers of a booke which I wrote in Laten to enforce myne entent herine. As the kynge our soverayne lorde be not harmed be theym in his titlis of Englonde or of Fraunce. Syr as to the fyrste poynte in whiche ye desyre my declaracion, I hope to finde not dyfficulte, for our lorde sayd not in his forsayd juggement that a woman shuld be under the power and lordshipp of all men, or of many men. But he sayd indiffinytely or indetermynably that she shuld be under the power and lordshipp of man. Which is true yf she be under the power or lordshippe of eny man, for logycions sayne:

Quod proposicio indiffinita est vera si in aliquo supposito illa sit vera [That an indefinite proposition is true if in any hypothesis it is true]. And by that reasonne she is undyr the power and lordshippe of man yf any kynde of subieccion she be undyr the power and lordshippe of any man. Wherfore howe be it that thar beth many kyndes of lordshippes called by dyverse names in laten as is: *Dominium Regale, Dominium Politicum* [f. 320b] *et Dominium Dispoticum* [Regal Rule, Political Rule and Despotic Rule] and such other. Yf a woman be under the power of man in oone of the kyndes of lordeshippes, she is undere the lordshipp of man. And that every woman is under the power and lordshippe of sume ['one' inserted] man, which alle that she is arted unto by the forsaid juggement in Genesis may not be denied. For every woman is under the power and lordshippe of the Pope whiche is a man and he vicer of Criste god and man. And though his power and lordshippe were but spirituell, yet ['the' inserted] beinge undyr that power and lordshippe is a beinge under the poure and lordshippe of man. Wherfor the forsaid texte of Genesis or eny thinge by me deduced therof may not prove that a woman may not reigne in a kyngdome of whiche the kinge hath no soveragne in temporalte sithen sche abidith always subget to the Pope. And by the same reasonne it may not hurte the kinge in his titles to his forsayd twoo roialmes.

Fortescu

[red in margin] The argument made agenst woman in the laten boke

Item, this matier is argued in the forsaid laten boke in this forme: God commaunded and by his juggement establysshed that every woman shalbe under the power and lordshipp of man. Than by the same commaundement and juggement he commaunded that no woman shalbe free or exempt from the power and lordshippe of man, for as I wrote there: *Precepto uno contrariorum eorum alterum prohiberi necesse est* [If one of two contraries is accepted, the other must be rejected]. But a woman to reigne in a kyngdome of whiche the kingdome is subget to no man in temporaltes is a woman to be fre and exempt from the power and lordshippe of man. Hit shall thanne necessarily ensue that no woman may reigne in any suche kyngedome for it were suppremely and soveraynly to reigne uppon man, wherthorougth she wer thanne [f. 321a] not undyr the power and lordshippe of man. This is the strength argument that is made in the said boke, by reasonne of the forsayd texte of Genesis. Wherfor yf this argument be clerely dystroyed, the fyrste matier whiche ye desyre me to declare is than clerely declared. Nowe truly I am right sory that ever I made eny suche argument, for it is an informyle tale and no kynde of silogisme, wherfor the minor is impossible and tharfor not true, and the consequent yf it might be callede a consequent is not necessarie, wherfore this maner of argument proveth no thinge.

Fortescu

[red in margin] Here is proved that no kyng is with oute soverayne in temporaltes

The forsaid minor is this: a woman to reigne in a kingedome of whiche the kinge is subget to noo man in temporaltes is a woman to be free and exempt from the power and lordshippe of man. Fyrste it nedyth that it be undyrstonde that alle that we speke of kinges and kingdomes in this disputacion muste be undyrstonde of crysten kynges and thaire kyngdomes, though tharin we name thayme not so. Thanne thus ther is not or may be by possibilite eny kingedome of whiche the kinge in temporaltes is subget to no man. For all kynges beth membres of Holy Chyrche of which our holy fader the Pope as vicare to Cryste is hede, saynge to the Appostell; *Omnis viri caput Cristus est* [The head of every man is Christ]. Tho whome alle the membres of the churche, and as to the hede tharof, beth and ought to be subgettes and obedyentes. Wherfor thanne it wolle be [f. 321b] followe necessaryly that any kinge to be not subget to any man is unpossible sythen every kinge is a membre of Holy Chirch, is subiecte to the Pope. Thanne whethir this subgetcione be only of his persone or also of and on his persone and his kingedome, which bothe by temporales, onely now remayneth to be proved. And to prove that he and his kingedome and also he in his kingdome, and in all other of his temporalties beth subget unto the Pope, I procede in this maner. Or Cryste was conceyved, God said ['sayd' repeated] to him by his aungell to his moder theis wordes: *Dabit illi dominus deus sedem David patris ejus et regnabit in domo Jacob in eternum et regni ejus non erit finis* [The lord God will give him the seat of his father David and he will reign in the house of Jacob for ever and of his kingdom there will be no end]. Of which wordes this is the sentence: God promitted by his aungell that Criste Jhesus shulde have the estate and dignite of David which was kynge of Israel. And that he shuld reigne in that kingdome, which in the forsaid worde the aungell called the house of Jacob. For Jacob was called Israell of whom all the people of that roialme were descended and tharfor by him and of him that roialme was called the kingdome of Israell, in whiche the aungell said that Criste shuld reigne for evermore and that ther shuld never be ende of his reigne. Israell by interpretacion is a man that seeth God, thanne is not the kingdome of ['Jewes' deleted] whiche the aungell thoo spake to the kingdome of Jewes, for thay seen nat God, and also thaire kingdome is endede. But it is the kingdome of all crysten men, which onely a monge almankynde seen God and evyr shall laste, and nowe is called all Holy Chyrche. In this kyngdome nowe reyneth Cryste by his vicare and ever shall reygne for he promitted to be with us unto the ende of the worlde. As somtyme reyned David in the kingdome of Israell while he lyvede and sithen all the princes and subiectes of kinge David were his subiectis in thair persones and in thair possessions, why than beth not now all the kinges and princes of the chirche fygured by the kingdome of David, also wele subiectes to the Pope in thaire persones as in thair temporaltes. [f. 322a] Kinge David toke not from his subetts thaire goodes or possessiouns with oute juste cause, but yit he compelled the princes of every tribe to rule justely thair subiectes and els he punisshed thayme for thaire neglygens and defautes. Thus Moyses hanged the princes that punysshed not thaire subiectes whanne thay hadde offended. Thus have popes punysshed emperours and kinggis when they have mysrulyd thaire subiectes as we rede in cronicles of olde dais, for thay ought to correcte thaire owne subiectes whanne thay offended. So ought the Pope to correcte theym whanne thay offende and els thaire defautes shalle remayne unpunysshed, which God wold not. And therfor Criste is kinge of all kinges and lord of all worlde, havynge in the handes of the Pope his vicare bothe swerdes, for which he is called *Rex et Sacerdos* [King and Priest], and compellith all princes as well spirituell as temporell to come to his gret councelles. By which matiers and by many moo which wolde aske grete trait of tyme yf thay shulde be specified, yf many [it may] undoutedly appere that ther is now noo kingdome in the erthe of cristen men of which the kinge is not subiecte also welle in temporaltes as spiritualtes, wherthorth the forsayd minor is nowe clerely proved impossible, and therfor it may not be tru.

Fortescu

[red in margin] Here is the consequent of the forsayd argument disproved

And sithen the minor of the forsaid argument is proved impossible and tharfor untrue, the conclucion called the consequent is not necessarye and therfor not good by logyke or eny other faculte. Wherthorough it maneth [maketh] no maner profe or evydence agenste the right of succession of woman in kingdomes as by the said argument was intended. And though the said minor hadde be possible and true yet [f. 322b] the consequent tharof wolde have made no good argumente, for though a kynge be not subiecte to any man in temporaltes, yet it folowith not tharof that such a kinge is not subiecte to any man: *simpliciter quia arguendo a quo ad simpliciter non valet argumentum* [For the very reason that arguing from what is correct under a certain respect to what is absolutely correct is not a valid argument].

['Fortescu' deleted] The lerned man

[red in margin] The lerned man holdyth him content

Then said the forsaid lerned man in this wyse: Truly Syr, ye have nowe declared thies matiers so openly and clerly that ['that' repeated] ther remayneth no matier of evydence a genste the kinge or his roialmes, by reasonne of the jugement ['of' deleted] goven by God a genste woman, whanne he said: *Eris sub potestate viri et ipse dominabitur tui*, [Thou shall be under the power of the man and he shall be thy lord] which was the mooste sore matier a genste the inherytaunce of woman in kingdomes.

The lerned man

[red in margin] The lyvere sued by the heires of the duke of Clarence

But Syr I remembre me well that I have redde a wrytinge made in your name, in whiche ye doubted whethir that Phelyppe, moder to Roger sometyme erle of Marche of whome the kynge is descended were the doughter of Syr Lyonell, duke of Clarence, and wheder the same duke had any issue that evir levid him or noo. For ye said that ye had not seen nor harde of any man that hadd seen any recorde provinge that the said Phillipp or eny of hire heres, or that other personne hadde evir any lyvere in the Chauncerie or otherwyse of any [f. 323a] lordeshippes or other lyvelode that were somtyme to the said duke of Clarence. Nathelesse I mervell not grettly of youre ignorance tharin, for I canne well suppose that be your departinge out of this londe ye delt not moche with that inheritaunce and tharfor made nevur serche for the lyverez tharof and while ye were by yonde the see ye might not se ['nd' deleted] eny suche recorde. But Sir now that ye beth come hider ye may with oute difficulte se recordes proving such liverez made also well to the said Phillipp as to diverse of hire issue as heires to ye for said duke, and also as heires to the dochesse his wyfe dame Elizabeth moder to said Phillippe, as here after ye shall never have doute or finde difficulte in that matier. Wherupone the same lerned man than schewyd unto the said Fortescu a copye of an accompte made in the Escheker in the dais of kinge Edward the thirde in thes wordes: *In compoto* ['Iho' deleted] *Johannis Gressingham escheatoris regis in comitatibus Norfolcie et Suffolcie computatur a xxvii die Novembris anno xlii usque xlviii de aliquibus exitibus maneriorum de Walsyngham seu Crecham quae Leonellus, nuper dux Clarenciae defunctus tenuit per legem Anglie poste mortem Elizabethae quondam uxoris suae de rege in capite ut de hereditate Philypae, filiae et heredis predictorum Leonelli et Elizabethae sicut continetur in transcripto cuiusdam inquisicionis et extentae coram dicto escheatore inde capta super hunc compotum liberatum xviio die octobris anno xlvi, quo die idem dux obiit. Et dictus escheator maneria illa per mortem ipsius ducis cepit in manum regis usque xxiiii diem augusti proximis sequentis, quo die dicta Philippa quam Edmundus de mortuo mari et comes Marchie duxit in uxorem aetatem suam sufficienter probavit. Et rex cepit fidelitatem ipsius comitis regi de omnibus terris et tenementis quae praedictus nuper dux tenuit tam in dominico suo ut de feodo, quam per legem Angliae post mortem praedictae Elizabethae, quondam uxoris suae matris ipsius Philippe de hereditate eiusdem Philippe debitam et eisdem comiti et Philippe omnes terras et tenementa praedicta cum pertinentiis reddidit, ac rex* [f. 323b] *per breve suum datum eodem xxiiii die augusti precepit dicto escheatori eisdem comiti et Philippe de omnibus terris et tenementis predictis plenam seisinam habere facere non R et cet.* [In the account of John Gressingham, the king's escheator in the counties of Norfolk and Suffolk, assessed from the 27th day of November, from the year 42 to 48, concerning certain revenues of the manors of Walsyngham and Crecham which the late Lionel, duke of Clarence, held by the law of England after the death of Elizabeth, his late wife, from the king in chief, as concerning the inheritance of Philippa, daughter and heir of the afoesaid Lionel and Elizabeth, as is contained in the transcript of a certain inquest and extent before the said escheator, thence recorded on this account issued on the 17th day of October, in 46th year, on which day the same duke died. And the said escheator took those manors, after the death of the Duke, into the hand of the King until the 23rd day of August the following year, on which day the aforesaid Philippa, whom Edmund Mortimer, earl of March, married, sufficiently proved her maturity. And the King received the fealty of the earl owed to the King for all lands and tenements which the aforesaid late Duke held, as much in his demesne as of fee, as by the law of England, after the death of the aforesaid Elizabeth, his late wife, mother of Philippa the rightful heiress. To the same earl and Philippa he gave back all the lands and aforesaid tenements with their appurtenances. And the King, through his writ, granted on the same 23rd day of August, ordered the aforesaid escheator to grant the same earl and Philippa full seisin concerning all the aforesaid lands and tenements.] By whiche recorde it clerely apperith that the forsaid Philippe was doughter and heire to the forsaid duke of Clarance and to Elizabeth his wyfe. And that sche and the erle of Marche, hire housband, had livere in the kinges Chauncerie of all tho landis and tenementes whiche the forsaid duke helde the day of his deth in his demeane as of fee. And also of all thoo landes and tenementes which he held by ye curtesy of Englonde after the deth of the forsayd dochesse. And ovir this the forsayd lerned man offered to have shewed to the forsayd Fortescu diverse other recordes aswell of the Escheker as of the Chauncerie proving all the premisses if he wold have goten with hym into the same couurtes.

Fortescu

Wherunto Fortescu said, I pray you Sir shew me no moo recordes of this matier. For this suffysith to put oute of my mynde alle the dawte that I hadde in this matier. For sithen the said Philippe and here husband hadde lyvere as heire to the forsaid duke in oone countee, hit may not be douted but that thay hadd lyke livere in every counte of Englonde, wher as the said duc hadd any lyfelode and thoughe thay hadd not yet it apperith that thay ought to have hadde.

The lerned man

[f. 324a] [red in margin] The wrytinge made in Scoteland touching kinge Stevyn et cet.

Then said the lerned man in this wyse Syr while ye were in Scotteland, ye wrote howe kinge Henry the firste hadde issue a doughter wedded to the emperoure of Almayne by whome she hadde non issue. But after his decesse she was wedded to the erle of Angeoy and hadd issue by him a sonne afterward called Henry Fitz Emperesse. And that kinge [Henry I] diede withoute eny other issue, after whos deth this londe wold not suffre his doughter to reygne apon hem by cause, as ye sayd, it was not inheritable by woman. And by the same reasonne thay wolde not suffre hire sonne to be thaire kinge by title of her. But they chase thanne Stephen erle of Boloyne suster sonne to the said kinge, to be thaire kinge, which by force of that eleccion was made and ennoynted kinge of Englonde and so reigned more thanne xviii yere. And after that whanne the sonnes which the said kinge Stephen hadde were dede, accorde toke bitwene him and Henry Fitz Empesse [*sic*] that the same Henry shuld after his decesse have the kingdome of Englonde to him and to his heires masles forevermore, of whiche estate he was thanne made sure by auctorite of parliament, by which title he and his issue hath reyned in this lande all way sethenne. Syr me semythe whanne ye wrote thus ye knewe not well the cronicles that beth wryten of kinge Stephen and of Henry Fitz Emperesse, for certaynly kinge Stephen come not to this londe by eleccionne, nor Henry Fitz Emperesse was entitled tharin by auctoryte of parlament. Wherfor sithen ye be now in this londe where ye may serche and finde the trouthe therof whiche ye knewe not then me thinketh it were for you nowe to make suche serche, and thanne to declare by your wrytinge the clernesse and trouthe of this matier, for els the kinges title as well as to this londe as to his roialme of Fraunce might be diffaymed and hurte by coloure of your sayd wrytinge, whiche I knowe well ye wolde not wer do in any wysse.

[sub-title of 'Fortescu' omitted]

[f. 324 b] [red in margin] The serche made touching the forsayd matier

I thanke you my frende for youre counceyll, but yet truly I have ['I have' repeated] done alle redy as ye now advyse me, and therfor I shalle schewe unto you in articles what I have founde in sondrye cronicles of this matier. Fyrste I finde in a cronicle wryten by a worshipfull clarke called Radulphus de Diceto sumtyme deane of Pawles how undyr the yere of our lorde ml cxxxv he wryteth the wordes: *Rex Anglorum Henrycus cum regnasset annis triginta quinque quatuor etiam mensibus decessit apud sanctam Dionisium in Silva Leonum* [in Normandy] *et in Anglia sepultus est apud Radingum* [Reading]. *Hugo Bygod senescallum regis veniens in Angliam coram archiepiscopo Cantuariensi sacramento probavit quod dum rex Henricus ageret in extremis, ortis quibusdam inimiciis inter ipsum et imperatricem, ipsam* ['exheredidavit' erased] *exheredavit et Stephanum Bolonie comitem heredem instituit. Willielmus Cantuariensis nimis credulus verbis senescalli, Stephani Moritonii comitem consecravit in regem apud Westmonasterium.* [After Henry king of England had reigned for thirty-five years and four months he died at St Denis in Silva Leonum [a camp the king had built in Normandy] and was buried at Reading in England. Hugo Bygod, the king's steward, came to England and swore on the sacrament to the archbishop of Canterbury that while king Henry was dying, influenced by a certain enmity between himself and the Empress [Maud, Henry's daughter], he disinherited her and made Stephen, count of Boulogne his heir. William of Canterbury, being too credulous of the words of the steward, consecrated Stephen, earl of Moretoil [in Normandy] king at Westminster.] By which wordes it apperith that kinge Stephen was made kinge of Englande and the Emperesse put from that astate oonely by the reporte of the stewarde of the kinges house to whiche the archebisshoppe gave to hasty credence. Wherthorough it apperith that the same kinge Stephen was not chosen to be kinge of Englonde as is conteyned in the forsayd wrytinge made in Scotelande et cet.

Fortescu

[red in margin] An other cronicle

Item I finde in the same cronicle howe that in yere of our lorde ml clii Henry Fitz Emperesse entred into this londe wherof the said cronicles wrytes under thees wordes: *Henricus dux Normanorum intravit Angliam in manu valida infra octavas Epiphanie castellum de Malmesbury obsedit et milites intus obsessos ad dedicionem coegit. Eustachius filius regis mortuus est.* [f. 325a] [Henry, duke of Normandy, entered England powerfully on the eighth day of Epiphany; he laid siege to the castle at Malmesbury and forced the besieged soldiers to surrender. Eustace, the king's son, died.] By which it apperith that in the lyffe of kynge Stephen and by fore any accorde made with him, Henry Fitz Emperesse claymed this londe in his owne right as inherytor tharoff, for at the tyme of his entre he hadd non othere tharto.

Fortescu

[red in margin] Item, a nother cronicle

Item in the yere of oure lord ml c liii the said cronicler writeth in this wyse: *Evenit quod minime credebatur deffencio regni non dirimitur in gladio. Partibus evocatis hinc et inde transaccio celebrata est, diligencia intervenit archiepiscopi Cantuariensis et auctoritas plurium operata est, Wintoniensis episcopi profuit solicitudo, coepiscoporum assensus non defuit, defuit procerum et consilium et concensus. Et ut nostri maiores videantur a legibus aliquid accipisse novi aliquid se sumpserunt a legibus. Ducem si quidem Normannorum rex in filium arrogavit et in eum jus suum transtulit et potestatem sibi quo adiunxerit regie dignitatis solam ymaginem referravit. Et si propheticum illud et attenderis iam se induit genitore iam ducem arrogavit in filium in participem regni et postmodum successorem universi ducem recipient et rege ducem et in duce regem singuli venerabuntur.* [Something happened that was scarcely credible, that the strife of the realm was not resolved by the sword. Thereupon, the parties were summoned and thence an agreement was reached by the careful intervention of the archbishop of Canterbury and the exercise of much effective authority. The solicitude of the bishop of Winchester was beneficial, the agreement of fellow bishops was not lacking, but the counsel and assent of the nobles was lacking. And our ancestors, so that they might seem to have received something new from the laws, took something from the laws. Since the King adopted the Duke of Normandy as his son and transferred his right and power to him, he reserved for himself only the image of royal dignity as long as he lived. If you also pay heed to that prophecy: 'now he has played the part of a father', he now adopted the Duke as his son, sharing the kingdom, and hereafter all will recognise the Duke as his successor and will venerate the Duke in the King and the King in the Duke]. By this cronicle it apperith that the accorde made betwene kinge Stephen and Henry Fitz Emperesse was a privat peas and covenaunt made betwene hem by thee meanys ['of'] spirituell men for terme of the lyffe of kinge Stephen. And toke no lenger any effecte for it was made by none auctorite of parlyament, as it expressely apperith by the same cronicle undir thees wordes: *Episcoporum assensus non defuit, defuit procerum et consilium et consensus* [The agreement of the bishops was not lacking, but the counsel and assent of the nobles was lacking]. What wordis may more clerly shewe that it was not made by auctorite of parliament than doon thies wordes that seyn ther lacked to this accorde the councell and assent of the nobles temporalx of the londe [f. 325b].

Fortescu

[red in margin] Another cronicle

Item in an other cronicle wrytten under the yere of oure lorde ml c liii is conceyved thus: *Stephanus rex Anglorum et Henricus dux Normannorum cognatus eius, viii^o^ idus novembris justicia de celo prospiciente concordati sunt hoc modo. Rex prius recognovit in conventu episcoporum et comitum et relinquorum obtimatum hereditarium jus quod dux Henricus habeat in regno Anglie, et dux benigne concessit ut rex tota vita sua si vellet regnum teneret.* [Stephen, king of the English, and Henry, duke of Normandy his cognate, the viiith November by the justice of heaven were providentialy reconciled in this way. The King first recognised in this meeting of bishops and earls to accept the hereditary right that Duke Henry had to the kingdom of England, and the Duke benevolently conceded that the King could hold the kingdom for his whole life if he wished.] And in lyke fourme is wrytten the same yere, *quasi de verbo in verbum* in the cronicle called Flores Historiarum, by which it expresely apperith that kinge Stephen knoleged that Henry Fitz Emperesse, which was thoo entred into Englonde, hadd right to the said londe as his inherytaunce. And that after that accorde the said king Stephen hadd no right tharin but by the graunte of Henry Fitz Emperesse.

The lerned man

[red in margin] Theffecte of the forsayd cronicles

Wheropon the forsaid lerned man than sayd in this maner: faithfully Syr me thinketh that ye have done good and effectuell diligence in the serch of thes cronicles, which be right playne and proven clerly that kinge Stephen was never chosen by this londe to be kinge tharof. And also that Henry Fitz Emperesse was kinge tharof of his owne inherytaunce as sonne and heire to the emperesse, doughter to kinge Henry the fyrste. And that he come not to this londe by title of eleccion or by auctorite of parlyament, as was supposed by the forsayd wrytinge made in Scoteland. Wherforth than it openly apperith that he had right tharin by his moder, whiche right he enioyned all his lyfe and so have done all his childer sithen. And by the same reasonne [f. 326a] Roger, sometyme erle of Marche, sonne to Philippe, doughter to the sayd duke of Clarence, elder brother to prynce Edward, fader to kinge Richarde ought to have hadd this roialme as next heire to kinge Richard, by which consideracione kinge Rychard made the same erle of Marche to be proclaymed in parlyament his heyre apparent beynge ther tho present the duke of ['Clarence' deleted] Lancaster and his sonne the sherle of Derby. Whiche after the dethe of kinge Richarde reyned as kinge of Englonde, callyd kinge Henry the iiii[th], which right to the crowne is descended from the sayd Roger, sometyme erle of Marche, to the kinge oure soverayne lorde, as to his cosynne and heire, that is to saynge sonne to Rycharde, sonne to Anne, doughter to the same Rogere, erle of Marche. As in an article before specially declarede and by lyke tytle, descent and right, oure sayd soveraine lorde ought to have the roialme of Fraunce by Isabell, moder to kinge Edwarde the iii[de], doughter and heire to the kynge of Fraunce.

The lerned man

Nowe truly Syr I am gladd that I have comenyd with you uppon all thes matiers, for howe so be it that when ye wrote them ye entended that thay shuld have been sore agayne the kinges title by which he tho claymed and now hath this londe. And so they sowned and wer so taken of many men, God ['g' erased] knowyth. Yet nowe blyssed be God, thay be taned to acontrarie entent and effecte, for thay [Harley 1757 'have causyd'] [f. 326b] alle your forsayd declaracione. By whiche the sayd title is nowe so clere and oppenne that ther remayneth to theym that wylle stryve therwith nother matier nor coloure to do so. And verely ye be worthy grete thanke for that ['sparinge' deleted] ye have thus planely sayd in thies matiers, not sparinge your owne ['owne' repeated] oppynions, which ye helde while ye ware aparcyalle man, but preferring right a bowe wylle and all effeccions. And where as late ye dredde that such maner of delynge might hurte your fame, truly Syr it may not do so, for ye have in no thinge sayd nay to such thinges as ye verely knewe. But in many thinges which he [Harley 1757 'ye'] provyd by argumentes, ye have now dysprovyd by gretter reasons. And many thinges which ye wrote by informacions wenynge thay hadd bene such as ye were tho informed ye hath sethen knowen by grete evydences and cronicles that thay were not such, which ye nowe knowledge as ye ought to do for els ye hadd doone a gen right which me thynketh ye be not so disposed to doo.

Finis

APPENDIX 3

Surviving Manuscripts of Sir John Fortescue's Works

Information concerning watermarks has been taken from C.M. Briquet, *Les Filigranes: Dictionnaire Historique des Marques du Papier, 1282–1600*, 4 vols (Paris, London, etc.: 1907).

In some of the manuscripts no watermarks are visible.

All the manuscripts are written on paper.

The Commodities of England

Oxford, Bodleian Library Laud Misc. 593, ff. 16b–19a, late fifteenth century. The only known copy of this work. Preceded by the *Governance of England*, ff. 1a–15b. See the *Governance* below for details.

De Titulo Edwardi Comitis Marchie

London, BL MS Additional 48063, ff. 4a–11b, early sixteenth century. The only known copy of this work. See above, Appendix 1, for details.

Of the Title of the House of York

No complete copy of this tract is known to survive. The report of the committee of 1732 on the burnt Cotton Manuscripts shows that Otto B i, which could have dated from the fifteenth century, contained a version of approximately ten sides, ff. 92a–96a.

One defaced, untitled fragment of the beginning exists in London, BL MS Cotton Vespasian F ix, f. 122a–b, dating from the late fifteenth century. The volume contains items mostly dating from the sixteenth and seventeenth centuries. It comes from a different, plainer manuscript than its near contemporary, BL MS Additional 48005.

London, BL MS Additional 48005 (Yelverton 6) f. 97a–b, late fifteenth century. Professionally written with ornate initials at the beginning of each paragraph, contains three fragments from the tract but not the beginning. It could be the original from which the two following manuscript fragments were copied. The leaves are stuck into the volume and are not part of the original binding.

London, BL MS Cotton Julius F vi, ff. 269a–271b, late fifteenth/early sixteenth centuries. This bears two copyist's observations, 'Hic desunt multa', f. 271a, and 'Alia multa hic desunt', f. 271b, showing that this version was incomplete at an early stage.

London, BL MS Lansdowne 205, ff. 137b–138a, 1581. 'A volume of heraldical and historical collections formerly belonging to Elias Ashmole Esq.' An inscription at the beginning provides the original provenance: 'The true copie of certayne leves that had ben torn out of a booke written as it shulde seeme by the hand in the days of king Edward the fourth on the behalf and in favour of the house of Lancastre against the said king. Which leves were found in a bookbyndere shoppe wheras the said booke ignorantly had ben putt to profane uses. 1581'. The fragments were probably copied from the one now bound in Julius F vi, since it contains identical Latin observations on missing parts. It can thus be inferred that the leaves were found in the bookbinder's shop considerably earlier than 1581 and that Additional 48005 contains the original fragment and that the two others are later copies.

Defensio Juris Domus Lancastrie

Oxford, Bodleian Library, MS James 28, pp.10–16, early seventeenth century, contains four fragments of the tract copied by Dr Richard James (1591–1638), an antiquary and librarian to Sir Robert Cotton. On p.16 there is a short piece in Scottish dialect alleging that Edmund Crookback, earl of Lancaster, was the oldest son of Henry III and thus the true heir to the English throne. Sir John Fortescue denied that he had ever written such a tract.

Another fragment was printed by G. Harbin, *The Hereditary Right of the Crown* (London: 1713) appendix, i–iii. This may still exist in the USA, Kansas MS C63 (formerly Phillipps MS 4284). L.H. and C. Nelson, 'A Lost Fragment of the *Defensio Juris Domus Lancastrie*', *Speculum*, 40, 290–3.

Replication against the claim and title of the duke of York for the crowns of England and France

London, BL MS Additional 48031A, ff. 134a–b, dated from 1480s. See the *Governance* for details.

London, BL MSS Harley 543, ff. 163b–164a and 545, ff. 136a–b, both copied by John Stow (1524/5) in the mid- to late sixteenth century.

London, BL MS Additional 38139, f. 234a from the seventeenth-century collections of Sir Walter Manwood.

Hatfield MS 230.4, half a page, late sixteenth century, bears the superscription, 'Out of Sir John Fortescue's book of defence of the title of the House of Lancaster'. This could be the book 'in the vulgar tongue' referred to in the *De Titulo*, which could be a work that has been lost or a reference to the full version of *Of the Title*. See above, Chapter 4, p. 160.

London, College of Arms, formerly Phillipps MS 13783, f. 8a, early seventeenth century, part of the estate of the late Sir Anthony Wagner, Garter King of Arms, now privately owned.

De Natura Legis Naturae

Oxford, Bodleian Library, MS Laud Misc. 585, pp.1–95, second half of fifteenth century. Written in a professional French hand. The anchor watermark could date from the 1460s. Contains only the first book. The reverse side of page 95, where the first book ends, is blank so there may have been no intention to write the second book there. No signs of ownership or dedication.

London, Lambeth Palace MS 262, ff. 1a–102a, late fifteenth century. A fine volume with calligraphic ornaments and marginal figures, one little monkey-like figure weilds a pot and supports a motto, 'mors in olla' (death in a pot, f. 27b). The quality of the work makes it possible that it could have been intended as a presentation copy for the Pope or the king of France. The script starts at the top of f. 1 and could originally have been preceded by a dedicatory page. This treatise was originally a separate volume owned by John Selden and bears his motto, 'Peri pantos ten Eleutherian'. It was bound by Archbishop Sancroft with the two other items in the late seventeenth century. See the *Governance* for details of the other two items.

An additional copy may still exist but its location is unknown. In the late seventeenth century it was in the library of Dr Benjamin Worsley, E. Bernard, *Catalogus Librorum Manuscriptorum Angliae et Hiberniae*, 2 vols (Oxford: 1679) vol. 2, 213a.

De Laudibus Legum Anglie

Cambridge, University Library MS Ff 5 22, ff. 1a–30b, written in a good, professional hand belonging to second half of the fifteenth century, contains a watermark of that period. It once belonged to Sir Robert Cotton. Like the two sixteenth-century versions, it omits three separate sentences as well as 500 between the middle of chapter XXIV and the middle of chapter XXV. All three were seemingly derived from a common source, either the manuscript that later became Cotton B i, which was therefore defective, or an intermediate defective copy. Whitechurch remedied the defects in his printed edition, presumably because he had access either to Cotton B i or another early complete copy. He probably produced it between 1545 and 1546, since Henry Smyth, who specialised in legal books and who is associated with him on the title-page, was active only for those two years (Chrimes, *De Laudibus*, lxxxiii, n. 2).

London, BL MS Harley 1757, ff. 208b–226a. Written in various hands dating from the mid-sixteenth-century and the watermarks bear this out. Sixty-five items altogether, including the *Declaration* and another copy of part of it and the *Governance*, which see for details.

Oxford, Bodleian Library MS Digby 198, ff. 1a–48a, first half of the sixteenth-century; part of the *Governance of England*, ff. 48a–75b; part of the *Declaration*, ff. 76a–90a.

The articles sent from the prince to the earl of Warwick his father-in-law

London, BL MS Additional 48031A, written by John Vale in the early 1480s, ff. 146a–148a, the earliest copy. For details see the *Governance*.

London, BL MS Harley 543, ff. 172a–173b copied from the above manuscript by John Stow in the mid- to late sixteenth century.

Example what good counsel helpeth

London, BL MS Additional 48031A, f. 148b, copied by John Vale in the early 1480s. See the *Governance* for details and *Vale's Book*, p. 226, for the proposed placing and purpose of this little piece.

London, BL MS Harley 542, f. 125a, copied by John Stow in the mid- to late sixteenth century.

Declaration upon certain writings sent out of Scotland

London, BL MS Royal 17 D xv, ff. 311b–326b, produced by John Multon in the early 1470s. See description in Appendix 2.

London, BL MS Harley 1757, paper; ff. 188a–195b; another incomplete copy, ff. 204a–207b, late sixteenth century. See *Governance* for details.

London, BL MS Harley 537, ff. 1a–8b, late sixteenth century.

London, BL MS Additional 48020 (formerly MS Yelverton 21), ff. 1a–18b, late sixteenth century.

London, BL MS Additional 48079 (formerly MS Yelverton 86), ff. 11a–29b, early seventeenth century.

London MS Lambeth 262, ff. 129a–140b, late fifteenth/early sixteenth century. See *Governance* for details.

Oxford, Bodleian Library MS Cherry 20, f. 2, seventeenth century.

Oxford, Bodleian Library MS Digby 198, ff. 76a–90a, first half of sixteenth century. Incomplete. See *Governance* for details.

Norfolk, Holkham MS, the earl of Leicester.

San Marino, CA, Huntingdon Library, MS Ellesmere 1131, ff. 31a–40a, seventeenth century. See *Governance* for details.

Keswick Hall, near Norwich, manuscripts of John Henry Gurney Esq., no. xxii, miscellaneous items dating from the fifteenth to the eighteenth centuries, ff. 37–39, 'Declaracion mad by Jo. Fortescue, Knt., upon certayne writings sent out of Scotland against the king's title to his realm of England'. May have formerly belonged to or been copied by Sir Henry Spelman (1563/4–1641), the Norfolk antiquarian (*HMC, Twelfth Report*, vol. ix, 134).

The Governance of England

Oxford, Bodleian, MS Laud Misc. 593, ff. 1a–15b, late fifteenth century, a small volume in poor condition, containing first the *Governance*, the unique copy of the *Commodities of Englond*, ff. 16b–19a, and, at the end, a list of the wards in the township of Stepney. The watermark in the paper is an elaborate crown, a popular motif in the fifteenth and sixteenth centuries, but no exact model has been found. This is likely to be the earliest surviving version of the *Governance*, although nothing in the jottings on the manuscript gives an indication of ownership before the sixteenth century, when there are references to the Bedingfields of Oxburgh, Norfolk (in 1568 both a Fortescue and a Bedingfield were officials in Lincoln's Inn, *Black Books*, vol. 1, 363). There are also also references to a Campion and a Tomlinson (see Gross, *Dissolution of the Lancastrian Kingship*, 105–6, for a discussion of these). It is written in a late fifteenth-century hand, which could date from the 1470s. The scribe appears to change on f. 3a and he may also have written the *Commodities*. The main reason for suggesting that this is the earliest copy, apart from the script, is that this manuscript has fewer chapter divisions than all the other surviving copies, as if it had not been fully prepared for presentation. There is no formal title: the first heading on f. 1a was adopted by later copies and it was also taken as the title of the work:

'The deference bi twene dominium regale and dominium politicum and regale'. This changed in the late sixteenth century, when Stow called it *The Governance of England* (see below, London, BL MS Harley 542). The next heading is given to chapter IV and thereafter, with the exception of chapter XVII, which is not marked, and with minor deviations, the titles are the same as in the other early version, BL Cotton Claudius A viii. Another feature which makes it likely that this text represents a very early version is the spasmodic highlighting of quotations which was done systematically in later professional copies and the one made by Sir Adrian Fortescue in 1532. The script seems to be the work of scribes, using secretary hand, rather than the author. It could, however, have been dictated by him, which would account for small errors in the text, or it could be a copy of such an original. Minor corrections have been added in a later hand, some taken from another text of the treatise, others which seem to reflect the whim of the writer. The treatise ends mid-sentence two-thirds of the way through chapter XIX: 'every wyse man mey well conseyve. The ffundacion …' , the result of at least one page having been torn out rather than, as in other copies, a deliberate ending. This means that no king is mentioned in the chapter.

London, BL MS Cotton Claudius A viii, ff. 175a–197b, not later than 1475. A well-preserved volume containing a number of items which were written professionally in the London shop of the stationer John Multon, who died in 1475 (see A.I. Doyle, 'An Unrecognised Piece of *Piers the Plowman's Creed* and Other Work by Its Scribe', *Speculum*, 24, (1959), 428–36). The watermark is hard to see as the pages are closely written, but it looks like a sun, a common device during the fifteenth and sixteenth centuries. The items are mostly documents on political and religious history. The *Governance* is untitled except by the first chapter heading and a partly visible inscription in a later hand at the top of f. 175b: 'was wrighten to King Henry the sixt by Sir Johani Fortescue Lord Chancelor. De Dominio Regale et politico Johani Fortescue Authore'. At the bottom of the page there is the autograph of the collector: 'Robert Cotton Bruceus'. Throughout the treatise is well written in secretary hand and meticulously presented, with all twenty chapter titles and quotations distinguished by a bolder script. It is complete, finishing at the end of chapter XX, although a later binder has clipped the pages so that some marginal phrases are partly lost. The king named in chapter XIX is Edward IV, yet the later inscription on the first page is Lancastrian in tone, mentioning Henry VI as the king to whom the treatise was dedicated and calling Fortescue 'Lord Chancellor', a title which was only recognised by the Lancastrians. Together with BL MS Additional 48031A (see next item) it has a unique peculiarity: at the end of chapter VI it is missing a phrase, which is present in Laud 593 and all later copies: '... also ferre as mey be possible to us'. This increases the probability that this version, or one very close to it, where the scribe had omitted a phrase from his original, was used by John Vale (an associate of John Multon) to copy the treatise into his book.

London, BL MS Additional 48031A (formerly Yelverton 35), ff. 149a–164a, early 1480s. This bears a watermark of the arms of France on a shield, dating from about 1471. A large collection of official and private letters, historical extracts and political papers which, from internal evidence, can be shown to have been written in the early 1480s, almost certainly by John Vale. He was a servant to Sir Thomas Cook, a rich and powerful London draper, and after his death to his widow, Dame Elizabeth. Vale signed several items in the volume, which was all written, apart from a few later insertions, in the same hand (ff. 94a, 119b, 187b; see Kekewich *et al.*, *Vale's Book*, *passim*). It is in a good, accurate secretary script and the general presentation is professional. The major variations which distinguish this text from other surviving copies have been noticed above: several different chapter headings, e.g. Chapter XI, 'The subsidie that the souldane takith of his subgiettes', and other subheadings in the margins and the fact that the king mentioned in chapter XIX is Henry VI. It is impossible to do more than speculate about why the collection was assembled, although its nature indicates that it might comprise the raw materials for an English history: Vale tried his hand at a short one (ff. 119b–121a). This precedes a collection of political papers that related to the troubled later reign of Henry VI and the civil wars. They include other works by Fortescue – as well as *Governance* there are the *Replication* against the duke of York (f. 134a–b) and two works which are only known from this manuscript and John Stow's later copies (respectively BL MSS Harley 542 and 543): *Example what good counsel helpeth* and *Articles sent by Edward, Prince of Wales, to the earl of Warwick concerning the government of England*. As Vale seems to have made the book for his own purposes, he probably felt free to adapt the contents of some of his material according to his own fancy. This seems the most likely explanation for the minor differences between this text of the *Governance* and the other versions.

Oxford, Bodleian Library MS Digby 145, ff. 131b–159a, copied by Sir Adrian Fortescue in 1532. It contains two main items: *The Vision of Piers Ploughman*, ff. 2a–130b, and the *Governance*, ff. 131b–159a. The watermark is a gloved hand holding a flower, samples of which, with various ornamentation, exist throughout the fifteenth and sixteenth centuries. Both items are written in a good secretary hand. An inscription at the end of the treatise on f. 159a reads: 'And God save the king. Explicit liber compilatus et factus par Johannem Ffortescue militem ... scriptus manu propria mei Adriani Ffortescu militis.1532.' On the next line Sir Adrian Fortescue drew his personal device: a shield containing the letters 'Fforti with an 'A' below them and a decorative line on either side surmounted by his motto 'Loyall pensee'. The letters 'Ihs' are written above the beginning of the text on f. 133a. This is an excellent copy, with all the standard chapter headings centred above the text and quotations distinguished in heavy type. There is a list of contents before the text starts on f. 133a but no title. The chapters run from I to XX and the king mentioned in chapter XIX is Edward IV. It seems likely that, with the exception of Stow's copy Harley 542, later complete versions were based on this manuscript or one very close to it. Of the three early versions described above, this one most closely resembles the stationer Multon's Claudius A viii, the only significant difference being the missing phrase at the end of chapter VI in the Claudius MS.

London, Lambeth Palace MS 262, ff. 106a–128b, late fifteenth and early sixteenth century. A watermark of a glove holding a flower is bound on a blank sheet f. 103. The manuscript, which is professionally written, contains three works by Fortescue, the unique copy of both books of the *De Natura*, ff. 1a–102a, the *Governance*, and the *Declaration*, ff. 129b–140b. The last two items are written by a different scribe from the copyist of the first text, probably in the early sixteenth century. The second part of the manuscript, ff. 106–140, originated from the Carew-Sheldon collection and was bound together with the *De Natura* by Archbishop Sancroft, whose tenure lasted from 1678 to 1691. The *Governance* is concluded at the end of chapter XVIII with the word 'Ffinis', which makes the intention of the copyist unambiguous. Plummer (*Governance of England*, 90–2) thought that this was the earliest of a group of three manuscripts which had a common source, although they differed in sufficient details not to have been copied from each other. (Descriptions of the other two follow.) All three were produced to duplicate the works of Fortescue and this provides evidence of the interest in his writings, especially the *De Laudibus*, which already existed by the sixteenth century. San Merino, CA, Huntingdon Library Ellesmere MS 1131 now makes a fourth, seventeenth-century member of this group which is characterised by ending at chapter XVIII (or earlier in the case of Harley 1757).

Oxford, Bodleian Library MS Digby 198, ff. 48a–75b, first half of the sixteenth century. Three watermarks: a gloved hand holding a crown, three fleur-de-lis with a flower contained within an open box and a flower surmounted by a crown (only the last two types of paper are used in the *Governance*): no exact models of the first two have been found, but the third is close to 6409 (Briquet, *Dictionnaire Historique*, vol. 1, 1544, Neuburg). The volume contains three works by Fortescue: *De Laudibus*, ff. 1a–48a, the *Governance* and an unfinished *Declaration*, ff. 76a–90a. Plummer (*Governance of England*, 91) remarked that on two occasions the Pope was referred to as 'the Bishop of Rome', a turn of phrase used after the beginning of the Protestant reformation in England. He thought that the writing was careless. The volume ends after chapter XVIII with the word 'ffinis'.

London, BL MS Harley 1757, ff. 196a–203b, mid-sixteenth century. The watermark is of of a gloved hand holding a flower. It contains a number of items including a sequence of works by Fortescue: the *Declaration*, ff. 188a–195b, the *Governance* (incomplete), a second incomplete middle section of the *Declaration*, ff. 204a–207b, and the *De Laudibus*, ff. 208a–226a. Clermont identified the script of the last text as belonging to Robert Glover (1543/4–1588) (*Works*, 366). If he was correct in this, as Plummer pointed out, and was referring to the first part (the second being in a different hand), then Glover must also have copied the *Governance*, which is in the same hand. The text finishes abruptly in the middle of chapter XV, which must have been a deliberate decision as the rest of the page is unmutilated and blank.

London, BL MS Harley 542, ff. 126a–139b, late sixteenth century. The watermark is an ornamental jug surmounted by a flower, a very common device in the sixteenth and early seventeenth centuries. A compendium of historical papers assembled by John Stow. The two documents by Fortescue were taken from MS Additional 48031A (see above) and agree with that version in all important respects. The *Governance* is written in Stow's own hand: at the end he wrote, 'Sir John Ffortescu upon the governance of England'. He may well be responsible for assigning this title to the work. This is the only known full copy of this type with its idiosyncratic chapter headings and mention of Henry VI rather than Edward IV. The *Example*, f. 126a, was treated as a preamble to the *Governance* rather than as a rider to the *Advice to Warwick* as it was in Stow's original. A hand, probably later than Stow's time, inscribed a title-page, f. 125a: 'H [Harley ?] Treatise compiled by Sir John Ffortescue knight cheife Justice of England Tempore Regis H 6 upon The Governance of England transcribed by Mr John Stow with his owne hand.'

Oxford, Bodleian Library MS Rawlinson D 69, ff. 1b–19a, third decade of the seventeenth century. The the watermark is an ornate vase bearing the initials 'V H' and surmounted by a flower. This volume contains the Remonstrance of the House of Commons and the Petition of the House of Lords, both made in June 1626; since the same hand seems to have written the *Governance*, it may be dated to approximately the end of that decade. This copy does not seem to have been identified previously by Fortescue's historians, indeed Macray in the Rawlinson Catalogue of 1893 remarks upon the fact that Clermont did not refer to it in his edition. On the cover of the volume there is a contents list which assigns a title to it: 'The difference between Dominium Regale and Dominium Politicum et Regale, made in the time of Edward the 4th'. It is complete although it only has eighteen chapters as the scribe has coalesced chapters XI, XII and XIII, this may simply be a case of the scribe tightening up his version by omitting two short chapter headings. The ending is the same as Digby 145 except that 'God save the king' is omitted. Given the other contents of this volume the omission of this loyalist exclamation is not surprising.

Oxford, Bodleian Library MS Rawlinson B 384, ff. 48a–62a, mid-seventeenth century. The watermark is an ornate jug bearing the initials 'M C' and surmounted by a crescent. The volume contains papers relating to English history. The text is very close to Digby 145 and may have been copied from it or from an intermediary manuscript. There are twenty chapters and the king mentioned in chapter XIX is Edward IV. As is the case with all the other manuscripts, there is no contemporary heading. The wording at the ending with 'God save the king' is identical to Digby 145. The only peculiarity to be found is that, like MS Rawlinson D 69, chapters XI, XII and XIII all share the same heading: 'What off the kinges livelod geven awey mey beste be taken a geyn'. Since, in common with all the other manuscript copies, the chapters are not numbered in the text, this does not appear anomalous. This indicates that the copyist may have taken his version from Rawlinson D 69 or vice versa.

Cambridge, University Library MS Ll. iii. 11, ff. 214a–240a, first half of the seventeenth century. The watermark is of two columns enclosing an ornate decorative motif, no model for which has been found. The volume is a collection of papers mainly relating to English history of the first half of the seventeenth century. At the beginning of the *Governance* the copyist wrote: 'Sir John Ffortescue, knight Lord Cheife Justice of the Kings Bench and as some have holden Lord Cheife Justice of England in the Raigne of King Henrie the 6th and of King Edward the 4th writt a Treatise intituled Jus Regale and Jus Politicum et Regale.' Plummer (*Governance of England*, 93–4), concluded that he must have had access to a copy of the type of Additional 48031A, as the treatise was preceded with 'Example what good councell helpith' and adopted its unique title for chapter XI. On the other hand, this version mentions Edward IV in chapter XIX and also shows signs of having copied certain modernisations of the text from Rawlinson B 384. It contains all the chapters, including XX.

San Marino, CA, Huntingdon Library MS Ellesmere 1131, ff. 2a–26b, seventeenth century. This manuscript was unknown to Clermont and Plummer but was mentioned by Chrimes. It has only been examined on microfilm so no information about watermarks has been gathered. It is written in a professional hand which does not change throughout. The contents of the 'first book' are given on ff. 1a–b, the end of chapter XVIII is concluded with 'Ffinis'. The *Declaration* follows, ff. 31a–40a. There are marginal notes which are in a different, unprofessional hand and which display an interest in the practicalities of government such as sources of revenue and the functions of the council.

Cambridge, Trinity College MS R. 5. 18, ff. 50b–55a, early eighteenth century. An Epitome of the *Governance* in Latin. Part of a volume of political papers written or collected by Mr Beaupre Bell. Thomas Hearne (1678–1735) wrote a note inside the cover, dated 1 September 1733, that Bell was its owner. It commences: 'Epitome singularis eiusdam politici discursus Edwardi 4ti temporibus scriptus ab aliquo magno viro: ad regem de maximis rebus quae ad praesentem suum statum spectabant potime instruendum.' Each of the chapters of the *Governance* was summarised until XIX and XX, when the author recorded in the margin that they had been treated together. It ends with a translation of the praise that Edward would receive if he carried out Fortescue's advice: 'Vivat Edw. 4. Anglorum. Rex.'

Oxford, Bodleian Library MS Rawlinson D 1171 (formerly Rawlinson D Misc. 326), ff. 43a–65b, early eighteenth century. Plummer described this as an 'Epitome' but it is, in fact, an incomplete transcription of the original text by Thomas Hearne. I could not find the heading Plummer described (*Governance of England*, 94), 'Sir John Fortescue prepared for the press. Thursday Jan. 19, 1726'. It ends at the foot of a page half-way through chapter XII and seems to have been derived from a version of the type of Digby 145. Hearne assigned it a title in his contents list: 'Sir John Fortescue's Discourse *de Dominio Politico et Regali* [imperfect]'.

APPENDIX 4

Works Referred to by Sir John Fortescue

Principal sources: Thomas Fortescue, Lord Clermont, *The Works of Sir John Fortescue, Knight* (London: 1869); *The Governance of England by Sir John Fortescue*, ed. C. Plummer (Oxford: 1885); *De Laudibus Legum Anglie*, ed. S.B. Chrimes (Cambridge: 1942); *Sir John Fortescue: On the Laws and Governance of England*, ed. S. Lockwood (Cambridge: 1997).

References are given in the form adopted by Sir John Fortescue or his editors. In many cases, Fortescue used unacknowledged compendia such as the *Auctoritates Aristotelis* and Roger of Waltham's *Compendium Morale*; subsequent opinions about his sources are not cited. See Chapters 4 and 5 for a discussion of his sources.

Of the Title of Edward earl of March (De Titulo Edwardi Comitis Marchie)

A number of references to the Old Testament

Chapter

III. 'the history of the English'.

VII. 'the chronicles and histories of England'.

X. *Compendium Morale*, quoting from Augustine, *De Civitate Dei.*

XII. Augustine, *Against the Manichees.*

Of the Title of the House of York

Old Testament, Genesis, 3.16.

'chronicles in the reaume of France'.

Augustine, 'Quid sunt regna nisi magna latrocina'.

Defensio Juris Domus Lancastriae

Old Testament, Genesis 3:16.

Replication against the claim and title of the duke of York for the crowns of England and France

'cronicles of France and of Seelande'.

De Natura Legis Naturae

Many references to the Old and New Testaments

Part 1

Chapter

I. Aristotle (often referred to as 'the Philosopher'), 'omnia amamus', not identified but there are similar phrases in *Rhetoric*, i, 38 and *Politics*, vii, 14–17. Seneca, Epist. 8.

IV. Augustine, *De Civitate Dei*, xv, xvi.
Josephus, *De Antiquitatum Historiis*, general reference.
Canon Law, *Decretum*, pars i. distinctio i. cap i.

V. Canon Law, *Decretum*, dist. viii. cap i; dist. ix; dist. v. cap i. and 'the gloss'; dist. i. cap. i.
St Thomas Aquinas, *Summa Theologica* in Prima Summae, quaestione xcvi. De Potestate legis humanae. articulo 2.
Varro (probably taken from Vincent of Beauvais, *Speculum Historiale*)
Vincent of Beauvais, *Speculum Historiale*, v, 59; *Eruditio Puerorum Regalium*, cap. iii.

VI. Josephus, *Antiquitatum Jud.* i.11
Civil Law, *Digests*, lib.i. tit.i. lex i.

VII. Canon Law, *Decretum*, pars i. dist. vi.
Augustine, *De Civ. Dei*, xvi.11.
Cicero, *De Officiis*, iii.4
Homer, *Iliad*, Σ.109.
Aquinas, *De Regimine Principum*, i. 10.
Aristotle, *Politics*, v.12.
Seneca, *Naturales Quaestiones*, vii.Ix.3.
Diodorus Siculus, *Bibliotheca Historica*, i. 44, 45.

VIII. Augustine, *De Civ. Dei*, xvi.17.
Vincent of Beauvais, *De Morali Institutione Principum*, and *Speculum Historiale*, i. 101.
Augustine, *De Civ. Dei*, xvi.3.

IX. Augustine, *De Civ. Dei*, xv.20.
Josephus, *Antiquitatum Jud.*, i.3.
Aquinas, *De Reg. Prin.*, i. 12.
Canon Law, *Decretum*, pars i. dist. vii. 1; dist. viii. cap. 3.

XV. Aquinas quoting Aristotle and Augustine in commentary on Peter Lombard, *In 2m librum Sententiarum*, dist. xxxvii.
Boethius, *De Consolatione Philosophiae*, lib. iii. prosa iv.
XVI. Aquinas, *De Reg. Prin.* ii.9.
Egidius Romanus (Giles of Rome), *De Regimine Principum.*
Aquinas, *De Reg. Prin.* iii.12.20; ii.8; iv.1.
XVII. Aquinas, *De Reg.Prin.*i.12.
XVIII. Aquinas, *De Reg.Prin.*i.1.
Aristotle, *Physics*.i.12.
Civil Law, *Digests*, ff. lib.i. tit.1.
Vincent of Beauvais, *De Morali Principum Institutione*, reference to St Gregory the Great, *Morals on Job*, lib. xvii.
XIX. Canon Law, *Decretum*, pars i. dist. v. cap. i.
Augustine, *De Civ. Dei*, xv.3.
XX. Civil Law, *Institutes*, lib. i. tit. 2; *De Jure Naturale gentium et Civili*, φ11.
XXII. Aquinas, *De Reg. Prin.*, ii.9.
XXIV. Egidius Romanus, *De Reg.Prin.*, lib. iii. pars 2, cap. 23.
Aristotle, *Ethics*, v.x.8.
Aristotle, *Politics*, iii, taken from the *Auctoritates.*
XXV. Aquinas, *De Reg. Prin.*, iii.11.
XXVI. Boethius, *De Cons. Phil.*, Iii. metrum, 5, iv. prosa 2.
'Metrista quidam', 'a certain rhymer'.
Boethius, *De Cons. Phil.*, iii. prosa 10.
Aquinas, *De Reg. Prin.*, i.3, 5, 6.
XXVII. Boethius, *De Cons. Phil.*, iii. prosa 5.
Jerome, 'in Glosa super xix. cap. ii *Libri Regum*'; 2 Samuel 19.
XXVIII. Aquinas, *De Reg. Prin.*, i.1.
XXIX. Augustine, *De Civ.Dei*, xix.13.
XXXI. Cicero, *De Officiis*, i.2.
Canon Law, *Decretum*, pars i. dist. viii.4, 'De Veritate'; cap.7, 'Frustra'.
Januensis (Joannes Balbus), *Catholicon*, under the article 'Diffinitio'.
XXXIV. Aquinas, in *Prima Summae*, quest. xcvi. art. 4.
Aquinas, *De Reg. Prin.*, iii.9.
Augustine, *De Civ. Dei*, xix.14, 13.
Aristotle, 'in Primo *Politicorum*' from *Auctoritates.*
Augustine, *De Civ. Dei*, xix.15.

St John Chrysostom, sermon 'Quomodo primus homo omni prelatus sit ...'

XXXV. Anselm. This definition of justice occurs in several if his works, e.g. *Dialogus de Veritate*, v.12.
Augustine, *De Civ. Dei*, xiv.11.

XXXVI. Civil Law, *Digests*, lib. i. tit.1; *De justitia et jure*, lex 1.
Augustine, *De Trinitate*, lib. ix.

XXXVII. Augustine, 'in libro *De Dignitate Conditionis Humanae*'.
Aristotle, *De Coelo et Mundo*, i.1.
Dionysius Areopagita, *De Divinis Nominibus*, chap. ii.
Augustine, 'in sole sunt substantia eius', probably quoted from a spurious source.

XXXVIII. Aquinas, *De Reg. Prin.* iii.9.

XXXIX. Augustine, *De Civ. Dei*, xiv.6.

XL. Peter Lombard, *Commentary* on 1 Cor.11:7.

XLI. Dionysius, *De Divinibus Nominibus*.

XLII. Isidore, *Etymologies*, lib. v. c.2.
Augustine, *Contra Faustum Manichaeum*, xxii.27.
Boethius, *De Cons. Phil.*, iv. prosa vi.
St John Damascene, *De Fide Orthodoxa*, ii.29.
Aquinas, *Summae*, in Prim. Sec. Quest. xci. art.2.
Boethius, *De Cons. Phil.*, iv. prosa x.

XLIII. Canon Law, *Decretum*, pars i. dist. viii. c.2.
Boethius, *De Cons. Phil.*, iv. prosa vi.

XLIV. Aquinas, *De Reg. Prin*, i.14, 15.
Aristotle, *Politics*, vii.
Boethius, *De Cons. Phil.*, iii. prosa. ii.
Aquinas, *De Reg. Prin.*, i. 8.
Aristotle, *Metaphysics*, iii, from *Auctoritates.*
Boethius, *De Cons. Phil.*, iii. prosa ii.
Aquinas, *De Reg. Prin.*, i. 8, 15; iii. 3.

XLV. Aquinas, *ibid.*
Aristotle, 'he who acts by the intellect works for an end'.

XLVI. Aquinas, *De Reg.Prin.*, i.14.
Aristotle, *Ethics*, i.1.

Part II

Chapter

IV. Augustine, *De Civ. Dei*, lib. xviii.
Josephus, *Antiquities*, general references
Aquinas, *De Reg. Prin.*, iii. 11.

VII. Aristotle, *Metaphysics*, i. 3.

VIII. Aristotle, *De Generatione Animalium*, ii.3.
Aquinas, *De Reg. Prin.*, iv.6.

IX. Aristotle, *Politics*, ii.6.
Aquinas, *De Reg. Prin.*, iv.6.
Civil Law, 'ff. *De Regulis Juris*, lege Feminae'.
Civil Law, *Digests*, lib.1. tit. xvii. lex 2.
Canon Law, *Decretum*, pars ii. causa xxxiii. quest. v. cap. 17.
Aristotle, *De Coelo et Mundo*, lib. ii.
Aquinas, *De Reg. Prin.*, i.1.
Aristotle, *Politics*, ii.13.
Aristotle, *Physics*, ii.2.

XVIII. Aristotle, *Politics*, i.2; ii.4.
Aquinas, *Summae*, Prima Pars, quest. xcvi. art 4.
Aquinas, *De Reg. Prin.*, iii.9.
Peter Lombard, *Commentary* on 1 Cor. 11:8, 9.
Aristotle, *Metaphysics*, xi.2.
Hugh of St Victor, *Eruditio Theologica*, De Sacramentis, lib.i. pars vi. cap. 35.
Canon Law, *Decretum*, pars ii. causa xxxiii. quest. 5, cap. 13.
Vincent of Beauvais, *Speculum Historiale*, i.41.

XIX. Hugh of St Victor, *De Sacramentis*, i.vi.34.
Canon Law, *Decretum*, pars ii. causa xxxiii. quest. 5.cap. 13.
Aristotle, *De generatione Animalium*, i.22, ii.2; *Metaphysics* vii.iv.4, 5.

XX. Augustine, 'in libro lxxxiii. quest.' *De Ideis. De Diversis Questionibus*, quest. xlvi.

XXII. Augustine, *De Civ. Dei*, xviii.2.
Aristotle, 'Turpis est pars quae non convenit suo toto', probably from *Metaphysics.*
Diodorus Siculus, ii.46.

XXIII. 'Auctor de Causis' (Alfarabius).

XXIX. Canon Law, *Decretum*, pars i. dist. v. i.
Isidore, *Etymolog.* v.2.

XXX. Boethius, *De Cons. Phil.*, iv. prosa ii.

XXXI. Civil Law, *Digests*, 'De Regulis Juris, lib.1. tit. xvii. lex 120.
Ibid., lex i.

XXXII. *Institutes*, lib. ii. tit. xix.

XXXV. Leonardo Bruni Arentino, *In Libros Morales Aristotelis Ysagogicum*, 'Hinc igitur vides tot esse fines quot sunt actus ...'

XXXVI. Aristotle, *Metaphysics*, chs 4 and 5.

Homer, *Iliad*, H, 18, 19.
Macrobius, *Somnium Scipionis*, lib.i. cap. xiv. para. 15.

XLII. Aquinas, *Prim. Summae*, quest. xcvi. art.4.
Aquinas, *De Reg. Princ.*, iii.9.
Augustine, *De Civ. Dei*, xix. 14, 16.
Aristotle, 'Semper esse aliquod primum et dirigens', an 'Auctoritas' from *Politics*, book 1.
Aquinas, *De Reg. Prin.*, ii.9.
Augustine, *De Civ. Dei*, xiv.10.

XLV. Augustine, *De Civ. Dei*, xix.15.
Aquinas, *Summa*, Prima pars, quest. xcvi. art 4.
Aquinas, *De Reg. Prin.*, ii.9.
Aristotle, *Politics*, i.2.
Augustine, *De Civ. Dei*, xix.15.
Aquinas, *De Reg. Prin.* ii.9.

XLVI. Augustine, *De Civ. Dei*, xviii.21.
Aquinas, *De Reg. Prin.*, i.1.
Aristotle, *Politics*, iii.7.
Augustine, *De Civ. Dei*, xv.8.
Canon Law, *Decretum*, pars ii. causa xxxiii. quest. 5.

XLVIII. Civil Law, *Novellae*, Collatio ix. tit. i. cap. 5 (true reference *Novella Constit.* cxviii).

XLIX. Augustine, *De Civ. Dei*, xix.21.

LI. Canon Law, *Decretum*, pars i. dist. i.

LII. Civil Law, *Codex*, lib. xii. tit. i. lex i.
Civil Law, *Digests*, lib. i. tit. 5.
Civil Law, *Institutes*, lib. i. tit. 15.
Civil Law, *Codex*, lib. x. tit. 31.

LIII. Civil Law, *Digests*, lib. v. tit. i.
Civil Law, *Digests*, lib. i.17. *De Regulis Juris*. lex 2. tit. 4. *De Muneribus et Honoribus*.
Civil Law, *Codex*, lib. x. tit. 40.
Civil Law, *Digests*, lib. i. tit. 9.
Civil Law, *Authenticae*, coll.iv
Civil Law, *Codex*, lib. x. tit. 62.
Civil Law, *Codex*, lib. v. tit. 4.
Civil Law, *Codex*, lib. xii. tit. viii.
Civil Law, *Digests*, lib ii. tit 1. lex 3.
Civil Law, *Digests*, lib. i. tit.iv.
Civil Law, *Codex*, lib. i. tit. xi.
Civil Law, *Digests*, lib. xlviii. tit. 2.

LIV. Civil Law, *Digests*, lib.i. tit. i.

LV. Canon Law, *Decretum*, pars ii. causa xxxiii. quest. v.c.17.
LVII. Augustine, *De Civ. Dei*, ii.1.
Dionysius Cato, '*moralis Catonis versiculus*', lib.i. dist.3.
LIX. Aristotle, *De Caelo et Mundo*, iii.2; *Metaphysics*, xi.x.2.
Augustine, *De Civ. Dei*, xv.22, xix.13.
LXII. Canon Law, *Decretum*, pars ii. causa xxxiii. quest. 5.
LXIII. St Gregory, *Third Letter to Augustine.*
Peter Lombard, lib. ii. dist. 22, G.
Augustine, *Commentary on John* 1:4.
Peter Lombard, lib. ii. dist. 23 G, Commentary on 1 Cor. 11:8, 9.

De Laudibus Legum Anglie

References to the Old and New Testaments

Chapter

I. Civil Law, *Institutes*, Preface.
Helynandus, *De Bono Regimine Principum.*
III. Civil Law, *Institutes*, 1, 2, 3, v.
Pseudo-Aristotelian *Liber de Causis.*
IV. Leonardo Bruni Arentino, *Isagogue of Moral Philosophy.*
Aristotle, *Politics*, 7, viii.5.
Bruni, *Isagogue.*
Aristotle, *Ethics*, 5 i.
William of Auvergne (Parisiensis), *Cur Deus Homo.*
V. Aristotle, 'Nothing is loved unless it is known', origin unknown.
Quintilian, 'The arts would be fortunate if artists alone were to judge them', origin unknown.
'A certain poet', 'All that he is ignorant of, the rustic declares, ought to be despised', origin unknown.
Aristotle, *Metaphysics*, vi. lect. i.
'It is commonly said that "Art has no enemy except the ignorant"', origin unknown.
Aristotle, *Ethics*, vii.x.
VI. 'A certain wise man', 'What a vessel takes when new it tastes of when it is old', origin unknown.
VII. Aristotle, *Ethics*, 1, xiii and *On Generation and Corruption*, II.
VIII. Aristotle, *Physics*, 1, i.
Averroës (The Commentator), Auctoritates, 143.
Aristotle, *Posterior Analytics*, II.

Aristotle, *Physics*, 1, v.
Aristotle, *Topics*, 1.
Aristotle, *Physics*, 1, ii.
Aristotle, *Ethics*, VI, viii.
Seneca, *Letter to Lucilius*.

IX. Civil Law, *Institutes*, 1, 2, 6; *Digest*, 1, 4, 1.
Aristotle, *Politics*, III, lect. 14.
Aquinas, *De Reg. Prin.*, 1, vi.
Fortescue, *De Natura*, I.xvi.

XI. Fortescue, *De Natura*, I.xxvi.

XII. Augustine, *De Civ. Dei*, v.12.
Augustine, *De Civ. Dei*, xvi.17.

XIII. Augustine, *De Civ. Dei*, xix.21.
Aristotle, *Politics*, 1.v.3.
Aristotle, *On the Parts of Animals*, II.iv.
Diodorus Siculus, *Library of History*, II, 35; IV, 76.

XIV. Fortescue, *De Natura*, I.xxvi.
Boethius, *De Cons. Phil.*, IV.ii.24.

XV. *Corpus Iuris Civilis*.

XVI. Aristotle, *Ethics*, V.vii.

XXIV. Aristotle, *Rhetoric*, III. ii.

XXXII. Bernard of Parma, *Glossa Ordinaria*, C.23, x, 2, 20.

XXXIV. Civil Law, *Institutes*, 1, 2, 6; *Digest*, 1, 4, 1.
Fortescue, *De Natura*, I.xxvi.

XXXV. Aristotle, *Rhetoric*, III.ii.

XXXVII. Aquinas, *De Reg. Prin.*, III.xi.
Fortescue, *De Natura*.
Aquinas, *De Reg. Prin.*, I.vi.

XXXIX. Civil Law, *Institutes*, I.10.13; *Corpus Iuris Civilis*, Code 5.27. 8, 10, 11.
Statute of Merton, 1237.
Civil Law, *Code* 6. x. 4. 17.
Civil Law, Accursian gloss, *Institutes*, 1,2, 3, v.

XL. Civil Law, *Institutes*, 1.10.12.
'A certain poet writes, "To whom the people is father, his father is to him nobody and everybody; to whom the father is the people, he has no father"', a Latin proverb.
Augustine, *De Civ. Dei.*, xvi.34.
Canon Law, *Decretal Gregor. IX*, lib. IV, tit. l, cap. xviii.

XLII. Civil Law, Accursian gloss, *Corpus Iuris Civilis*, Code 6, 7, 2.
Civil Law, *Code*, 10, 40. 9.
Littleton's Tenures

XLIII. Civil Law, Accursian gloss, *Digest*, 14, 6, 9, 4.
XLIV. Civil Law, *Novels*, 118, 5.
Aristotle, 'Everyone does boldly what he knows himself to be not deficient in', source unknown.
XLVI. Civil Law, *Institutes*, 4. 1. 5; 1. 16. 1.
XLVIII. Statute, 36 Edward III, st. I, ch. 15.
LIV. Vegetius, *De Re Militari*.
Vincent of Beauvais, *De Princ. Mor. Instit.*
Robert II of France, hymn, 'The grace of the Holy Spirit be with us'.
Vincent of Beauvais, *De Princ. Mor. Instit.*, ch. 15.
Civil Law, *Code* 6. 23. 19.

The Governance of England

Chapter
I. Aquinas, *De Reg. Prin.*
Roger of Waltham, *Compendium Morale*.
Giles of Rome (Egidius Romanus), *De Reg. Prin.*
Aquinas, *De Reg. Prin.*
II. Civil Law, *Institutes*, lib.i. tit.ii.
Aristotle, *Politics*.
Diodorus Siculus, *Library of History*, bk i (ii), bk iii (iv).
IV. Aquinas, *De Reg. Prin.*, i.c.1.
V. Aristotle, *Ethics*, I.viii.
VI. St Bernard of Clairvaux, *Letters*.
VIII. Aquinas, *De Reg. Prin.*, iii.c.11.
IX. Aristotle, *Politics*, vii.17, 13.
'The cronicles of every reaume, and in especiall of Spayne and Denmarke'.
XII. Aristotle, *De Generatione et Corruptione*, i.2.
XIV. The wise man, 'Ubi multa consilia ibi salus' (where there is much advice, there is security).
XVI. 'the cronicules of the Lacedemonyes and of the Atheniences'.

Declaration upon certain writings late sent out of Scotland

St Alban's Chronicle.
Flores Historiarum.
Policronicon.
Petrus Pictavensis, *Chronicle*.

Nicholas Tryvet, *Chronicle.*
Old Testament, Judges 11.
Canon Law, Gratian, *Decretum.*
Aquinas, *Summa Theologica,* secunda secunde, 'and in all his bokes, where as he asketh eny questions'.
Old Testament, Genesis 3:16.
Apostle, 'Omnis viri caput Cristus est'.
New Testament, Luke 1:32, 33.
Exchequer Account 42–48, Edward III.
Ralph de Diceto, *Chronicle.*
Flores Historiarum.

APPENDIX 5

Modern English-Language Editions Containing Works by Sir John Fortescue

S.B. Chrimes, *Sir John Fortescue. 'De Laudibus Legum Anglie'* (Cambridge: 1942).

M.L. Kekewich, 'The Lancastrian Court in Exile', *The Lancastrian Court*, ed. J. Stratford (Donington: 2003) 95–110, appendix 2, translation of four memoirs sent by Fortescue to the French chancellor.

M.L. Kekewich, *Sir John Fortescue and the Governance of England* (Woodbridge, 2018). Appendix 1, 'Of the Title of Edward, earl of March'; Appendix 2, 'Declaration upon certain writings late sent out of Scotland'.

M.L. Kekewich, 'Thou shalt be under the power of the man': Sir John Fortescue and the Yorkist Succession', *NMS*, 42 (1998) 188–230, appendix 1, 'Of the Title of the House of York'.

M.L. Kekewich, C. Richmond, A.F. Sutton, L. Visser-Fuchs and J.L. Watts, eds, *The Politics of Fifteenth-Century England: John Vale's Book* (Stroud: 1995). *The 'Replication' against the claim of the House of York*, 202–3; *Articles sent by Edward, Prince of Wales, to the earl of Warwick concerning the government of England*, 222–5; *Example what good counseill helpith*, 225–6; *The Governance of England*, 226–50.

S. Lockwood, *Sir John Fortescue on the Laws and Governance of England* (Cambridge: 1997) also appendix A, 'Extracts from On the Nature of the Law of Nature'; appendix B, 'Example of how good council helps'; appendix C, 'Articles to the Earl of Warwick'.

Bibliography

Manuscripts

Cambridge

University Library

MS Ff 5 22, Ll iii 11

St John's College

MS 76 D1

Chicago

Newberry Library

MS f 37, Ry 20

Exeter

Devon County Record Office

1262 M/FS 1; 1262 M/T 570; 1262 M/T 571; 1262 M/T 708; 1262 M/TG 6; 1262 M/TG 7; 1262 M/TG 9; 1262 M/TN1; 1262 M/TSU 2; 1262 TG 10

Hatfield

Hatfield House

MS Hatfield 230.4

Kansas

University of Kansas, Watson Library

MS C 63

London

British Library

MSS Additional 4696, 36682 B, 48005, 48031 A, 48063; MSS Cotton Vespasian F ix, Vitellius E x, Claudius A viii; MSS Harley 542, 543, 545, 889, 1091, 1538, 1757, 4763, 7353; MS Lansdowne 205; MSS Royal 17 D xv, App. 89

Corporation of London Record Office

'London Journal'

Lambeth Palace Library

Lambeth MS 262

Lincoln's Inn

Black Books

The National Archives

Chancery, Inquisitions Post Mortem C 139/43/6; C 140/41/39; C 145/323/50
Close Rolls, C 54/23
Common Pleas 25/1/293/73/411
Exchequer, Issue Rolls, E 101/586/10, E 403/64, Tellers' Rolls E 405/53
Fine Rolls, C 60/189
King's Bench, Term Indictment Files KB 9/255/1; KB 9/269
Patent Rolls, C 66/322, 324
Sion College, MS L 40.2/E 43

New Haven

Yale Law School Lillian Goldman Library

MSS G & St 11 no. 1

Oxford

Bodleian Library

MSS Digby 145, 198; MS James 28; MS Laud Misc. 585; MS Laud Misc. 593; MS Rawlinson A 398

Magdalen College

MS Fastolf 42

Paris

Bibliothèque nationale de France

Collection de Lorraine Ms 26
Fonds fr. MSS 3887, 4054, 6602, 6964, 6975, 6977, 20685, 20936,32511

Printed Primary Sources

Accounts and Papers Printed by Order of the House of Commons, vol. 62 (London: 1878)

Ancient Kalendars and Inventories of His Majesty's Exchequer, ed. F. Palgrave, 3 vols (London: 1836)

Ashby, George, *Poems*, ed. M. Bateson (London: 1899)

Atkins, R., *The Ancient and Present State of Gloucestershire* (London: 1712), republished in 1974 with an introduction by B.S. Smith

Les Auctoritates Aristotelis. Un florilège medieval. Étude historique et édition critique, ed. J. Hamesse (Louvain: 1974)

Basin, Thomas, *Histoire des règnes de Charles VII et de Louis XI*, 4 vols (Paris: 1859)

Bentley, S. ed., *Excerpta Historica or Illustrations of English History* (London: 1831)

Bernard, E., *Catalogus Librorum Manuscriptorum Angliae et Hiberniae*, 2 vols (Oxford: 1679)

Bibliotheca Historica of Diodorus Siculus translated by John Skelton, ed. M. Salter and H.L.R. Edwards, 2 vols (London: 1956)

Bolingbroke: Political Writings, ed. D. Armitage (Cambridge: 1997)

Briquet, C.M., *Les Filigranes: Dictionnaire Historique des Marques du Papier, 1282–1600*, 4 vols (Paris, London, etc.: 1907)

Calendar of Close Rolls, Henry V, 1, Henry VI, 1–6, Edward IV, 1–3, HMSO (London: 1929–1953)

Calendar of Entries in the Papal Registers Relating to Great Britain and Ireland, vol. 9, *Papal Letters, 1455–64*; vol. 13, *Papal Letters, 1471–84*, parts I and II, ed. J.A. Twemlow (London: 1921, 1955)

Calendar of Fine Rolls, Henry VI, 15–19, HMSO (London: 1935–1939)

Calendar of Inquisitions Post Mortem Preserved in the Public Record Office, Henry VI, 22–26 (London: 2003–2009), Henry VII HMSO second series, 1–3 (London: 1898–1989)

Calendar of Patent Rolls, Henry V, 1–2 (London: 1910), Henry VI, 1–6 (London: 1901–1910), Edward IV, 1–3 (London: 1897–1901)

Calendar of the Plea and Memoranda Rolls Preserved Among the Archives of the Corporation of the City of London at the Guildhall, 1437–1457, ed. P.E. Jones (Cambridge: 1954)

Calendars of the Proceedings in Chancery in the Reign of Queen Elizabeth with Earlier Proceedings from Richard II (London: 1830)

Calendar of State Papers and Manuscripts Existing in the Archives of the Collection of Milan, ed. A.B. Hinds, vol. 1 (London: 1912)

Catalogue of Ancient Deeds in the Public Record Office, ed. H.C. Maxwell-Lyte (London: 1890–)

Chartier, Alain, *Fifteenth-Century English Translations of Alain Chartier's 'Le Traité de l'Espérance' and 'Le Quadrilogue Invectif'*, ed. M.S. Blayney, EETS original series 270, 281 (London: 1974, 1980)

Chastellain, G., *Oeuvres*, ed. K. de Lettenhove, 8 vols (Brussels: 1863–66)

——, *Le Temple de Bocace*, ed. S. Bliggenstorfer, *Romanica Helvetica* 104 (Berne: 1988)

Commentaries of Pius II, ed. L.C. Gabel, trans. F.A. Gragg (Northampton, MA: 1936–40)

Diodorus Siculus, *Bibliotheca Historica*, ed. F.M. Salter and H.L.R. Edwards, 2 vols (1956, 1957)

Dunstan, G.R., ed., *Register of Edmund Lacy, Bishop of Exeter, 1420–1455, Registrum Commune*, 5 vols (Torquay: 1963–72)

England and France in the Fifteenth Century: The Contemporary French Tract entitled 'The Debate between the Heralds of France and England', ed. and trans. H. Pyne (London: 1870)

Escouchy, M. d', *Chronique*, ed. G. du Fresne de Beaucourt, 3 vols (Paris: 1863–64)

Fabyan, Robert, *The New Chronicles of England and France*, ed. H. Ellis (London: 1811)

Fortescue, J., *De Politica Administratione; et legibus civilibus florentissimi regni Anglie commentarius*, pub. E. Whitechurch (London: 1545/6)

——, *A Learned Commendation of the Politique Laws of England*, trans. Robert Mulcaster (London: 1567)

——, *De Laudibus Legum Anglie*, ed. J. Selden (London: 1616)

——, *The Difference between an Absolute and a Limited Monarchy as it more particularly regards the English Constitution by Sir John Fortescue Knight*, ed. J. Fortescue Aland (London: 1714)

——, *De Laudibus Legum Anglie*, trans. into English by Francis Gregor who attached notes by John Selden (London: 1737)

——, *De Laudibus Legum Anglie*, ed. A. Amos (Cambridge: 1825)

——, *The Commodities of England*, ed. T. Fortescue, Lord Clermont, privately published (1863)

——, *The Declaration upon certain writings late sent out of Scotland*, ed. T. Fortescue, Lord Clermont, privately published (1863)

——, *De Natura Legis Naturae*, ed. T. Fortescue, Lord Clermont, privately published (1864)

——, 1: *The Works of Sir John Fortescue Knight*; 2: *A History of the Family of Fortescue in all its Branches*, ed. Thomas Fortescue, Lord Clermont, 2 vols (London: 1869), also the same reproduced by University Microfilms International (Ann Arbor, MI: 1981)

——, *The Governance of England by Sir John Fortescue*, ed. C. Plummer (Oxford: 1885)

——, *De Laudibus Legum Anglie*, ed. S.B. Chrimes (Cambridge: 1942)

——, *On the Laws and Governance of England*, ed. S. Lockwood (Cambridge: 1997)

Forty-Fourth Annual Report of the Deputy Keeper of the Public Records (London: 1883)

Forty-Eighth Annual Report of the Deputy Keeper of Public Records (London: 1887)

Four English Political Tracts of the Later Middle Ages, ed. J.P. Genet, Camden Society (London: 1977)

Great Chronicle of London, ed. A.H. Thomas and I.D. Thornley, microprint (Gloucester: 1983)

Gregory's Chronicle, The Historical Collections of a Citizen of London, 'William Gregory's Chronicle of London', ed. J. Gairdner, 3 parts (London: 1876) vol. 3, 57–239

Haenel, G., *Catalogi Librorum Manuscriptorum qui in Bibliothecis Galliae etc. Asservantur* (Leipzig: 1830)

Hall, E., *Chronicle Containing the History of England during the Reign of Henry IV and Succeeding Monarchs to the End of the Reign of Henry VIII*, ed. H. Ellis (London: 1809)

Hingeston, F.C., ed., *Register of Edmund Stafford, Bishop of Exeter, 1395–1419* (London: 1886)

Historical Manuscripts Commission, *Report on the Manuscripts of the Late Reginald Rawdon Hastings*, 4 vols (London: 1928–47)

Historie of the Arrivall of Edward IV in England, ed. J. Bruce (London: 1838)

Hotman, F., *Antitribonianus sive dissertatio de studio legum*, ed. G. Beyer (Lipsiae: 1704)

Issues of the Exchequer, Henry III to Henry VI, ed. F. Devon (London: 1837)

John Benet's Chronicle for the Years 1400–1462, ed. G.L. and M.A. Harriss, Camden Miscellany 24 (London: 1972)

Kingsford, C.L., *English Historical Literature in the Fifteenth Century* (Oxford: 1913)

Kingsford's Stonor Letters and Papers, 1290–1483, ed. C. Carpenter, 2 vols (Cambridge: 1996)

Letters and Papers Illustrative of the Wars of the English in France, ed. J. Stevenson, 2 vols (London: 1861, 1864)

Letters and Papers of John Shillingford, Mayor of Exeter, 1447–1450, ed. S.A. Moore (London: 1871)

Libelle of Englyshe Polycye, ed. G. Warner (Oxford: 1926)

Literae Cantuarienses: The Letter Books of the Monastery of Christ Church Canterbury, ed. J.B. Sheppard, 3 vols (London: 1887–89)

Machiavelli, N., *The Prince*, ed. M.L. Kekewich, trans. C.E. Detmold (Ware: 1997)

Manors of Norton St Philip and Hinton Charterhouse, 1535–1691, ed. C.J. Brett, Somerset Record Society (Bristol: 2007)

Medieval Account Books of the Mercers of London, ed. L. Jefferson, 2 vols (Aldershot: 2008)

On the Government of Rulers, 'De Regimine Principum': Ptolemy of Lucca with Portions Attributed to Thomas Aquinas, ed. and trans. J.M. Blythe (Philadelphia: 1997)

Parliament Rolls of Medieval England, 1275–1504, ed. C. Given-Wilson, 16 vols (Woodbridge/Leicester: 2005).

Paston Letters and Papers, ed. J. Gairdner, 6 vols (London: 1904)

Paston Letters and Papers of the Fifteenth Century, ed. N. Davis and vol. 3, R. Beadle and C. Richmond, 3 vols (Oxford: 2004, 2005)

The Politics of Fifteenth-Century England: John Vale's Book, ed. M.L. Kekewich, C. Richmond, A.F. Sutton, L. Visser-Fuchs and J.L. Watts (Stroud: 1995)

Prétensions des Anglois à la Couronne de France, ed. R. Anstruther (London: 1847)

Prince, J., *Danmonii Orientales Illustres or the Worthies of Devon* (Exeter: 1701)

Proceedings and Ordinances of the Privy Council of England, ed. H. Nicholas (London: 1835)

Rapin de Thoyras, *History of England* (London: 1751)

Records of the Honourable Society of Lincoln's Inn: The Black Books, vol. 1, *Admissions from 1422 to 1586* (London: 1897)

Report from the Committee Appointed to View the Cottonian Library (London: 1732)

Rotuli Parliamentorum, ed. J. Strachey, J. Pridden and E. Upham, 7 vols (London: 1832)

Rotulorum Patentium et Clausorum Cancellarie Hiberniae Calendarium, vol. 1, part 1 (Dublin: 1828)

Rymer, T., *Foedera*, 20 vols (London: 1641–1713)

Sallust, *The Catiline of Sallust*, ed. G.H. Nall (London: 1948)

Seipp, D.S., *Medieval English History: An Index and Paraphrase of Printed Year Book Reports, 1268–1535* (Boston: 2007)

Short Scottish Prose Chronicles, ed. D. Embree, E.D. Kennedy and K. Daly (Woodbridge: 2012)

Statutes of the Realm, Record Commission, 11 vols (London: 1810–23)

Stow, J., *The Annales of England* (London: 1605)

Supplications from England and Wales in the Registers of the Apostolic Penitentiary, 1410–1503, ed. P.D. Clarke and P.N.R. Zutshi, 3 vols, Canterbury and York Society (Woodbridge: 2013, 2014)

Tanner, T., *Bibliotheca Britannico-Hibernica sive de scriptoribus* (London: 1748)

Three Fifteenth Century Chronicles, ed. J. Gairdner (London: 1880)

Trevelyan Papers Prior to 1588, ed. J. Payne Collier (London: 1857)

Vaesen, J. and E. Charavay, eds, *Lettres de Louis XI, roi de France*, 11 vols (Paris: 1883–1909)

Warkworth, John, *A Chronicle of the First Thirteen Years of Edward the Fourth*, ed. J.O. Halliwell (London: 1839)

Waterhouse, E., *Fortescutus Illustratus or a Commentary (with large portions of the text) on that Nervous Treatise 'De Laudibus Legum Anglie'* (London: 1663)

Wauvrin, Jean de, *Anchiennes Chroniques d'Angleterre*, ed. E. Dupont, 3 vols (Paris: 1858–63)

Westcote, T., *View of Devonshire in MDCXXX with a Pedigree of Most of its Gentry*, ed. G. Oliver and P. Jones (Exeter: 1845)

Yearbooks of Henry VI, vols 1–20 (London: 1552–82)

Secondary Sources

Albanès, J.H., 'La bibliothèque du Roi René', *Revue des Sociétés Savants des Départements*, 8 (1875) 301–11

Alexander, J.J., 'Devon County Members of Parliament: The Later Plantagenet Period (1399–1485)', *Report and Transactions of the Devonshire Association*, 46 (1914) 478–96

Allen, A., 'Yorkist Propaganda: Pedigree, Prophecy and the "British History" in the Reign of Edward IV', *Patronage, Pedigree and Power in Later Medieval England*, ed. C.D. Ross (Gloucester: 1979) 171–92

Anglo, S., 'The British History in Early Tudor Propaganda', *BJRL*, 44 (1961) 17–48

Armstrong, C.A.J., 'The Inauguration Ceremonies of the Yorkist Kings', *TRHS*, 30 (1948) 51–73

Baker, J.H., *The Order of Sergeants* (London: 1984)

——, *The Legal Profession and the Common Law: Historical Essays* (London: 1986)

——, *An Introduction to English Legal History* (London: 1990)

——, *Readers and Readings in the Inns of Court and Chancery* (London: 2000)

——, 'Westminster Hall, 1097–1997', *The Common Law Tradition: Lawyers, Books and the Law* (London and Rio Grande: 2000) 247–62

——, *The Men of Court, 1440–1550*, 2 vols (London: 2012)

——, 'Tudor Pedigree Rolls and Their Uses', *Heralds and Heraldry in Shakespeare's England*, ed. N. Ramsay (Donington: 2014) 105–24

Barron, C., 'London and the Crown', *The Crown and Local Communities in England and France in the Fifteenth Century*, ed. J.R.L. Highfield and R. Jeffs (Gloucester: 1981) 88–109

Beddard, R.A., 'Thomas Allen and John Selden and the 1616 Edition of Fortescue's *De Laudibus Legum Anglie*', *Book Collector*, 53, 4 (2004) 533–41

Bedford, H., *The Hereditary Right to the Crown of England Asserted* (London: 1713)

Bennett, M., 'Edward III's Entail and the Succession to the Crown, 1376–1471', *EHR*, 113 (1998) 580–607

——, 'Henry IV, the Royal Succession and the Crisis of 1406', *The Reign of Henry IV, 1403–1413*, ed. G. Dodd and D. Biggs (York: 2008) 9–27

Berkowitz, D.S., *John Selden's Formative Years: Politics and Society in Early Seventeenth-Century England* (London and Toronto: 1988)

Blayney, M., 'Sir John Fortescue and Alain Chartier's *'Traité de l'Espérance'*', *MLR*, 48 (1953) 385–90

Blatcher, M., *The Court of King's Bench, 1450–1550: A Study in Self-Help* (London: 1978)

Blomfield, F., continued by C. Parkin, *An Essay Towards a Topographical History of the County of Norfolk*, 11 vols (London: 1805–10)

Blythe, J.M., *Ideal Government and the Mixed Constitution in the Middle Ages* (Princeton: 1992)

Bolton, J.L., *Money in the Medieval English Economy, 973–1489* (Manchester: 2012)

Born, L.K., 'The Perfect Prince: A Study in Thirteenth-Century and Fourteenth-Century Ideals', *Speculum*, 3 (1928) 470–504

Britnell, R.H., *The Commercialisation of English Society, 1000–1500* (Manchester: 1996)

Briggs, C.F., *Giles of Rome's 'De Regimine Principum': Reading and Writing Politics at Court and University, c.1275–c.1525* (Cambridge: 1999)

Broadway, J., *'No historie so meete': Gentry Culture and the Development of Local History in Elizabethan and Early Stuart England* (Manchester: 2006)

Brooks, C.W., *Lawyers, Litigation and English Society since 1450* (London and Rio Grande: 1998)

Brown, A.L., *The Governance of Late Medieval England, 1272–1461* (London: 1989)

Brown, L., 'Continuity and Change in the Parliamentary Justifications of the Fifteenth-Century Usurpations', *The Fifteenth Century VII: Conflicts, Consequences and the Crown in the Late Middle Ages*, ed. L. Clark (Woodbridge: 2007) 157–73

Bryce, W. Moir, 'The Black Friars of Edinburgh', *The Book of the Old Edinburgh Club*, vol. 3 (Edinburgh: 1910) 13–104

Burns, J.H., 'Fortescue and the Political Theory of *dominium*', *Historical Journal*, 28 (1985) 777–97

——, *Lordship, Kingship and Empire: The Idea of Monarchy, 1400–1525*, Carlyle Lectures 1988 (Oxford: 1992)

Callahan, E.T., 'Blood, Sweat and Wealth: Fortescue's Theory of the Origin of Property', *History of Political Thought*, 17 (1996) 21–35

Calmette, J. and Périnelle, G., *Louis XI et l'Angleterre, 1461–1483* (Paris: 1930)

Campbell, J., *Lives of the Lord Chancellors*, 10 vols (London: 1845–7)

——, *Lives of the Chief Justices of England*, 2 vols (London: 1849)

Carpenter, C., *Locality and Polity: A Study in Warwickshire Landed Society, 1401–1499* (Cambridge: 1992)

——, *The Wars of the Roses: Politics and the Constitution of England, c.1437–1509* (Cambridge: 1997)

Castor, H., *The King, the Crown and the Duchy of Lancaster: Public Authority and Private Power, 1399–1461* (Oxford: 2000)

——, *Blood and Roses: The Paston Family in the Fifteenth Century* (London: 2004)

Cawse, G.A., *Modbury* (London: 1860)

Cherry, M., 'The Courtenay Earls of Devon. The Formation and Disintegration of a Late Medieval Aristocratic Affinity', *Southern History*, 1 (1979) 71–97

——, 'The Struggle for Power in Mid-Fifteenth-Century Devonshire', *Patronage, the Crown and the Provinces*, ed. R.A. Griffiths (Gloucester: 1981) 123–44

Chrimes, S.B., *English Constitutional Ideas in the Fifteenth Century* (Cambridge: 1936)

Clark, L. and Carpenter, C. eds, *The Fifteenth Century IV: Political Culture in Fifteenth Century Britain* (Woodbridge: 2004)

Clifton, M., *Three English Martyrs, Knights of St John: Venerable Thomas Dingley, Blessed Adrian Fortescue, Blessed David Gonson* (Liverpool: 1991)

Cole, A., 'Staging Advice in Oxford, New College MS 288: On Thomas Chaundler and Thomas Bekyngton', *After Arundel: Religious Writing in Fifteenth-Century England*, ed. V. Gillespie and K. Ghosh (Turnhout: 2011) 245–63

Coleman, J., '*Dominium* in Thirteenth and Fourteenth-Century Political Thought and its Seventeenth-Century Heirs: John of Paris and Locke', *Political Studies*, 33 (1985) 73–100

Colley, L., Review of A. Blick, *Beyond Magna Carta: A Constitution for the United Kingdom* (London: 2015) *TLS*, 18 September 2015, 4

Cromartie, A., 'The Common Law, Counsel and Consent in Fortescue's Political Thought', *The Fifteenth Century IV: Political Culture in Late Medieval Britain*, ed. L. Clark and C. Carpenter (Woodbridge: 2004)

——, *The Constitutionalist Revolution: An Essay in the History of England. 1450–1642* (Cambridge: 2006)

——, 'The Idea of Common Law as Custom', *The Nature of Customary Law: Legal, Historical and Philosophical Persectives*, ed. J.B. Murphy and A. Perreau-Saussine (Cambridge: 2007) 203–27

Cron, B.M., 'Margaret of Anjou and the Lancastrian March on London, 1461', *The Ricardian*, 11 (1999) 590–615

Dawson, J., *John Knox* (New Haven and London: 2015)

Dodd, G., *Justice and Grace: Private Petitioning and the English Parliament in the Late Middle Ages* (Oxford: 2007)

Doe, N., 'Fifteenth-Century Concepts of Law: Fortescue and Pecock', *History of Political Thought*, 10 (1989) 257–80

——, *Fundamental Authority in Late Medieval English Law* (Cambridge: 1990)

Doyle, I.A., 'An Unrecognised Piece of *Piers the Plowman's Creed* and Other Work by Its Scribe', *Speculum*, 24 (1959) 428–36

Dumont, C.E., *Histoire de la ville de Saint Mihiel*, 4 vols (Paris and Nancy: 1860–64)

——, *Les ruines de la Meuse*, 5 vols (Paris and Nancy: 1869)

Elrington Ball, F., *The Judges in Ireland*, 2 vols (London: 1926)

Favier, J., *Le Roi René* (Fayard: 2008)

Ferguson, A.B., 'Fortescue and the Renaissance: A Study in Transition', *Studies in the Renaissance*, 6 (1959) 175–94.

Ferster, J., *Fictions of Advice: The Literature and Politics of Counsel in Late Medieval England* (Philadelphia: 1996)

Fortescue, T., Lord Clermont, *A History of the Family of Fortescue in All Its Branches* (London: 1880)

Friedrichs, R.L., 'Ralph Lord Cromwell and the Politics of Fifteenth-Century England', *NMS* (1988) 32, 207–27

Genet, J.P., 'Les idées sociales de Sir John Fortescue', *Économies et sociétés au Moyen Âge: Mélanges offerts à Edouard Perroy* (Paris: 1973) 446–61

——, 'New Politics or New Language? The Words of Politics in Yorkist and Early Tudor England', *The End of the Middle Ages? England in the Fifteenth and Sixteenth Centuries*, ed. J.L. Watts (Aberystwyth: 1996) 23–64

——, 'Empire and the English Identity: Reflections on the King of England's *Dominium*', *The Plantagenet Empire*, ed. P. Crooks, D. Green and W.M. Ormrod, Harlaxton Medieval Studies 26 (Donington: 2016) 35–48

Gill, P.E., 'Politics and Propaganda in Fifteenth-Century England: The Polemical Writings of Sir John Fortescue', *Speculum*, 46 (1971) 333–47

Gillespie, J.L., 'Sir John Fortescue's Concept of the Royal Will', *NMS*, 23 (1979) 47–65

Gilson, J.P., 'A Defence of the Proscription of the Yorkists in 1459', *EHR*, 26 (1911) 512–25

Green, J.R., *A Short History of the English People*, ed. R. Hudson (London: 1992)

Green, R.F., *Poets and Princepleasers: Literature and the English Court in the Middle Ages* (Toronto: 1980)

Greenfield, L., *The Spirit of Capitalism: Nationalism and Economic Growth* (Cambridge, MA: 2002)

Griffiths, R.A., *The Reign of King Henry VI: The Exercise of Royal Authority* (London: 1981)

——, 'Local Rivalries and National Politics: The Percies, the Nevilles and the Duke of Exeter, 1452–1454', *King and Country: England and Wales in the Fifteenth Century* (London: 1991) 321–64

Gross, A., *The Dissolution of the Lancastrian Kingship: Sir John Fortescue and the Crisis of Monarchy in Fifteenth-Century England* (Stamford: 1996)

Guy, J., 'Sir Thomas More and Christopher St German: The Battle of the Books', 95–120; 'The King's Council and Political Participation', 121–47, *Reassessing the Henrician Age: Humanism, Politics and Reform, 1500–1550*, ed. A. Fox and J. Guy (Oxford: 1986)

Hammond, P.W., *The Battles of Barnet and Tewkesbury* (Stroud: 1990)

Hanham, A., 'Pleas, Pigs and Peascods: Three Unpublished Stonor Accounts', *The Ricardian*, 24 (2014) 113–19

Harriss, G.L., 'Medieval Doctrines in the Debates on Supply, 1610–1629', *Faction and Parliament: Essays on Early Stuart History*, ed. K. Sharpe (London and New York: 1985) 73–103

——, *Cardinal Beaufort: A Study of Lancastrian Ascendancy and Decline* (Oxford: 1988)

——, 'The King and His Subjects', *Fifteenth-Century Attitudes: Perceptions of Society in Late Medieval England*, ed. R. Horrox (Cambridge: 1994) 13–28

——, *Shaping the Nation: England 1360–1461* (Oxford: 2005)

Harvey, I.M.W., *Jack Cade's Rebellion of 1450* (Oxford: 1991)

Hastings, M., *The Court of Common Pleas in Fifteenth-Century England: A Study in Legal Administration and Procedure* (Ithaca, NY: 1971)

Head, C., 'Pope Pius II and the Wars of the Roses', *Archivum Historiae Pontificae*, 8 (1970) 139–78

Hepburn, F., 'The Queen in Exile: Representing Margaret of Anjou in Art and Literature', *The Fifteenth Century XI: Concerns and Preoccupations*, ed. L. Clark (Woodbridge: 2012) 61–90

Hicks, M., 'The Case of Sir Thomas Cook, 1468', *EHR*, 93 (1978) 82–96

——, *False, Fleeting, Perjur'd Clarence: George, Duke of Clarence, 1449–1478* (Gloucester: 1980)

——, 'St Katherine's Hospital, Heytesbury: Prehistory, Foundation and Re-foundation, 1408–72', *Richard III and His Rivals: Magnates and Their Motives in the Wars of the Roses* (London: 1991) 119–32

——, *Bastard Feudalism* (London: 1995)

——, *Warwick the Kingmaker* (Oxford: 1998)

——, 'A Minute of the Lancastrian Council at York, 20 January, 1461', *Northern History*, 35 (1999) 214–21

Hinton, R.W.K., 'English Constitutional Theories from Sir John Fortescue to Sir John Eliot', *EHR*, 75 (1960) 410–25

History of Parliament, The House of Commons, 1386–1421, ed. L. Clark, C. Rawcliffe and J.S. Roskell, 4 vols (Stroud: 1992)

Holdsworth, W.S., *The History of English Law*, 17 vols (London: 1922)

Holmes, G.A., 'The Libel of English Policy', *EHR*, 76 (1961) 193–216

Hudson, J.G.H., *F.W. Maitland and the Englishness of English Law*, Selden Society (London: 2007) 3–31

Hughes, J., *Arthurian Myths and Alchemy: The Kingship of Edward IV* (Stroud: 2002)

Ibbetson, D., 'Custom in Medieval Law', *The Nature of Customary Law*, ed. J.B. Murphy and A. Perreau-Saussine (Cambridge: 2007) 151–75

Ives, E.W., *The Common Lawyers of Pre-Reformation England, Thomas Kebell: A Case Study* (Cambridge: 1983)

Jacob, E.F., 'Sir John Fortescue and the Law of Nature', *Bulletin of the John Rylands Library*, 18 (1934) 359–76

——, *The Fifteenth Century, 1399–1485* (Oxford: 1961)

Jenks, S., 'Bills of Custody in the Reign of Henry VI', *Journal of Legal History*, 23 (2002) 197–222

Johnson, P.A., *Duke Richard of York, 1411–1460* (Oxford: 1988)

Judd, A., *The Life of Thomas Bekyngton* (Chichester: 1961)

Kekewich, M.L., 'The Attainder of the Yorkists in 1459: Two Contemporary Accounts', *BIHR*, 55 (1982) 25–34

——, 'John Fortescue Junior: An Upwardly Mobile Gentleman, *c.*1400–1442', *Southern History*, 17 (1995) 1–23

——, '"Thou shalt be under the power of the man": Sir John Fortescue and the Yorkist Succession', *NMS*, 42 (1998) 189–230

——, 'The Lancastrian Court in Exile', *The Lancastrian Court*, ed. J. Stratford (Donington: 2003) 95–110

——, 'The Mysterious Dr Makerell: His General Pardon of 27 November 1469', *Much Heaving and Shoving: Late Medieval Gentry and Their Concerns. Essays for Colin Richmond*, ed. M. Aston and R. Horrox (Lavenham: 2005) 45–54

——, *The Good King: René of Anjou and Fifteenth-Century Europe* (Basingstoke: 2008)

Kelley, D.R., *Foundations of Modern Historical Scholarship: Language, Law and History in the French Renaissance* (New York and London: 1970)

——, *History, Law and the Human Sciences: Medieval and Renaissance Perspectives* (London: 1984)

——, *The Human Measure: Social Thought in the Western Legal Tradition* (Cambridge, MA, London: 1990)

Kelly, M.R.L.L., 'Sir John Fortescue and the Political Dominium: The People, the Common Weal and the King', *Constitutions and the Classics: Patterns of Constitutional Thought from Fortescue to Bentham*, ed. D. Galliga (Oxford: 2014) 51–85

Kempsall, M.S., *The Common Good in Late Medieval Thought* (Oxford: 1999)

Kendrick, T., *British Antiquity* (London and New York: 1970)

Kingsford, C.L., 'Historical Notes on Medieval London Houses', *London Topographical Record*, 10 (1916) 44–144

——, *English Historical Literature in the Fifteenth Century* (Oxford: 1913)

Kleineke, H., 'Why the West was Wild: Law and Disorder in Fifteenth-Century Cornwall and Devon', *The Fifteenth Century, III: Authority and Subversion*, ed. L. Clark (Woodbridge: 2003) 75–93

——, 'The Widening Gap: The Practice of Parliamentary Borough Elections in Devon and Cornwall in the Fifteenth Century', *Parchment and People: Parliament in the Middle Ages*, ed. L. Clark (Edinburgh: 2004) 121–35

——, '"Þe Kynges Cite": Exeter in the Wars of the Roses', *The Fifteenth Century VII: Conflicts, Consequences and the Crown in the Late Middle Ages*, ed. L. Clark (Woodbridge: 2007) 137–56

Klinck, D.R., *Conscience, Equity and the Court of Chancery in Early Modern England* (Farnham: 2010)

Kumar, K., *The Making of English National Identity* (Cambridge: 2013)

Lander, J.R., *Conflict and Stability in Fifteenth-Century England* (London: 1969)

Lapsley, G., 'The Parliamentary Title of Henry IV', *EHR*, 49 (1934) 423–9, 577–606

Laynesmith, J.L., *The Last Medieval Queens: English Queenship 1445–1503* (Oxford: 2004)

Lecoy de la Marche, A., *Le Roi René: Sa vie, son administration, ses travaux artistiques et littéraires*, 2 vols (Paris: 1875)

Levy, F.J., *Tudor Historical Thought* (San Marino, CA: 1967)

Lewis, P.S., 'War Propaganda and Historiography in Fifteenth-Century France and England', *Essays in Later Medieval French History* (London and Ronceverte: 1985) 193–213

Lingard, J., *The History of England from the First Invasion by the Romans to the Accession of William and Mary*, 10 vols (London: 1856)

Litzen, V., 'A War of Roses and Lilies: The Theme of Succession in Sir John Fortescue's Works', *Annales Academiae Scientiarum Fennicae*, 173 (1971) 2–73

Lurie, G., 'Sir John Fortescue's Legal Prestige' *History of Political Thought*, 32 (2011) 293–315

McFarlane, K.B., 'William Worcester', *Studies Presented to Sir Hilary Jenkinson*, ed. J. Conway Davies (Oxford: 1957)

——, 'The Hungerford Family and the Hundred Years War', *The Nobility of Later Medieval England: The Ford lectures for 1953 and related Studies* (Oxford: 1973) 196–221

——, *England in the Fifteenth Century: Collected Essays* (London: 1981)

McGerr, R., 'A Statute Book and Lancastrian Mirror for Princes: the Yale Law School Manuscript of the *Nova Statuta Anglie*', *Textual Cultures: Text, Context and Interpretation*, vol. 2 (2006) 6–59

——, *A Lancastrian Mirror for Princes: The Yale Law School 'New Statutes of England'* (Indianapolis: 2011)

McGlynn, M., *The Royal Prerogative and the Learning of the Inns of Court* (Cambridge: 2003)

McIlwain, C.H., *The Growth of Political Thought in the West* (New York: 1968)

Maddern, P., *Violence and Social Order: East Anglia 1422–1442* (Oxford: 1992)

Maitland, F.W., *English Law and the Renaissance* (Cambridge: 1901)

——, *The Constitutional History of England: A Course of Lectures* (Cambridge: 1908)

Malcolm, J.L., 'Magna Carta in America: Entrenched', *Magna Carta: The Foundation of Freedom*, ed. N. Vincent (London: 2014) 120–35

Maurer, H.E., 'Margaret of Anjou and the Loveday of 1458: A Reconsideration', *Traditions and Transformations in Late Medieval England*, ed. D. Biggs, S.A. Michalove and A. Compton Reeves (Leiden, Boston, Cologne: 2002) 109–24.

——, *Margaret of Anjou: Queenship and Power in Late Medieval England* (Woodbridge: 2003).

Meekings, C.A.F., 'Thomas Kerver's Case, 1444', *EHR*, 90 (1975) 331–46

——, 'King's Bench Files', *Legal Records and the Historian*, ed. J.H. Baker (London: 1978)

Mitchell, R.J., 'English Law Students at Bologna in the Fifteenth Century', *EHR*, 52 (1936) 270–87

Munro, J.H.A., 'An Economic Aspect of the Collapse of the Anglo-Burgundian Alliance, 1428–1442', *Bullion Flows and Monetary Policies in England and the Low Countries, 1350–1500* (Aldershot: 1992) 225–44

Nederman, C.J., *Lineages of European Political Thought: Explorations along the Medieval/Modern Divide from John of Salisbury to Hegel* (Washington, DC: 2009)

Nelson, L.H. and C., 'A Lost Fragment of the *Defensio Juris Domus Lancastrie*', *Speculum*, 40 (1965) 290–3

Nicholson, R., *Scotland: The Later Middle Ages* (Edinburgh: 1974)

Nuttall, J., *The Creation of Lancastrian Kingship: Literature, Language and Politics in Late Medieval England* (Cambridge: 2007)

Orme, N., *From Childhood to Chivalry: The Education of the English Kings and Aristocracy 1066–1530* (London: 1984)

Ormrod, W.M., 'The Use of English: Language, Law and Political Culture in Fourteenth-Century England,' *Speculum*, 78 (2003) 750–87

Palmer, R.C., 'The Construction of an Online Digital Archive: The Anglo-American Legal Tradition Website Project', *Law, Lawyers and Texts: Studies in Medieval Legal History in Honour of Paul Brand*, ed. S. Jenks, J. Rose and C. Whittick (Leiden: 2012) 361–78

Payling, S., 'The Amptill Dispute: A Study in Aristocratic Lawlessness and the Breakdown of Lancastrian Government', *EHR*, 104 (1989) 881–907

——, *Political Society in Lancastrian England: The Greater Gentry of Nottinghamshire* (Oxford: 1991)

——, 'The Rise of the Lawyers in the Lower House, 1395–1536', *Parchment and People: Parliament in the Middle Ages*, ed. L. Clark (Edinburgh: 2004) 103–20

——, 'The "Grete Laboure and Long and Troublous Tyme": The Execution of the Will of Ralph, Lord Cromwell and the Foundation of Tattershall College', *The Fifteenth Century XIII: Exploring the Evidence: Commemoration, Administration and the Economy*, ed. L. Clark (Woodbridge: 2014) 1–30

Plucknett, T.F.T., *A Concise History of the Common Law* (London: 1956)

Pocock, J.G.A., *The Ancient Constitution and the Feudal Law* (Bath: 1974)

——, *The Machiavellian Moment: Florentine Political Thought and the Atlantic Revolution* (Princeton: 1975)

Pollard, A.J., *Warwick the Kingmaker: Politics, Power and Fame* (London: 2007)

Postan, M.M., *Medieval Trade and Finance* (Cambridge: 1973)

Potter, H., *Law, Liberty and the Constitution: A Brief History of the Common Law* (Woodbridge: 2015)

Powell, E., 'Settlement of Disputes by Arbitration in Fifteenth-Century England', *Law and History Review*, 2 (1984) 21–43

——, *Kingship, Law and Society: Criminal Justice in the Reign of Henry V* (Oxford: 1989)

Prince, J., *Danmonii Orientales Illustris* or *The Worthies of Devon* (Exeter: 1701)

Ramsay, N., 'Retained Legal Counsel, *c.*1275–1475', *TRHS*, 35 (1985) 95–112

Reeves, A.C., 'Adam Moleyns, Bishop of Chichester', *Lancastrian Englishmen* (Washington, DC: 1981) 203–63

Rex, R., 'Blessed Adrian Fortescue: A Martyr without a Cause?' *Analecta Bollandiana*, 115 (1996) 307–53

Richmond, C., 'English Naval Power in the Fifteenth Century', *History*, 52 (1967) 1–15

——, *The Paston Family in the Fifteenth Century: The First Phase* (Cambridge: 1990)

Rodger, N.A.M., *The Safeguard of the Sea. A Naval History of Britain, 660–1649*, vol. 1 (London: 1997)

Rose, S., *England's Medieval Navy, 1066–1509: Ships, Men and Warfare* (Barnsley: 2013)

——, *The Wealth of England: The Medieval Wool Trade and its Political Importance, 1100–1600* (Oxford and Havertown: 2018)

Roskell, J.S., *Parliament and Politics in Late Medieval England*, 3 vols (London: 1981–83)

Ross, C.D., *Edward IV* (London: 1974)

Roxburgh, R., *The Records of the Honourable Society of Lincoln's Inn: The Black Books*, vol. 5, *Two Postscripts* (London: 1977)

Ruddick, A., *English Identity and Political Culture in the Fourteenth Century* (Cambridge: 2013)

Saul, N., *Knights and Esquires: The Gloucestershire Gentry in the Fourteenth Century* (Oxford: 1981)

Scofield, C.L., 'Sir John Fortescue in February 1461', *EHR*, 27 (1912) 321–3

——, *The Life and Reign of Edward IV*, 2 vols (London: 1923)

Sharpe, K., *Sir Robert Cotton, 1586–1631: History and Politics in Early Modern England* (Oxford: 1979)

Skeel, C.A.J., 'The Influence of the Writings of Sir John Fortescue', *TRHS*, 10 (1916) 77–114

Skemer, D.C., 'Reading the Law: Statute Books and the Private Transmission of Legal Knowledge in Late Medieval England', *Learning the Law: Teaching and the Transmission of English Law, 1150-1900*, ed. J.A. Bush and A. Wijffels (London and Rio Grande, 1999) 113–31

Skinner, Q., *The Foundations of Modern Political Thought*, 2 vols (Cambridge: 1978)

Somerville, R., *The History of the Duchy of Lancaster*, vol. 1, *1265–1603* (London: 1953)

Storey, R.L., *The End of the House of Lancaster* (Stroud: 1986)

Strohm, P., *England's Empty Throne: Usurpation and the Language of Legitimation, 1399–1422* (New Haven and London: 1998)

——, *Politique: Languages of Statecraft between Chaucer and Shakespeare* (Notre Dame, IN: 2005)

Stubbs, W., *The Constitutional History of England*, 3 vols (Oxford: 1878)

Sutton, A.F., 'Sir Thomas Cook and His "Troubles": An Investigation', *Guildhall Studies in London History*, 3(1978) 85–108

Tanner, T., *Bibliotheca Britannico-Hibernica sive de scriptoribus* (London: 1748)

Taylor, Craig, 'Sir John Fortescue and the French Polemical Treatises of the Hundred Years War', *EHR*, 114 (1999) 112–29

——, 'War, Propaganda and Diplomacy in Fifteenth-Century France and England', *War, Government and Power in Late Medieval France*, ed. C. Allmand (Liverpool: 2000) 70–91

——, *Debating the Hundred Years War: 'Pour Ce Que Plusieurs' and 'A Declaracion of the Trewe and Dewe Title of Henry VIII'* (Cambridge: 2006)

Thielemans, M.R., *Bourgogne et Angleterre: Relations politiques et économiques entre les Pays-Bas bourguignons et l'Angleterre, 1435–1467* (Brussels: 1966)

Thorne, S.E., *Readings and Moots at the Inns of Court in the Fifteenth Century* (London: 1954)

Tierney, B., *Religion, Law and the Growth of Constitutional Thought* (Cambridge: 1982)

Tite, C.G.C., 'The Early Catalogues of the Cottonian Library', *British Library Journal*, 6 (1980) 144–57

——, *The Manuscript Library of Sir Robert Cotton* (London: 1994)

——, *The Early Records of Sir Robert Cotton's Library: Formation, Cataloguing, Use* (London: 2003)

Toomer, G.J., *John Selden: A Life in Scholarship*, 2 vols (Oxford: 2009)

Tucker, P., *Law Courts and Lawyers in the City of London, 1300–1550* (Cambridge: 2007)

Tullis, S., '*Glanvill* after Glanvill: The Afterlife of a Medieval Treatise', *Laws, Lawyers and Texts: Studies in Medieval Legal History in Honour of Paul Brand*, ed. S. Jenks (Leiden: 2012) 327–59

Vanderjagt, A., 'The Princely Culture of the Valois Dukes of Burgundy', *Princes and Princely Culture, 1450–1650*, ed. M. Gosmam, A. Macdonald and A. Vanderjagt, 2 vols (Leiden: 2003) vol. 1, 51–79

Vickers, K., *Humphrey, Duke of Gloucester, a Biography* (London: 1907)

The Victoria History of the County of Bedfordshire, vol. 1, ed. H.A. Doubleday (Westminster: 1904)

The Victoria History of Hertfordshire, vol. 2, ed. William Page (London: 1908); vol. 3, ed. William Page (London: 1971)

The Victoria History of the County of Middlesex, vol. 5, ed. T.F.T. Baker and R.B. Pugh (London: 1976)

The Victoria History of the County of Somerset, vol. 10, ed. Mary Siraut (London: 2010)

Virgoe, R., 'Some Ancient Indictments in the King's Bench Referring to Kent, 1450–52', *Documents Illustrative of Medieval Kentish Society*, ed. F.R.H. Du Boulay (Ashford: 1964) 214–65
——, 'The Composition of the King's Council, 1437–1461', *BIHR* (1970) 43, 134–60
——, 'William Tailboys and Lord Cromwell: Crime and Politics in Lancastrian England', *BJRL*, 55 (1973) 459–82
Viroli, M., *From Politics to Reason of State: The Acquisition and Transformation of the Language of Politics, 1250–1600* (Cambridge: 1992)
Wakelin, D., *Humanism, Reading and English Literature, 1430–1530* (Oxford: 2007)
——, 'England: Humanism Beyond Weiss', *Humanism in Fifteenth-Century Europe*, ed. D. Rundle (Oxford: 2012) 265–305
Walker, S., *The Lancastrian Affinity, 1361–1399* (Oxford: 1990)
Watts, J., '"A New Ffundacion of is Crowne": Monarchy in the Age of Henry VII', *The Reign of Henry VII*, ed. B. Thompson (Stamford: 1995) 21–53
——, *Henry VI and the Politics of Kingship* (Cambridge: 1996)
——, *The Making of Polities: Europe 1300–1500* (Cambridge: 2009)
Wedgwood, J.C. and A.D. Holt, *History of Parliament, 1439–1509*, 2 vols (London: 1936–38)
Weiss, R., *Humanism in England during the Fifteenth Century* (Oxford: 1957)
Williams, E., *Early Holborn and the Legal Quarter of London*, 2 vols (London: 1927)
Wolffe, B.P., 'Acts of Resumption in the Lancastrian Parliaments, 1399–1456', *EHR*, 73 (1958) 583–613
——, *The Crown Lands* (London: 1970)
——, 'The Personal Rule of Henry VI', *Fifteenth-Century England, 1399–1509: Studies in Politics and Society*, ed. S.B. Chrimes, C.D. Ross and R.A. Griffiths (Manchester: 1972) 29–48
——, *Henry VI* (London: 1981)
Wood, D., *Medieval Economic Thought* (Cambridge: 2002)
Wright, S.M., *The Derbyshire Gentry in the Fifteenth Century* (Chesterfield: 1984)

Unpublished Theses

Kekewich, M.L., 'Books of Advice for Princes in Fifteenth Century England with Particular Reference to 1450–1485', unpublished PhD thesis (Open University: 1987)
McGovern, C.M.J., 'Lancastrian Diplomacy and Queen Margaret's Court in Exile, 1461–1471', unpublished BA dissertation (University of Keele: 1973)
Marcuzzi, S., 'Sir John Fortescue on Law and Regal Power', unpublished PhD thesis (University of Cambridge: 2011)

Index